Post-Traumatic Stress Disorder
and the
War Veteran Patient

Brunner/Mazel Psychosocial Stress Series
Charles R. Figley, Ph.D., Series Editor

1. Stress Disorders Among Vietnam Veterans
   Edited by Charles R. Figley, Ph.D.
2. Stress and the Family Vol. 1: Coping with Normative Transitions
   Edited by Hamilton I. McCubbin, Ph.D., and Charles R. Figley, Ph.D.
3. Stress and the Family Vol. 2: Coping with Catastrophe
   Edited by Charles R. Figley, Ph.D., and Hamilton I. McCubbin, Ph.D.
4. Trauma and Its Wake
   Edited by Charles R. Figley, Ph.D.
5. Post-Traumatic Stress Disorder and the War Veteran Patient
   Edited by William E. Kelly, M.D.

Editorial Board

BRUNNER/MAZEL PSYCHOSOCIAL STRESS SERIES NO. 5

Post-Traumatic Stress Disorder

and the

War Veteran Patient

Edited by

William E. Kelly, M.D.

Associate Chief of Staff for Education
Veterans Administration Medical Center
Coatesville, PA, and
Clinical Professor of Psychiatry
Medical College of the Thomas Jefferson University
Philadelphia, PA

BRUNNER/MAZEL, *Publishers* • New York

Library of Congress Cataloging in Publication Data

Main entry under title:

Post-traumatic stress disorder and the war
  veteran patient.

  (Brunner/Mazel psychosocial stress series; vol. 2)
  Based on the proceedings of the 25th Annual
Neuropsychiatric Institute, held at the Veterans
Administration Medical Center, Coatesville, Pa., in
1982.
  Bibliography: p.
  Includes index.
  1. Post-traumatic stress-disorder—Congresses.
2. Veterans, Disabled—Mental health—United States—
Congresses. 3. Vietnamese Conflict, 1961-1975—
Psychological aspects—Congresses. I. Kelly, William E.
II. Neuropsychiatric Institute (U.S.) (25th : 1982 :
Veterans Administration Medical Center, Coatesville, Pa.)
III. Series. [DNLM: 1. Stress, Disorders, Post-
Traumatic—congresses. 2. Veterans—psychology—
congresses. W1 BR917T v.2 / WM 184 P8567 1982]
RC552.P67P667 1985   616.85'212   84-26839
ISBN 0-87630-386-6

Copyright © 1985 by Brunner/Mazel, Inc.

Published by
Brunner/Mazel, Inc.
19 Union Square West
New York, New York 10003

MANUFACTURED IN THE UNITED STATES OF AMERICA

Editorial Note

The purpose of the Psychosocial Stress Book Series is to develop and publish books which in some way make a significant contribution to the understanding and management of the psychosocial stressor–stress reaction paradigm. The books are designed to advance the work of clinicians, researchers, and other professionals involved in the varied aspects of human services.

The first volume in the Brunner/Mazel Psychosocial Stress Series, *Stress Disorders Among Vietnam Veterans* (SDVV), published in 1978, alerted the nation to the difficulties of coping with one's war experiences and provided guidance to professionals working with these men and women. It was common then to read popular accounts in newspapers and magazines about the startling problems of Vietnam veterans: high divorce and suicide rates; the frequency of drug and alcohol abuse; the characteristic violence against others; and an assortment of other emotionally based problems. All this, we were led to believe, was a direct result of the war. Yet in the professional publications in the mid-1970s, with few exceptions, the immediate and long-term emotional effects of the war were minimized or dismissed entirely. With the publication of SDVV, mental health professionals and policymakers began to recognize the complexity of the postwar readjustments of Vietnam veterans. Soon a national outreach program emerged within the Veterans Administration and across the country to help Vietnam veterans cope. As a result, thousands of professionals became aware of the special circumstances of war veterans and how to help them.

The next two volumes in the Series, *Stress and the Family, Volume I: Coping with Normative Transitions* and *Stress and the Family, Volume II: Coping with Catastrophe*, edited by Charles R. Figley and Hamilton I. McCubbin, provide a comprehensive summary of the available information about how families cope with psychosocial stress. The former volume attends to the typical and predictable stressors of family life, while the latter volume focuses on how families cope with extraordinary and unpredictable stressors. Volume #4 in the Series is *Trauma and Its*

Wake: The Study and Treatment of Post-Traumatic Stress Disorder, edited by Charles R. Figley. It is the first in a series of books that review the latest innovations in theory, research, and treatment of this disorder, caused by a wide variety of stressful life events.

This fifth volume in the Series represents the latest advances in both understanding and treating the war veteran patient. The contributions of leading clinical scholars in this area are effectively organized beginning with a brief history of Congressional initiatives in this area. Each of the 15 chapters is built on the important work of the past. Perhaps more than any other work to date, *Post-Traumatic Stress Disorder and the War Veteran Patient* provides a specific blueprint for conceptualizing and treating war veterans' stress disorders. Moreover, the reading list assembled in the appendix is the most comprehensive bibliography ever published on this topic.

There will be future volumes in the Series that will focus on the special circumstances of military veterans and build on the important contributions of *Post-Traumatic Stress Disorder and the War Veteran Patient*. Most of the volumes in the Series, however, will be concerned with other populations and sources of stress. These include, for example, psychosocial stress of crime victims, emergency/crisis workers, and victims of family abuse.

Although the history of stress disorders began with the earliest medical writings, only today are we beginning to understand the complex interaction between mind and body, between the human being and context. Indeed, the future holds exciting mysteries to marvel, ponder, and solve!

CHARLES R. FIGLEY, Ph.D.
Series Editor

Foreword

Coincident with the rise of industrial and technological societies men, women, and children have been increasingly exposed to massive traumata from powerful and destructive man-made forces as well as from those ongoing and uncontrollable natural disasters. Modern warfare, wherein millions are killed, maimed, and psychologically tortured, continues to provide stark reality to the existence and unleashing of the brutal forces innate in mankind. In this century the acute consequences of war-induced stress always demanded attention that dwindled on each occasion after peace was declared. Little attention was given to these chronic sufferers until Kardiner studied a group of World War I patients in a veterans hospital and others after World War II examined surviving prisoners of war and victims of the Nazi concentration camps.

Vietnam's aftermath presents still another aspect of induced psychological trauma: the surprising eruption within many individuals of "delayed" expressions of combat-induced stress—a phenomenon puzzling and often doubted by the public at large as well as by clinically trained mental health workers. While delayed reactions had been identified before Vietnam, but were seldom studied, the reasons for their now frequently observed occurrence have stirred much reflection. Their serious study may offer means for prevention in the future as well as for treatment. Much will be found in the chapters of this book which address the matters considered significant to persistence of the post-traumatic stress disorders as well as the eruption of the "delayed" forms. Many logistical, political, social, and psychological factors impinged upon the Vietnam veteran as he was returned home. The war itself—a continuous guerrilla exposure—now is recognized as more stressful and longer in duration in terms of individual exposure than had previously been thought.

To prepare these chapters, Dr. William E. Kelly, the editor, has admirably assembled some of the most knowledgeable and experienced men and women in terms of direct work and observation of the sufferers of war-induced stress disorders. He has arranged the chapter groupings to encompass various aspects of the subject. Thus, within the first two chapters Richard B. Fuller describes the background and position of the federal legislative bodies and the U.S. Veterans Administration that led to the development of Operation Outreach to assist the Vietnam veterans, and Chaim F. Shatan writes upon and illustrates the "perceptual dissonance" between the veteran's experience of current reality and his ongoing conflicting memories.

Chapters three through seven provide definitions of the syndrome, its variations, including various explanatory psychological and psychoanalytic interpretations of the Post-Traumatic Stress Disorder (PTSD). Tanay describes the effects of training for and involvement in violence in war and the resulting pathological consequences in the guilt suffered by returning veterans denied social support for their wartime actions. Silver considers both the constructive and destructive potential of the Vietnam combat experience for the veteran and the significant strengths within veterans which may be used for change. Sarah Haley has a fine section on psychodynamics and a particularly insightful case history. This section ends with Hendin and his colleagues' report on the reliving experiences of these veterans and Marr's review of the veterans' problems in relating to wives and children and the critical need for a family support system to promote reintegration.

Emphasis in the succeeding three chapters focuses on matters of prediction and the particular problems of veteran minority groups. Amongst these chapters is a report of a particularly fine and seminal research study done by Wilson and Krauss which identifies the major sources of stress amongst the Vietnam veterans in which such variables as exposure to death and loss of a buddy, the "short-term syndrome," homecoming experience, premorbid personality, hospitalization, symptoms of PTSD, and isolation have all been weighed and assessed. Two fine chapters by Van Devanter and Parson deal with minority issues as they pertain to women and blacks.

In the final five chapters, writers address the use of various psycho- and sociotherapies, including hypnotherapy and narcosynthesis. Also included as treatment interventions are plans for the development of inpatient units for Vietnam veterans in Veterans Administration Medical Centers so as to provide a specialized therapeutic milieu. Selection and training of staff to man these units and a model for an in-hospital individualized approach to therapy are also described.

For a "state of the art" presentation of theoretical, administrative, and therapeutic understanding of the chronic and delayed post-traumatic stress disorders induced in many young Americans under the unique, conflictful, and indeed confused sociopolitical catastrophe of armed intervention in Southeast Asia and its aftermath, the reader will find much here for thought and practical guidance.

LAWRENCE C. KOLB, M.D.
Distinguished Physician in Psychiatry
Veterans Administration Medical Center
Albany, New York

Contents

Editorial Note by Series Editor, Charles R. Figley, Ph.D. v
Foreword by Lawrence C. Kolb, M.D. vii
Preface xiii
Acknowledgments xvii
About the Contributors xix

1. War Veterans' Post-Traumatic Stress Disorder and the U.S.
   Congress 3
   by Richard B. Fuller, M.A.
2. Have You Hugged a Vietnam Veteran Today? The Basic Wound
   of Catastrophic Stress 12
   by Chaim F. Shatan, M.D.
3. The Vietnam Veteran—Victim of War 29
   by Emanuel Tanay, M.D.
4. Post-Traumatic Stress and the Death Imprint: The Search for
   a New Mythos 43
   by Steven M. Silver, Ph.D.
5. Some of My Best Friends Are Dead: Treatment of the PTSD
   Patient and His Family 54
   by Sarah A. Haley, L.I.C.S.W.
6. The Reliving Experience in Vietnam Veterans with Post-Traumatic Stress Disorders 72
   *by Herbert Hendin, M.D., Ann Pollinger Haas, Ph.D., Paul
   Singer, M.D., William Houghton, M.D., Mark F. Schwartz,
   Ph.D., and Vincent Wallen, Ph.D.*
7. Why the Pain Won't Stop and What the Family Can Do to
   Help 85
   by Robert Marrs, M.A.
8. Predicting Post-Traumatic Stress Disorders Among Vietnam
   Veterans 102
   by John P. Wilson, Ph.D., and Gustave E. Krauss, M.A.

9. The Unknown Warriors: Implications of the Experiences of
   Women in Vietnam 148
      by Lynda M. Van Devanter, R.N.
10. The Black Vietnam Veteran: His Representational World in
   Post-Traumatic Stress Disorders 170
      by Erwin Randolph Parson, Ph.D.
11. The Use of Hypnosis in Post-Traumatic Conditions 193
      by Joel Osler Brende, M.D.
12. Hypnotherapy of Post-Traumatic Stress Disorder in Combat
   Veterans from WW II and Vietnam 211
      by Steven M. Silver, Ph.D., and William E. Kelly, M.D.
13. Establishing a Post-Traumatic Stress Disorder Inpatient
   Program 234
      by W. Peter Sax, M.D.
14. Management and Implementation of Nursing Care for the Post-
   Traumatic Stress Disorder Patient 249
      *by Gertrude C. Woods, R.N., Thomas A. Sherwood, R.N.,
      and Rose Marie Thompson, R.N.*
15. An Approach to Treatment of Post-Traumatic Stress Disorder 276
      by William D. Racek, Ph.D.

*Appendix A: A Suggested Reading List on Vietnam Veterans and Post-
   Traumatic Stress Disorder, by Chaplain Ray W. Stubbe* 293
*Appendix B: A Guide to Self-History-Taking with Particular Reference
   to Post-Traumatic Stress Disorder (PTSD), by W. Peter Sax,
   M.D.* 323
*Appendix C: A Suggested Overview Reading List of Material on Vietnam
   Veterans and PTSD, by Steven M. Silver, Ph.D.* 326
Name Index 329
Subject Index 332

Preface

The enigma of post-traumatic stress reactions has attracted the interest of observers of human behavior as far back as recorded history can take us. Ancient Greek and Roman literature contains accounts of reactions of warriors after surviving severe battlefield experiences. Shakespeare described the syndrome in accurate terms in King Henry the Fourth. Freud was greatly intrigued by post-combat psychological reactions. World War II physicians were so fascinated by the combat neuroses which they were called upon to manage and treat while in the service that many returned to civilian life and devoted the rest of their professional lives to the study of the human psyche. But what has created an even greater amount of interest, concern, and controversy is the unusually high incidence of post-traumatic stress reactions among the returned Vietnam veterans, especially where their appearance has been delayed for long periods of time, in some cases not becoming evident until some 20 years after the original trauma.

In the past few years the Veterans Administration Medical Centers have begun to see an increasing number of these reactions, many of which at first were not recognized as such. For the most part these presented extremely difficult problems in both management and treatment. It was primarily to deal with these problems among its own patient population that the Coatesville Veterans Administration Medical Center devoted its Twenty-fifth Annual Neuropsychiatric Institute (1982) to the study of this area of concern. An unusually large attendance at this symposium made it obvious that there is a substantial need for more enlightenment on this subject. Therefore, we were encouraged to collect and augment the material available from the proceedings of our Annual Institute and present it in published form. Beginning with a nucleus of these papers, additional contributions were sought from a carefully selected group of knowledgeable professional therapists and researchers in an effort to develop an up-to-date, wide-ranging, and comprehensive study of this serious social and medical problem.

It is hoped that this volume will be read with profit by therapists, researchers, veterans, and their families as well as interested others. Some of the chapters deal with the broad social issues involved; others with intricacies of psychodynamics and mental functioning, while still others deal with methods of treatment. Some survey the problems faced by the spouses, children, and close acquaintances of the victims of the disorder. Other chapters deal with the problems faced by the therapists in trying to manage not only these difficult and unusually powerful emotional reactions in their patients, but the therapists' own disturbing emotional responses and countertransferences. Special problems faced by women veterans and minority groups such as blacks are studied. A sophisticated program of research undertaken in an effort to diagnose and predict the likelihood of developing post-traumatic stress reactions and what factors tend to precipitate them is carefully reviewed. Some parallels and differences between civilian, concentration camp, and military settings for the development of post-traumatic stress reactions are explored. Treatment approaches, from storefront centers to special in-hospital units, are discussed. Group versus individual therapies are examined. Hypnotherapy and narcosynthesis are described. Selection and preparation of the treatment staff for the management of these problems are included.

Throughout all the chapters there are generous examples of case histories showing the patient's responses to the efforts of their therapists. All the authors are outstanding professionals with wide experience and fully credentialed in their fields of endeavor, so that the information presented here is firmly based on a foundation of knowledge and experience. While the editor does not necessarily agree with every opinion expressed by the authors, he has encouraged the free expression of divergent points of view in order to expose all sides of the issues and to promote dialogue.

One of the most striking aspects of this volume is the dedication of the authors to their work with this type of patient. Post-traumatic stress disorder patients are extremely difficult to work with, require an unusual degree of commitment on the part of the therapist, and their treatment exacts a heavy toll of emotional drain upon the therapist. Yet when requested, every contributor was immediately willing to join in the effort to put together this volume. Not a single individual approached refused to participate. And no one, including the editor, has or will receive one cent of remuneration for their literary efforts.* This volume is truly an

---

*The original Institute presenters were paid a modest honorarium for participating in the seminars. All the other papers were prepared gratis.

expression of concern for one's fellowmen, with a full appreciation of their suffering and a wish to help.

The generous sharing of their scientific efforts and accomplishments is typical of the spirit of the entire group engaged in the study and treatment of this disorder. This volume throws open to you, the reader, a rare opportunity to share intimately in the therapeutic experiences and scientific endeavors of these authors in their efforts to understand the true nature of post-traumatic stress reactions in a war setting. It constitutes an open invitation to join with them in their further study and efforts to alleviate the human suffering and modify the social attitudes that underlie this all too common affliction of our veteran population.

August, 1984   WILLIAM E. KELLY, M.D.

Acknowledgments

The production of a volume such as this requires the efforts of many individuals besides the editor and the contributors. On the part of myself and the authors, I wish to acknowledge our indebtedness to these significant others. First our appreciation goes to James L.G. Parsons, II, Director of the Coatesville Veterans Administration Medical Center for his support and encouragement through the continuation of Coatesville's fine tradition of Annual Neuropsychiatric Institutes and the publication of their proceedings. Next, we are indebted to Paul J. Fink, M.D., Chairman of the Department of Psychiatry and Human Behavior of the Thomas Jefferson University College of Medicine and Chairman of the Coatesville V.A. Medical Center Dean's Committee, for his support and assistance in planning this our Twenty-fifth Annual Neuropsychiatric Institute. We are most in debt, however, to Steven M. Silver, Ph.D., himself a survivor of the Vietnam experience and chief psychologist assigned to Coatesville's Post-Traumatic Stress Disorder Unit, which he helped to establish, staff, and supervise. His encouragement and assistance in developing the program for the Institute, as well as selecting and soliciting many of the contributors to this volume, have been central to its accomplishment.

Also of great significance in this undertaking has been the assistance of Chaim F. Shatan, M.D., not only as a contributor but in suggesting others actively involved in treating post-traumatic stress disorders as contributors of additional chapters for inclusion in this book. Appreciation goes also to James R. Harris, M.D., Chief of Staff at the Coatesville V.A. Medical Center, for his enthusiastic support of the Institute as well as the publication of its proceedings. Thanks go also to Makis J. Tsapogas, M.D., Director of the Veterans Administration Northeast Regional Medical Education Center at Northport, L.I. and his staff for their guidance and support for Coatesville's educational endeavors. Support given by W. Peter Sax, M.D., William P. Racek, Ph.D., Thomas A. Sherwood, R.N., Gertrude C. Woods, R.N., and Rose Marie Thompson, R.N., and others of the staff of the Coatesville Medical Center involved in the treatment of post-traumatic stress reactions of our veteran patients is also acknowledged—support manifested not only by the preparation of their manuscripts but also by their warm backing of the efforts of the editor.

Appreciation is due Ms. Alice Vonderlindt, chief librarian, and Glenn Brown, Chief of Medical Media, at the Coatesville V.A. Medical Center for their services in preparing the material for this publication as well the assistance at times from Mrs. June Strickland, librarian for the Institute of the Pennsylvania Hospital. Great credit goes to Ms. Ruth Poteet who did much of the arranging for the Institute and handling of the correspondence with the contributors. An especially important contribution was made by my wife Martha who typed and word-processed most of the manuscripts after each of numerous editings and corrections for spelling and punctuation.

It goes without saying—but should be said—that the authors who have shared their years of experience and understanding with you, the reader, most deserve to have their contributions acknowledged. Special thanks go to Lawrence Kolb, M.D., who made time in his busy schedule of scholarly activities to read the manuscripts and prepare the Foreword for this volume. And lastly, the editor wishes to express his deep gratitude to John P. Wilson, Ph.D., for his invaluable assistance in finding a suitable publisher and to the Senior Editor, Charles R. Figley, Ph.D., for his guidance in the choice of material to be included in this volume. Special thanks go to Chaplain Ray W. Stubbe for allowing us to include his extensive reading list on Vietnam veterans and post-traumatic stress disorder.

W.E.K.

About the Contributors

Joel O. Brende, M.D., received his psychiatric training at the Menninger Foundation. He began his clinical work with Vietnam veterans in 1977 while a staff psychiatrist at the Topeka, Kansas, Veterans Administration Medical Center and has been a consulting psychiatrist to the V.A. National Outreach Program since 1979. He has produced a number of publications pertaining to the diagnosis, treatment, and psychophysiology of PTSD. Currently he serves as the Clinical Director of the PTSD Treatment Unit for Vietnam veterans at the Bay Pines Veterans Administration Medical Center in Florida and is Assistant Professor of Psychiatry at the University of South Florida in Tampa.

Richard B. Fuller, M.A., has been a Professional Staff Member with the U.S. House of Representatives Committee on Veterans Affairs since 1979. He has served with its Subcomittee on Education, Training, and Employment and presently serves with the Subcommittee on Hospitals and Health Care under its Chairman, the Hon. Robert W. Edgar (D-Pa). He is a 1968 graduate of Duke University and served with the U.S. Air Force in Vietnam. He participated in the design and passage of the original legislation calling for the Readjustment Counseling Program for Vietnam era veterans through P.L. 96-22 and the subsequent extension and expansion of the program through P.L. 97-72 and 98-160.

Sarah A. Haley, L.I.C.S.W., is Associate Clinical Professor of Psychiatry, Tufts Medical School, Boston, and is associated with the Boston V.A. Outpatient Clinic. She was a member of the Vietnam Veterans Working Group, a sub-task force of the DMS-III Task Force which researched and wrote the section on "post-traumatic stress disorder." She is a member of the National Advisory Committee on the Readjustment of Vietnam Veterans. Ms. Haley has treated Vietnam veterans since 1969 and has written on the potential for a negative countertransference in the treatment of the survivors of catastrophic stress. She has published widely and is at work on a book, *Incoming: Psychotherapy with Vietnam Veterans*.

Herbert Hendin, M.D., is Director of the Center for Psychosocial Studies at the V.A. Medical Center in Montrose, New York, and Professor of Psychiatry at New York Medical College. During the past five years he and his colleagues at the Center have been studying post-traumatic stress disorders in Vietnam veterans and are the authors of a number of articles on the subject. Dr. Hendin (with Dr. Ann Pollinger Haas) is also the author of the recently published *Wounds of War: The Psychological Aftermath of Combat in Vietnam* (Basic Books, 1984).

William E. Kelly, M.D., is Associate Chief of Staff for Education at the Coatesville V.A. Medical Center, Coatesville, Pennsylvania. His professional background includes experience as a military psychiatrist, private practice of psychiatry and psychoanalysis, and as a consultant for several Army, Veterans Administration, and civilian hospitals in the Philadelphia area. He is a Clinical Professor of Psychiatry at the Thomas Jefferson University School of Medicine and a faculty member of the Institute of the Philadelphia Association for Psychoanalysis. He has published several journal articles and book chapters, in addition to editing three other books on psychiatric subjects.

Lawrence C. Kolb, M.D., a graduate of Johns Hopkins Medical School, studied briefly in London before entering the Navy during WW II where he saw hospital ship duty in the South Pacific. During his distinguished career, he has been associated with the National Institute of Mental Health, the Mayo Clinic, and the Veterans Administration. He has served as Professor of Psychiatry at the University of Minnesota, Chairman of the Department of Psychiatry at Columbia University's College of Physicians and Surgeons, Director of Psychiatric Services at Presbyterian Hospital, Director of the New York Psychiatric Institute, and Commissioner of the New York State Department of Mental Hygiene. He was elected president of the American Psychiatric Association in 1969 and in 1983 received its Distinguished Service Award. Dr. Kolb is well known for his contributions to the psychiatric literature, particularly as author of his popular text book in psychiatry, *Modern Clinical Psychiatry* (Sanders,1977). Presently he serves as Professor of Psychiatry at Albany Medical College and as Distinguished Physician in Psychiatry at the Albany Veterans Administration Medical Center where he has researched, taught, and published widely on the subject of post-traumatic stress disorders.

Gustave E. Krauss, M.A., is a graduate student in psychology at Cleveland State University and an outreach worker in the Veterans Administration readjustment counseling program for Vietnam veterans. He and Dr. John P. Wilson co-authored the *Vietnam Era Stress Inventory*.

Robert L. Marrs, M.A., Professor of Student Services and Placement Counselor at Macomb Community College, is currently employed as a psychotherapist with Square Lake Mental Health Center P.C., a contractor for the V.A.'s Outreach Program. Since 1970, he has made local and national presentations aimed at increasing the understanding of delayed post-traumatic stress symptoms among the helping professions. He developed the videotape, *Stress and Human Misery*, and helped establish the Detroit Metro Task Force on Vietnam Veterans' Concerns, which sponsored an Agent Orange Workshop and cooperated in Public Television's Vietnam Veteran Call-a-thon.

Erwin Randolph Parson, Ph.D., is a Vietnam veteran and clinical psychologist who served as a medic in Vietnam. He is the Regional Manager of the 23 Veterans Administration's Vietnam Veterans Readjustment Counseling Centers for the Northeastern United States, which includes Puerto Rico and the United States Virgin Islands. He is Director of the Institute for Psychological Testing and Occupational Guidance at Long Island Consultation Center. He is also a practicing psychoanalyst in Long Island, New York, and does forensic work with Vietnam veterans. He has written a number of papers and book chapters on psychological trauma, and is co-author of *Vietnam Veterans: The Road to Recovery* (Plenum, 1985).

William P. Racek, Ph.D. is a veteran of 23 years of military service in the Infantry and Armored Cavalry which encompasses WW II, the Korean, and the Vietnam campaigns. His extensive combat experience both as an enlisted man and officer, along with his studies at Kansas State University (where he prepared a master's thesis on counseling in the military and a doctoral thesis on drug abuse in the military), led quite naturally to a career in counseling. Following his graduation in 1972 he became the Director of the Drug Abuse Clinic at Ft. Riley, Kansas, and taught at Kansas State University. His extensive clinical experience with veterans and their families during his work as ward psychologist at the Coatesville V.A. Medical Center forms the basis of his highly successful treatment program for PTSD.

W. Peter Sax, M.D., following graduation from the Harvard Medical

School and residency training at the Institute of the Pennsylvania Hospital, maintained a private practice in psychiatry for the next 25 years, teaching at Hahnemann Medical School and the Institute of the Pennsylvania Hospital, before joining the Veterans Administration Medical Staff in 1976. He is an Assistant Clinical Professor of Psychiatry at the Thomas Jefferson University College of Medicine and currently serves as coordinator of the Post-Traumatic Stress Disorder Program at the Veterans Administration Medical Center at Coatesville, Pennsylvania. Psychoanalysis, genetic epistemology, linguistics, and Gestalt therapy have contributed to his eclectic orientation.

Chaim Shatan, M.D., is the recipient of the First Annual Holocaust Memorial Award (1974) and a member of the Vietnam Veterans Working Group which insured the inclusion of PTSD in DSM-III. In 1970, he organized 40 volunteer therapists to work with "rap groups" of Vietnam Veterans Against the War. The unifying thread of his clinical research and publications is the impact of man-made catastrophic stress. He was a committee member of the DSM-III Task Force and is a faculty member of "Operation Outreach." He is a Clinical Professor and Training Analyst in the Postdoctoral Psychoanalytic Training Program, New York University. Dr. Shatan is in private practice in New York City. Besides psychoanalysis, he also practices group therapy and hypnosis. Currently he is working on books on *War Babies* and *The Psychology of Combat*.

Thomas A. Sherwood, R.N., holding three Master's degrees and currently completing course work towards his Ph.D., is Chief of Nursing Services at the Veterans Administration Medical Center, Coatesville, Pennsylvania. He has taught at the Columbia University School of Public Health, worked as a consultant in New York City drug programs, practiced as a psychotherapist, and serves as a consultant in psychiatric, medical, and nursing services administration. He has published in the areas of Nursing Services, Health Administration, and Quality Assurance.

Steven M. Silver, Ph.D., received his Ph.D. in Counseling Psychology from Temple University. As an officer in the Marines, he served in the Vietnam War with Fighter-Attack Squadron 115 and had 316 combat missions in North and South Vietnam, Laos, and Cambodia. He has worked with Vietnam veterans and their families, as well as other trauma survivors, since 1971. He holds an academic appointment in the Department of Psychiatry at the Thomas Jefferson University School of

Medicine. Currently he is Program Psychologist for the Post-Traumatic Stress Disorder Program at the Veterans Administration Medical Center, Coatesville, Pennsylvania.

Emanuel Tanay,M.D., is Clinical Professor of Psychiatry, Wayne State University, Detroit, Michigan, and a psychiatric consultant to the U.S. Veterans Administration, Detroit Regional Office. Dr. Tanay was a speaker at the Fourth International Psychoanalytic Forum, New York, 1972, and was a member of the panel on Post-Vietnam Syndrome. In 1973 he received the Detroit Institute of Technology Award for "Outstanding Recognition in Assisting Vietnam Veterans." Dr. Tanay authored a paper in 1976 entitled, *The Dear John Syndrome During the Vietnam War.* He is a contributor to *Massive Psychic Trauma* (International Universities Press, 1968).

Rose Marie Thompson, R.N., attended Los Angeles County General Hospital School of Nursing and received her B.A. from California State University. She is Head Nurse/Supervisor on the Post-Traumatic Stress Unit at the Coatesville Veterans Administration Medical Center. She has held several administrative and supervisory positions in nursing. She is taking courses in administrative sciences towards an M.S. degree at West Chester State University, West Chester, Pennsylvania.

Lynda M. Van Devanter, R.N., is the National Women's Director of Vietnam Veterans of America. She earned her R.N. degree in 1968 from Mercy Hospital School of Nursing in Baltimore, and her B.A. in Psychology in 1980 from Antioch University in Los Angeles. She served as a U.S. Army Nurse in Vietnam in 1969 and 1970, and is the author of *Home Before Morning: The Story of an Army Nurse in Vietnam* (Beaufort Books, 1983), as well as numerous journal articles. She has been a consultant to government and private sector mental health researchers and clinicians for several years on the subject of Post-Traumatic Stress Disorder and women veterans.

John P. Wilson, Ph.D., is a Professor of Psychology at Cleveland State University and a National Consultant to Vietnam Veterans of America. He is the founder and director of The Forgotten Warrior Project which has been studying the nature and dynamics of post-traumatic stress syndrome in Vietnam veterans since 1974. He also serves as a consultant to the Veterans Administration readjustment counseling program for Vietnam veterans. His current research focuses on a comparative analysis of PTSD among different survivor groups. His most recent book (with Joel Aronoff) is *Personality in the Social Process* (Erlbaum, 1984).

Gertrude C. Woods, R.N., is a Clinical Specialist in psychiatric nursing at the Veterans Administration Medical Center, Coatesville, Pennsylvania. She has been a nursing instructor with the Chicago Board of Education and a member of the teaching faculty at the Malcolm X Community College in Chicago. For the past two years she has worked with Vietnam veterans in Coatesville's Post-Traumatic Stress Disorder Program. In this role, she performs psychotherapy (both individual and group), teaches, consults, and speaks on Vietnam issues. She frequently gives workshops on "Transactional Analysis and Burnout" and on "Conducting Group Therapy."

Post-Traumatic Stress Disorder
and the
War Veteran Patient

VIETNAM ILIAD

Anger be now your song,
for the gentle ballad of youth
were hushed in the roar of fire,
soul-eating flames,
leaving bitter ashes.

Your rage sings
like a whistling sword,
cleaving the tenuous hold
others made on you.

You do not feel the gentle wind
of home—this soil
does not hold the print
of your foot.

What war do you now fight?
Who is your enemy,
when you face you?

Stilling the guns
only stops the killing:
the dying continues
as you destroy you.

A Vietnam War Veteran

1

War Veterans' Post-Traumatic Stress Disorder and the U.S. Congress

RICHARD B. FULLER, M.A.

On April 26, 1979, the Senate Veterans Affairs Committee filed the formal report on legislation S-7, which authorized the Veterans Administration to recognize and treat post-traumatic stress disorder (PTSD) among Vietnam Era veterans. This was not the first time the Senate Committee had recommended this proposal. The provision had been included in legislation and approved by the Senate as a whole in every Congress since 1972 where it had been introduced with regularity by Senator Alan Cranston, Committee Chairman. In each instance the House Veterans Affairs Committee had blocked the proposal from passing out of the Congress. However, the political pressures were too great in 1979 for the proposal to be ignored further, and, for various reasons discussed below, the House conceded to the Senate and the provisions of S-7 were signed into law through P.L. 96-22 later that year.

The Congress set aside a miniscule $9.9 million out of a total V.A. budget of $23 billion to authorize for two years a network of storefront peer group counseling centers to help Vietnam veterans "readjust." The entire concept was vague. The term "post-traumatic stress disorder" was hardly even known or used in connection with the legislation. Vietnam veterans' problems were referred to as "Post Vietnam Syndrome" or "Delayed Stress." In 1977 the Congress authorized a major $1.2 million study, commissioning the Center for Policy Research in New York to determine the extent of readjustment difficulties among Vietnam era veterans. However, the results of that study were not even available at the time the law was approved by the Congress. The House and Senate Committees were reacting in good faith to the idea that a considerable problem did exist as they enacted a program that no one was completely certain could actually work.

The Senate Veterans Affairs Committee, in its report accompanying S-7, described the problem and the program as follows:

> Section 103 of the Committee bill would add a new section 612A to Title 38 U.S.C. to provide for the establishment of a new program of readjustment counseling and follow-up mental health services for veterans who served on active duty during the Vietnam era (August 5, 1964 through May 7, 1975) to assist such veterans with psychological problems in readjusting to civilian life . . . the purpose of the readjustment counseling provision is to make fully available and to encourage and facilitate the full use of the resources of the V.A. health care system to those Vietnam Era veterans who feel the need for counseling to help them in their readjustment to civilian life.
>
> The Committee construes a "readjustment problem," as that term is used in section 103 of the committee bill, to be a low-grade motivational or behavioral impairment which interferes with a veteran's overall ability to cope reasonably effectively with his or her daily life problems. A readjustment problem does not usually amount to a definable psychiatric illness requiring extended professional services but could become such an illness in the absence of early detection and counseling and follow-up care where necessary.

> *Readjustment Counseling Program for Vietnam Veterans S-7*
> *96th Congress 1st Session*
> *Senate Report 96-100*
> *Page 27*

The Congress was breaking new ground in authorizing this program. Traditional sources in the Veterans Administration and in the House of Representatives had consistently refused to accept that returning Vietnam veterans were any different in their needs from the remaining 20 million living veterans who had returned from wars before them. They felt that the programs enacted for their fathers and grandfathers, notably the G.I. Bill and basic health care services, would suffice for the youngest generation of veterans as well. To suggest that something "different" might have happened during the Vietnam War to those who served in Southeast Asia, or that Vietnam veterans might have reacted differently to the experiences of war and the homecoming than previous service-men, pressed a very sore nerve. Recognizing that Vietnam veterans could be unique, in the minds of many, served as a reminder of the controversy, of the unrest, of the political turmoil and other images that swirled around our last and longest war.

For both the World War II generation in Congress, and the rest of the country deep in its own amnesia over Vietnam, the rallying cry against such programs as readjustment counseling became: "A veteran is a veteran is a veteran." They were eager to wrap the Vietnam veteran into the same cloak as those who fought in previous wars, even though many Vietnam veterans were not ready, or even able, to accept that characterization themselves.

Apart from societal and generational prejudice, the critics of the program also cited legal precedents in objecting to specialized treatment for post-traumatic stress disorder through the Veterans Administration under Title 38 U.S. Code (Veterans Law). Health care benefits and services provided by law through the Veterans Administration are categorized in two areas: service-connected disabilities and non-service-connected disabilities. Within these categories special criteria determine certain groups and a hierarchy of priorities as to who shall receive these services. The Veterans Administration does not, and subject to appropriations by law cannot, provide equal services for each of the 28 million living veterans. On the other hand, the new Readjustment Counseling Program authorized priority treatment and the availability of all V.A. health care services for any of the current population of 9 million Vietnam era veterans seeking that assistance. To the horror of the critics as well, the program also offered collateral treatment and counseling to the families and even certain friends of those veterans to assist in the overall readjustment of the individual veteran. This definitely was a departure from the norm. The concept was a serious threat—to the health care professionals in the Veterans Administration, to budget planners in the President's Office of Management and Budget, and to Members of Congress and their committee staff on Capitol Hill.

With such strong opposition, it is no wonder that readjustment counseling and the recognition of post-traumatic stress disorder were blocked in the Congress for nearly 10 years. Even final passage of the legislation did not stop the critics and detractors from trying to undermine the program within its limited authorized two-year life time.

To compound the problem further, special rights and special programs for Vietnam veterans since the early 70s were more often than not promoted by a relatively small handful of inexperienced "town criers." Early proponents of post-traumatic stress disorder were characterized by critics as "crackpot, screwball, self-serving psychologists and psychiatrists who were probably all against the war anyway and were only looking for a surefire way to get some money out of the Veterans Administration." Or worse, in the minds of the traditionalists, these proponents were part of the most visible and activist symbol of the antiwar movement in the United States: the Vietnam Veterans Against the War who were "probably all crazy before they got into the service in the first place."

With this background, there was no single force to push special programs for Vietnam veterans in a country that was desperately trying to forget Vietnam. Many Vietnam veterans were trying to do the same thing for better or for worse. As a result, the Vietnam veterans movement faltered and fragmented into many separated and competing groups.

The political realities of the ebb and flow of veterans' benefits in Washington center on what is aptly called the "Iron Triangle" formed by the Congress, the Veterans Administration, and the Veterans Service Organizations. Little can be accomplished without the acquiescence of each. Depending on politics and budgets, each corner of the triangle pushes and tugs at its neighbors until a consensus is reached. Each corner of the triangle went through a metamorphosis during the late 70s which led to enactment of the readjustment counseling program and the elevation of Vietnam veterans issues into general prominence.

In 1974, following Watergate, a whole new class of men and women were swept into Congress eager to question old values and old concepts. Many of those Congressmen, such as Rep. Bob Edgar of Pennsylvania, and those that subsequently followed them, were of the Vietnam generation itself. They challenged the old ways, the seniority system, patronage, and porkbarrel politics. Some of them managed to stay in Congress and gradually became more effective. Over the years they attained seniority and leadership positions themselves on key committees. For instance, in 1982 Edgar became chairman of the prestigious House Veterans Affairs Subcommittee on Hospitals and Health Care with jurisdiction over all V.A. medical programs. After years of struggle, Vietnam veterans' issues finally became the top priority of the House Committee.

There are currently 55 members of the House who served in the military during the Vietnam era. Within the context of the "New Politics" in Congress, they banded together to form a coalition to isolate those issues of most concern to Vietnam veterans and to pressure the authorizing committees on these points when momentum seemed lax. As a group they represent a formidable force of influence for the legislative activity of the Veterans Affairs Committees in the House and Senate. Readjustment counseling and post-traumatic stress disorder became one of their top priorities.

During the 60s and 70s, the traditional veterans organizations, with their powerful representation in Washington and across the country, still remained wrapped in the flag of previous wars. While acknowledging the Vietnam veteran from a distance, these organizations set their sights on the huge expansion of the V.A. medical, compensation, and pension programs during this period. Ironically, returning Vietnam veterans, amputees, and paraplegics were used very effectively by politicians and the media. Portrayed as living in rat- and roach-infested V.A. hospital wards, these returning veterans were used as examples to boost V.A. budgets and expand programs with new hospitals, clinics, and services. As a result the V.A. now has the largest medical system in the free world with 172 hospitals and 227 outpatient clinics. Much of that growth has occurred since the beginning of the Vietnam war.

Thousands of Vietnam veterans benefited from these improvements. But the basic issues of concern to the vast majority of the Vietnam veterans remained unaddressed, namely, adequate education benefits and effective and meaningful employment and readjustment programs. Apart from the 300,000 wounded in Vietnam, how many of the remaining 9 million Vietnam era veterans were seeking care at V.A. hospitals? In 1975, at an average age 29, how many of these veterans would seek those services in the following 10 to 20 years?

The traditional veterans organizations, the most powerful and most frequent voices before the House and Senate Veterans Affairs Committees, were not ready to recognize the problems, nor the promise and potential that Vietnam veterans could bring to their constituency. Likewise, as with all good politicians, the traditionalists in Congress and the Veterans Administration mirrored the thought patterns of their most vocal constituency.

However, this too began to change in the late 70s. Vietnam veterans represented nearly one-third of the then total of 30 million veterans in the United States, a membership target and a constituency that could not be overlooked for long. By gradual degrees, veterans organizations began promoting Vietnam veterans to visible leadership positions within the organizations and espousing their concerns, including the readjustment counseling program.

The third corner of the "Iron Triangle," the Veterans Administration, fell into step behind Vietnam veterans with the confirmation of Max Cleland as V.A. Administrator during the Carter Administration. As the youngest V.A. Administrator in history, he joined the ranks of his younger counterparts and progressives in the Congress to make improvements in a wide range of programs, with Vietnam veterans as his primary objective. He too used post-traumatic stress disorder and the V.A.'s readjustment counseling program as the springboard for this movement.

In 1979 the House Veterans Affairs Committee finally caved in and accepted the Senate amendment to create the readjustment counseling program. The program was agreed to by the House as a bargaining chip in the final conference on S-7 in exchange for the Senate accepting a House provision calling for the committees to have the jurisdiction and the ultimate powerful authority to directly review and approve all major V.A. renovation and construction. The Administration strongly opposed this infringement on the authority of its own Office of Management and Budget, but with readjustment counseling in the legislation, the bill was virtually veto proof.

The media blitz which accompanied the opening of the 91 Storefront Counseling Centers, charged with the responsibility for dealing with post-traumatic stress disorder, was unprecedented in recent V.A. history. This positive attention surprised both proponents and detractors of the program. Vet Centers became a rallying point for Vietnam veterans across the country. Politicians jumped to cut the ribbons at Center openings. Furthermore, the readjustment counseling program began to accomplish what it set out to do. The gamble had paid off. Vietnam veterans were using the Centers and receiving help. The Centers and the program had identified an entire patient population that the Veterans Administration had not previously known to exist.

This attention was surpassed in 1981 only when the Reagan Administration announced its plans to terminate the program. In one of the first and most publicized defeats of his Administration, the President received the news in the Spring of that year that the Congress had unanimously approved a three-year extension of the program with a current yearly budget of $31 million. Readjustment counseling was extended again for four more years in 1983 and expanded in size in 1984.

The program not only was successful in providing direct services to Vietnam veterans, but also sparked discussion and a wide range of study into the whole issue of post-traumatic stress disorder. The Center for Policy Research finally released its study in 1981. This became one of the most intensive and reliable documents on the readjustment of an entire generation of veterans. While that information is already aging, the study documents in clear detail that 500,000 to 800,000 Vietnam era veterans, particularly those who had endured the most severe combat-related stress and psychic trauma, were still encountering varying degrees of inability to adjust successfully to civilian life. These experiences were indeed affecting their social orientation and economic stability.

The American Psychiatric Association recognized post-traumatic stress disorder as a definable disorder. Likewise, the Veterans Administration officially defined post-traumatic stress disorder as a service-connected disability and began approving claims for compensation, not only for Vietnam veterans, but for older veterans from previous wars as well.

The program also sparked one of the largest volunteer efforts within the federal government as a call went out to health care professionals and community leaders across the country asking for their assistance to augment the work of the Vet Centers.

The program was designed to identify and treat so-called "troubled" Vietnam veterans. However, the early controversy and ensuing debate over the Vet Centers served as a forum for millions of Americans to discuss and come to grips with the Vietnam experience themselves. Included in that number are the vast majority of Vietnam era veterans who remained unscathed by their experience, but until recently were not able to openly acknowledge that veterans' experience.

But perhaps the most lasting benefit from the program has been its impact on the Veterans Administration itself. When Max Cleland and V.A. psychologist and Vet Center director, Dr. Donald Crawford, sat down in the Summer of 1979 to design the program, they decided that to be successful, Readjustment Counseling (*Operation Outreach*) would have to be placed outside the physical and administrative structure of the V.A. The plan was submitted and approved to place the centers in communities in storefront settings with a chain of command and budget process totally apart from the traditional bureaucratic function of the V.A.'s Department of Medicine and Surgery.

This was done for two reasons: 1) to overcome the inherent distrust of the V.A. "organization" felt by the client Vietnam veteran population; and 2) to overcome the distrust of the program felt by those within the

V.A. itself who had long questioned from the traditional perspective the nature of post-traumatic stress disorder and the new treatment methods being implemented under the program.

Separating the Readjustment Counseling Program from the mainstream of traditional V.A. mental health services served to heighten the visibility of the program and the impact it could have on the V.A. itself. The visible lines had to be drawn in order that they could eventually be erased when the program had proven its worth. In any issue of debate, particularly in politics, it is first necessary to build a barrier delineating differences in order that the barrier can later be broken down through compromise. The issues are clearly separated so as to define their differences and share the benefits of each. In this regard the Readjustment Counseling Program has served as an entry point for thousands of Vietnam veterans seeking assistance and understanding from the Veterans Administration. It has also served as a training ground for an entire new generation of V.A. health care professionals eager to share new technology, new treatment methods, and increased concern for the veteran population within the V.A. system.

In designing and approving legislation calling for a treatment program for post-traumatic stress disorder, the House and Senate Veterans Affairs Committees were faced with the usual quandary. The members of these committees and their staff are not psychologists, not psychiatrists, and not scientists. Yet they are in direct control of millions of dollars directing the day-to-day operation of the V.A. medical system and research operation. There is certainly ample and constant advice from all quarters as to how those dollars should be spent, but in the end, the ultimate decision is theirs, accompanied by the same questions.

How do you approach human suffering with a checkbook? There are certainly more health problems than there are dollars to pay for treatment. How do you judge the cost effectiveness of certain research and certain programs over others? More importantly, what will the taxpayer tolerate?

In the case of the Readjustment Counseling Program and its pioneering efforts in the field of PTSD, the Congress took a gamble. The gamble arose in certain quarters from political motivation, but has paid off handsomely in terms of lasting benefits for the health, image, and welfare of the Vietnam veteran and the advancement of medical science.

TABLE 1
Legislative History—Documents on Hand

I. SENATE
    A. Hearing—Senate Veterans Affairs Committee (SVAC)—96th Congress—First Session on S-7
        January 25, 1979
    B. Report—SVAC—to accompany S-7
        April 27, 1979: Report #96-100
    C. Hearing—SVAC—97th Congress—First Session on S-26, etc.
        April 30, 1981
    D. Congressional Record
        May 16, 1979: S 5998-S6047
        June 4, 1979: S 6781-6786
        February 6, 1981: S 1188-S1196

II. HOUSE
    A. Hearing—House Veterans Affairs Committee (HVAC)—96th Congress—Oversight South Dakota
        May 29, 1979
    B. Hearing—HVAC—97th Congress—Readjustment Counseling
        April 8, 1981
        Serial No. 97-20
    C. Report—HVAC—to Accompany H.R. 3499
        May 19, 1981
        Report No. 97-79
    D. Hearing—HVAC—Issues Concerning Vietnam Veterans
        July 16, 1981
        Serial No. 97-32
    E. Hearing—Committee on Government Operations
        October 19, 1981
    F. Hearing—HVAC—Veterans Administration Programs in Montana
        June 19, 1982
        Serial No. 97-68
    G. Hearing—HVAC—Adequacy of Care Through Vet Centers
        August 26, 1982
        Serial No. 97-76
    H. Congressional Record
        May 21, 1979: H3453-H3471
        June 24, 1981: H3303-H3304

III. LAW
    A. PL 96-22
    B. PL 97-72
    C. PL 98-160

CHAPTER

2

Have You Hugged a Vietnam Veteran Today? The Basic Wound of Catastrophic Stress

CHAIM F. SHATAN, M.D.

Most of you have seen the bumper sticker which asks, "Have you hugged a Vietnam veteran today?"

If you have ever responded, you may have been shoved aside (especially if you are a woman), or you may have been hugged back and wetted by silent tears. Many a veteran has trouble with intimacy and tenderness—as well as with such other intense feelings as rage and grief. "Serious and prolonged" readjustment problems "have been markedly greater for Vietnam veterans than for other veterans," according to the V.A. (1973).

Massive psychic trauma clothes survivors with a perforated, tattered, sometimes even shattered ego. The emotional context of catastrophe persists after the trauma seems over. And this wounded ego has to cope with the traumatic sense of reality.

To confront this reality, psychiatry needs a language to transmit what was, what is, and what might be again; a knowledge to help ease the crippling, though invisible, wounds. We cannot get away with abridging complexity. We all know from our own experience that there is always something beyond words and evidence.

"The Troubled Vietnam Veteran" was the title of a *Newsweek* cover story (March 30, 1981). Lindy (1981) wrote about the reluctance of survivors to use psychiatric resources. Then there was this news story:

MAN ATTACKS V.A. HOSPITAL
West Los Angeles (AP). A man shouting that Agent Orange had destroyed his brain drove a jeep . . . (into) a V.A. hospital and opened fire . . .The man claimed . . . that he was deaf because of Agent Orange, a . . . defoliant used . . . during the Vietnam War (*Houston Post*, March 15, 1981).

James Clavell, the author, spent four years in a Japanese prison camp. Fourteen out of every 15 prisoners died. For 15 years afterwards, he had to restrain the impulse to forage for food in garbage, and he was never without a tin of sardines. And for 15 years he told no one.

Such bizarre behavior can persist for decades or emerge decades later. And these survivors tend to avoid human contact. They retreat into the interstices of society, especially when asked about the atrocities they survived or carried out. As professionals, we may find no adequate frame of reference for confronting these issues. Staring such events in the face, we may feel unable to achieve empathy, unable to put ourselves in the shoes of victimizer or victim. Nor can we listen. Or speak. To try to convey this actuality is "like a blind man talking about color" (Amery, 1980).

MAN-MADE STRESS AND UNHEALED PSYCHIC REALITY: THE BASIC WOUND

Many symptoms and syndromes have been assigned to these victims. However, at their core they share a common wound: the fact that their entire cultural or social unit has been torn asunder—and by *man-made*, socially sanctioned destructiveness, not by natural disaster. *The man-made nature of this overwhelming event determines the intensity and duration of stress, as well as any susceptibility to later psychopathology.*

Every facet of the survivors' daily existence had been governed by total persecution or total combat—privations, mutilations, massacres, killing or being killed. Coming home did not always bring the horror to an end. Homecoming is stressful: it can spell coming home to die, or coming home with a "thousand mile stare."

I propose that all the specific disturbances are emblems of a marked personality change founded upon the *unending threat of death at human hands.* The outcome may be murderous rage or suicidal resignation without means or chance for mastery or coping. Commonly, there is a new, constricted adaptation to life. Chronic disorders may erupt years later—stemming from the time of catastrophe and from the interweaving of unimagined savagery with unrelieved anxiety.

The survivor's tattered garment is *unhealed psychic reality*—reality that he has not restructured in full. This is his specific wound. His ego remains deformed, and his perceptions are still based on the conditions from which he returned. There, psychotic reality was the norm, eclipsing everyday living. Imminent death and destruction had become the new "reality principle." In counterinsurgency warfare, as in a Nazi death camp, a person had a chance to live only by so distorting his ego that he could make the new, deadly reality his own. A Vietnam medic said that, in an ambush, he had "to permit . . . old reality to slide away . . . through a membrane" (K.P., 1972).

After penetrating the "membrane" between the two realities, perception of events is utterly changed. The individual adopts the paranoid stance and mentality of survival in combat. Styles of action, affect, and cognition are transformed. Even when the stress ends, a return to the status quo is unlikely. Each survivor's inner world is still permeated with traumatic reality. In fact, its malevolence may overthrow the reality perceptions of ordinary life: the world suddenly feels "bereft of order; . . . as though the whole reasonable and decent constitution of things, the sum of all he had experienced or learned to expect, were . . . mislaid somewhere . . .; no outrageous circumstance . . ., no new, mad thing . . . could add a jot to the all-encompassing chaos that shrieked about his ears . . ." (Waugh, 1934, pp. 136-137).

The new overriding mentality is paranoid only in the eyes of outsiders, outsiders who have never faced a ghetto railroad line, nor ever needed to kick an adversary in the face to live. A flash of combat may alter someone's life forever. Haunting experiences are woven into the tapestry of these lives: from the vantage point of the *other* reality, there is no deficit in thinking, and *no* inappropriate behavior.

That other reality means "to be a dead man on leave . . . who only by chance is not yet where he belongs . . ." He continues to feel "condemned to be murdered in due time" (Amery, 1980). The survivor finds more wisdom in his Marine dog tag or in the number on his arm than in all the Geneva and genocide treaties.

To reenter, the survivor must pass through the torn interface between the two universes of reality perception—that of catastrophic reality and that of daily reality, from the reality of massacre to everyday reality. But *incorporated traumatic reality* remains an unpredictable threat. As a rule, we are only aware of segments of possible realities. The ego fashions an integrated realm out of reality by selectively dissociating vast territories of experience. In combat veterans and survivors, the two reality perception systems co-exist and overlap. Awareness is blurred. I suggest that we call the clash between these two systems *"perceptual dissonance"* (P.D.). Once the triumph of survival has worn off, "symptoms" may arise from this clash. These "symptoms" represent impulses which need to be restrained, yet which continue to press for utterance (Shatan, 1974).

Case 1. "Highway One" (An Example of Perceptual Dissonance)

A "pure" instance of perceptual dissonance was presented by a veteran who had been a truck driver in Vietnam. He survived by driving Vietnam's Highway One "like a bat out of hell." In 1979, seven years after discharge, he became a coppermine truck driver. The one lane, snaking dirt road felt like Vietnam's Highway One. In a year, a split image "appeared" in his rearview mirror: on the right, the coppermine road, on the left, Highway One. He knew that one image belonged to the past. Yet, its grip was so inexorable that he had to battle panic with all his might to avoid a smash-up. Sweating, shaking, he was exhausted at the end of each day. This case was one of the first to gain a V.A. hearing for psychotherapy and disability. His claim was based on *combat-related stress disorder*, although symptoms did not appear until seven years after discharge.* Since his new job duplicated his Vietnam job, it carried him back to the war zone as inevitably as if he had sighted North Vietnamese soldiers. Was he secretly attracted to the new job? That question remains unanswered.

NEW ADAPTIVE LIFESTYLES

Scratch many returnees from total war and you will find, under their differences, one striking common denominator—a new, permanent adaptive lifestyle (Kardiner, 1941).

Impaired adaptability is the central feature of this new lifestyle. Feel-

---

*Until recently, the V.A. did not consider symptoms arising more than two years after discharge to be service-related.

ing, thinking, and action are fundamentally changed: They become tighter, more rigid, hemmed in.

Can the behavior of combat veterans change so drastically in only a year or two? The outcome depends upon the intensity and totality of their experience, rather than its duration. Being uprooted, dislocated, and transplanted are disorienting experiences. They render young men, in particular, peculiarly vulnerable to fragmentation. Automatic surrender to authority during training predisposes them to new inflexible styles of reacting. There is unique *imprinting* value in dedicating every hour to the repetition of a small spectrum of activities. Then, unpredictable shifts—in leadership, group, pace, and setting—evoke regressive patterns. And, when the newcomers are treated as "F.N.G.'s"* in action, they may retreat into even narrower modes of response.

Overnight, the "freedom bird" (this designates the homebound plane from Southeast Asia after discharge) suddenly jets men back to "the World." ("The World" designates the U.S.A., just like "the world" outside the jail walls in prison slang. The jailhouse argot "lifers," "short-timers," etc. is not a result of chance. It is an appropriate response to a one-to-three-year sentence in the 'Nam.). This speed helps newly acquired traits to set almost with the rapidity of plaster. "The mind becomes wax to receive impressions, but marble to retain them" (Grant, 1946) in both combat and post-combat adaptation.

PERCEPTUAL DISSONANCE

The earliest known concepts of psychic "integration" were framed in the Eastern Mediterranean about 500 B.C. Only a few centuries ago, the simultaneous perception of multiple dimensions of reality, as well as hallucinations, were commonly accepted as belonging within the boundaries of normal experience. We can still find such "unintegrated" or dissonant psychic awareness in population "pockets" in advanced societies, as well as in the South Pacific or the South American jungle.

Am I being irrelevant or am I digressing? I think not. The new adaptive lifestyles are not simply due to individual psychological regression. Entire social groups, such as death camp inmates or counter-guerrilla warriors, can regress. The resulting mental states can admit dissociated phenomena into partial awareness. Each individual also senses the dissociated material as a frightening incursion of the past into the present.

---

*"F.N.G.'s," a standard Vietnam war phrase, which meant "F———'n New Guys."

This is the essence of "flashback." One of the most transparent examples is that of the truckdriver *(Case 1)*.

How is the groundwork prepared for such developments? Abrupt, dramatic shifts in time and place do not allow for necessary periods of transition. Orderly integration and reintegration cannot occur. New and old sets of experiential information are not sorted out. Multilayered systems of reality perception from both civilian and military milieux, or from the worlds of persecutory and pre-war reality, are—so to speak—"stored alongside" still other reality perception systems of childhood and adult life (Jaynes, 1976).

Suppose we conceive of the "Ego," the Psyche, the "I," as the seat of perception of this reality. This "eye" is then always confronting, not merely a multilayered reality but a "multichambered reality." It scans both connections and separations between different segments of the possible spectra of human reality.*

The survivor's tattered** ego is unprepared for such tasks of bridging and separating. The new adaptive lifestyle is "dedicated" to defending the delicate organization of the survivor's self. Although incomplete, the tattered garment protects the veteran as well as it can. It guards the individual from sudden onslaughts of what was once the core of perceived reality. However, this new way of life lacks flexibility. Hence, there can be "breakthroughs" (flashbacks) to previous life events, or "breakdowns" (syndromes) to previous ways of life. True, the person remains oriented in current time and space. Yet, because of this rigid imprinting, his inner resources cannot relieve the residual tensions. As a result, many a veteran may come close to desperation upon reentry from Vietnam. The symptoms and syndromes are the post-traumatic stress disorders (PTSD) described under "Reactive Disorders" in DSM-III*** (American Psychiatric Association, 1980).

FEATURES OF MAN-MADE STRESS

Disbelief still greets the notion that Vietnam veterans and K'Z,**** or death camp, survivors share many traits. Yet, we made this assertion

---

*For simplicity, I omit "right" and "left" brain research from this discussion.

**The Yiddish or German word "zerissen" is more apt as it comprises: torn, torn apart, full of holes, in shreds. The noun "Zerissenkeit" signifies "torn-apart-ness."

***The section on PTSD was formulated by the "Reactive Disorders" subcommittee of the DSM-III Task Force, with the collaboration of the Vietnam Veterans Working Group (Coordinator, C.F. Shatan, M.D.).

****K'Z = "Konzentrationslager," i.e., concentration camp.

in 1971, not as theory but because of similar clinical symptoms and findings (Shatan, 1972). The gap between victimizers and those once destined for the ovens is narrower than might be expected.

Both were plucked from their peacetime habitats, relocated, and de-individuated. Both were dispersed again and again, and designated by numbers. Both felt surrounded, like fish in a hostile sea, by death, mutilation, and starvation. Drugs, from amphetamines to heroin (and alcohol), lowered the G.I.'s resistance to orders. Besides being wasted by snipers, booby traps, and "friendly fire," grunts were shot by some officers if they refused to go into action (S.T.J., 1980). Terror (and counterterror) were the daily diet for K'Z's* and veterans alike.

Extremes of climate were a shared experience. The few escapees roamed the forests or jungles, in mortal danger, sometimes in small groups, offering what resistance they could to all comers. "Apocalypse Now" (Coppola, 1980) situations have been confirmed by a number of combat veterans as well as by some psychotherapists who work with veterans. Computerized R & R was not only a hollow mockery, but tantalizing torture, a brief interlude in hair-raising "reality." From 600,000 to 1,000,000 veterans are still burdened by less-than-honorable discharges or "SPN" ("spin") numbers, often inflicted vindictively. This "bad paper" is fraught with *unemployability*. So is the legacy of the forced labor camps.

DELAYED STRESSORS AND MAN-MADE STRESS

The man-made quality of this stress leads to protean manifestations, which saturate its every difference from random natural disaster. The effects of man-made "injury," even an urban ambush (a mugging or a rape), are far more enduring and disabling than those following a sudden "act of God."

When a person loses his entire town ("shtetl"**) or his whole combat unit, he becomes "unplugged" from his network of communal relationships. Unplugging predisposes to delayed stress disorders, which may be triggered—even decades later—by *traumatic triggering factors* (T.T.F.). At first, these "delayed stressors" seem autonomous, but it is easy to recognize in them fragments or symbols of an appalling reality—the

---

*K'Z's is used here as short-hand for concentration camp inmate.

**"Shtetl" (literally "tiny city") means any village or town in Eastern Europe which was a predominantly Yiddish center of population and communal life.

original stress-related or combat-related stimuli. The people they affect are in a state of latent endocrine and autonomic hyperarousal. This hyperalertness exists alongside a state of unconsummated mourning—the persistent effects of denied and unexpressed loss, which I call "impacted grief." The recurrent nightmares, the irritability, the startle reactions have all been catalogued and summarized in DSM-III. They are much more severe and lasting in survivors of combat and persecution than in noncombat veterans or survivors of earthquakes and hurricanes. Twenty-five years later, combat veterans still show baseline respiration, pulse, and E.E.G. readings which are significantly elevated compared to non-combat veterans or nonveterans (Archibald & Tuddenham, 1965).

POST-COMBAT ADAPTATION AND OTHER POST-TRAUMATIC LIFESTYLES

Counterinsurgency war or Holocaust is followed by post-traumatic adaptation. This is—at bottom—a continuation of the death factory or guerrilla war position into the postwar era. It is the paranoid stance, still unceasingly watchful against the threat of death, yet ill at ease without enemies. When there is friction, or "perceptual dissonance" (Shatan, 1974), between "everyday life" on the one hand and readiness for action on the other, "war participation symptoms or syndromes" (Tanay, 1979) may appear.

Such syndromes and symptoms obviously represent peacetime persistence of the wartime personality. However, each person has his own "breaking point" under stress. Accordingly, one may live a lifetime without showing the full range of one's newfound lifestyle. Other people are simply aware that a man is "not the same," that he is "changed forever," that "he's a different person."

Features of Post-Traumatic Adaptive Lifestyle

1) Veterans and survivors both experience early interludes of *euphoria,* but these feelings generally fade. They are replaced by feelings of being scapegoated, problems with security and secretiveness, and problems with work and intimacy. A pervasive hyperalertness is punctuated by startle reactions, flashbacks, and intrusive fears (American Psychiatric Association, 1980; Shatan, 1972, 1974).

2) *Constant vigilance* is the hallmark of the Vietnam *combat survivor* (a term I prefer to combat veteran). A startle reaction is a reflex *tactical*

response to *any* sudden change in the surroundings. But it represents a failure of peacetime adaptation; the veteran feels ambushed by sudden change. He may adopt elaborate precautions to avoid being taken by surprise. He stands with his back to the wall to protect his rear. If a leaf trembles, he knows if it has been swayed by a breeze or shaken by a squirrel. He keeps to the inside of a park path. ("Any man who's been on patrol knows that that way you're less visible to hostiles" [K.P., 1972].)

Sleeping with a weapon nearby—knife, pistol, machete—is no guarantee against nightmares. Sleeping on the floor to be unseen (below window level) provides no certainty because one may be awakened by the special silence which foretells an attack. (In the 'Nam, bird, animal and insect sounds would vanish before a night attack—a *deathly* stillness.) A sudden hot, humid spell—like jungle weather—may trigger nightmares, as does cold for the K'Z survivor. During heavy snowstorms, survivors and their American-born children may hoard food—without consulting each other (Rustin, 1973).

3) During combat *nightmares,* veterans may strike their wives or sweethearts yet remember nothing once they wake up. When a veteran becomes a parent, his child may appear in his combat nightmares: "I dreamt I was near Dakto. I was trying to save my kid. A bunch of guys in black pajamas were chasing him." A woman, who was born in a ghetto in 1939, gave birth and dreamt regularly that her child was with her in the wartime ghetto.

4) Basic combat training actively discourages both intimacy and grief since they are the most antimartial of sentiments (Shatan, 1977). The result is a *guarded attitude toward showing feeling* and emotion. Strict military bearing is the preferred mode at a funeral, not public mourning. *Tenderness* towards women and children is to be avoided. Warriors' women say, "We just couldn't get close." Some add, "It frightened the baby to see him beating me." One veteran said, "I wish I could learn to love as much as I learned to hate in Vietnam. And I sure hated, man. But love's a pretty heavy word." Yet combat veterans—survivors of *so many "separations"*—find even brief separations from their wives to be torture.

5) *Moving,* whether around the corner or to another state, is stressful. It is uprooting and transplanting again. Anxiety grows, as do hyperarousal, security measures, and flashbacks. The veteran may say: "You don't know what to expect in the new locale. *If you feel threatened, you become threatening, just like you did in the 'Nam"* (S.A., 1976).

6) *International crises* can precipitate panic or retreat into "mental fox-

holes." The 1975 helicopter evacuation from the U.S. embassy roof in Saigon evoked flashbacks in Holocaust survivors of rescue ships off the Balkan coast in 1944. The 1982 Falklands war provoked a rash of phone calls from Vietnam veterans. They were both scared and spellbound.

7) However, both types of survivors also acquire *positive values*. Many K'Z survivors value children highly, and in a concerned, not always overprotective, way. Many a Vietnam veteran feels a deep, often unspoken, comradeship with other veterans, even though the war was computerized. They also adopt the Vietnamese sense of being one with the natural kingdom. Seeds and apple cores are not rubbish, but food for small animals and birds.

DOES TIME HEAL ALL WOUNDS? DELAYED TRAUMATIC STRESS DISORDERS

Man-made stress, new forms of adaptation, perceptual dissonance, and permanent change in self-definition shape the substrate for "delayed" traumatic stress disorders (Reactive Disorders in DSM-III). Such disturbances follow the "symptom-free" incubation period. They may be neither transient nor reversible. The furnace of adaptation is the womb which gives birth to a new personality. This new personality harbors the predispositions to delayed stress disorders.

Follow-ups of World War II veterans (Archibald & Tuddenham, 1965; Nefzger, 1970), survivors (Niederland, 1972; Eitinger, 1972), and Vietnam combat veterans (Shatan, 1973) all lead to one conclusion: Perceptual dissonance may not disclose itself as disorder until years after the original stress. May we speak of "permanent psychological implants" (Zea, 1974) which must work their way to the surface—like shrapnel—before damage is apparent?

We need such concepts, however inadequate, to understand and alleviate suffering. We must grasp the twofold matrix of the basic wound of post-traumatic stress. *First,* we specify that the stress was "social" catastrophe, not "natural" disaster. Man-made stress tears the fabric of human trust asunder. *Secondly,* the same or similar monumental disruption of community affects the entire group—a loss of communality.

After such massive man-made stress, preexisting disorder is irrelevant. The specific stress itself constitutes the crucial predisposition. This stress is generally predictive of the nature and degree of morbidity and of symptoms.

The *"latent"* period which follows post-traumatic stress is a time of *chronic susceptibility.* *Natural* disaster, however, is quickly succeeded by *acute* emotional reactions and rapid recovery after rescue and rebuilding. *There has been no human agency, no chronic threat, no coercion.* Witness the rapid recovery of the city of Darwin, Australia, after its 1975 tidal wave.

Once disorder does emerge, adaptive traits turn into "symptoms," while disturbed adaptive patterns become clinical "syndromes." "Time does *not* heal all wounds" (Shatan, Haley, & Smith, 1977).

COMBAT VETERANS AND SURVIVORS IN PSYCHOTHERAPY

Many treatment centers seldom take a military history from a veteran, nor do they obtain the full story of persecution from survivors (Haley, 1974). Yet this information is the foundation of *healing.* Therapy can only proceed in a *multi-axial framework:* Catastrophic life events are the defining guideline, and symptoms and course are the other two dimensions (Shatan et al., 1977). Then, as veterans and survivors repair their shattered faith in human beings, they will tell "war stories" and talk of persecution.

We have shown how deeply connected victims and victimizers can be (Shatan, 1972). Now, let us talk about aspects of "cure"—especially the uncovering of the facts of man-made disaster and the excavation of buried feelings.

Case 2. "Who Should Live and Who Should Die?" (Loss of Communality)

H.S., a Warsaw Ghetto survivor, developed suicidal depression and terror. Chief pathologist in a major Eastern hospital, he had fallen afoul of the director, who wished to dismiss him. He was sure that he would be blackballed and that "no one in the East would touch" him. Suicide seemed the only alternative to unemployment—a rather extreme solution.

Reluctantly, he spoke of the death factories and of "selections" made between those "who should live and those who should die." It emerged that, under his depression, was a dread of becoming *unemployable.* This was a criterion for instant extermination in the death camps, for joining those who had not survived. His depression slowly lifted. He made connections with other hospitals and was elected head of the state pathology society.

He had loathed his son's college—one of the best in the East—since his first sight of it. He now grasped that the train tracks nearby had precipitated a flashback, which he repressed, to the transports carrying Jews to the *"East."*

In the Ghetto, the conviction that hospitals were havens of safety endured. One day, an S.S. raid was impending. The family packed off the grandfather and three infants to the hospital. Imagine their horror when the S.S. invaded the hospital and slaughtered all the patients. For his first 10 years here, this doctor would work only in black and Puerto Rican "ghetto" hospitals.

After a survivors' rap session, he had a recurrent nightmare. He was being observed in a performance, which would "have a bearing on his future." (The observers were "like Nazis making 'selections.' ") He had to reassemble a machine, but couldn't find the "important missing parts." His "frantic search prevented an orderly job." All such dreams ended in frustration.

Working in ghetto hospitals is an attempt at restitution. It is also a "frantic search for a safe "haven." He is hunting for the *"missing parts,"* the relatives who vanished *in* the ghetto hospital. Without them, he cannot reconstitute the family machine. At work, however competent he may look, inwardly he feels "disorganized before observers." Yet he is a brilliant pathologist—at great psychic cost.

Case 3. From Qui Non to Appalachia: "How Many Limbs Does a Child Have?"

Thirteen years after Vietnam, John B., a former medic, started having flashbacks when friends got pregnant. Later, he became anxious the day before any visit to children. He would become panicky en route. No sooner would he see that the children's limbs were all intact than relief would sweep over him. He counted the arms and legs of any child, and would lean over the car seat to verify the presence of limbs hidden from view. Although he recalled no atrocities, he insisted that "my eyes must have seen what my hands may have done."

Hypervigilance was second nature. He wanted to drop out of college to "become a cop like other vets." He would jump at the sound of firecrackers, especially on (*Civil War*) Memorial Day. Ten years after homecoming, he honeymooned in Northern Ireland (he was of Irish Protestant descent) although his first choice was the 'Nam.* This trip strengthened his siege mentality and combat stance. He said, "I take another route each time I come to see you just as I did in Belfast to avoid both the Orangemen and the Catholics." He typed a detailed biography, in which the only mention

---

*cf. "Easy Rider" trips through the American South by combat vets.

of Vietnam was about two relatives being hospitalized while he was there.

Evidence of atrocities against children never emerged. The children were symbolic, *literally* ("the Vietnamese looked like small kids") and figuratively ("kids are such easy targets that I have trouble keeping control because I want to take action to protect them"). The random violence of male toddlers was provoking: "They made me feel like hitting out indiscriminately . . . Once, I wanted to spray the tree line to protect my 4-year-old niece and her little brother from danger."

After these insights, he began to sleep better, felt more comfortable when he held children, and stopped counting their limbs. When infertility, perhaps due to Agent Orange, was found, he viewed this as "more punishment" for his part in the War. Paradoxically, this magnified his *guilt* feelings: He felt the infertility was a "mark of Cain," proving he was a criminal. "On my first day in Saigon, I saw hundreds of kids without arms or legs. It socked me in the guts. I knew I shouldn't be there."

Flashbacks decreased in frequency, intensity, and length. When he got ready to leave for medical school, and knew that he would have no therapy for awhile, he feared that flashbacks might come back. He had learned to master certain anxieties through self-hypnosis, except for flashbacks. He *missed* his flashbacks, and wanted to keep them! "A flashback is pure hell, but I feel relief afterward." Perhaps, repetition of the massive trauma permitted some "working through." We decided "not to push progress," and he arranged to visit an "Operation Outreach"* center on a preliminary trip to his new state.

Our observations can be extended beyond these atrocities to civilian life. Take, for instance, an unexpected menace to the existence of even one or a few families. I refer to threats from higher human authority, not from natural phenomena.

---

*The rap group movement has been coordinated by the volunteer "Vietnam Veterans Resource Project," John Russell Smith, coordinator. The publication of DSM-III and activity of Vietnam veteran congressmen led to "Operation Outreach," an outgrowth of the self-help movement. Over 100 centers, funded by the V.A. but with professional autonomy, include many Vietnam veterans on their teams. The chief psychiatrist, Arthur Blank, a Vietnam veteran, now directs the entire program. The author, Chaim F. Shatan, has been on the faculty of "Operation Outreach" training conferences, has consulted with Outreach staff, and has appeared on T.V., radio, and other public forums, together with veterans, as part of therapeutic advocacy. The Disabled American Veterans and Vietnam Veterans of America also operate outreach programs. The V.A. has renamed Operation Outreach as Readjustment Counseling Services.

Case 4. A North American Community in Peacetime: The Airport at Chatham, Ontario (Canada) and Three-Mile Island

A farm family near Chatham, Ontario, developed a clearcut, stress disorder: startle reactions, nightmares, suspiciousness, fear of strangers, trouble concentrating, and impulsiveness. These symptoms followed a 1981 offer by the Chatham airport to buy a strip of their land (Montreal Gazette, September 1, 1981). Chatham planned to slice the farm in two to lengthen a runway. Seven other farm families were affected. They saw their farms as bridges between past and future. The airport threatened to disrupt the chain of future generations. This felt far more damaging than a flood ever had. These eight farmers had embodied their life in a living present, but *other people* had decided that that present would be devoid of a future.

What links these farmers with the people near Three Mile Island? They share a determination to keep their status as members of an intact community, not marked off from it, not dismembered, but plugged into a common matrix. Both groups are suspicious of people—with good reason, vested authorities have questioned their perceptions of reality. Yet these powers are tampering with the very basis of that reality by planning to divide and fragment it. Their suspicion and their symptoms make perfect sense.

A NOTE ON THE TREATMENT OF DISRUPTED COMMUNITIES: A CULTURAL PROCESS

I regard counterguerrilla warriers as *"combat survivors."*

1) During *"the talking cure,"* survivors must know that someone listens to each account and each recollection of every aspect of their cataclysm. But talk is not enough.

2) *Gathering together* the human remnants is another facet of cure. Broken ties are mended. Mutual support systems are social equivalents of ruined communal or military groups. V.V.A.W.* rap groups, therapeutic collectives, the 1981 assembly of survivors in Jerusalem, the Disabled American Veterans, and bars which cater to veterans can all help

---

*Vietnam Veterans Against the War (V.V.A.W.) (founded 1967) was the largest antiwar veterans organization, boasting 20,000 members. It originated rap groups, therapeutic communes, sociopolitical theater, newspapers, and poetry as treatment (WHAM—*Winning Hearts and Minds* was a bestselling book of poetry [Crumb, 1973]).

to reconstruct the shattered *symbiotic units*. These can invent social and political action on their own behalf, and play an active part in defining their future.

Both sides of this *cultural treatment process* combine to relieve the "impacted grief" (Shatan, 1973), the *shame* and *guilt* of being alive when others have died.

3) A veteran's fear of sudden, uncontrollable rage and violence can be "stepped down" in small increments. As a rule, he sees no middle ground between withdrawal and physical violence. In session, he is asked to fantasy additional alternatives between these two extremes, e.g. hitting a wall or a punching bag, *imagining* hitting a wall, and so on. This *"basic training in reverse"* may be quite effective, and can be carried over into daily life.

4) As for *duration* of treatment, it took me two years to learn the meaning of the college railroad tracks (*Case 2*) and four years to learn about returning to Vietnam via Northern Ireland (*Case 3*). Many veterans and survivors suffer in private, reluctant to communicate their pain. Perhaps only poets and writers can speak for them. A novelist writes:

> A patient used to his illness . . . a sick person subject to acute crises . . . that . . . may seize him at any moment, lives prudently, walks gingerly . . . ready to withdraw into himself . . . The pain is there somewhere; he doesn't know how it will pounce on him, and so he's . . . on his guard, feeling his way . . . hoping to cheat fate. (Simenon, 1978)

A poet laments:

> *Memory* is the enemy now,
> Again and again his first wife dies
> In his second wife's embrace.
>
> The chase is still on.
> He hides behind the busyness of days
> And is captured each night
> When the enemy moves on with
> The slippery ease of dreams. (Suhl, 1972)

The unendingness of persecution, the unexpectedness of ambush, equipped survivors with another system for interpreting reality. It is a frame of reference which does not fit everyday psychosocial frameworks, a system in close touch with dark timeless depths. The slightest echo from that encapsulated past—a helicopter on T.V. or a Nazi emblem—can easily explode into Tet, 1968, or Auschwitz, 1944. Then there is no present, no past, and no future.

By activating our imagination, we can appreciate the uneasy stirrings in many blacks at the resurgence of K.K.K. paraphernalia. They are also children and grandchildren of survivors, who trembled in the shadow of lynching, of that "strange fruit" whose "sudden smell" was "burning flesh" (Holiday, 1949). *Yesterday's tragedy*—be it booby-trap or death factory—*is today's inner oppression.* "A catastrophe that occurred yesterday cannot be ruled out for tomorrow" (Amery, 1980).

5) But for historical accident, this could afflict any of us. Trust in the human world must be rebuilt every day—and may be lost every day. Each day, these people fear that their essential identity is threatened. They are not deranged, and were not deranged. The disorders which may engulf them exist as internalized historical events. These events were on T.V. as they occurred. For many ex-soldiers whom we saw on T.V., "the awareness of catastrophe . . . remains the dominant force of (their) existence" (Amery, 1980). Recently, several World War II and Korean War veterans have phoned me to find an outreach program or a rap group to help them cope with continuing or delayed symptoms from *their* wars.

Concentration camp survivors, however badly off, have fared better than Vietnam combat veterans due to the early support of the United Nations Relief & Rehabilitation Administration, the support of world Jewry, the support of Israel, and compensation from German reparations. The hostages who recently returned from Iran, *and* their families, were treated along lines similar to those we adopted in 1970 in our volunteer "rap group" program. We recommended these measures long ago to the V.A., Congress and the Pentagon. They are now being adopted in "Operation Outreach."

Statistics from the V.A. hospital system on the high suicide rate among Vietnam veterans and data from penal systems on the high percentage of Vietnam veterans in jail are only the most ominous yardsticks. They require us to recognize and define combat survivors so that we may intervene appropriately.

To some people they may appear bent and unfit—physically, psychically, socially. But perhaps they are better able to recognize the inner and outer dimensions of their reality. We dare not turn away from them and their unique knowledge. Otherwise, tomorrow we may walk in their footsteps.

REFERENCES

Amery, J.: On the necessity and impossibility of being a Jew. *New German Critique*, 20:15-29, Spring-Summer, 1980.

Archibald, H.E., & Tuddenham, R.D.: Persistent stress reaction following combat: A 20-year follow-up. *Archives of General Psychiatry, 12*:475-481, 1965.

Coppola, F.: *Apocalypse now*. A movie, 1980.

Crumb, J. (Ed.): *WHAM—Winning hearts and minds*. New York: McGraw-Hill, 1973.

Diagnostic and statistical manual of mental disorders, third edition (DSM-III). Washington, D.C.: American Psychiatric Association, 1980.

Eitinger, L.S.: *Concentration camp survivors in Norway & Israel*. London: Allan & Unwin, 1972.

Grant, J.C.B.: *A method of anatomy*. Baltimore: W.B. Saunders, 1946.

Haley, S.: When the patient reports atrocities. *Archives of General Psychiatry, 30*:191-196, 1974.

Holiday, B.: *Strange fruit*. Blues song, 1949.

Jaynes, J.: *The origin of consciousness in the breakdown of the bicameral mind*. Boston: Houghton Mifflin, 1976.

Kardiner, A.: *The traumatic neuroses of war*. New York: P.B. Hoeber, 1941.

K.P.: Former corpsman in Vietnam, personal communication, 1972.

Lindy, J.D., Grace, M., & Green, B.: A general survivor's reluctance to utilize mental health resources. *American Journal of Orthopsychiatry, 51*:468-478, 1981.

Nefzger, M.D.: Follow-up studies of World War II and Korean War prisoners. I. Study plan and mortality findings. *American Journal of Epidemiology, 91*:123, 1970.

Niederland, W.: The guilt and grief of Vietnam veterans and concentration camp survivors. Workshop, IVth International Psychoanalytic Forum, October 2, 1972, N.Y.: Shatan, C. (Chair): Combat survivors & holocaust survivors compared.

Rustin, S.: Personal communication, 1973.

S.A.: Vietnam veteran, personal communication, 1976.

Shatan, C.: The guilt and grief of warriors and concentration camp survivors. IVth International Psychoanalytic Forum, October 2, 1972, N.Y. Round Table. Adapted from chairman's remarks.

Shatan, C.: The grief of soldiers: Vietnam combat veterans' self-help movement. *American Journal of Orthopsychiatry, 43*:640-653, 1973.

Shatan, C.: Through the membrane of reality: "Impacted grief" and "perceptual dissonance" in Vietnam combat veterans. *Psychiatric Opinion, 2*(6):6-15, 1974.

Shatan, C.: Bogus manhood, bogus honor: Surrender and transfiguration in the U.S. Marine Corps. *Psychoanalytic Review, 64*(4):585-610, 1977.

Shatan, C., Haley, S., & Smith, J.: Johnny comes marching home: Post-combat stress & D.S.M. III. Presented at the meeting of the American Psychiatric Association, Toronto, May 1977.

Simenon, G.: *The family lie*. New York: Harcourt Brace Jovanovitch, 1978 (Paris: Gallimard, 1940).

S.T.J.: Vietnam combat veteran, personal communication, 1980.

Suhl, Y.: Survivor (poem). *New York Times*, April 13, 1972.

Tanay, E.: Personal communication, 1979.

V.A., Department of Medicine Memorandum. Reprinted in *Congressional Record*, Oct. 12, 1973.

Waugh, E.: *A handful of dust*. Harmondsworth, England: Penguin Books, 1934.

Zea, P.H.: Personal communication, 1974.

CHAPTER

3

The Vietnam Veteran—Victim of War

EMANUEL TANAY, M.D.

My personal and clinical experiences have provided me with many opportunities to observe war victimization. As a young adolescent I experienced World War II and Nazi persecution of Jews in Eastern Europe. During my late adolescence and early adulthood I observed the ravages of war in West Germany. Throughout my professional career, I have been actively involved with evaluation and treatment of victims of wars. I have functioned as a consultant and therapist for the survivors of German concentration camps. I have evaluated and treated innumerable World War II veterans in my capacity as consultant to the Veterans Administration. During the last 15 years I have been actively involved with Vietnam war veterans. A trip to Vietnam in 1968, on the "Invitational Order" of President Johnson, provided direct, though brief, exposure to the Vietnam experience. As a forensic psychiatrist I have had occasion to evaluate a great many Vietnam veterans who have committed a variety of violent acts for which they were criminally prosecuted.

There has always been condemnation of the misery of wars imposed upon innocent victims like women, children, and the noncombatant population. The forgotten victims of wars are the soldiers who have managed to survive the wars without mutilation.

The victims of war are not only the vanquished, but also the victors, if any. Individuals and societies show long-lasting psychic sequelae of involvement in war. Each war invariably leads to social pathology in the societies involved and produces clinically visible pathology in most, and possibly all individuals who participated in the war. Yet, the soldiers who return home with intact bodies are viewed as untouched by the perils of war.

CITIZEN TO SOLDIER

The ideal wartime soldier has acquired talents which are obsolete in peacetime and, in fact, constitute handicaps in a peaceful society. The victims of Nazi persecution and the demobilized soldiers have certain skills and psychic changes in common which are impediments to normal living. The paranoid-like sensitivity of the victims of Nazi persecution, for example, had adaptive value since it protected the victims from the mortal danger with which they were constantly confronted. It frequently meant the difference between life and death. These adaptations invariably carry on in peacetime and interfere with work and daily life.

The victims of war (concentration camp survivors, soldiers, prisoners of war) are liberated or demobilized and society feels that it has fulfilled its responsibility to them. There is a striking absence of preparation of war survivors for the adaptive crisis which awaits them upon return to the civilized world. Survivors of Nazi concentration camps were often given a normal diet after their liberation which was, in a great many cases, responsible for illness and even death. There has been little effort made to assist in the process of reintegration of war's victims into normal life. Similarly, the demobilized, discharged soldier is given almost no assistance in the psychic adaptation required of him.

This is particularly true of the Vietnam War veterans who were transported, often within hours, from the jungles of Southeast Asia to the streets of American cities. The process of reintegration of the soldiers cannot take place without the acknowledgment that the soldier has undergone profound psychic changes as the result of his military experience. Inmates of prisons speak of having lost their "street personality." Similarly, the soldier loses his "civilian personality" when he enters military life, particularly during war.

TRAUMA AS TRAINING

An infant undergoes a separation-individuation phase at 18 months (Mahler, 1968). A second separation-individuation phase has been described as occurring around the age of 13. There is a third separation-individuation phase around the age of 18. This is, in fact, the final phase.

In this crucial and sensitive period, many young men are inducted into the military setting, which involves a separation without individuation. The separation is followed by an incorporation into an organization which constitutes an ambivalent symbiosis (Mahler, 1968). Military induction at this particular age is a major psychosocial intervention which frequently leads to devastating results.

• Military life initiates a process of major psychic reorganization. The traumatic consequences of military life range from those which are universal to symptoms which are a result of individual vulnerability. Military life frustrates individual gratification. Such basic needs as food, personal hygiene, sleep, the need for privacy, sexual and aggressive gratifications, and constancy of objects are all frustrated in the military setting. The sexual deprivation is unavoidable. Military life creates an aggressive overload and leads to aggressive frustration.

Even if we assumed that no mistreatment occurs in the armed forces induction centers, it should be recognized that military training requires submission to the aggression of superiors. It involves infliction of aggression upon subordinates. Sadomasochistic relationships develop to a varying degree in the proper training of soldiers. Neither sadism nor masochism, as forms of sexualized aggression, are effective means of discharge of aggression. Sadomasochistic relationships lead to ever-increasing accumulation of aggression within the psychic apparatus, primarily the superego, which becomes cruel and corruptible. Military training thus predisposes the individual for the perpetration of atrocities which are guilt provoking.

From the standpoint of mental life of the individual, the design of the military setting is ideal for the development of neurotic conflicts. The individual becomes totally submerged in the goals and needs of the military organization. Military life is not only frustrating to the sexual needs of the individual but it is also degrading of sexuality. It would, indeed, be naive to explain the antisexual atmosphere of the military setting as deriving from morality. Love and war are not compatible. The antisexual stance of the military was recognized by Freud:

Two people coming together for the purpose of sexual satisfaction, insofar as they seek solitude, are making a demonstration against the herd instinct, the group feeling. (Freud, 1955, p. 140)

The military requires herd instinct and opposes libidinal strivings. At another point Freud states:

In the great artificial groups, the church and the army, there is no room for women as a sexual object. The love relation between men and women remains outside these organizations. (Freud, 1955, p. 141)

The survivors of Nazi concentration camps relate that "little" humiliations, like having one's head shaved and standing naked, have made profound traumatic impact upon them, frequently just as much as facing the crematoria. Military life is full of such "little" humiliations which are devastating and traumatic.

The military training, at times called survival training, is alleged to prepare the individual for encounters with overwhelming experiences. It is my impression, based upon many cases, that military training makes the individual more vulnerable to stress. Military training often induces experimental traumatic neurosis or psychosis.

Dehumanization of the enemy and attenuation of guilt are among the goals of military training. Guilt interferes with killing, and is, therefore, maladaptive to a soldier. Dehumanization promotes killing and, therefore, is an adaptive quality in a warrior. The psychic trauma associated with being an actual or potential killer has to be recognized in order to understand the conflicts confronting the soldier. Every death witnessed leads to some guilt. Being an accidental survivor of a death situation leads to a specific guilt, namely, the survivor guilt. Being a killer in the defense of one's own life also leads to remorse and guilt. Being a killer "without a reason" leads to profound remorse and guilt, which frequently becomes unbearable and has to be dealt with defensively through denial or projection. Guilt is experienced by the soldiers subjectively and/or manifested objectively through self-destructive behavior. However, the absence of guilt awareness should not be mistaken for lack of guilt. Very few survivors of concentration camps verbalize survivor guilt; however, none that I have encountered are free of it. I have never seen a perpetrator of homicide who failed to show some manifestation of guilt.

There is a form of conscious guilt which is experienced by the individual as unrealistic and egodystonic. These are reproaches by the superego rejected by the ego. Then there is a form of guilt fully accepted by the ego, which is identified with the superego. An extreme form of it is seen in delusional self-reproaches.

Vietnam veterans who have participated in atrocities have frequently experienced a transformation of guilt of one form into another. In Vietnam, involvement in cruel, sadistic behavior was egosyntonic at the time and was not experienced as a transgression. Upon return to the United States, and some integration into peaceful society, this behavior becomes egodystonic and now the guilt is egosyntonic. In other words, when the behavior is not acceptable the guilt becomes acceptable.

THE TRAUMA OF FOREIGN WAR

Veterans describe the unreality of their Vietnam experience. This was a strange and foreign culture to which they were sent without preparation. The military training anticipated combat in jungles, but there was no effort made, to my knowledge, to prepare the veterans for exposure to a strange and new environment.

Prior to my visit to Vietnam in 1968, I read a number of books about Vietnam and learned a few Vietnamese phrases. I was astonished that I knew more Vietnamese and more about Vietnam than many of the officers who were there.

The usual separation of frontline and rear echelon did not exist in Vietnam. There was neither the intense danger of the frontline nor the safety of being behind frontlines. There was almost total absence of interaction with civilians, which the soldier needs as a reassurance that life still goes on.

The military service in Vietnam was more comparable to a prison term than to a military expedition. It is not surprising, therefore, that many of the terms used by American soldiers in Vietnam were borrowed from prison terminology. Regular army members were referred to as "lifers," whereas draftees and enlisted personnel were called "short timers." The United States was referred to as "the world." Phrases like "back in the world" were constantly used.

The racial tensions existent in the United States were tremendously magnified in Vietnam, to a point where they were intolerable. This could have been due to the intense aggressive build-up which was experienced by individuals and then displaced into racial confrontation. Furthermore, it might have had more to do with the racial aspect of the war itself, where the killing of "gooks" was emphasized.

THE WAR AT HOME

The soldier who returned from Vietnam was burdened with collective and individual guilt. The society did not share in the blame by proclaiming him a war hero. His individual guilt was not diminished by suffering or destruction at home. He found that the people at home had not suffered from war with Vietnam; only he and his buddies had been at war with that remote country. His guilt was augmented by the rage he experiences against those back home who neither suffered nor assisted him.

All we gave him was military hardware, but no emotional or ideological support. Now he feels he has been duped, taken advantage of, or—to use the common phrase of Vietnam veterans—he has been "fucked over." The Vietnam veteran is full of rage; he is mistrustful and guilt-ridden, frequently experiencing the symptoms of the War Participation Syndrome. He needs help but he avoids contact with the Veterans Administration, which he regards as part of the establishment responsible for his suffering.

The Vietnam war veterans are often depressed, unable to enjoy life, undergoing existential crisis, questioning the meaning of life, etc. Frequently they express cynical attitudes, but when one scratches the surface one finds a great deal of sensitivity and vulnerability. The soldiers experienced the Vietnam situation as an assault upon their value system. The veterans I have seen, regardless of their background, complained about the assault upon their values. Even veterans who have criminal backgrounds, and entered the military service to escape criminal prosecution speak of the unnecessary killings and meaningless death, and express disgust with their own behavior and the behavior of other soldiers.

Inhibitions against killing other human beings are universal, and the fact that they are frequently transgressed should not be interpreted as an absence of such an inhibition. The violation of this prohibition activates the pathogenic potential of the inhibition. In order to kill with a minimum of pathological consequences, an individual needs certain specific protective factors. One of them is the belief that the killing was essential; that it served some useful purpose; that it was done against one's wishes, etc.

The Vietnam war veterans have participated in, perpetrated, witnessed, or at least heard about killings which they consider to be unnecessary from a military standpoint. When I asked one veteran what troubled him most about his Vietnam experience, his response was, "I have killed." I asked how this affected him and his response was, "It leaves me with not too many damned principles."

The veterans I have interviewed are a random, unselected sample. Yet I have never encountered one who was not critical of the U.S. involvement in the Vietnam war. This is in contrast to some soldiers who were in favor of the war in Vietnam when I visited there.

Innumerable veterans refer to the fact that the war "wasn't right." They emphasize that if the war had been justified, then the reactions which they have suffered would have been different. A number of veterans referred to the absence of a cause as if they were talking about military supplies.

Over the years I made the observation that survivors of severe combat situations in World War II would, most reluctantly, talk about where they had been. A typical interview would begin with my suspecting that the particular veteran was, in fact, a survivor of some death situation and I would inquire indirectly about it. For example, I would ask, "Did you serve during wartime?" The answer was "Yes, during wartime." "Where were you stationed?" The veteran would give various places in the U.S. Then I would ask, "Were you stationed overseas?" Answer: "Yes." Ultimately, I would ask about combat experiences, and only then would some traumatic events be related. This reluctance is even more apparent in Vietnam veterans.

I find it amazing that staff members at the V.A. are often unaware of combat experiences of an individual with whom they are working. A psychologist at the V.A. can relate details about the veteran, but when asked specifically if the individual was in Vietnam, more often than not he doesn't know. Some veterans have been in psychotherapy for years without any discussion of war experiences.

Some veterans are able to verbalize the relationship between their traumatic experiences and the symptomatology which they experience. Other veterans have no such intellectual insight and engage in massive denial. They will describe a perfect correlation between their experiences in Vietnam and the onset of symptoms. At the same time, they maintain that the two are unrelated. These are all examples of massive denial of psychic trauma of war.

PSYCHIC TRAUMA OF VIETNAM

Every disaster causing psychic trauma has some unique features; therefore, one can expect event-related modifications of traumatic neurosis based upon unique symptomatology or causation.

There are obvious differences between survivors of Hiroshima, survivors of Auschwitz, and the American soldiers who survived the Vietnam experience. On the other hand, there are significant experiential and phenomenological similarities. All three were overwhelming, life-threatening situations. A pathologist might make a differentiation of wounds, depending upon whether they were inflicted by an ax, a bayonet, or a straight razor. To a physiologist, studying the consequences of blood loss, such differentiation might be of little practical consequence.

When psychic trauma reaches certain levels of intensity, maladaptive consequences are inevitable and one is justified in referring to the event as absolute trauma (Furst, 1967).

Traumatic experiences of a soldier differ from those of a civilian. The Vietnam war, as wars go, was unique in many respects. It is, therefore, of value to speak of Post-Vietnam Syndrome as long as we recognize that we are not dealing with a new psychopathological entity. It is old wine in a new bottle (Furst, 1967).

Soldiers are perpetrators and recipients of egosyntonic violence. The egosyntonic quality of violence during war has some protective function. Egosyntonic violence occasions little guilt since it meets with superego sanction and peer approval (Tanay, 1969). The capacity of a soldier to experience his own violence as egosyntonic depends upon a variety of psychosocial factors which were discussed earlier in this chapter. The Vietnam war was unique in that soldiers had great difficulty experiencing their behavior as egosyntonic. In the absence of ideological and emotional commitment to a cause, and without significant support by the country as a whole, even normal military operations would be difficult to experience as egosyntonic. In Vietnam, the activities of American military units often were directed against targets not acceptable to the average soldier.

The dehumanization of the enemy contributed to a high incidence of behaviors which can only be described as atrocities. Even though such atrocities might have temporarily been experienced as egosyntonic while in Vietnam, in a great many cases upon return to the United States they would be experienced as egodystonic.

In view of the fact that violence played such a significant role in the causation of traumatic neurosis among Vietnam veterans, it is not surprising that violence is one of the striking symptoms of the Post-Vietnam Syndrome. I have extensive experience in evaluating and treating concentration camp survivors and Vietnam war veterans. There is virtual absence of overt violence among concentration camp survivors. There is high incidence of overt violence in Vietnam war veterans. Concentration camp survivors and Vietnam war veterans are both full of rage and self-destructiveness. There is, however, on a behavioral level a significant difference in the expression of this rage. I do not have a satisfactory explanation for this difference.

WAR AND ATROCITIES

War atrocities are a group phenomenon. The search for the individual wrongdoer is an effort to deny the collective complicity of a society. It is part of the denial of war atrocities as a phenomenon in itself. It is an insistence that nothing has changed during the war from the peacetime operation. An effort is made to create the illusion that one deals with an evil person who does his evil deeds in a foreign land. The banality of evil was the central theme of the book *Eichmann in Jerusalem* by Hannah Arendt. This very theme is an effort to deny the psychopolitical nature of war atrocities. It is an effort to personify war crimes. It is a desire to decollectivize a mass phenomenon.

After World War II, Professor Heuss, the first president of the German Federal Republic, spoke of collective shame of the German people for the atrocities perpetrated during World War II. The German people were reluctant to assume the responsibility for the deeds perpetrated in their name. Professor Heuss emphasized that collective shame could not be rejected just because one did not actively participate in the atrocities.

Nations are eager to assume collective credit for cultural achievements of individuals. We do not speak of the music of Mozart and Beethoven only, but also of German music. We speak of the Dutch school of painting, French impressionism, or Yankee ingenuity. There is little doubt that major cultural achievements of the individual are rooted in the collective resources of a society. However, there is understandable reluctance to claim collective credit for the atrocities perpetrated by members of a particular society.

We still speak of German music, but we no longer speak of German atrocities; rather we use the subgroup designation, "the Nazi atrocities." Increasingly, in fact, an effort is made to associate the Nazi atrocities with a few individuals like Hitler, Borman, Eichmann, etc. The personification of evil of that era will be completed when the atrocities will be linked in our minds with individual names only. Few dare to speak of atrocities perpetrated by G.I.s as American atrocities. Bertrand Russell, who in the mid-sixties conducted war crime trials against America, was considered "a kookie gook lover." It is, however, much more difficult to dismiss the judgment of Gunnar Myrdal, who is considered to be one of the foremost students of American society. He said:

> Take world public opinion about America over the past seven years—what really amounts to a hate America campaign. It is partly due to the very cruel, immoral, and criminal war that the American government is carrying on. I am chairman of the Committee on U.S. War Crimes where we listen to witnesses, many of them from America . . . Well, there was tremendous publicity here in all the newspapers about this committee. We covered it on television and radio, but there was not a word in the American press because of your self-censorship. You should know there is a "hate America campaign" going on in the world, and I am afraid it is going to increase tremendously in the future. (Mydral, 1972)

Germany has undergone a dramatic transformation since World War II. It has experienced an industrial, political, and social renaissance. Is it possible that the destructive, collective guilt was replaced by constructive, collective shame, of which Professor Heuss spoke? Germany suffered collective punishment which, after all, is an excellent remedy for guilt. The United States, on the other hand, has only its guilt.

DENIAL OF PSYCHIC TRAUMA

We eliminate the victims we are guilty of creating on a symbolic level by denying the existence of the condition from which they suffer. The endless debates over whether there is shellshock, combat neurosis, or concentration camp survivor syndrome fulfill our manifestations of denial.

The first line of defense is the denial that a traumatic event actually took place. This is a rather primitive defense and if maintained in the face of overwhelming evidence it requires psychotic distortion: "There are no concentration camps" or "There is no Vietnam war."

The second line of defense is based upon denial of the meaning of the event. Unfortunately, reality has the disagreeable quality of relentlessly asserting its existence.

The following is the story of a man who returned from Vietnam "whole." Hopefully it will serve to animate the reality of the post-traumatic stress disorder I have been discussing. Tom was a victim—first, of the Army, then of the Detroit Police Force, and finally of himself.

Tom completed high school and went on to a community college for one year before enlisting in the Air Force reserves at 19 years of age. After a year and a half in the reserves, not wishing to serve out the lengthy reserve commitment, he decided to enlist in the regular armed forces.

Tom was sent to serve in Vietnam as a helicopter pilot. His mission was to fly into battle zones, as often as four times a day, taking troops out on patrol. On occasion, some of those he delivered to the battlefield returned dead, or not at all. One mission to which he was assigned required that he evacuate corpses of American soldiers from the battlefield. When he saw the large stack of bodies in plastic bags, he burst out crying, unable to regain his composure for nearly half an hour. Yet he managed to complete the several flights required to evacuate the numerous corpses.

After several months of these assignments, Tom began having difficulty sleeping. He began to treat his insomnia by drinking himself to sleep each night.

Tom continued flying, sometimes experiencing a loss of control of the aircraft due to unknown mechanical difficulties. On two occasions, these losses of control led to crash landing the helicopter. On a third occasion, Tom was shot down over a battle zone. He survived all three crashes without major physical injury.

Tom persisted in drinking heavily and after several months began experiencing blackouts. He, nevertheless, continued flying for the remainder of the two years he was stationed in Vietnam, completing over 600 flights.

Upon his return to the United States, Tom was welcomed home only by the cab driver who drove him from the airport.

During the year following his return from Vietnam, Tom met a woman whom he subsequently married. On their honeymoon, Tom began having nightmares in which he saw with remarkable clarity a young Vietcong whom he had killed during his tour of duty, particularly his eyes.

Though, as a soldier, he had killed numerous people, this particular killing stood out in Tom's mind. The young Vietcong had penetrated a U.S. military compound. He was shot in his legs but continued crawling toward a fuel tank with a satchel of dynamite. Tom had him at gunpoint, hesitated as he looked at the man, and finally shot him dead.

Retrospectively, Tom experienced considerable guilt over this killing. "Maybe I waited too long. I looked at him too much . . . He was a conscript just like me." The approval of his military supervisors for preventing this act of sabotage did not help to abate his guilt, however. The nightmares during which Tom relived this event recurred every four to five weeks.

Tom's drinking persisted after his return home. His wife observed that though his drinking appeared moderate, just a couple bottles of beer would bring about intense, overt hostility. At times, he would begin disjointedly relating his Vietnam experiences. However, when he went to sleep drunk, Tom would at least be spared his nightmares.

In addition to his nightmares and drinking, Tom was frequently depressed. He tried to get some help from the Veterans Administration but was merely advised that this "Vietnam syndrome" would simply go away in time. Tom never bothered to return.

Two years after his return from Vietnam, Tom was honorably discharged from the Army with a Purple Heart and 27 other medals. A few months later, he was accepted for training at the Detroit Police Academy.

He completed his training and after three months on the police force was assigned to the highly controversial tactical police unit, STRESS. The controversy surrounding the STRESS unit, as well as the life-threatening situations, contributed to the reliving of the Vietnam experiences.

On one occasion during the year he was with STRESS, he was involved in chasing a man and suddenly realized that the man had fired a sawed-off shotgun at him at close range. Tom realized that had it not been for the defective firing pin, he could very well have been killed.

When the Detroit Police instituted their Aviation Division, Tom was assigned to it as the chief pilot and was charged with training, testing, and supervising new pilots for the unit.

His duties also included flying Medevac operations and night patrols, similar to those duties he had in Vietnam. One rescue mission he was involved in required that he rescue a young boy from a floating piece of ice even though the helicopter was not equipped with flotation gear. In another rescue, Tom succeeded in pulling a civilian pilot from a crashed plane despite the fact that he had become drenched with fuel from the ruptured gas tanks and was at great risk of being burned.

Tom was responsible for inspection of the helicopters for safety and, based on his flying experience, recommended that the police helicopters be equipped with strobe lights for night flying. His recommendation was ignored. Tom was then devastated when a pilot whom he had just completed training was killed in a midair collision which might have been avoided with the strobe lights. He became depressed and began having nightmares about the dead pilot, and his drinking continued.

The police helicopters began going out of control in midair, just as they had in Vietnam. Tom became intensely preoccupied with death but continued to inspect and test the helicopters which were subject to the "falling out of the sky syndrome."

Tom's nightmares, depression, and drinking persisted during the eight years he flew for the police department until finally one day he suffered a blackout while driving and got into an auto accident.

He was admitted to a hospital and treated for his depression and alcoholism and discharged after four weeks with the comment that he "was doing very well in the hospital" and would be followed up by the Substance Abuse Clinic.

The following Monday he returned to his job at the Aviation Division despite the fact that aviation regulations mandate an examination by a flight physician after hospitalization for alcoholism before return to work. Tom's supervisor, not being a pilot, was not aware of this and Tom avoided such review because it could take up to two years for his license to be reinstated.

The next day, Tom pulled into the Aviation Division parking lot, pulled out his service revolver and shot himself in the head. The suicide attempt left Tom quadriplegic.

He attempted to obtain compensation from the Detroit Police Department and the Veterans Administration on the basis that his disability was related to his service to both organizations. Each tried to blame the other for the stresses which led to Tom's suicide attempt. Finally, after a lengthy legal battle, Tom was awarded compensation from both the Detroit Police and the U.S. Army.

Tom survived attempts on his life in Vietnam, on the streets of Detroit, and in the air. He even survived his own attempt on his life. He no longer sees the eyes of the Vietcong he killed, nor is he depressed about Vietnam, Now, at 33 years of age, he is merely depressed over having to spend the rest of his life in a wheelchair.

Yes, Tom was a victim—first, of the army, then of the Detroit Police Force, and finally of himself. And the tragedy of his life is played out to varying degrees in the life of each and every returning soldier. All are examples of the soldier as victim.

REFERENCES

Freud, S. (1917-1919): Psychoanalysis and the war neurosis. In J. Strachey (Ed.), *Standard edition*, Vol. 16. London: Hogarth Press, 1951.

Freud, S. (1921): Group psychology. In J. Strachey (Ed.), *Standard edition*, Vol. 18. London: Hogarth Press, 1955.

Furst, S.S.: *Psychic trauma*. New York: Basic Books, 1967.

Mahler, M.: *On human symbiosis and the vicissitudes of individuation*. New York: International Universities Press, 1968.

Mydral, G.: An interview with Dr. Frank L. Keegan. *World*, August 29, 1972.

Tanay, E.: Psychiatric study of domicile. *American Journal of Psychiatry, 125:* 9, March 1969.

CHAPTER

4

Post-Traumatic Stress and the Death Imprint: The Search for a New Mythos

STEVEN M. SILVER, Ph.D.

"Why are you going to Vietnam?" the young man was asked.

"I owe it to my country" was his reply.

"Why are you here in Vietnam?" the young man was asked after six months of combat. "Why don't you turn in your wings and leave?"

"I cannot leave my friends" was his reply.

"Then you are not doing it for your country, for the Vietnamese, for God, apple pie, and mother?"

"No—I feel as if I do not have a country; all I have is a family."

"And who are they?"

In reply the young man gestured towards the other young men with old eyes who were walking towards their aircraft.

"There they are."

"What are you a part of now?" the no longer young man was asked 10 years after Vietnam, 10 years after Tchepone, the A Shau Valley, the DMZ, and more.

"For a long time, I haven't been a part of anything, just an outlaw." He paused. "But now, I don't know, something's changing . . ."

43

The purpose of this chapter is to point out the contribution of a Vietnam veteran mythos to the development and maintenance of reactions generally referred to as the Post-Traumatic Stress Disorder (PTSD). It is suggested that the erosion of America's older warrior mythos led to the adoption of a distorted one in which warriors became outlaws and which served to exclude Vietnam veterans not only from the mainstream of society but even from the society of one another. This exclusion, by prolonging and making more severe the problems of Vietnam veterans, only made matters worse. This outlaw mythos, however, is structurally flawed by the very exclusion it permits and it is now in the process of crumbling. We can see the gradual development by society of a newer mythos which offers, at last, an opportunity for the integration of Vietnam veterans with society. Concurrently, Vietnam veterans themselves are developing a mythos which gives an opportunity for both integration with society and therapeutic change.

A mythos, as *Webster's* (1973) points out, is "a pattern of beliefs expressing, often symbolically, the characteristic or prevalent attitudes in a group or culture" (p. 762). We will examine more closely the usefulness of a warrior mythos. It is enough to say at this point that a mythos can provide a relatively stable psychological reference point for people caught up in the chaos of prolonged and massive trauma.

The trauma of the Vietnam War experience for its participants has been well documented. Popular books and films have effectively communicated that there was, indeed, a war in Southeast Asia whose ferocity was at least a match for the other wars in our history (e.g., Caputo, 1977; Herr, 1978). The doubt as to whether it was really a war has faded as the realization has emerged that our people in Southeast Asia had a greater chance of becoming a combat casualty, killed or wounded, than in any war in our history except the fratricidal bloodletting of the Civil War.

Within the professional mental health community, there has been a gradual shift away from the indifference and even hostility of some to a more objective understanding of the nature and functioning of traumatic stress reactions. Much of the reason for this change is due in no small way to the work of several of the people contributing to this volume. Indeed, the very fact of this gathering of papers is indicative of the gradual changes which have taken place within the mental health community.

The phrase "gradual changes" is used deliberately, for it has not been sudden. The early reluctance to change in the recognition of Vietnam veterans and their psychological reactions was not entirely due to corruption, as has been charged (Lifton, 1976). Also present was the difficulty inherent in a shift of paradigms.

As Kuhn (1970) has indicated, the adoption of a paradigm is an often difficult though useful process, as it permits the recognition of previously ignored phenomena. However, once a paradigm is adopted—such as when diagnostic criteria for a particular mental disorder are accepted —phenomena which do not fit the definitions of the paradigm tend to be discounted or ignored. This state of affairs tends to continue to exist until the unaccepted though still occurring phenomena can no longer be ignored or accommodated. This results in the collapse of the old paradigm and the beginning of the building of a new one. Psychiatry, especially military psychiatry, attempted to use the paradigms for combat-related reactions evolved out of the experiences of the two World Wars. This led to the conclusion that comparatively less stress was experienced in Vietnam than in our other wars (Bourne, 1972). The flaw lay in the ignoring of phenomena which did not meet the paradigmatic definitions needed for inclusion in the old paradigms.

Additional difficulty in recognizing the combat-related reactions of Vietnam veterans came from the reality that psychology and psychiatry are not separate from the society in which they exist. Despite our sometime tendency to view the rest of the human race as if it were somehow distant from us—note, for example, our tendency to use psychological terminology to describe patients' behavior and cognition but never our own—the reality is that we are actually a part of the cultural environment and we tend to share many of the same assumptions, perceptions, and values as others in our society.

And the assumptions and perceptions of many in our society concerning Vietnam veterans reflected the national trauma incurred in the Vietnam War. Vietnam veterans serve as symbols of an event which was a severe stressor on the social fabric of our country. In an ontogenetic macrocosm of an individual's reaction, society turned away from those symbols of the stressor event.

Vietnam veterans could not be incorporated into the social body of America because the belief and value system which would have permitted this to occur, the warrior mythos, had been destroyed. Devastated by the nightly and necessarily incomplete images of war, the old picture of the American warrior could not survive. John Wayne's movie *The Green Berets* might have been acceptable in World War II, but during the Vietnam War its Hollywood simplification was too distant from the nightly news to be acceptable.

The warrior mythos had in the past served a number of functions. It helped the individual to rise above self for the good of the group by becoming a member of an élite, thereby increasing the effectiveness of society's armed forces. Perhaps the classic example of this aspect of the traditional warrior mythos is to be found in the conduct of Japanese warriors in World War II. Calling upon the samurai mythos, in which life became as a feather compared to the mountain which was duty, they, as kamikaze, fought us with a ferocity and success out of proportion to their strength in material.

The warrior mythos served to set warriors apart from others in society while at the same time guaranteeing their place within it. By setting warriors apart from others, the mythos permitted a denial of war's reality. Besides denying the consequences of war, setting warriors apart permitted the rest of society to pretend that killing, particularly in the savage manner often required by combat, was an ability which resided only in those who had been particularly trained for it. Warriors aided this process when they, like other professionals, developed their own language, traditions and customs which served to give the impression that war was a concern of a relative few.

In virtually all countries and cultures, warriors have been placed into a separate but included caste, one outranked often only by royalty and the priesthood. This was due, in simple terms, to the unique role played by warriors—they killed people. Soldiers endured war and approached and encountered the ultimate unknown, death. Those who have worked and lived with death have always occupied a position apart from others. This is a "death imprint" always worn by warriors.

The perceived need for a society to be protected from enemies without obviously required the inclusion of warriors within its structure; why else would they fight to defend it? Combat effectiveness required the warriors to be disciplined and able to submerge their concern for self. The warrior mythos supplied the rationale for this submergence. The more a society felt, and feels, threatened by exterior enemies, the more it pays homage to the warrior mythos. One has only to examine the change in attitude of American society towards its military over its 200-year history to recognize this fact.

Obviously, the collapse of the old warrior mythos had begun in America before the war in Vietnam. As Campbell (1975) has noted, the disintegration of the old warrior mythos had begun in some degree well before World War II and had been marked by a shift away from sagas which were focused on the struggle of the individual against nature on behalf of the group. The internal struggle within the individual began to occupy the greater part of society's attention. It is quite likely that, even without the Vietnam War to act as the final challenge, the traditional psychological value to be found in the identity of society's warrior would have largely eroded away.

The hero now recognized by society was the individual whose struggle was with and for him- or herself. This new perception was influenced by many factors, of which the rising mythos of psychology was among the most important. Nonetheless, the paradigm of the traditional warrior mythos could be and was expanded to include the emphasis on the internal struggle. The literature coming out of the experiences of World War II and the Korean War reflects this expansion of the paradigm. The individual struggles not only against the exterior and obvious enemy but within, with that portion of the self which opposes submergence and acceptance of the warrior mythos.

But we also see a growing cynicism in such literature in regards to the warrior mythos which testifies to its weakening. As the technological fury of war increased, the contribution of the individual was both increased and lessened—increased in terms of power and destructiveness now available, decreased in terms of the individual's efforts. Anyone could push a button, and buttons were more powerful than bodies or virtues. Both the feather and the mountain of the kamikaze burned at Hiroshima.

With the weakening of the old warrior mythos, the old regard and support began to fade as well. This state of affairs, it is important to point out, existed well before Vietnam. Vietnam, or, more precisely, society's perception of it, was the capstone. The perception was so traumatic that it became important for society to have some way of distancing the Vietnam experience from itself.

Vietnam War veterans were reminders of that traumatic experience; the weakened old warrior mythos could have required maintaining a place for warriors within society. However, the societal trauma was so severe that this was unacceptable and the old mythos was destroyed. There could be no recognition by society of any commonality existing between Vietnam veterans and the rest of society. The implications for self-doubt, guilt, and failure in such commonality, as well as the shared potential for inflicting horror, were intolerable.

Vietnam veterans, like almost everyone subjected to severe stressor events, had to cope not only with their own tendencies to withdraw but with the turning away of society from them. It may very well be, then, this abandonment by society was responsible for the greatest portion of the post-traumatic stress reactions experienced by our veterans. Certainly it denied catharsis, emphasized guilt, and encouraged repression, thus at the very least prolonging the problem. The existence of even the weakened warrior mythos which World War II veterans could depend upon was denied to Vietnam veterans.

This is not to say that a new mythos did not come about; one did, albeit incomplete and inherently weak in structure. This interim mythos served the useful and perhaps psychologically necessary function of separating these particular warriors from their society. Vietnam veterans became outlaws, pariahs, whose distinctiveness from society was emphasized. As separate symbols, projection of guilt, failure, and other feelings too powerful to be maintained individually could now be accomplished, relieving the psychological burden carried by people within society. Such is the purpose of scapegoats.

Unlike earlier warriors, the Vietnam veterans were not placed in a caste within society to avoid recognition of the common ability to kill. They were separated, and a mythos was created to maintain this separation and exclusion, in order to project onto them the negative feelings held by their fellow citizens.

Parts of the old warrior mythos were used in the construction of the outlaw mythos. These parts were enhanced and emphasized. The part reflecting the killer, the amuck-berserker, for example, was particularly emphasized.

The outlaw mythos, as do all mythos, had utilized some elements of reality in its structure. These elements were exaggerated and distorted, forming an ultimately unreal picture but one which permitted the exclusion of Vietnam veterans.

The elements of the outlaw mythos were such items as war atrocities, drug abuse, poor discipline, and, of great significance to Americans, loss of a war. Into this simmering brew various mental health professionals added the element of insanity—the Vietnam veteran mythos came to include an uncontrollable potential for violence. These returning young men and women were walking time bombs. That this mythos was readily acceptable to society is clearly demonstrated by such examples as the refusal of employers to hire Vietnam veterans on the basis of their image. The public clearly accepted this image. In a study of television, Brewin (1975) noted that virtually every portrayal of Vietnam veterans was one of drug abusers, killers, or potential if not actual psychotics, and frequently all three.

Think for a moment what the reaction would have been if such a steadily negative treatment had been accorded to, for example, women, or blacks, or World War II veterans, or even psychiatrists and psychologists. Lawsuits, marches, demonstrations, denunciations from pulpits, newspapers, and the offices of politicians surely would have resulted. However, in the case of the Vietnam veteran, few raised any protest—the subscription to the outlaw mythos was almost total.

Paradoxically, for two major reasons the outlaw mythos began to fail as it succeeded. First, it would not permit the denial of the horror of war. To the contrary, to picture the Vietnam veteran as outlaw it became necessary to emphasize the horror of war in a manner unique in our history. Since society in adopting the outlaw mythos could not avoid the reality of war and its consequences, it was only a question of time before yet another mythos which would permit this became required. Feelings of outrage over the Iranian hostage incident were difficult to express in terms of striking back by force, by military force, unless the horror of the deaths of thousands in exchange for the possible return of dozens could be glossed over and denied. Such is the world we live in that such considerations are seriously made.

The second reason for the failure of the outlaw mythos lay in its success in separating Vietnam veterans from society. An awareness of the actual lack of distinction between society and its Vietnam veterans was coming about, and not only because the elements of the outlaw mythos were challenged. Most importantly, the Vietnam War was a shared trauma. The same media which permitted and encouraged the exaggeration of the outlaw mythos also made the viewers participants. Individuals were forced to choose sides. Unlike World War II, when war was thrust upon this country and people felt they had no choice in the matter, this war gave the American people a sense of choice. Even when opposed to the war, they were caught up in it. In a very real sense, *all* Americans became Vietnam veterans. This result of the national trauma meant that eventually, over time, this universally shared dichotomy originally existing between Vietnam veterans and other Americans would have to give way.

With the distinction between Vietnam veterans and their society partially merged by the shared psychology of trauma, it is becoming possible for society to build a new mythos. This is one which society can partially identify with and has as its key element the shared experiences of the Vietnam War. We see slowly emerging new themes describing Vietnam veterans in the popular and professional media. The murderer and other negative images fade as too uncomfortable for society to maintain for more than a decade and a half. Now the mythos begins to emphasize the shared experiences of betrayal—and so were we all during the

war—and abandonment—and so were we all after the war. There is also
a reemergence of the traditional warrior attributes customarily a part of
earlier mythos, such as courage and loyalty.

What of Vietnam veterans? What new mythos, if any, have they
evolved of themselves? We would expect them to develop one as a
natural rebellion of the human spirit against oppression—the experience
of blacks, women, and other groups in this country give many clear
examples of the usefulness and even necessity of developing a mythos
of one's peer group when struggling against the isolation often imposed
by society. Further, the perception of Vietnam veterans by their society
was so negative for so long that these veterans could not endure the
pain. Forced to take on the negative perception as a self perception was
a burden which could not be carried forever. To throw it off required
something to take its place.

As noted previously, an essential foundation for any mythos is that
it have some basis in fact. Thus, within the Vietnam veteran mythos is
an element of the outlaw. Reality requires an acceptance of the differences in experiences between them and society and, most importantly,
a recognition of the turning away of society. Here we see a vehicle for
therapeutic intervention. If isolation and withdrawal are components of
the post-traumatic stress disorder, then the acceptance of the element
of outlaw may indeed contribute to the isolation. However, by so doing,
the individual Vietnam veteran has now, in effect, joined a group of
outlaws. If reintegration is to take place, it will be a gradual process
requiring the gradual expansion of the Vietnam veteran's social network.

Here we see a major reason for much of the success of Vietnam veteran
rap groups and inpatient programs, such as the Post-Traumatic Stress
Disorder Program at Coatesville VAMC. The emotional and often physical isolation of the past is altered by joining with others sharing basically
the same experiences (Shatan, 1972).

This process is aided by the desire of most veterans to see their relationships in Vietnam as positive and supportive, and in many cases
more so than they actually were. This makes joining with other sharers
of the trauma easier—it is a return to a supportive system, rather than
an initiation of one. It is not necessary that it once did exist, or that it
did to the degree the mythos presents. It is only necessary that it exist
now.

Interestingly enough, the other major element in the Vietnam veterans' mythos, that of being a survivor, is also useful in therapuetic change.
The survivor element, like the outlaw element, is based upon an un-
deniable reality—these people survived. The very fact of survival carries

with it two facets aiding change. The first is the clear recognition that to have survived the violence of war is to admit to the existence of powerful control mechanisms within the individual. People who cannot control their reactions in a firefight are less likely to survive than those who can. This is not to say, incidentally, that those who did not survive lacked such controls. This is to say that such control increases the probability of survival, while not guaranteeing it. Survival also hinges upon deliberate enemy action and random chance.

The recognition of such controls and the ability they represent is vital. Many veterans have come to believe that they cannot approach their memories of their stressor events because they would not be able to handle them. Since it is clear that they did handle them once when trauma was happening, it is also clear that the potential exists for handling the memory of the trauma. This assists greatly in therapeutic technique of hypnosis and desensitization, which calls for a return to the events of the trauma.

The second facet of survival aiding change is that survival generates sensitivity. Much has been made, and appropriately, of the impact of Vietnam on the development of the young people caught up in it. Building on some of the work of Wilson (1980), references are often made to interruption and possible retarding of psychological development. Overlooked is the accelerated development which took place in Vietnam. These veterans had to confront the ultimate issues of human existence, life and death. This kind of confrontation ordinarily does not take place in human development until near the end of life (Erikson, 1980). I submit that such a confrontation forced a coming to grips with the reality of mortality and was at the same time both a source of trauma and the birth of human understanding.

This understanding, this unique sensitivity, may be undirected, poorly articulated, and even consciously denied, but those who have seen the tears of Vietnam veterans shed for one another understand its reality.

Survivor strength and sensitivity support therapeutic change. They are critical for the resolution of the existential search for meaning. The hunt for the awesome "why" of survival is no easy journey and it requires much in the way of both strength and sensitivity. The answer, for a particular veteran, may range widely: to serve as a legitimate spokesperson for those who did not survive so they shall not be forgotten; to prevent the tragedy from again happening; to instruct and teach others the lessons learned; to serve yet again in some way, such service perhaps atonement but never punishment.

Is the acceptance of this evolving mythos by Vietnam veterans taking

place or are they still hiding themselves away, trying to deny the existence of a part of their selves? One has only to look around. Out of the
closets and duffle bags are coming the berets and faded camouflage
shirts; seen again are the dusty and stained jungle boots. Out of their
fire, agony, and triumph their published words form the structure of
the new mythos (Caputo, 1977). In Vet Centers and new veterans organizations the outlaws are ending their isolation from one another.

Society's mythos and the Vietnam veterans' mythos permit, through
acceptance on the one hand and a recognition of the need to join on the
other, a convergence. Slowly, the torn fabric is rewoven, even as we
watch, and the very existence of this volume is a part of that process.

This convergence of society and its latest generation of warriors aids
the veterans in their changing, as well as aiding society on a macro scale
to go about its change. Viewed by others and by self differently, these
new self-perceptions permit and encourage a return to the experiences
of Vietnam. Slowly, these experiences are becoming no longer simply
a heavy, painful burden which one longs to discard. Rather, they become
what they are potentially and in reality—a source of purpose, strength,
and sensitivity in a world in need of all three.

It is appropriate to conclude as I began, with the words of that no
longer young Vietnam veteran. These words, a fragment of a poem,
reflect much of what I have tried to say. He dedicated the poem to his
brother, who served in Vietnam also.

> Like the Ohio
> we've rolled on,
> rolled on—
> the river, at the
> same point
> is changed,
> changing,
> never the same.
> What do I see
> in my brother's eyes—
> is that flicker
> rage's ember,
> left from the
> burning elephant grass?
> Or is it,
> just,
> the reflection of my own eye?

> Our brothers and sisters are
> many, now,
> a bloodline
> broader than the
> Ohio;
> from here to the
> Mekong—
> our family is larger
> and lonely.

REFERENCES

Bourne, P.G.: The Vietnam veteran: Psychological casualties. *Psychiatry in Medicine*, 3:23-27, 1972.

Brewin, R.: TV's newest villain: The Vietnam veteran. *TV Guide*, 23:4-8, July 19, 1975.

Campbell, J.: *The hero with a thousand faces*. London: Abacus, 1975.

Caputo, P.: *A rumor of war*. New York: Holt, Rinehart & Wilson, 1977.

Erikson, E.H.: *Identity and the life cycle*. New York: W.W. Norton, 1980.

Herr, M.: *Dispatches*. New York: Avon, 1978.

Kuhn, T.S.: *The structure of scientific revolutions* (2nd ed., rev.). Chicago: University of Chicago Press, 1970.

Litton, R.J.: Advocacy and corruption in the healing profession. In N.L. Goldman & D.R. Segal (Eds.), *The social psychology of military service*. Beverly Hills: Sage Publications, 1976.

Shatan, C.F.: Soldiers in mourning (Vietnam veterans self-help groups: The "Post-Vietnam Syndrome"). *American Journal of Orthopsychiatry*, 42:300-301, 1972.

Webster's new collegiate dictionary. Springfield, MA: Merriam, 1973.

Wilson, J.P.: Conflict, stress, and growth: The effects of war on psychosocial development among Vietnam veterans. In C.R. Figley & S. Leventman (Eds.), *Strangers at home*. New York: Praeger, 1980.

5

Some of My Best Friends Are Dead: Treatment of the PTSD Patient and His Family

SARAH A. HALEY, L.I.C.S.W.

Man-oh-man, Cowboy looks like a bag of leftovers from a V.F.W. barbecue. Of course, I've got nothing against dead people. Why, some of my best friends are dead. (Hasford, 1979)

In previous papers (1974, 1978), I have shared my experiences of the past 15 years in the treatment of Vietnam combat veterans. My interest in—but actually my need to write about the treatment of these veterans—initially stemmed from anxiety provoked in me by "the patient who reports atrocities." In a paper (1974) by that name, I called attention to the potential for a negative countertransference reaction in the therapeutic exchange wherein the patient revealed participation in war atrocities.

In this chapter, I will present a brief historical review of combat psychiatry and argue the insufficiency of earlier psychoanalytic theories to fully appreciate the deforming impact of catastrophic stress, particularly combat, on psychic structures. The expanded conceptual framework available to clinicians today draws on our greater understanding of: stress response syndromes (Horowitz, 1976), object relations theory (Kernberg, 1976), issues of narcissism (Kohut, 1972), and the work of investigators such as Mahler (1968) on separation-individuation. Since Vietnam veterans served in combat during late adolescence, it is crucial for clinicians to become knowledgeable about adolescent psychology and to assess the impact of combat (killing, fear of dying, loss of buddies, atrocities) on the ego and, in particular, the superego and the ego ideal on the still fluid adolescent psychic structures. I will offer a conceptual framework regarding one aspect of catastrophic stress, namely the loss of a soldier's buddy, his sustaining transitional object, as a potential precipitant to the unleashing of sadistic impulses and actions in the surviving soldier. Case material will be presented to demonstrate the potential for regression to a state of annihilation anxiety and primitive rage and the impact of this experience on one combat veteran.

The literature on combat psychiatry from WWI (Salmon, 1919), WWII (Grinker & Spiegel, 1945), and Korea (Glass, 1954) demonstrates the clinician's interest in and attempts to intervene therapeutically with men who during or at some point after combat exhibited a range of symptoms which were varyingly called "shell shock," "adrenal depletion syndrome," or "traumtic war neurosis." Most of the literature, however, concerns itself with the numerical incidence of casualties and brief case vignettes. Following WWII there were descriptions of brief dramatic interventions. These were generally the sodium amytal interview or hypnosis, which were thought to bring symptom relief and resolution through "abreaction/catharsis." In the absence of a psychodynamic follow through, or in those cases where psychotherapy was thought indicated or attempted, the clinician's assumption, typified by Zetzel (1970), was that "external events, no matter how overwhelming, precipitate a neurosis only when they touch on specific unconscious conflicts."

In a recent review of 120 years of reactions to combat, from the Civil War through to Vietnam, Smith (1981) argues that, historically, reactions to catastrophic stress focus on causality: i.e.individual differences or the conditions of the event. "With both predisposition and occasion, it is the question of where to lay blame that is critical. Fundamentally, each view compels an underlying *moral judgment,* and is not merely a neutral scientific investigation of causality."

Utmost respect is due to the clinicians cited above for their exhaustive efforts with the combat soldiers of previous wars. I believe, however, that the theoretical constructs available to them, even the burgeoning appreciation of ego psychology, were not sufficient to fully understand the etiology of the presenting disorder and its treatment. In discussions with some senior Boston analysts and in a daylong consultation with Dr. Peter Blos (1980), it would appear that not merely the "state of the art" influenced their capacities to fully comprehend the degree of psychic regression required to maintain ego intregity under catastrophic stress. Many clinicians were in one way or another affected personally by WWII, either as refugees or as military psychiatrists. The scope of this chapter permits the author only to point out that quite a few were themselves dealing with alternating psychic numbing, intrusive recollections, and survivor guilt. Some also appeared to be in a philosophical watershed in the years following WWII. Many now discuss having been in delayed grief following the death of Freud in 1939 and some also shared his disillusionment in those final years as to whether man's nature, contrary to the theory of the "pleasure principle," was more drawn to nihilism—the death instinct.

The case of a WWII combat veteran suffering traumatic war neurosis (Wexler, 1973) is illustrative. Wexler states, "the patient presented a great number of diagnostic and therapeutic problems which were not easy to resolve. Similar issues have arisen with the emotional casualties of the current war in Vietnam, and it seems to me, these are as puzzling to the therapist today as they were 30 years ago" (p. 565).

In 1973, Wexler reviewed his patient's symptomatology and treatment of 20 years earlier wholly from a drive theory orientation, emphasizing regressions to oedipal issues with his father as paramount to his traumatic war neurosis. This in spite of an observation that "if he had seen no combat, he would have served (in the military) uneventfully and been discharged with a good conduct ribbon" (p. 586).

My clinical observations during 15 years of evaluating and treating Vietnam combat veterans are that the psychic regressions induced by combat and necessary to the preservation of psychic integrity propel the combatant much farther down the developmental scale. Cognizance of the varying levels of psychic regression is crucial to structural reintegration in the therapeutic process. Wexler (1973) came close but did not develop further a sense of the possibility of regressions to pregenital levels. "His loneliness and sense of isolation were intense. Perhaps it was ultimately this sense of being abandoned which made it impossible for him successfully to handle the sadism of the super ego" (p. 585).

The following conceptual framework, case material, and dynamic formulations are offered in the hope that they will enlarge the therapeutic tools available to clinicians struggling with men suffering from the often devastating assault to psychic structures that combat can induce. Work with such men generates a frustration and urgency in the clinician to understand the dynamics more fully and to bear up under the intensity of the transference-countertransference interface more effectively. This sense of frustration and urgency in the healer often arises because as Horowitz (1976) has painfully concluded, "for some (victims of catastrophic stress) the damage appears irreversible; the horror was too great, and treatment can become only a reliving but not a dispelling of the nightmares" (p. 121).

The availability of an ever enriched conceptual reservoir makes clearer to the clinician the nature of the trauma of combat and indicates pathways towards healing. Today as yesterday, however, we, like Wexler, have often worked intensely with men suffering from post-combat stress disorders only to become passive witness to the patient's ultimate choice to resolve his trauma through suicide.

NORMAL ADOLESCENCE AND THE SOLDIER

Because the majority of Vietnam combat soldiers were between the ages of 17-21, I will be concentrating on a view of them as late adolescents. Blos (1962) states that under normal environmental conditions, the adolescent ego is subject to temporary regressions as it attempts to consolidate ego functions and form an integrated sexual identity, self-object representations, and a stable, autonomous ego. According to Blos, aggressive and sexual drives are intensified in part by the adolescent's increasing social freedom and responsibilities. The interaction between these instinctual drives and the environment can "stimulate certain ego functions toward accelerated development, (as well as) stunt and retard other ego functions." Further, he states that typical American adolescents display the defenses of identification, denial, isolation, and impulsivity—a "rushing into danger." Oedipal and separation issues are reworked during the adolescent years, and resolution of the separation/individuation stage is achieved by late-adolescence. For such development to occur, two elements are essential: 1) clearly defined societal/familial values, ethics, and rules to guide the adolescent, and 2) consistent, caring, and supportive parents and peer groups.

For the soldier, the combat experience in Vietnam placed additional burdens on the adolescent ego's needs for this first requirement, i.e. rules to guide him. The Vietnam war itself also placed burdens on the soldier's parents, community, indeed the nation as a whole to provide the second requirement of consistency and support. Most adolescent soldiers went to Vietnam with an amalgam of family, religious, and cultural values which would be called the "good warrior ethos." An awareness that "thou shalt not kill" except with the sanction of a higher authority and the moral support of family and society were thought to be present.

The stress of combat brings all soldiers, but particularly the more vulnerable adolescent ego, face to face with annihilation anxiety. The guerrilla warfare of Vietnam, however, assaulted the adolescent ego as it attempted to utilize the "good warrior ethos" as a coping device and a defense against precipitous ego regressions, particularly to identification with the aggressor and pleasurable, albeit guilt-provoking anal sadism. The stress of combat on the adolescent ego caused an adaptive split within the ego. This phenomenon, according to Horowitz (1976), occurs in any person exposed to extreme stress. With this split, Vietnam became the "bad" environment, and home became good and idealized, the "world." This splitting of good and bad introjects, however, stirred up inevitable feelings of loneliness, aloneness, and vulnerability in the young men who were often experiencing their first real separation from home. As the realities of combat became more apparent, the soldier relied heavily on his combat unit for support, limits, and values, in much the same way that the adolescent relies on his peer group—which becomes even more valued than the parents themselves during adolescence.

The continued stress of guerrilla warfare, and most often the lack of good leadership, led to a regression to earlier, preadolescent and pregenital levels of psychic organization, particularly, transitional phenomenon and separation-individuation tensions and anxieties. The soldier often turned to a single buddy, who then took on the role of a transitional object, as in childhood the first "not me" object. This buddy, this friend, thus served to assuage anxiety, fear, and abandonment panic because of the magical belief that this buddy—as long as the soldier stayed physically close to him—could protect him and love him enough to endure the dangers around him.

Modell (1968) describes these regressed dyadic relationships as having the "capacity for magical thought (to) mitigate . . . the danger of catastrophic anxiety through the creation of (a) lack of separateness between self and the object" (p. 148). In *Totem and Taboo,* Freud (1913) noted that the concepts of magic and omnipotence were equal. Freud felt that this magical omnipotence compensated for the realities of prolonged biological helplessness that all infants face from time to time, and by extension are faced by some/all survivors of catastrophic stress.

Combat psychiatry and literature attest that combat buddies are of major importance to the cohesiveness of both the group and the individual members. Since Vietnam soldiers entered the country as individuals, rather than with their unit, they were referred to as the FNG (fucking new guy) until they had proved themselves. The combat imperative propelled them to "buddy up" as soon as possible. The utilization of the transitional phenomenon has been stressed by Fox (1974) who emphasizes the importance of the buddy to the soldier. He describes soldiers who wore their buddy's socks or other clothing into battle for good luck, and in our own clinic we have treated many Vietnam veterans as well as World War II and Korean War veterans who wore their buddy's clothing into combat, and many who have kept articles from their deceased buddy, even years after the war. Another indicator of the magical nature of the buddy-soldier relationship is that following their military service, most veterans do not contact their buddy. It is as though that special, magical, and idealized relationship would be shattered were the soldier to really know the mundane realities of his buddy's life: what his buddy really loves and values, independent of the soldier.

The buddy's death in combat served as a premature loss of an essential and life-sustaining transitional object. With the transitional object/buddy's death, the not-me components of the transitional object were destroyed, and the soldier was vulnerable to more fragmented coping styles as he felt abandoned, alone and faced with the unbearable realities of danger, loneliness, possible death and annihilation anxiety. However, whereas initially he regressed in the service of the ego (by adaptive splitting of good and bad images, and comforting reveries about home), the adolescent ego, once it reached the transitional object stage, was vulnerable and frail. Thus, as Fox (1974) indicates, the loss of the buddy did not arouse mature responses to object loss (i.e. hypercathexis and decathexis of the lost object with that object always being perceived as separate from the self), but aroused very early, primitive reactions to separation and loss, similar to Bowlby's (1973) construct of childhood attachment and separation.

In particular, the death of the buddy produced the states of "protest," "despair," and "detachment," all of which Bowlby states are predictable responses when a child is faced with the loss of an important love object, usually the mother. Uncontrolled rage is unleashed in the child, so that the heretofore obedient, content toddler suddenly bites other children, or mistreats a favorite toy (transitional object). There is a tendency for "anger and hostility directed towards a (lost) loved person to be repressed and/or redirected elsewhere, and also for anger to be attributed to others instead of the self." This anger eventually gives way to a despairing pining for the lost object, similar to mourning, and eventually is replaced by a numbed detachment. Lifton (1973) has described this same phenomenon with survivors of catastrophic stress as "psychic numbing."

In the face of annihilation anxiety where no inner nor outer good objects are experienced, the ego may become totally disorganized. Bowlby's stages of loss and mourning come into motion. The enemy or anyone else in the soldier's path, including women and children, could be targets for unleashed aggressive impulses. Loss of the buddy led many to the need to avenge the buddy's death through displacement, by repetitive aggression against anyone and anything that represented a reminder of the lost buddy, or who exposed the vulnerability of the surviving soldier. Mourning became suspended in animation, and repetitive self-defeating aggression and/or atrocity became for many the only restitution for a disintegrating ego and the shattered transitional object/buddy bond. In his paper "Militarized Mourning," Shatan (1980) explores the evolution of combat grief into ceremonial vengence.

In previous papers, (1974, 1978, 1984) I have delineated the nature of countertransference resistances and the therapeutic task with combat veterans. I stressed that as in all therapies, but most crucial in the treatment situation to be discussed in this paper, is the imperative of the development of a strong, trustful therapeutic alliance. Such an alliance enables the veteran to tolerate remembering, reexperiencing, understanding, and working through his stressful combat experiences and their symptomatic sequelae. Psychotherapy with Vietnam combat veterans is difficult for the veteran but sometimes equally difficult for the therapist. For the therapist, war is hell for three reasons: 1) confrontation with one's own personal vulnerability to catastrophe; 2) the challenge to one's moral attitudes toward aggression and killing; and 3) the almost unbearable intensity of the countertransference and the transference (Haley, 1974, 1978, 1984).

Because of the ambiguous nature of the Vietnam war, one of the most damaging effects of the stress of combat for veterans was the stripping away of their adolescent illusions and the tarnishing of their ego ideals. The deforming of psychic structures under stress, especially superego regressions to identification with the aggressor, have occurred in all wars; such regressions and the taking on of the group superego permitted preservation of psychic integrity in the face of catastrophe. Returning from combat, the veteran was expected to forge a realignment of psychic structures, with the ego once again predominant in the management of affects and instincts. Vietnam veterans, however, are associated in the public imagination with the loss of "their" war and have had few societal sanctions and reentry rituals to aid them in this realignment which is most crucial in the reinstatement of a viable ego ideal (Haley, 1974, 1978, 1984).

In our clinic, we have been particularly concerned with the pervasiveness of a seeming trade-off to passivity in our Vietnam veteran population in order to counter fears of their past and potential aggressiveness (Morrier, 1983). With few societal ego supports and an impoverished ego ideal, the regressed superego stands virtually unopposed. Activity, initiation, assertion, aggression, and murder have clearly become and remain fused in a dynamic continuum for many veterans (Haley, 1984). Although Vietnam veterans have been characterized in the public and clinical media as having explosive aggressive reactions, Morrier (1983) has noted that these episodes are often punctuation marks in a more stultifying passivity.

In the case for discussion in this paper, I hope that some of the theoretical therapeutic parameters delineated above will come alive in the case material.

Case Report

At the time of his referral in April, 1974, Mark was a 25-year-old black, married, Marine combat veteran, with an excellent work history for the preceding two and a half years, despite some earlier job failures in his first year back from Vietnam. He had presented himself at the local V.A. hospital seeking admission for two intersecting stresses: 1) he had discovered that his wife of seven years was having an affair (in fact, one which had started while he was in Vietnam), and that she wanted a divorce; and 2) he was about to be promoted to supervisor. He was held in very high esteem as an electrician on his job where men worked under very dangerous conditions on highrise buildings. Mark commented that it was one thing for him to risk his life daily, but it would be "too much like Vietnam to choose the dangerous assignments for men under my command." He had both homicidal impulses toward his wife and suicidal impulses on the job.

Mark was a tall, handsome man, who was visibly agitated, anxious, and enraged. The intensity of his affects and the severe depression underlying the surface presentation convinced me that his suicidal/homicidal potential was severe. After some initial resistance to talking to a "honky" and further evaluation by a black psychiatrist (who placed him on an antidepressant and a phenothiazine for daytime use for his agitation), the veteran returned to me and embarked on a four-year treatment that profoundly affected both of our lives.

Mark was the oldest son of four children in an upwardly mobile Southern family. An emphasis on schooling and church involvement characterized a family where both parents emerged as strong and loving. The father owned his own small farm but when he wanted to expand and buy some adjacent land owned by a white family, he was shot by a group of hooded men who drove into the family's front yard. The father was left a quadriplegic, and remained at home for two years until his care became too complicated for the mother.

Remarkably, after the father was transferred to a nursing home, the family was able to keep and work their farm. Mark, by then age 16, began to run with a rough crowd, was truant from school, and his excellent grades fell drastically. His mother feared for him because of his increasing insolence towards white people. Faced with school failure and increasingly provocative behavior in his hometown, he enlisted in the Marine Corps in 1967. Also, an older cousin had been in Vietnam and had suffered a nervous breakdown. The family was embarrassed by his medical discharge and his "crazy" and aggressive behavior.

Mark's approach to basic training, after his initial naivete and shock, was an identification with the drill instructors and a posture of "you can't break me." He excelled in Advanced Infantry Training and had achieved a grade of E4 before being sent to Vietnam. During this time he also met and married his wife who had two children by a previous marriage. By his description, she was dependent and immature, unlike the women in his own family. She reacted with rage when he received orders for Vietnam and she wrote to him only twice during his first tour of duty. During this tour, he had the Red Cross contact her and he learned she was living with another man.

At the end of his first tour he returned home to his wife, effected a reconciliation and established her in a home in Boston where she had relatives. He stated that he "reuped" for a second tour in Vietnam because his company was being replaced with new recruits and the upper command level was disorganized and demoralized. Later, in therapy, he acknowledged that he was tight with his Lieutenant and wanted to be with him, "to look out for him." During the second year, he attained a grade of E7 and was awarded two Bronze Stars and a Navy Commendation Medal.

The first year of Mark's treatment was an obsessive, nearly day-by-day account of his two years in Vietnam, coupled with painful ambivalent feelings of love and hate engendered by the separation from his wife. The regression to identification with the aggressor, which had begun following the attack on his home and his father's injury, and which had continued during his stateside service time, escalated gradually but steadily during his first year in Vietnam.

As a therapist who had evaluated, treated or supervised the treatment of nearly 100 combat veterans and who felt she had "heard it all," I was not prepared for the descent into psychic hell that awaited me. As in Philip Caputo's "Rumor of War" (1977), I felt myself being dragged, kicking and screaming for release down every jungle trail, burned out village, and terrorizing night patrol until the thin line between control and its loss, between combat killing and murder/atrocities, had been crossed. The veteran's combat nightmares, night terrors and startle responses which had plagued him since his return from Vietnam and which he had heretofore told to no one were alive and shared in the treatment hours. I came to dread those hours, to have sleepless nights before them, and often an episode of crying or dry heaves following them.

In a symposium on trauma at the Beth Israel Hospital in Boston, Dr. Paul Russell (unpublished), commenting on my experiences with combat veterans, stated, "One of the difficulties in understanding childhood traumata when treating adults is the fact that a great deal has intervened in the meantime. There is a lot to learn, therefore, when the trauma is recent . . . Ms. Haley's experience is such that she can tell, sometimes in advance, when a patient is going to begin to bring himself to describe an atrocity. There is a dread and foreboding and a stealing oneself against it, along with a sense that it is absolutely imperative to hear what is going to be described. Then, as the horror of the act emerges, the therapist is thrown back: 'This cannot be! He is a monster, an animal! No human could have done that.' But the treatment process requires that the therapist be able to feel, 'I could well have done that.' It does not have to be said, just felt; but there is a clear difference between being able or not able to feel it. And the patient can tell. No matter how experienced, it is always in some measure costly to the therapist each time it is felt, but the treatment process requires that the therapist be able to. One cannot understand the trauma unless one can feel what the patient felt."

During this first year of treatment, Mark relived his combat experiences from a regressed posture with no reaction formation evident. Gradually, however, as his affects were shared and tolerated, he appeared to take strength from the therapeutic relationship and to develop necessary narcissistic defenses. He revealed that he had not seen his parents nor returned to his hometown since discharge. He feared his parents would "see the change in me, in my eyes—my mother didn't raise me to be a killer." In fact, the early history only emerged slowly, in fragments, during the second year of treatment.

The following excerpt from Mark's combat history is illustrative of the regression from a state of separation anxiety on through to annihilation anxiety and its atrocious sequelae. Mark had cut himself off physically from his parents following his return from Vietnam but my impression is that most veterans feel emotionally separate and split off from their families despite geographical proximity.

Case Report (continued)

Mark served in Vietnam between 1966-1968 and was at Quang Tri at the start of the Tet offensive. He was a platoon sergeant and his CO, his "LT," was a white officer named Alan. Their friendship had been forged over the past two years across the abyss of race and family backgrounds that separated them.

Returning to their base camp from a seemingly routine patrol, they came under three-sided fire. Some died instantly, others crumpled like rag dolls, the Lt. was hit. Those who could carried or dragged the wounded and Mark brought up the rear as they moved towards the safety of the base camp.

Approximately 50 yards from the camp, Mark was thrown to the ground by the impact of a rocket grenade. Shrapnel and dirt hit Mark's face and eyes. Unable to see, he pressed his body to the ground holding his machine gun. The air continued to be shattered with small arms and rocket fire.

Pinned down, the surviving Marines inside the camp were unable to assist Mark. They yelled out to him that Alan "wasn't going to make it." As the next wave of Vietcong massed to attack, the surviving Marines shouted directions to the blinded Mark. Through their instructions, Mark was able to direct his machine gun towards the advancing Vietcong. He fired, changed position at the directions of the survivors, and was resupplied with ammunition belts thrown to him from inside the camp. For the next 24 hours, the surviving Marines and Mark successfully held off the Vietcong until the arrival of reinforcements ended the battle. Mark was returned to the camp where his injuries were treated. His sight gradually returned, because there had been only blood and dirt in his eyes, no direct injury. For his heroism, he received several military awards.

He sought out Alan and was overwhelmed at the extent of his friend's injuries and the inevitability of his death. As helicopters arrived to evacuate the wounded, Mark became panicked and enraged as he realized that because Alan was near death, he would be one of the last to be evacuated. Although Mark had seen and understood the rationale for the medical triage of casualties, his despair drove him to rage tearfully at the triage officer. Restrained and comforted by his fellow survivors, he sat on the launch pad with Alan for two hours awaiting evacuation.

His most vivid memory of those hours was Alan's hand, which had been rendered nearly skeletal, holding a cigarette, while Alan made jokes about the risks of lung cancer. Mark remembers that their final conversation was similar to many they had had in the past: family, friends, girlfriends, memories of R&R, and ethnic slurs and jokes leveled at one another. This "gallows humor" continued even as Alan was loaded into the helicopter and they parted, eyes riveted on each other saying, "See you around."

Within the hour, Mark learned that Alan had died during the flight. He remembered returning to Alan's hootch, looking at and touching his belongings. He then threw himself on his friend's cot, sobbing. He fell asleep for a number of hours and then awoke feeling in a dreamlike state. His awareness of Alan's death and his anger at himself for "not having the guts to say, 'I love you; don't leave me' " were experienced in a numbed, detached manner. Outside, newly arrived troops were busy fortifying the camp and guarding 30 Vietcong who had been taken prisoner. As he joined his fellow survivors, he noticed that most of them appeared dazed and detached, some were crying. The survivors quietly, calmly, and collectively gathered weapons, mostly machine guns, and approached the 30 prisoners who were in a wired enclosure. One survivor, another lieutenant who was the ranking officer in the camp, motioned the guards to leave the enclosure. Without a word being spoken, the majority of the survivors, including Mark, surrounded the prisoners and killed them to the last man.

Although Mark and Alan had seen atrocities committed by their fellow soldiers, they had never participated. Mark's involvement in atrocity followed a battle of overwhelming threat to his own survival and the death of his closest friend.

I refer once again to the Beth Israel Hospital symposium on trauma. Dr. Edward Payne stated, "When the veteran, or any of us, has committed acts which violently conflict with his values, which he regards as atrocities, he is indeed alienated from the internal representatives of his first-loved objects, whose values he has violated, and is deprived of the protective shield which the relationship confers. The vulnerability to guilt is of course increased when he leaves the group which supported his acts, and is once more dependent on the group which shares the values that he violated." The necessity for the therapist, therefore, to be able genuinely to empathize with and tolerate the experiences of the veteran who has committed atrocities, allows for the "restoration of the protective relationship (real or internalized) which was ruptured, making dissociation necessary. It is this which permits the toleration of the assimilation of previously unacceptable experiences."

Mark's parents painfully suffered his injunction that they not meet, although he kept in regular telephone contact with them. Midway through his second year of treatment, however, his mother arrived unexpectedly much to Mark's shock and disbelief. His mother stated that despite his evident distress about his upcoming divorce, she had noted a change, a softening in his voice, and had decided to "take matters into my own hands." Mark's mother stayed two weeks. She was supportive to him during his nightmares, night terrors, and harassing phone calls from his wife, but was most curious about his "therapy" and this "white lady" he talked to. She insisted on accompanying him to the clinic and asked if she could join us in the interview. A born psychotherapist, Mark's mother said the family had expected that war would leave its scars on him, as it had on the other Vietnam returnees in their hometown, indeed, on the combat veterans of World War II and Korea. She then asked why Mark was so "touchy" about coming home. I did my best to explain and she seemed reassured he was "on the road back." I had apparently passed muster but this diminutive, powerful lady had an agenda of her own. I was made aware, in detail, of Mark's scholastic and athletic achievements and honors. She and the family hoped that Mark would soon feel comfortable enough to visit them. Throughout the exchange, Mark was visibly moved and for the first time in his treatment he wept. He sealed a transference merger between mother and myself by stating to his mother, "Isn't she all I told you," and to me, "I told you my mother was good people—the best."

Over the following months, the veteran was able to disengage from the combat-like, sadomasochistic relationship with his wife (Haley, 1983b) and began to reflect on the boy he had been raised to be and the man into which he had been deformed. Gradually, a reaction formation to his combat atrocities and instances of overkill emerged and for the first time consciously he asked how I had tolerated his earlier presentation and affects. He began to fear that I would be repulsed by him and ultimately reject him.

On the third anniversary of beginning treatment, Mark sat silent throughout the interview and then told me quietly that he loved me and wanted to marry me. After berating myself for having botched the treatment and having precipitated a psychotic transference, I took a deep breath and trusted to another voice inside: perhaps rebirth—not regression—was in progress. I told Mark that I was "overjoyed he loved me . . . that I loved him also and the we had cause for celebration." Simply put, "the man"—or any of society's impersonal opposers—had not won! I told him that, despite the catastrophic assault on his father, the dehumanizing stresses of combat, and the darkest forces within him which had been unleashed, a spark of his humanity—his capacity for concern—had remained. It had required a tolerant atmosphere in which to rekindle. That he now experienced himself as loveable and able to love within the treatment meant that he could use this rebirth (dynamically this return of a viable ego ideal and a realignment of a strengthened ego with superego) to allow available love objects into his life once again. As could be expected, the veteran took the fact that I would remain his therapist and not his woman as a rejection of his love.

There followed months of rage, depression, and the revelation of his pleasure and guilt at watching atrocities, particularly ones involving women. As Mark tearfully argued that no one else could love him if they knew the things I knew about him, I found myself awash with feelings of revulsion. The negative countertransference reaction that I cautioned fellow clinicians to be wary of threatened to overtake me. Gradually, though, I began to hear less about Vietnam and more about beginning friendships with men and some tentative dating. Just as I thought I saw closure in sight, however, the veteran suffered a severe industrial accident, falling 40 feet, rupturing four lumbar vertebrae. There followed a year of severely limited activity, three operations, extensive physical therapy and, in the veteran's words, "Time alone to think with no place to run." I, of course, was "left alone" to wonder to what extent the struggles in the transference/countertransference interface had contributed to renewed suicidal impulses in Mark and his subsequent "accident."

To recapitulate: Under the impact of catastrophic stress, especially combat, psychic structures regress and deform to more primitive levels of organization. Superego regressions to identification with the aggressor and the temporary taking on of the group superego preserve psychic integrity in the midst of catastrophe. Establishment of a close relationship, "a buddy," is an effort by the combatant to contain the panic of separation anxiety and to ward off exposure to overwhelming annihilation anxiety. In a consultation with Blos in 1980, he pointed out that regression under stress to earlier modes of psychic organization and the revival of earlier childhood trauma are quite common and well understood. He pointed out, however, that under catastrophic stress, as in combat, the revival of those childhood traumata will take place at a higher level of action without any restraining environmental forces. The revived trauma becomes more devastating than the original because the child had a supportive system that took responsibility for the child. The second edition of the trauma, where one has not only murderous fantasies but murderous actions, is much more devastating to the psychic organization. Dr. Blos stressed the deformation of psychic structures in the wake of superego transgressions, and the disillusionment of the ego ideal.

Combat may render the power of the superego forever compromised because despite its temporary regression and alignment with the group superego, return to one's primary group with its original superego injunctions renders the ego overwhelmed with the awareness that one can "get away with murder." It is questionable whether the superego ever again can resume its powerful control over the ego. The ego, with a superego stripped of its magical, retributive, punitive properties, will experience panic in the face of future aggressive impulses; hence, the clinical picture with so many combat veterans of a stuck, passive aggressive posture and episodic, unconstructive, self-defeating outbursts of aggressive behavior.

A psychotherapy wherein both veteran and therapist are "at risk" strengthens the ego's ability to reestablish conscious, cognitive controls over heretofore terrifying aggressive impulses. The therapist becomes a model of concern for others and rekindles this capacity in the veteran. Strengthened ego ideals stand as a counterforce to a perhaps permanently compromised superego and offers hope for renewed mastery of both affects and instincts. A psychotherapy wherein the therapist becomes a new "buddy" enables the veteran to reconstruct a bridge back to his family and their values.

Dr. Blos suggested that the therapist might think of the post-combat trauma as an encapsulated borderline condition embedded in the veteran's ego image. In therapy, Blos believed, and my experience bears him out, that the treatment proceeds in phases and that the veteran takes "parts" from the therapist and incorporates them into himself. The veteran is bombarded by his insights and needs to take strength from the therapist, "transmitting internalizations" in language of "self psychology" (Kohut, 1977) and the "reparation of the self" described by Parson (1983).

Drawing on his vast experience with adolescents, Dr. Blos stressed how much at risk the therapist is in the treatment of combat veterans. They will need to borrow and sometimes take some quality from the therapist. As with some adolescents, they may even need to take something tangible, even if its only a matchbook. "Tell them they can return it when they don't need it anymore" (Blos, 1980).

In the case of Mark, treatment continued during the years following his accident as his physical condition permitted. Toward the middle of the fourth year, having returned to work at a desk job, the veteran presented himself for an interview appearing calm and commenting on his physical condition and a recent visit to his family. Imperceptibly it occurred to me that his eyes were "clear" and that no talk of Vietnam had intruded. I commented on these changes. Mark stated that Vietnam and what had happened there would always be with him but that somehow "It's in a far place in my heart. You're some place in the middle, but now there's someone right up front. I brought her to meet you."

REFERENCES

Blank, A.: Discussion of earlier draft, APA Meeting, San Francisco, May 8, 1980.
Blos, P.: *On adolescence: A psychoanalytic interpretation*. New York: The Free Press, 1962.
Blos, P.: Personal communication. New York, March 1, 1980.
Blos, P.: Private consultation. New York, March 1, 1980.
Bowlby, J.: *Attachment and loss. Vol. II: Separation, anxiety and anger*. New York: Basic Books, 1973.
Caputo, P.: *A rumor of war*. New York: Holt, Rinehart & Winston 1977.
Fox, R.: Narcissistic rage and the problem of combat aggression. *Archives of General Psychiatry*, 31:807-811, 9174.
Freud, S. (1913): Totem and taboo. In J. Strachey (Ed.), *Standard edition*, Vol. 14. London: Hogarth Press, 1957.
Glass, A.U.: Psychic therapy in the combat zone. *American Journal of Psychiatry*, 110:725-731, 1954.
Grinker, R.R., & Spiegel, J.: *Men under stress*. New York: McGraw-Hill, 1945.
Haley, S.A.: When the patient reports atrocities. *Archives of General Psychiatry*, 30:191-196, 1974.
Haley, S.A.: Treatment implications of post-combat stress response syndromes for mental health professionals. In C. Figley (Ed.), *Stress disorders among Vietnam veterans: Theory, research and treatment implications*. New York: Brunner/Mazel, 1978.
Haley, S.A.: "Warriors Women"—a film review. *Community Mental Health Journal*, 19(1):85-87, 1983.

Haley, S.A.: The Vietnam veteran and his pre-school child; Child rearing as a delayed stress in combat veterans. *Journal of Contemporary Psychotherapy, 14,* Spring/Summer 1984.

Hasford, G.: *The short timers.* New York: Harpr & Row, 1979, p. 153.

Horowitz, M.J.: *Stress response syndromes.* New York: Jason Aronson, 1976.

Kernberg, O.: *Object relations theory and clinical psychoanalysis.* New York: Jason Aronson, 1976.

Kohut, H.: Thoughts on narcissism and narcissistic rage. *Psychoanalytic Study of the Child, 27:*360-400, 1972.

Kohut, H.: *The restoration of the self.* New York: International Universities Press, 1977.

Lifton, R.: *Home from the war: Vietnam veterans neither victims nor executioners.* New York: Simon & Schuster, 1973.

Mahler, M.: *On human symbiosis and the vicissitudes of individuation.* New York: International Universities Press, 1968.

Modell, A.: *Object love and reality.* New York: International Universities Press, 1968.

Morrier, E.: Passivity as a response to psychic trauma. *Journal of Contemporary Psychotherapy, 14,* Spring/Summer 1983.

Payne, E.: Psychic trauma. Unpublished manuscript.

Parson, E.: The separation of the self: Clinical and theoretical dimensions in the treatment of Vietnam combat veterans. *Journal of Contemporary Psychotherapy, 14,* Spring/Summer 1983.

Russel, P.: Trauma and the cognitive function of affects. Unpublished manuscript.

Salmon, T.W.: The war neuroses and their lessons. *NY State Journal of Medicine, 109:*933-944, 1919.

Shatan, C.: Militarized mourning and ceremonial vengeance. Paper presented at the American Psychoanalytic Association, December 21, 1980.

Smith, J.R.: *A review of one hundred and twenty years of the psychological literature on reactions to combat from the civil war through the Vietnam war.* Durham: Duke University, 1981.

Wexler, H.: The life master: A case of severe ego regression induced by combat experience in WW II. *Psychoanalytic Study of the Child, 27:*565-597, 1973.

Zetzel, E.R.: *The capacity for emotional growth.* New York: International Universities Press, 1970.

6

The Reliving Experience in Vietnam Veterans with Post-Traumatic Stress Disorders

HERBERT HENDIN, M.D., ANN POLLINGER

HAAS, Ph.D., PAUL SINGER, M.D.,

WILLIAM HOUGHTON, M.D., MARK F.

SCHWARTZ, Ph.D., and

VINCENT WALLEN, Ph.D.

One of the most dramatic manifestations of post-traumatic stress disorders in Vietnam veterans is the reliving experience—the sudden acting or feeling as if traumatic combat events were recurring. The symptom was considered of sufficient significance that DSM-III (1980) listed it, together with recurrent dreams and recurrent intrusive recollections, as evidence of reexperiencing the trauma—one of the criteria which must be present for the diagnosis of post-traumatic stress disorder to be made.

In reliving experiences, the individual is awake but appears to be in a state of altered consciousness and often has subsequent amnesia for what takes place. The experiences last from a few minutes to several hours and can usually be distinguished from startle reactions in response to environmental stimuli that momentarily reinvoke traumatic combat events, in which misperceptions are quickly corrected.

Work on post-traumatic stress disorders resulting from exposure to traumatic combat events has given relatively little attention to reliving experiences or their psychodynamics. Several clinicians have reported that dissociative states were frequent among veterans of World War I and II (Nemiah, 1975; Futterman & Pumpian-Midlin, 1951; Lidz, 1946; Rado, 1942), and a recent, large-scale survey of Vietnam veterans found that 17 percent have had combat-related "flashbacks" since returning home (Egendorf et al., 1981). However, neither the behavior nor its functions in terms of postwar adaptation has been elaborated.

In civilian life the alteration of consciousness seen in fugues and multiple personalities seems to have some similarities to what occurs in combat-related reliving experiences, with the striking difference that the combat veteran usually does not assume another identity during such episodes. Past work on dissociative states among civilians has tended to view the alteration of consciousness either as a defense against conflicted and unacceptable feelings, or as resulting from a failure in the development of the individual's sense of his own and others' separateness and an accompanying inability to integrate unpleasant or disparate emotional experiences (Fisher, 1947; Luparello, 1970; Berman, 1981; Stolorow & Lachman, 1980). In cases described in such work, traumatic childhoods, often with physical abuse, frequently appear to have been precursors of later episodes of altered consciousness.

Several observers have described dissociative states following traumatic experiences during adulthood. Sonnenberg (1972) and Burnstein (1983), for example, described hallucinatory experiences or "revisualizations" following such stressful experiences as the traumatic loss of a spouse or a severe accident. Barnes (1980) reported the occurrence of partial dissociative reactions resulting from the stress of travel in a foreign country.

Jaffe (1968) and Niederland (1968) described more extreme and persistent dissociative states among former concentration camp inmates, in which traumatic experiences would be reenacted. Jaffe noted that among many concentration camp survivors, precursors of the later dissociative behavior were evident in the altered states of consciousness they experienced during imprisonment as a result of extreme terror and fatigue.

Howard's (1976) account of his own experiences in Vietnam similarly suggests that the fatigue and threatening environment encountered by soldiers during combat produced alterations of consciousness and contributed to their subsequent inability to integrate the trauma with the rest of their lives. While such observations suggest factors which may contribute to later reliving experiences, the paucity of well-developed case material has limited our understanding of the psychodynamics of this phenomenon.

Our work with large numbers of Vietnam veterans evidencing symptoms of post-traumatic stress disorder subsequent to intense combat (Hendin et al., 1981, 1983a; Hendin, 1983, 1984; Hendin & Pollinger, 1984) has put us in touch with a sizable subgroup of men with active reliving experiences. Of the more than 100 post-traumatic stress cases with whom we have worked, about 20 percent have or have had episodes in which they suddenly acted or felt as if traumatic events which they had experienced in Vietnam were recurring. In almost every case such episodes were repetitive across a period of time ranging from a matter of weeks to several years. Access to this population has allowed us an opportunity to begin to explore the psychodynamics and adaptive functions of reliving experiences, about which little is currently known.

Presented below are summaries of three combat veterans who have had repeated reliving experiences since returning from Vietnam. Each of these men participated in our Post-Traumatic Stress Evaluation and Treatment Program at the Veterans Administration Medical Center, in Montrose, N.Y. Following our usual evaluation (Hendin et al., 1983b), each veteran completed a life history questionnaire and a series of five semistructured interviews prior to being diagnosed as having a post-traumatic stress disorder. Each man was also administered a battery of psychological tests, including the Rorschach, and was subsequently followed in ongoing stress-oriented psychotherapy for a minimum of one year. As the case summaries illustrate, even though in all three veterans the stress disorder was manifested in periodic reliving experiences, the frequency and duration of these experiences varied considerably, as did their relationship to what the veterans had been through in combat and the ways they tried to cope with this in their postcombat lives.

Case I: Mr. M

Mr. M was a stocky, muscular man in his mid-30s who was married, had four children, and had worked for 14 years for the highway department as a bulldozer operator. He had grown up in an intact farming family and had shown no evidence of social or emotional difficulty prior to his combat experience. He had been in Vietnam in 1966, and had served with various infantry units primarily in the northern provinces. His major assignment was as a machine gun operator on an armored personnel carrier.

He married soon after his return from Vietnam, but during the postwar years he gradually withdrew from his family, spending more and more time alone in his bedroom thinking and reading about Vietnam. In the last few years he had also begun to drink heavily and had increasingly thought of taking his own life.

Although he related his combat experiences with a good deal of affect, at times becoming angry and at other times tearful, he was vague and claimed not to remember any details. Outstanding in his recollections were the revulsion he felt at being exposed to dead and mutilated American soldiers whose bodies he and his comrades often carried back to the base in their vehicle, his awareness that in "free fire zones" they had killed unarmed civilians, and his vague descriptions of sexual involvements with Vietnamese prostitutes in which he had been physically abusive.

His post-traumatic stress disorder was characterized by reliving experiences which he described as "weird things I do that I have no memory of." When initially seen, he had been hospitalized for the first time after getting drunk at a friend's house, wrecking furniture, and then running out and shooting at imaginary Vietcong in a nearby field. A few months earlier, also while intoxicated, he had set a fire in his kitchen, claiming he was burning out Vietcong. He was sorrowful and upset in discussing this incident, saying he had a lovely family and expressing the fear he might do something to harm them.

Not all of his reliving experiences took place when he had been drinking. After he went to sleep at night, he had often been found by his wife crawling around the house with a gun as though he were back in combat. Once when hunting he felt another hunter was firing at him and started to fire back, but his brother who was with him told him to stop. Several times during sex he had referred to his wife as "mama san." During one reliving experience, he pointed a gun at her while speaking to her in a sexually derogatory manner.

When not reliving his Vietnam experiences, he avoided talking about them, particularly with his wife. Yet, the reliving appeared to be a way of communicating to her and to others things he was unable to talk about.

In therapy he gradually became able to discuss his combat experiences in detail, as well as his reaction to them. Virtually all of his reliving experiences turned out to be elaborations of those aspects of combat over which he was most troubled. His random shooting in the field was connected to a sense he had had in the last months of his tour that he was out of control and firing at "anything that moved." His setting the fire in his kitchen related to an incident where he had refused to crawl down an underground tunnel in pursuit of Vietcong and had persuaded his sergeant to burn them out instead. The hunting incident in which he almost shot another hunter bore a striking similarity to an incident where, during a firefight, he had killed another American whom he had mistaken for a Vietcong. The incident with his wife and the gun bore a direct parallel to his behavior with a Vietcong prostitute whom he had hit over the head with his gun after discovering her going through his friend's wallet.

He seemed to feel that his behavior in Vietnam had been a true reflection of the sort of person he really was. As he became aware of his guilt over his combat behavior and the ways in which he needed to confess and be punished, he began to make Vietnam a part of his life over which he had some control. He stopped drinking and became able to share with his wife the details of his combat experiences and the emotions he felt with regard to them. In the process he stopped having reliving experiences. After several months his mood lifted considerably, and he was able to leave the hospital and return to his family and his job. He was seen once a week for the next six months and showed considerable abatement of his stress symptoms and no return of his reliving experiences.

Case 2: Mr. B

After a distinguished tour as an Army helicopter pilot in Vietnam, for which he received a Presidential Unit Citation, a Valorous Unit Award, 14 air medals, and a Purple Heart, Mr. B when first seen at the age of 41 was a prison inmate serving a two-to-six-year term for bank robbery. He had grown up in a warm supportive family in a rural area of New York State. He had done well in school, had a good administrative job, and was happily married with two children when he entered the service in early 1965, hoping to later use service benefits to go to veterinary school.

Several particularly traumatic combat experiences played a role in the reliving episodes which were a major feature of the posttraumatic stress disorder he developed after his return from Vietnam. He had once been ordered, along with several other pilots, to fly a mission in a storm which resulted in the loss of one of the planes and several of his friends. While he was caught in the center of the storm, ice formed on the wings of his own helicopter, the rotor stalled several times, and the plane was sucked up and down at the will of the storm. His base was unable to pick him up on radar, his instruments failed, and he thought he would not survive. Finally, he was able to contact a ground unit that fired flares to direct him to a landing.

Two of his traumatic combat memories involved women. On one occasion he was shot many times by a Vietcong woman who fired directly at him after his helicopter had landed in a combat assault, and he survived only because of the armor in his flight jacket. During another combat assault into Cambodia he had been shot at by a woman who fired nails at him from point-blank range. He escaped injury by ducking behind his seat until someone else was able to kill the woman. The latter incident had occurred on a particularly hot day on which his unit had wiped out an entire village while everyone was taking a midday rest. He felt the woman was justified in defending her village and regretted having been part of an assault which he believed should never have taken place.

Another of his horrifying memories was of the severed head of an American soldier which he had seen from his plane in the light of exploding artillery shells. The head, which seemed to be frozen in the expression of a scream, was later put in a body bag with the rest of the soldier's body, and was flown back to the base in Mr. B's helicopter.

Although he had been faithful to his wife during his marriage, while in Vietnam Mr. B used constant sexual involvements with Vietnamese prostitutes to relieve his anxiety. He described himself as having used sex the way other soldiers used drugs or alcohol.

On one occasion during his tour of duty, he could not be fully aroused to go on a mission. He told the man awakening him to go to hell, went back to sleep, and when he awoke later he had no recollection of what had occurred. The doctor who then spoke with him considered sending him home, but Mr. B persuaded him not to and the episode was not repeated.

He returned home with the intention to pursue his flying through a career in the Army. Almost immediately, however, he began to experience severe insomnia, nightmares, reliving experiences, and an explosive temper that made his functioning in both the Army and his marriage impossible. He tried to get psychiatric help but was told that "pilots don't see shrinks." His promiscuous sexual behavior continued and eventually his involvements with the wives of several officers at the base led to legal difficulties and a less than honorable discharge which made him ineligible for veterans benefits.

For the next several years, he intermittently worked as a pilot for several small companies, and during this period he became addicted to heroin which he had initially used in order to sleep. Bitter and angry with the government, he joined several other Vietnam veterans in committing a number of bank robberies from 1969 to 1976. The last robbery was done with his second wife who, in the course of their marital breakup in 1980, turned him in to the police in exchange for immunity for herself.

The reliving experiences which characterized Mr. B's post-traumatic stress disorder involved several of his combat traumas although the thunderstorm experience and the time he was wounded were predominant. These experiences were frequently set off when he was driving his car and would suddenly begin reexperiencing his helicopter being tossed back and forth in the thunderstorm. Thinking he was actually flying, he had several times driven the car off the road. On other occasions he would relive being shot by the Vietnamese woman and would become so totally swept up in the experience that he would feel the impact of the bullets and fall backward.

Periods of insomnia characterized by combat nightmares would make him more prone to reliving experiences. Sometimes he would go from the nightmares to the reliving experiences with no clear-cut period of wakefulness.

For the first 10 years after returning from Vietnam, Mr. B also had a more prolonged type of dissociative episode in which he was unable to account for his actions or whereabouts for periods of several days or even weeks. Sometimes he would find himself with a woman in another city and would not recall how he got there. He was also amnestic for most of the details of the bank robberies. In some cases he could recall planning them; in others he could recall only waking up with a gun and large amounts of money on his bed.

In 1978, when he stopped working as a pilot and was able to get off heroin, the dissociative episodes for which he would have amnesia ceased. Since that time he had also gained greater control of his reliving experiences. When he would become caught up in reliving combat events, he would have a sense that what was happening was unreal and he would not act on the experience. In time he developed the ability to recognize that the events "were only taking place in my head." Gradually he was able to tell when the experiences were about to develop and would protect himself by staying in his room.

During once-a-week treatment over the course of a year it was possible to observe some of the events that triggered his reliving experiences. The most apparent was the time of the year. Around the anniversary of the episode when his helicopter was caught in the storm and that in which a combat assault had cost his company many lives and left him with the memory of the severed head, he would grow increasingly apprehensive and have nightmares and reliving experiences concerning these events. Very hot weather would trigger reliving experiences of the combat assault that was done on a hot day.

On several occasions it was ascertainable that the reliving experiences were caused by events that were only symbolically associated with the original traumatic experience. When he was turned down on a parole request, his sense of helplessness and rage triggered reliving experiences concerning the thunderstorm and the severed head. When a woman was critical of him during a church meeting held at the prison, he had a reliving experience in which the Vietnamese woman fired the gun containing nails at him.

His anger toward everyone he felt should have helped him and did not was pervasive. In leaving his family and robbing banks he had acted on this anger, but his conflict over his feelings caused much of this behavior to take place in a dissociated state.

Case 3: Mr. R

Mr. R was a tall, well-built man of 35 who was married, had three children, and worked as an ambulance driver. He grew up in a small town where his father was a factory worker and his mother worked nights as a telephone operator. As a child he was sickly and strove to make himself tough from an early age. He described neither parent as having been very involved with him but related this factually with no expression of bitterness or anger toward either of them. Although he participated in varsity athletics and had a number of friends, he said he had always been shy, which he attributed to a bad case of acne. In late adolescence he became involved in a gang that trained with knives and had numerous fights.

After several years in the Coast Guard, he had volunteered for an assignment in Southeast Asia, and had served from 1965-66 as a member of a covert intelligence unit which mainly operated along the Thai-Cambodian border. After completing this tour, he was given a stateside assignment in which he handled classified material and during this period he became afraid that agents from Southeast Asia were following him in pursuit of information.

In the years after leaving the service, he became increasingly isolated and alienated from his family, his parents, and friends, and spent almost all of his time at home and at work obsessed by images and memories of his war experiences. He was perfectionistic with his wife and children and jumpy outside the home, assaulting men on several occasions. He also became a heavy drinker and this, together with his reclusiveness, had led to severe marital problems. He and his wife fought in a tortured way about his lack of involvement around the house. Although he had had affairs with other women, he was jealous of his wife talking to other men and this was a source of conflict between them as well.

Although initially he was extremely reluctant to discuss his war experiences, he eventually revealed that he had killed 26 individuals with a knife during the course of his combat tour. He explained that his unit had standing orders to kill anyone who happened to come up to them as they were installing secret signalling devices used to guide American bombers in attacks against enemy positions. Because of the need for secrecy, a knife rather than firearms was used in all the killings. Although insisting that all the killings were strictly within the line of duty, he did admit to having removed gold fillings from the teeth of those he had killed. He claimed to be bothered only by the last killing which he said had involved a woman, something he had not realized until he was searching the body.

Mr. R's post-traumatic stress disorder was characterized by recurrent reliving experiences. He had had brief reliving spells at work but his most frequent and prolonged experiences occurred while out in the woods behind his house. He would spend hours there in a dissociated state, dressed in his combat fatigues and carrying his gun and military knife. When he returned to the house following these incidents, he would have only vague memories of what he had been doing, but would often be breathing heavily and perspiring as if he had been running or trying to escape from some unknown threat. On occasion he also awoke from his sleep in the middle of the night and went from one room of his house to another as if he were being pursued and was trying to hide and escape.

He reported that the sight of bloody, mangled, or dismembered bodies which he sometimes encountered in the course of his current work triggered episodes in which he thought he was back in combat. Also, when he hunted deer he said he would often think he was back in the jungle stalking the enemy. In the course of skinning and slaughtering deer he had just shot, he described sometimes thinking that he was cutting up human bodies. Once he cut out a deer's eyes and brains, boiled them in water, and then ate them, to the amazement and horror of his hunting companions. Anger at women in his present life seemed to trigger both nightmares and reliving experiences. In one dream, he began to make love to a woman, realized she was an enemy, and cut her throat. In other dreams, he relived his killing of the woman in Vietnam.

The reliving experiences in which Mr. R was running or escaping, turned out to be related to an incident in which he and a companion were hidden from enemy soldiers by the chief of a friendly village. They had watched helplessly as the enemy soldiers hung the chief from his feet, slit open his stomach, and laughed as pigs ate his intestines as they fell to the ground. Mr.R and his comrade managed to escape from the village but were pursued by the enemy. Mr. R, who was more experienced than his companion, split up with him out of the fear that he would accidentally give away their whereabouts. From his hiding place in the jungle he heard the other man's screams and subsequently found his decapitated and mutilated body.

Elaboration of the experiences he had had while hunting eventually led him to reveal the true nature of most of the killing he had done during the war. Only the first eight of his 26 kills had actually occurred in the line of duty; the rest had taken place in the course of his own unauthorized forays into the jungle. During these secret missions he had hidden in the bushes and had sprung out and knifed anyone who had walked down the trail. His thought on recent hunting trips that he was slaughtering humans rather than animals was related to his having tortured and butchered a number of those he caught on the trails. He admitted that in some cases he had dismembered his victims while they were still alive. Eating the deer's eyes and brains was connected to episodes in which he had swallowed handfuls of his victim's blood, mimicking an Asian ritual in which parts of the corpse were ingested in order to acquire the powers of the dead person.

His overall level of functioning at home and at work, and the absence of clinically manifested delusions and hallucinations, did not permit a DSM-III diagnosis of schizophrenia. His limited ability to repress traumatic imagery and ideation, and the bizarre nature of his frequent reenactment of experiences from Vietnam, suggested, however, an encapsulated and circumscribed psychotic response to combat, or what might be called a "traumatic psychosis."

Given the fragility of Mr. R's defenses, therapy involved a slow and difficult exploration of his war experiences. He looked to his therapist as a safe person to whom he could express his violent ideas, and an ally in his struggle to control them. In therapy his dreams gradually moved from unemotional killing to killing with remorse, and he became more aware of the fear and guilt connected with his reliving experiences. Although he has remained obsessed with violent urges, and has maintained considerable rigidity in his personal relationships, he has been successful in controlling his drinking, and his reliving experiences have diminished considerably.

DISCUSSION

Reliving experiences express in dramatic ways aspects of the combat experience which, although usually not consciously recognized by the veteran, continue to dominate his life because they are so unresolved. The men who have reliving experiences have recurrent nightmares of their traumatic experiences as well. All of the cases discussed above went at times from a sleeping/dreaming state to a somnambulistic state in which they relived combat experiences. The fact that combat events were reexperienced in their waking life suggests a greater permeation of their adaptive processes by the trauma with a lesser ability to repress traumatic recollections and the associated affect.

The Rorschach responses of these men provided some confirmation of this permeation. Mr. M saw periodic explosions in a Vietnam-related context throughout the testing. Mr. B had frequent Vietnam-related responses and even more frequent sexual responses that reflected his way of dealing with his anxieties associated with combat. He had a brief quasi-reliving experience during the testing when the blood he perceived on one of the cards took him back into a situation in which blood of a man hit by the blade of a helicopter in front of him had been splattered on his windshield. Mr. R, from his second response on, provided nothing but Vietnam-related material across the entire spectrum of Rorschach cards, with numerous references to tortured and mutilated bodies. That traumatic experiences will be reflected in Rorschach responses has long been observed (Rorschach, 1942; Beck, 1945; Kardiner, 1941; Bersoff, 1940; Van der Kolk et al., 1983), but for each of these three individuals, combat was a much more predominant theme than we have observed among the Rorschach records of Vietnam veterans with post-traumatic stress who do not have reliving experiences.

The three veterans, like most of those who relive combat events in civilian life, experienced psychic trauma under conditions of terror and fatigue. We have not yet been able to definitively distinguish the role of these particular factors in contributing to subsequent reliving experiences, as others who suffer from post-traumatic stress disorder but do not show this particular symptom have had similarly disorienting combat tours. What is clear from the cases discussed above, however, is that fatigue due to insomnia as well as drug and alcohol abuse in civilian life can trigger reliving experiences in those veterans who are prone to them.

Similarly, veterans who have reliving experiences do not appear to be distinguishable from those who do not on the basis of precombat variables. Although some men who have reliving experiences, like Mr. R, came from difficult family situations, in general we have not found this to be more true of them than of veterans whose post-traumatic stress disorders do not include reliving experiences. Veterans with post-traumatic stress disorders have often been so transformed by their combat experiences that they have difficulty in reconciling who they were with what they have become. This dimension of the disorder appears to be particularly acute in those veterans with reliving experiences.

Although Mr. M *(Case 1)* showed no particular precombat evidence of identity problems or of any vulnerability to dissociative episodes, the stress of combat and his resultant behavior had badly shaken his picture of who he was. His reliving experiences appeared related to a conflict over whether to hide, confess, or even remember actions over which he felt guilty. He responded well to being helped to become aware of his guilt, his conflict between repression and confession, and the ways in which he was punishing himself.

Mr. B *(Case 2)* came from a warm supportive family and was a well-functioning, stable individual prior to his singularly arduous combat experiences. He struggled during the war and subsequently to repress the fear, pain, and loss he experienced in combat. His reliving experiences were a reflection of his inability to do so. Mr. B felt no guilt over his combat behavior and was not amnestic for those events or for his reliving experiences. His post-traumatic stress disorder resulted in changed behavior of such magnitude that he was hardly recognizable as the person he had been before, and he did feel the need to block from consciousness the worst of his antisocial behavior. His dissociative episodes and antisocial behavior paralleled in severity his reliving experiences and disappeared when he gained greater control over those experiences.

Mr. R *(Case 3)* was not in touch with the frustration and anger he must have experienced in regard to his parents. His social adjustment had been poor prior to combat, and in the war he became eager to kill in a way that neither of the other two veterans had. He needed to hide more than to repress both his combat actions and his reliving experiences, and revealed them only after some months in treatment. He mainly feared punishment for his actions, although some remorse developed as his therapy progressed. The reliving experiences appeared to enable him to privately reenact bizarre and destructive combat behavior, without having to assume full responsibility for it. His drinking the blood of the individual he killed in Vietnam and later eating the deer's brains suggested some wish to merge with his victims. His need to isolate these experiences from the rest of his life resulted in his being removed from family, friends, and co-workers. The other two veterans struggled against what they saw as unwanted changes produced in them by their combat experiences. Mr. R, at least in part, seemed to want to remain what he had become.

The reexperiencing of traumatic events in a waking state is not without adaptive value. Mr. M was able through the reliving experiences to communicate what had happened to him in Vietnam which he could not otherwise do. Even before treatment Mr. B had gradually gained increased control over his stress disorder, starting with his reliving experiences in which he moved from acting as if they were real to recognizing that what was happening was actually taking place in his head. Mr. R seemed to need to induce and control the experiences in which he expressed destructive impulses and escaped retaliation. Sharing them in therapy resulted in his feeling less isolated. For all of these veterans, understanding the origin of their reliving experiences, the events that triggered them, and the adaptive functions they served was a valuable lever in treating the post-traumatic stress disorder.

REFFRENCES

Barnes, F.: Travel and fatigue as causes of partial dissociative reactions. *Comprehensive Psychiatry*, 21:55, 1980.
Beck, S.: *Rorschach's test*. New York: Grune & Stratton, 1945.
Berman, E.: Multiple personalities: Psychoanalytic perspectives. *International Journal of Psychoanalysis*, 62:283-300, 1981.
Bersoff, D.: Rorschach correlates of traumatic neurosis of war. *Journal of Projective Techniques and Personality Assessment*, 37:194-200, 1940.
Burnstein, A.: Post-traumatic visualizations. *Psychosomatics*, 24:166-167, 1983.
Diagnostic and statistical manual of mental disorders, Third Edition. Washington, D.C.: American Psychiatric Association, 1980.
Egendorf, A., Kadushin, C., Laufer, R., Rothbart, G., & Sloan, L.: *Legacies of Vietnam: Comparative adjustment of veterans and their peers*. Washington, D.C.: U.S. Government Printing Office, 1981.
Fisher, C.: The psychogenesis of fugue states. *American Journal of Psychotherapy*, 1:211-220, 1947.
Futterman, S., & Pumpian-Mindlin, E.: Traumatic war neurosis five years later. *American Journal of Psychiatry*, 108:401-408, 1951.

Hendin, H.: Psychotherapy for Vietnam veterans with posttraumatic stress disorders. *American Journal of Psychotherapy, 37*:86-99, 1983.

Hendin, H.: Combat never ends: The paranoid adaptation to posttraumatic stress disorders. *American Journal of Psychotherapy, 38*:1, 1984.

Hendin, H., & Haas, A.: *Wounds of war: The psychological aftermath of combat in Vietnam.* New York: Basic Books, 1984.

Hendin, H., Haas, A., Singer, P., Gold, F., & Trigos, G.: The influence of precombat personality on posttraumatic stress disorder. *Comprehensive Psychiatry, 24*:530-534, 1983a.

Hendin, H., Haas, A., Singer, P., Gold, F., & Ulman, R.: Evaluation of posttraumatic stress in Vietnam veterans. *Journal of Psychiatric Treatment and Evaluation, 5*:303-307, 1983b.

Hendin, H., Pollinger, A., Singer, P., & Ulman, R.: Meanings of combat and the development of posttraumatic stress disorders. *American Journal of Psychiatry, 138*:1490-1493, 1981.

Howard, S.: Vietnam warrior: His experience and its implications for psychotherapy. *American Journal of Psychotherapy, 1*:121-135, 1976.

Jaffe, R.: Dissociative phenomena in concentration camp inmates. *International Journal of Psychoanalysis, 49*:310-312, 1968.

Kardiner, A.: *War stress and neurotic illness.* New York: Paul Hueber, 1941.

Lidz, T.: Psychiatric casualties of Guadalcanal. *Psychiatry, 9*:193-213, 1946.

Luparello, T.: Features of fugue: A unified hypothesis of regression. *Journal of the American Psychoanalytic Association, 18*:379-398, 1970.

Nemiah, J.: Dissociative disorders. In A. Freedman, H. Kaplan, & B. Sadock (Eds.), *Comprehensive textbook of psychiatry.* Baltimore, MD: William & Wilkins, 1975.

Niederland, W.C.: Clinical observations on the "survivor syndrome." *International Journal of Psychoanalysis, 49*:313-315, 1968.

Rado, S.: Psychodynamics and treatment of traumatic war neurosis. *Psychosomatic Medicine, 4*:4, 1942.

Rorschach, H. *Psychodiagnostics.* New York: Grune & Stratton, 1942.

Sonnenberg, S.: A special form of survivor syndrome. *Psychoanalytic Quarterly, 41*:58-62, 1972.

Stolorow, R., & Lachmann, F.: *Psychoanalysis of developmental arrests.* New York: International Universities Press, 1980.

Van der Kolk, B., Blintz, R., & Sherry, S.: Clinical implications of Rorschach data in posttraumatic stress syndrome. Presentation at the meeting of the American Psychiatric Association Convention, New York, 1983.

CHAPTER

7

Why the Pain Won't Stop and What the Family Can Do to Help

ROBERT MARRS, M.A.

As I continue to work with Vietnam veterans and their families, I am increasingly troubled by the interaction of the veterans' history, i.e., the period of their childhood to adolescence, the particular and sometimes unique war experiences, usually the years between 19 and 23, and their return home with all its implications for lack of support and alienation. While a powerful trauma in any of the three phases can have serious consequences for the veteran in his effort for readjustment, paralleling negative experiences of a lower magnitude in two or more of these periods are just as likely to result in maladjustment. In many cases the negatives seem to compound one another to form a stranglehold of degradation and self-defeat from which escape is difficult (Argeropoulos, 1970). The concept might be likened to the bola weapon used by South American Indians which squeezes the life from their victims. Shorr et al. (1980) speak to the principle of addressing the existence of psycho-logical parallels.

To pierce the wall erected by a veteran subjected to that stranglehold requires skill of intervention in all three life phases as well as a strong humanistic philosophy which can be experienced by the veteran as positive regard for his person in spite of his attitudes or actions. Most of the veterans I have worked with are extremely sensitive about how they will be received by the therapist. Their feelings of anger and betrayal at having been scapegoated and deserted by the American public are strongly internalized and often result in overt distrust and alienation (Lifton, 1971). It is deeply etched in most of their minds and often communicated in the form of disrespect of people in general and the "establishment" in particular (Polner, 1971). In discussing the following case histories, one of my intentions will be to detail the existence of these parallels and show they can contribute to produce very negative reactions and assumptions which will cloud a person's whole life (Shatan, 1974).

Case 1: Rick, The Doubting Thomas

Rick is a former marine, now 37 years of age, who was wounded in action. Rick is married and has two children. He is self-employed, is well regarded in his community, and gives the impression of a well adjusted person. In spite of outward success, Rick feels dissatisfied with his career direction and has difficulties with decision making as is required in his line of work.

During his childhood Rick was often abused by his alcoholic father and, from statements made by him, it becomes evident that Rick allowed himself to believe that he himself was to blame for his father's abuse. His negative assumption formalized itself into a powerful negative statement: "Somehow my actions must produce a problem for others." A strong reinforcement of this statement came in Vietnam when Rick was required to radio in the position of his squad to a supporting helicopter for suppressing fire power. Somehow a mistake was made and the wrong position was fired upon. This mistake, as often happened in Vietnam, cost the life of one of Rick's buddies. Rick again blamed himself for the death, finding it impossible to suppress the possibility that an action or attitude of his had interfered dramatically with a vital relationship.

In another significant situation, two Vietnamese boys appeared to be marking Rick's position, perhaps to assist enemy mortar fire later that night. In his need to protect his squad, Rick killed them both. Children and civilians were used in this war on many occasions, and one could not afford to take chances. And yet, when reviewing this decision later, inevitable questions surfaced: Were the boys burning old huts for other reasons? Did he really need to kill them to safeguard himself and his men? Especially as his own children grew to the age of the two he killed, the horror and atrocity of his action loomed larger.

This tendency to repeatedly question oneself about traumatic events that happened in Vietnam seems to plague many veterans. Each time the scene comes to mind again, the emotions attached to it—guilt, grief, or rage—are increased. Rick reports sleeping much better following a confrontation of his feelings in a rap group for veterans. They must learn not to "second guess" past actions during their war years. At that time, the rules for survival were "shoot first, ask questions later." Any other action could have meant death.

Case 2: Tom, The Grounded Pilot*

Tom's story should be seen in the light of his Catholic upbringing which encouraged him to be strong and obedient. He translated this into being a hero in Vietnam where he was shot down twice while piloting a helicopter. On the second occasion he lost his copilot while trying to keep supplies coming to an Airborne Division in the Central Highlands. While the fighting was still raging, his was the first helicopter to land there and resupply the ground troops. He took out several wounded and one body while the mortars were being "walked" toward his aircraft. "You had to be a hero!" said his wife when she was told of the incident.

After the war Tom joined a large city police department helping to establish a helicopter squad. He became the trainer for the pilots involved, and the stress continued for him when one of his students was killed in an accident while flying. His early upbringing had left a framework of guilt and responsibility, and Tom found it hard to overcome the loss of his colleague. He was still in pain over the many deaths he had witnessed in Vietnam, and he was using alcohol to relieve the stress and pressures building within him. When the alcohol was removed following a detoxification program in a hospital, he had no protection from feelings of helplessness and depression within him. A suicide attempt followed shortly thereafter. He is now confined to a wheelchair with a quadriplegic handicap resulting from the gunshot he directed to his head. His wife has emotionally divorced him, and after about four years he has only just started to take charge of his life again, accepting himself as a fallible, worthwhile human being.

---

*This is the same patient described by Tanay (see p. 39), who was also involved in the effort to assist this severely disturbed veteran.

To encourage other Vietnam veterans to free themselves from the trauma of unresolved pain and remorse stemming from that war, a poster was developed (Figure 1). It illustrates that pressures exist, both internal (through personal history) and external (from family, health, friends, or employment situations), interacting to form a potentially explosive situation (Polner, 1971). We have to be mindful of the extent to which both factors may contribute to promoting the risk of suicide, or to bringing about stages of rage and hostility which may be outward directed. I believe that for veterans who experience problems in three or four of the external areas, the risk of suicide increases dramatically (Argeropoulos, 1969).

Family members and spouses can tell you if internal pressures relate to Vietnam by monitoring, for instance, nightmares and emotional outbursts while the veteran is drinking. One wife related these comments:

> My interest in the problems of the Vietnam vet has opened the doors of communication with my husband. Letting him talk at his own pace is important. He can't be pressed to reveal what is on his mind. Closeness is very important while he's talking. He needs to be held and reassured that he did nothing wrong in Vietnam.
>
> We watch TV specials about Vietnam together. He often opens up after something someone else says. He related to the movie *Deer Hunter* when Michael found his friend back in Vietnam and pleaded with him not to play Russian Roulette. He remembers telling a couple of his boys in Vietnam that it wasn't necessary for them to patrol their camp at a particular time—one never returned.
>
> He is haunted by the fact that he lost three men there. He feels responsible for that. He blames it on the fact that he was in command at such a young age. He feels guilty about enjoying the killing. He thinks about Vietnam all the time, no matter what he is doing. He is haunted by the young Vietnamese boy who killed one of his buddies with a grenade, and having to kill the boy and his mother because of it. The memories of spending Christmas in Vietnam are sad. The time of the TET offensive is painful.

For Vietnam veterans, spouses, family, or close friends are the last line of defense against the hostile world and death. Many times veterans will push away their spouse although loving them, because their negative self-image is so strong they cannot stand to be loved. This self-repudiation has been intensified by such accusations as "beast," "baby killer," or "monster" people hurled at them at the height of the antiwar

FIGURE 1
THE VIETNAM VETERAN AND A MATRIX FOR SUICIDE

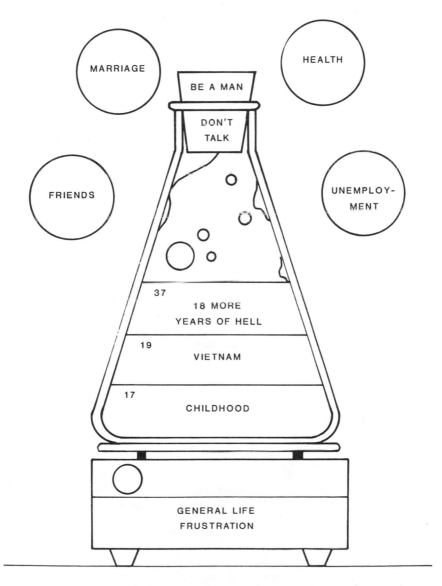

Figure 1. The Vietnam veteran and a matrix for suicide.

sentiment (Polner, 1971). We kept the men in a war they could not win, and tried one of them (Lieutenant Calley) for actions that were utilized and accepted by many (Lifton, 1971). Finally, when the American public turned away from a hawkish stance with regard to Vietnam, they set up a psychological nightmare for the men who were sent to fight in that war, a nightmare which continues to deeply trouble veterans, their families, and the nation in terms of loss of potential and human suffering (Shatan, 1973).

Case 3: Milt, The Pallbearer

Milt's story begins in his sixth year. His father, depressed because of health problems, committed sucide in their living room while the rest of the family was out shopping. Excited over some trinket, Milt runs into the house to show the purchase to his father, finding him in the last throes of death, jerking, gasping, and bleeding profusely. Alerted by his screaming, the mother was able to protect the other children from this terrible scene, but little was done to alleviate the trauma experienced by Milt as the entire family was in shock. While his brothers and sisters were able to overcome the death, the story is different for Milt who depreciated his abilities by making unwise and unwarranted comparisons with his siblings. He manufactured for himself a fantasy that his father had been killed by a murderer, and the scenes he conjured up in his mind filled him with fear.

A stepfather brought Milt an additional standard to meet because of medals he had earned in the Second World War. Repeatedly, veterans have spoken of the lack of respect they have received from their own fathers, especially if these men had fought in some of the heavy battles of World War II. Milt's training as an altar boy, and later as the pallbearer for several of his aunts and uncles before his tour of duty in Vietnam, left him with strong sentiments of death and helplessness.

Milt's experiences in Vietnam were mild compared to those of many combat troops, but they added negative components to undermine his emotional well-being. Many of his buddies lost their lives. A chieftain in one of the villages adjacent to Milt's encampment was killed by Viet Cong, and his young daughter witnessed the killing. This incident brought up Milt's own pain at the time of his father's suicide. He reported long periods of sleepless nights and emotional turmoil from that day on.

Upon his return to the United States, he married a woman who was beset by problems of her own. Following a period of disagreements with his boss, he was fired from his job after nine years with that company. Finding himself unable to cope with this additional stress, he was admitted to a local hospital for psychiatric treatment. While Milt was in the hospital, his wife announced her intention to divorce him.

Milt pulled himself together, avoided close investigations by his doctors, and left the hospital after two weeks. He did not realize that while his body was able to function, his unconscious mind remained in an overload position. A few months after his release he attempted suicide, but was fortunate that his brother-in-law was nearby and able to talk him into giving up the rifle before a fatal shot was fired.

It took three years for Milt to overcome his depression and bring his life back on course. During this time he began attending one of the Outreach Centers in his city. Through talking with other members he found he was not alone in his need to open up about his experiences in Vietnam. He learned how subsequent life-stressors will interact with the unresolved problems remaining from that time. Since finding help, he has in turn spent many hours helping other veterans with their own problems by being available when it was most needed.

Case 4: Jim—Finding Solace in the Bottle

Rather than the childhood or military parallels which exist in Jim's situation, the focus of the following case is the wife's efforts to get her husband help for the post-Vietnam syndrome that threatened to destroy their marriage and family.

Options available to wives are as varied as the imagination. Jim's wife tried them all. They are improvements in communication, support, pressure from other veterans in or out of rap groups, counseling, therapy, separation, and, finally, if all else fails, divorce. Sometimes it is necessary to secure help for the veteran by bringing about an enforced stay in the hospital for detoxification, or, if domestic violence is involved, sign a warrant leading to a jail sentence. It is suggested that these steps be used one by one, with ample time between each to allow for some integration or acceptance to occur. Rarely is the road to healing of the wounds taken in a steadily upward manner. Rather, as Jim's case illustrates, progress can be painstakingly slow and halting.

In utilizing communication, the wife or family members must assess the readiness of the veteran to open up blockages. Just because a need for openness is perceived by one does not mean that the veteran is ready to talk. He has learned to suppress his feelings under life-threatening events, and such lessons are not easily forgotten (Shatan, 1973; Caputo, 1977). Many of the men who have served in the Vietnam conflict seem to have chosen one of two alternatives in their efforts to live with the post-traumatic stress brought on by their war experiences. One is to numb themselves with drug or alcohol abuse, the other is to "flip out," or become as crazy as the war itself was. Boscarino (1980) discussed the former at a meeting and stated: "Veterans who served in Vietnam may have developed a level of alcohol problems which is not found among comparable veterans and nonveterans who did not serve in that conflict." He also stressed that there is a great need for special clinical treatment and early intervention efforts to prevent the list of casualties from this war from growing even longer.

During a period of more than six years Jim's wife tried everything in her power to turn Jim from the effects of his post-traumatic stress. Her attempts ranged from filing charges for assault to serving him with divorce papers. She repeatedly involved Jim in counseling, but he was not ready to let go of the alcohol, physical abuse, and general neglect of his family. He lost several jobs during this time, making their economic survival more and more doubtful. Jim seemed unable or unwilling to deal with the various traumas he had experienced during his childhood and in Vietnam. With some finality his wife decided to remove herself and their children from his reach. She left no means for him to contact her or the children. Only after she was sure that he had chosen to allow counseling and to confront his war experiences did she give information regarding herself and her children.

Severe communication problems are one of the factors increasing the veterans' alienation, thereby causing them to further distance themselves from their support systems. The following outline (Table 1), developed by John and Renée Smith of Duke University, would be an example of how communications might be improved when supporting or living with a Vietnam veteran.

Case 5: Steve, The Angry Brother

Steve's tragic introduction to the hell of Vietnam began with the notification that his brother had been killed in action while on duty in Vietnam. This happened in November, shortly after Steve had completed basic training. He was given emergency leave.

How does a family celebrate Thanksgiving when they are waiting for their son's body for burial? How does this affect their subsequent holidays? In working with veterans I have come to under-

TABLE 1
Communication Outline for Family and Friends of Vietnam Veterans

The communication with Vietnam veterans can be assisted by serious consideration of the following topics and suggested dialogue. This was developed by a Veterans Support Group consisting of wives, family, and friends of Vietnam veterans at Center Campus, Macomb County Community College, Mt. Clemens, Michigan 48044. It is hoped that this outline can serve as a resource for further discussion in this area and any reactions to it would be greatly appreciated.

SITUATION

1. *Expections:*
Knowing what to expect from a veteran.

1. a) *Ask* the veteran what he sees himself doing regarding his life career decisions. It does not help to oppose his initial views or continually "press" him to make a decision.

b) You could attempt to think of yourself as a sounding board at this point in his life.

2. *Communication:*
Communicating to him your concern for what he has been through.

2. a) Indicate that *you care* and wish to hear if *he desires* to share his experiences and concerns with you. Is it necessary to know the specific war experiences, in order to understand your veteran?

b) Do not make sharp negative or positive generalizations about Vietnam.

c) If you find that you cannot hear him talk about his experiences, seek help from those who can.

3. *Listening:*
His need to have a caring person or persons to hear and understand.

3. a) Attempt to understand his ideas as well as his feelings (i.e., "You're frustrated because you didn't get promoted.")

b) Be available and accepting.

c) Be more interested in expanding his beliefs and feelings.

4. *Comparing Experiences:*
All experiences are unique!

4. Do not compare your own war experiences or other heavy emotional experiences with those of the veteran even though they appear similar.

5. *Dreams and Nightmares:*
Most veterans experience dreams and nightmares directly related to their war experiences.

5. a) Dreams are an especially important release for the veteran. Dreams allow for feelings of guilt, fear, and frustration to be lessened. (You might say, "It's OK, honey. I'm with you.")

b) Afterwards, ask if he would like to discuss the dream with you. Dreams are the mind's way of freeing itself from conflict.

6. *Loving Without Controlling:*
The need to express your love and concern for the veteran without controlling him.

6. a) Allow him the right to make *his own* mistakes.

b) Allow him to be himself without forcing on your judgments or beliefs.

c) Be there, yet allow for distance at times that he requires it.

7. *Reentry and Readjustment:*
The veterans task of coping and meeting the expectations of society.

7. a) As much as possible try to remove pressure such as making important decisions that could wait awhile.

TABLE 1 (continued)

	b) Allow him the necessary time and psychological "space" to readjust.
	c) Your expectations must be in line with his ability to perform at that time.
8. *Grief*	8. a) To ask why him and not you is to ask an unanswerable and guilt-producing question. The simple answer "chance" has profound implications for anyone who has experienced war.
	b) The pain and sorrow won't help either the lost person or you.
9. *Guilt*	9. a) "I and the whole country share the responsibility for what you did."
	b) "War is a terrible thing. Human beings are required to do inhuman acts against other human beings and the general population often denies this reality."
10. *Anger and/or Withdrawal*	10. The hardest thing to do is not take it personally. The veteran's anger is more than likely directed at himself and the Hell that he has experienced.
	Establish ground rules of:
	1. No physical abuse.
	2. Agree to talk when problems occur. What did I do? What did you do? What could each of us have done differently?
11. *Substance Abuse*	11. Listen for repetitive "themes" of anger. Avoid arguing. Explore the "themes" when the person is straight (i.e., Say, "When you are drinking, you repeat this concern with *anger* and I'm worried that it just continues to torment you. I feel it steals your potential.")

stand that anniversary dates are very important. They may act like trip-wires, often resulting in emotional outbursts or setbacks even for those believed on the road to recovery. Anyone involved in providing counseling or therapy for Vietnam veterans should consider their own motivation and capacity to hear another person's pain. If a willingness is expressed to hear it all, but during the counseling or therapy session it becomes clear there is hesitancy to be with the veteran emotionally, it will leave the patient further alienated and frustrated.

Some therapists using the psychoanalytical approach may—when confronted with a veteran's pain—inquire into the patients relationship with his mother or with siblings, leaving the current issues for the most part untouched. Or, if a therapist finds himself becoming overwhelmed or horrified by the gory details, he may tell the veteran that he must "forget" about the war. But how does one forget witnessing comrades being blown up by a grenade, the obliteration of one's company in an ambush, or a murder committed in a craze for retaliation? Alcohol barely keeps these images at bay. Many veterans still wonder if the war has really ended, especially if they have to deal with the indifference or ineptitude of "the system," be it courts, lawyers, medical facilities, etc. These examples have been reported by my clients on more than one occasion. War is never pretty, or even glorious. We all bleed, and when the killing becomes too much, even the best intentioned man may commit acts he would not have allowed himself to think about under normal circumstances (Shatan, 1974).

Steve was nineteen years old at the time of his brother's death. He had shared his dreams, successes, and fears, and now he was en route to identify his body. After arriving at the airport he was met by an officer who escorted him to the military casket. The officer asked Steve if he was ready to see the body of his brother. When the casket was opened there was no body—or at least not what one would expect to see. There were three, clear plastic bags in the casket, each containing some of the many pieces of a mutilated body. The Viet Cong knew the value of horrifying U.S. troops. Steve was able to identify a ring on a hand, perhaps recognize a vague likeness. Who could describe the feelings Steve went through in seeing his brother's desecrated body, his rage at this senseless act of hostility, his concern for his parents who were never to find out about this sight? He could not even allow them to see the depth of his pain for fear of letting them know more about the circumstances of his brother's final hours.

Steve had been an exceptional recruit during basic training, and he received an assignment that would have kept him safe in the United States. All that was meaningless now. He volunteered for an elite reconnaissance unit with the Special Forces. This unit operated in small groups of men to gather information on the enemy. Sometimes a single man was dropped behind enemy lines—and in Vietnam that could have been anywhere the U.S. troops were not. One would need some knowledge about what it is like in the jungles of Vietnam to appreciate what it means to operate there without any support—and to like it better that way. After the first few kills, Steve began to be able to kill without remorse. When a friend lost his life, another anniversary date for him, it reopened the pain from his brother's death and resulted in Steve's completing a form of combat brutalization so that killing became second nature (Shatan, 1974). Soon it became a necessary function of daily existence—eating, sleeping, and killing.

While his hatred was immense, there was still duty, compassion, and much, much more in him. The ultimate test came when his company of Special Forces landed on top of the division headquarters of North Vietnamese Regulars. The death and destruction that followed were beyond belief. It would be impossible to block out the screams that night of injured and captured men who have been staked out close to the firing line, and not be affected by it.

Steve made three trips that night to free the injured and captured men. During one trip he met one of the enemy face to face and cut the man's throat. While he did, the soldier's head turned so that Steve was staring the man in the face. In such a situation, it is impossible not to experience the other person's death. Steve brought numerous soldiers off the hill that night, yet his superiors still asked him for additional trips.

Mortars caught him during his second tour in Vietnam. He nearly died. When a doctor closed the curtain around him—giving up—he became angry. He cursed the doctor for being weak and fearful. He again fought the doctors when they tried to take his leg. He won and uses it today.

After his wife got tired of too many sleepless nights, she got up one night and made some coffee. She said, "We have to talk," and so it started to come out. He continued to talk in therapy for another two years and is still talking to groups whenever there is an opportunity to let them hear about one man's HELL in Vietnam.

The following outlines, (Tables 2 and 3), developed by John and Renée Smith of Duke University, have been found very helpful to veterans and their families in enabling them to recognize that they are not alone in their struggle to overcome post-Vietnam trauma.

TABLE 2
Veterans' Problems Described by Their Partners

The following is a list of Vietnam veterans' problems as related by their partners. Their descriptions are consistent with the delayed stress symptoms commonly presented by the veterans themselves. Although it has not been possible to specify which or how many of these concerns affect any one woman, those which seemed to be most universally shared within our sample are indicated by (*).

1. He seems always to be in a crisis state although the identified reasons may vary from week to week.

*2. He is irresponsible in terms of holding a job, staying in school, and contributing in child care or household chores.

*3. He exhibits erratic behavior without specific reasons, such as rage reactions which alternate with remorse (Jekyll/Hyde Syndrome).

4. There is heavy use of alcohol and drugs, as well as suicidal ideation.

5. He is extremely demanding, considering his needs only or that they are more important.

6. He isolates himself from his partner, family, and others with a "leave me alone" attitude.

7. He is unable to handle frustrations or even to identify them.

8. He is unable to express or share his feelings.

9. He seems unable to handle it when things are going well, from a standpoint of not feeling worthy.

*10. There is lack of self-esteem, great insecurity, and feelings of worthlessness and help-lessness.

11. There is jealousy of the partner's relationships and activities.

TABLE 3
Problems of Veterans' Partners

In describing their own experiences, the partners of veterans relate the following problems. Again, what seems to be central issues are indicated by (*).

1. She is overwhelmed by pressures and feelings of having assumed total responsibility, i.e., strain of financial insecurity because of the man's job instability.

*2. She feels guilty that she somehow is responsible for the man's rage reactions.

3. She experiences many self-doubts which are generated by emotional and job instability of the man; she is caught up in continual crisis-responding, losing sight of her own needs or overall patterns.

4. She is afraid to say anything to him and in not knowing how to respond feels frustrated in her ability to help.

*5. She experiences confusion as to whether the problems are Vietnam related or not and whether there will ever be any resolution of the man's conflict.

6. She feels responsible for "making it all better," having to "mother" or "nurture" and hence creating greater resentment and irresponsibility on the part of the man.

7. Or she feels the converse—that it is all "his problem" and refuses to be involved (seemingly, a defensive position or survival stance when all else has been tried and failed).

8. She feels that he has separated from her and their children with little sense of family and poor father-child relationships.

9. She feels that support is not welcomed by the man, that she is being discounted.

10. She is subject to emotional, verbal, and physical abuse.

*11. Both partners are building defensive barriers in the relationship and are unable to be supportive of one another.

12. The men frequently engage in extramarital affairs.

13. She feels dragged down by the man's negative attitudes.

*14. She suffers from low self-esteem, is anxious, and feels a sense of hopelessness.

CONCLUSION

In 1970, while conducting sensitivity groups for Vietnam veterans at Macomb County Community College, Mt. Clemens, Michigan, I recruited a veteran who had served part of his tour of duty in Vietnam on a riverboat patrol. Mike, a very bright and intuitive person, told the group when asked about his feelings now that he was back home: "People don't understand, and people don't care!" A co-ed present at the time responded: "Why should we care? You decided to go!"

That interaction has come back to haunt me many times since then. For veterans it represents the type of response they often received from a hostile or unsympathetic society, and it also is a prime example of their dilemma. Where can they turn to unload the cancerous pain they have brought home with them if they know at the outset that people will neither understand nor care? "You decided to go" is seldom the individual veteran's or the selective service board's view of the serviceman's obligation. A very vocal antiwar movement forced the veteran to accept blame for having been there, conveniently forgetting that government power to assign someone to serve there was never abridged by the American people. Every veteran will remember his rites of induction into the Armed Forces when he has to swear he will serve "God and Country." These words are not taken lightly when a life is on the line.

The veteran's bitterness is understandable, but more important are the questions: Where does this leave me? How can I be a winner in life when I am still bitter and angry? Against whom can this bitterness be directed? Will it go away when I get into fights in neighborhood bars or on street corners, with "the man" at the police station, or with my wife at home? Vietnam veterans have been comparatively more often involved in acts requiring law enforcement, and their involvement in drugs and alcohol abuse is higher than for veterans of other wars. How can they be winners if they are angry at themselves and at God? Veterans have cursed God as the result of some horror they have had to witness or be part of, believing that God should have stopped this terrible evil.

Considerable value conflicts also undermine the veteran's support base within his family. "Tell it like it is" and "Grin and bear it" are mutually exclusive concepts. Many fathers who fought in the Second World War cannot understand their sons' alienation, and are thereby preventing them from seeking relief and understanding. Marty, another group member, was called home on leave following his father's heart attack. While visiting in the hospital, Marty was asked by his father, "How is the war really going?" Marty's response, "It is a lousy war," made his father furious. "We are losing because of men like you," he responded. After all, the fathers had been victorious. Their sons must not be less than they were. Nobody wins in such interactions, and the battle for respect and understanding continues in many families today.

Yellow ribbons are a popular way of greeting returning heroes from Grenada or the released hostages from Iran. Yellow ribbons are more often tied around the coffins of Vietnam veterans who are victims of the cruel aftermath of their involvement with Vietnam. Yet another aspect of the conflict existing between Vietnam veterans and society is that there are some definite distinctions of social class involved. Many of the men who were able to avoid the draft during the Vietnam conflict are today in positions where they can make the decisions of concern to veterans in employment, law enforcement, medicine, financial matters, etc. Some feelings of hostility and envy are only to be expected, along with increased alienation. From those able to avoid the war, there is often either callous indifference or a certain hostility based upon guilt and lowered self-esteem. Neither group wins and all Americans lose.

The plight of the Vietnam veteran continues to trouble many who are involved in care-providing roles. All of the men mentioned in the cases reported in these pages have experienced severe emotional overload situations at the present time, 10 to 15 years after their return from the fighting. The problems relating to Vietnam persist, and the destruction of human lives has cost this nation dearly. My hope is that as more veterans realize the need to open and heal old wounds, they will find caring people and professionals with enough insight and love to warm cold hearts and alienated souls.

The following poem written by Nancy A. Selaty expresses the feelings of sorrow, but also of hope, shared by many wives who have gone through the long period of readjustment with their husbands.

October 27, 1983

FROM A WIFE*

My soldier boy of Vietnam
You went away so proud
To fight the war for everyone
When the battle cry was loud.
They taught you how to march and fight
And stand brave and tall,
But when you came home again
They treated you so small,
And some of you couldn't walk at all.

You, my dear, came home to us
With all your limbs intact

---

*Reprinted with permission from Nancy A. Selaty. Copyright © 1983.

But only I will ever know
Of the load upon your back.
You came home anti-everything
Which soon included me,
And kept all your pain inside
Where you thought I couldn't see.

The horrors that you suffered
Were put away you said,
But every night you tossed and turned
As you laid upon our bed.
Like a wedge it laid between us
And surrounded you with pain
You didn't see our little home
Or the sons that we have made.

For ten long years I prayed to God
To set my husband free
To laugh, to sing, to love again
So we could be a family.
He wondered why he came home alive
What could the reason be?
The reasons were: your not yet born sons
And, yes my love, me.

You did what you had to
And the road wasn't smooth.
You suffered more than you should have
But only a wife knows the truth.
For wives of Vietnam Veterans
It's not an easy path,
But hold on tight and love him true
Thru the shaky aftermath.

Nancy A. Selaty
Wife of a Vietnam Veteran

REFERENCES

Argeropoulos, J.: Emotional dilemma. *Chronical Guidance*, Mental Hygiene File, Se 3, pp. 69-70, 1969.

Argeropoulos, J.: Posters: Self Realization and Self Defeat, (November 19, 1970), Northern Michigan University, Marquette, Michigan.

Blank, A.S. Jr.: The unconscious flashback to violence of the war in Vietnam veterans—Clinical mystery, community problems and legal defense. Presented at the meeting of the American Psychological Association, 1980.

Boscarino, J.: Excessive drinking among Vietnam veterans: A possible symptom of post-traumatic stress. Presented at the meeting of the Eastern Sociological Association, 1980.

Caputo, P.:*A rumor of war*. New York: Holt, Rinehart & Winston, 1977.

Fallows, J.: What did you do in the class war, Daddy? *The Washington Monthly*, October, 1975.

Litton, R.: *Home from the war*. New York: Simon & Schuster, 1971.

Marrs, R.L.: The Vietnam war: Stress and human misery. Macomb Community College, Mt. Clemens, Michigan, 1973.

Polner, M.: *No victory parades: The return of the Vietnam veteran*. New York: Holt, Rinehart & Winston, 1971.

Rogers, C.R.: *The therapeutic relationship and its impact*. Westport, CT: Greenwood Press, 1976.

Shatan, C.F.: The grief of soldiers: Vietnam combat veterans' self-help movement. *American Journal of Orthopsychiatry*, 43:640-653, 1973.

Shatan, C.F.: Through the membrane of reality: "Impacted grief" and perceptual dissonance in Vietnam combat veterans. *Psychiatric Opinion*, 2(6):6-15, 1974.

Shorr, J.B., et al. (Eds.): *Imagery: Its many dimensions and applications*, Vol. 1. New York: Plenum, 1980.

CHAPTER

8

Predicting Post-Traumatic Stress Disorders Among Vietnam Veterans

JOHN P. WILSON, Ph.D., and

GUSTAVE E. KRAUSS, M.A.

It is a fact of history that extraordinarily threatening and stressful life-events can leave lasting psychic effects among those who become survivors. When we study carefully the nature of man-made and naturalistic disasters, it readily becomes evident that they are defined and characterized by varying degrees of catastrophic stressors in which the victim is exposed to profound life-death encounters which transcend the boundaries of everyday social existence.

Lifton (1967) has observed that in catastrophically stressful situations the survivor typically gets immersed in the death experience in which he witnesses the painful injury of others, the destruction of life and property, intense suffering, mutilation of human and other life-forms,

The authors wish to thank Dr. Walter Knake, Mary Ann Eustace, Ken Smith, Joe Felix, Dr. S.D. Zigelbaum, Dr. Art Blank, Jr., Dr. James Schuerger, and Robert O. Muller of Vietnam Veterans of America for the help and encouragement in making this study.

and the grotesque and seemingly meaningless death of loved ones. As a consequence of immersion in the death experience, the survivor universally confronts the difficult task of justifying the meaning of the event and eventually assimilating it into his or her self-structure. However, as medical and psychological research has shown (e.g., Lifton, 1967; Niederland, 1968; Gleser, Green, & Winget, 1981), catastrophically stressful events can produce long-term stress response syndromes which characterize the attempts the survivor makes to assimilate the traumatic episode.

Clearly, one major dimension of this process of gradual assimilation of the profoundly threatening event is that of reexperiencing the original trauma (or elements of it) in a variety of forms which include intrusive recollections, dreams and character changes as manifest in identity and personality traits, ego-defenses, and individual coping strategies. Simply stated, profoundly stressful events can produce changes in all dimensions of the self-structure following termination of the trauma. As Lifton (1981) has noted, extremely life-threatening events often lead to traumatic survivor syndromes in which there are massive changes in *psychoformative* processes. The changes in psychoformative functioning can range, at one extreme, from zombie-like psychic numbing and the diminution of humanness, to a positive, healthy adaptation characterized by creative self-animation and prosocial strivings.

Similarly, Wilson (1980) has argued that the residual effects of catastrophic stress also extend to core motivational and developmental processes such that the entire personality structure of the individual may be altered in various ways. Briefly, he has suggested that, as a consequence of the trauma, ego development may: (1) retrogress to earlier modes of psychosocial adaptation; (2) undergo psychosocial acceleration in which new ego-strengths and capacities emerge prematurely into the character structure in self-actualizing directions which guide the process of reformulating the meaning of the trauma; (3) exacerbate predominant psychosocial developmental stages and therefore intensify and compound the psychosocial task itself; and (4) produce changes in the ordering of motives within a hierarchical order such that some individuals become chronically obsessed with safety, predictability, and order in their world, whereas others manipulate in Machiavellian power-oriented ways and still others seem to channel the energy associated with the traumatic conflict into prosocial humanitarian behaviors which are best characterized by being strongly concerned with nurturance and generativity.

The growing body of descriptive, clinical, epidemiological, and quasi-experimental research on the effects of massive psychic trauma has accumulated to the point where many scholars and practitioners now recognize that post-trauma stress syndromes appear to be the normal consequence of abnormally stressful events that, by definition, far exceed the usual stressors of daily living. Perhaps for this reason the Diagnostic and Statistical Manual of the American Psychiatric Association (DSM-III) (1980) has acknowledged Post-Traumatic Stress Disorder (PTSD) as a valid clinical entity which characterizes a well-defined syndrome of behavioral adaptation following profoundly stressful life-events.

The core feature of PTSD, as noted in DSM-III and in much earlier studies (e.g., Freud, 1959; Titchener & Kapp, 1976; Niederland, 1964; Lifton, 1967), is that the survivor reexperiences elements of the trauma in dreams, uncontrollable and emotionally distressing intrusive images, and dissociative states of consciousness, as well as in unconscious behavioral reenactment of the traumatic situation. In addition, many survivors also feel numb to themselves and others, experience a loss of normal affect, and manifest symptoms of depression and a loss of interest in previously meaningful work and interpersonal relationships. As Horowitz (1976) has theorized, the reexperiencing of the trauma (intrusion) may alternate with periods of denial to produce cycles during which the person is more or less symptomatic. Further, many studies have also reported that survivors experience post-trauma physiological symptoms which include excessive autonomic nervous system arousal, startle response, hyperalertness or hypervigilance, memory impairment, paresthesia, hysterical-conversion symptoms, etc. (e.g., Lifton, 1967; Gleser et al., 1981).

It is also typical for victims to report survivor guilt, moral guilt, loss of capacity for intimacy, sleep disturbances, anger, rage, mistrust, feelings of helplessness, tendencies to overgeneralize, and approach or avoidance tendencies to stimuli with trauma-related associational value. Taken as a set, these symptoms or behavioral responses define post-traumatic stress syndromes in a general way as clinical phenomena. Clearly, when the symptoms become either frequent or severe enough to impair normal psychosocial functioning, they can be considered to constitute a disorder signifying a pathological condition. However, what is not well understood scientifically are the specific factors which would predict the onset, duration, and severity of Post-Traumatic Stress Disorder.

What dimensions or attributes of the traumatic situation or of the person are associated with psychological difficulty in assimilating the trauma? Why do some persons seem to return to normal functioning rather quickly after the trauma whereas others reexperience it for many years? Are some persons strengthened in self-actualizing directions by extraordinarily stressful life-events? Clearly, the answer to these and other questions will help us to understand the nature and mechanisms of post-trauma psychological functioning.

Therefore, it is the purpose of this chapter to examine factors predictive of PTSD among Vietnam combat veterans participating in the Veterans Administration's program Operation Outreach, a network of storefront, community-based counseling centers whose sole function is to assist Vietnam era veterans experiencing emotional difficulties related to their military service in the Vietnam war. The chapter is organized in several sections, the first of which presents a general theoretical model of PTSD. The second section presents a conceptual framework for predicting post-trauma stress syndromes among Vietnam veterans. The third section presents some of the research findings from our current study of PTSD in a volunteer sample of male veterans participating in the outreach program.

GENERAL THEORETICAL OVERVIEW

Recently, my colleagues Bonnie Green and Jacob Lindy and I developed a conceptual framework for understanding post-traumatic stress syndromes among survivor groups (Green, Wilson, & Lindy, 1985). Figure 1 shows our working model for the development of PTSD. This model was developed after reviewing Horowitz's (1976, 1979) seminal work on stress syndromes. Specifically, he has developed an information processing model of PTSD which assumes that a major mechanism of human cognitive processes is the *completion tendency* in which "the mind continues to process important new information until the situation or the models change, and reality and models reach accord" (1979, p. 249). Until a traumatic life-event can be assimilated and successfully integrated into existing schemata, the psychological elements of the event will remain in active memory storage. They will stimulate thought representation and images of the traumatic events on all levels of cognitive functioning, which periodically emerge into consciousness as emotionally upsetting intrusive and uncontrolled images of the event. According to Horowitz (1976) ". . . repeated episodes of intensely conscious representations occur because (1) active memory tends towards repeated representations and (2) because representations of stress-related information are recognized as important and as hard to process to comple-

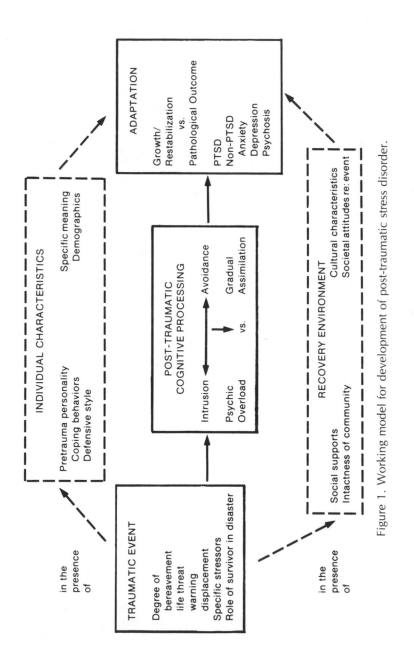

Figure 1. Working model for development of post-traumatic stress disorder.

tion" (pp. 103-104). Further, Horowitz's model includes an alternation feature between intrusive reexperiencing of the event and denial or defensive blocking of the images to constrict cognitive processing in general and thought representations of the trauma, in particular. Eventually, however, the survivor may succeed in processing the trauma to completion at which point it becomes a part of his or her self-structure in nondebilitating ways. "As assimilation and accommodation occur, there is a gradual reduction in the intensity, preemptoriness, and frequency of the repeated representation" (1976, p. 104).

In our model we have proposed that until the individual successfully assimilates the trauma, he or she experiences psychic overload, a state in which the nature, intensity, and meaning of the experience(s) are not readily understandable in terms of the existing conceptual schemata of reality. We propose that the normal ego-defensive and coping mechanisms have been overwhelmed and therefore are not adequate to process the trauma. However, if conditions are favorable, especially if there is a supportive recovery environment, the individual may gradually assimilate and "work through" the trauma to a successful outcome. On the other hand, if conditions are not favorable, the survivor may need help in the working-through process in order to learn how to "de-code" intrusive episodes and understand precisely how defensive functioning works against the painful and unbidden aspects of the trauma that are reexperienced consciously or unconsciously.

It is also the case, at least theoretically, that some persons may not experience psychic overload for reasons that are not well understood and yet are extremely important to understand. In these cases, we speculate that the individuals would be able to assimilate the traumatic event in such a way that it does not become part of active memory storage but rather is integrated in a congruent manner into existing cognitive schemata. It may be that persons with this capacity have greater ego-strength and the ability to frame a meaningful perspective of the event when it occurs. Alternatively, it could be the case that some persons have been inoculated against the trauma either by being "hardened" by the reexperiencing of many small scale traumas or by specific training designed to prepare them for the events by cognitive and behavioral rehearsal of the expected consequences in the threatening life-event.

In Figure 1 we present the major variables and their interactions which influence post-trauma processing of the event. To begin, it is necessary to conceptualize the nature of the traumatic event. Clearly, traumatic events differ along many dimensions which include the degree of: 1) bereavement; 2) life-threat; 3) speed of onset or advanced warning; 4) displacement of persons from the community; 5) severity of stressors in the environment or situation; 6) control over reoccurrence; 7) duration of trauma; 8) moral conflict over actions; 9) passivity or activity of the person relative to being a victim or agent in the event; and 10) the community directly affected. Thus, the nature of the trauma determines to a large degree how much cognitive processing of the event will be necessary. The processing of the event in terms of the perception of threat, the appraisal of one's resources to cope with it, and the subsequent cognitive requirements, including whether or not it reaches a state of psychic overload, are affected by both *individual dispositional* variables (e.g., premorbid personality traits, ego-strengths and weakness, behavioral tendencies, educational level, etc.) and *situational* variables (e.g., whether trauma is experienced alone or with others, at home or in a foreign place, etc.). After the trauma, the recovery environment to which the survivor returns is thought to constitute an important factor affecting the post-traumatic cognitive processing of the event. Under optimal conditions the recovery environment would contain high degrees of social, medical, psychological, emotional, and community support for the survivor. In a maximally supportive environment it is likely that individual processing of the trauma can occur as fast as possible without undue additional stressors which might lead to further denial, numbing, blocking, or other defensive operations that would likely lead to a sense of psychological isolation.

In terms of post-trauma adaptation we have broadly delineated two outcome categories: growth and restabilization versus pathological disorder. The pathological outcomes range from PTSD, perhaps the "purest" response and outgrowth of psychic overload, to other forms of psychopathology, including character disorders, neuroses, psychoses, and mixed pathological states which might include PTSD as an overlay to preexisting pathological processes. On the other hand, gradual assimilation of the trauma would lead to personal growth and restabilization. By restabilization we do not wish to imply that the survivor simply returns to "normality" and previous modes of mastery and coping. Rather, restabilization indicates that a non-pathological integration of the experience has occurred even though the individual may manifest some symptoms that are dynamically connected to traumatic events (e.g., hypervigilance, occasional nightmares, positive character changes, etc.).

In sum, then, the working model presented in Figure 1 is an attempt to construct a useful, general theoretical paradigm which might apply to different disaster situations. At present Bonnie Green, Jack Lindy, and I are continuing our work and hope to expand the model just presented into a more elaborate one which would allow predictions to be made of the precise ways in which dimensions of the trauma interact with dimensions of the person to produce specific post-trauma clinical syndromes. However, as the next section discusses, the utility of our model is that it enables researchers to begin testing specific hypotheses regarding the prediction of PTSD.

A CONCEPTUAL FRAMEWORK OF THE VARIABLES PREDICTIVE OF POST-TRAUMATIC STRESS DISORDERS AMONG VIETNAM VETERANS

Figure 2 presents a summary analysis of the major classes of variables thought to be related to psychological assimilation of the traumatic effects of combat in the Vietnam war. Building on the general model presented in the preceding section of this paper, it can be seen by examining Figure 2 that there are some five major classes of variables hypothesized to affect post-Vietnam adaptation and psychosocial functioning.

1) Pre-Trauma Personality Characteristics

First, it is necessary to understand what the person was like before being exposed to the traumatic situation. Included here, of course, are measures of personality traits and motives, ego-identity, ideological beliefs and values, predominant coping and defensive mechanisms, premorbid pathological processes, and relevant demographic and biographical factors. Stated simply, the soldier in combat brings these dispositional and characterological traits with him to the combat situation. Clearly, these variables may affect the way he performs his military duties as well as the way he evaluates the stressors which impact on his functioning. However, most central to the prediction of post-trauma adaptation is the specification of which premorbid attributes are associated with pathological consequences or healthy growth and restabilization.

2) Combat Roles

In the Vietnam war as well as other wars, there exist both combat and noncombatant roles. Previous research (Wilson, 1978, 1980) has dis-

Person Before Exposure to Traumatic Situation

PRE-MORBID PERSONALITY DIMENSIONS

Personality Traits & Motives
Ego-Identity
Ideological Beliefs & Values
Coping and Defensive Mechanisms
Pre-Morbid Pathological Processes
Specific Meaning of Demographics

Nature of Stressors in the Vietnam War

SPECIFIC STRESSORS IN THE VIETNAM WAR

I. Exposure to Injury & Death

Killing enemy in firefights, etc.
Seeing injury, death, dying, atrocities
Participating in body count of dead.
Survival life/death situation.
Ineffective high ranking military leadership

II. Lack of Personal Comforts & Jungle Terrain

Unpredictable environment (landmines)
Unpredictable enemy (guerrilla war)
Unpredictable attacks, ambush, etc.
Difficult physical environment–jungle, bugs.
Separation from loved ones & community
Repetitive capture and loss of objectives
Failure of ARVN troops in combat

III. Short-timer Syndrome

Twelve month tour of duty
Constantly changing unit membership
Development of Survival Mentality
Problem of ideological justification for action

**Homecoming Experience:
Social Support vs. Psychological Isolation**

RETURN FROM WAR ZONE

DEROS
Outprocessing
Twenty-day leave
Initial re-entry

HOMECOMING: 1ST SIX MONTHS

Nature of recovery environment.
Degree of Support from significant others.
Degree of discussion of traumas.
Degree of acceptance by society
Degree of social-psychological-medical
   support mechanisms.
Degree of economic support.

Post-Vietnam Adaptation

ASSIMILATION

Positive adaptation
Integration of experience
Normal personality functioning
Positive character changes

NON-ASSIMILATION
PATHOLOGICAL OUTCOME

Post-trauma stress
Character disorder
Psychoses
Neurotic traits

Figure 2. A conceptual framework of the major variables affecting the psychological assimilation of the traumatic effects of combat in the Vietnam war.

cussed the fact that active combat roles exposed the soldier to more life-death threats as well as the aftermath of fighting, killing, and destruction. Therefore, it is likely that combat roles vary in the frequency, duration, and intensity of exposing the soldier to the stressors that arise out of combat. For example, the infantry ground soldier who is part of a platoon which conducts search and destroy missions in heavy jungle terrain and encounters surprise ambush attacks must face a life-threatening situation that is different from that of a pilot of an attack helicopter (e.g., Cobra gunship) who flies aerial missions in which he fires machine guns and rocket launchers at the enemy below.

Although both combat roles are dangerous and life-threatening, the ground soldier must fight on the ground against an enemy whose method of fighting was predicated on hit-and-run guerilla tactics. In a sense, then, the foot soldier in Vietnam often was placed in a *reactive* combat role whereas the attack helicopter pilot initiated and controlled his combat role in a powerful, high-speed helicopter. Therefore, we thought it important to assess the number of different combat roles an individual performed in the Vietnam war, the number of weeks he executed them, and how subjectively stressful he perceived the roles to be. Further, by factor analyzing the combat roles it is possible to determine whether or not different combat roles are associated significantly with post-traumatic stress syndromes.

3) Nature of Stressors in the Vietnam War

Since PTSD is a clinical syndrome whose hallmark feature is the reexperiencing of a traumatic event, it is necessary to conceptualize the nature and dimensions of the stressors which were indigenous to combat in the Vietnam war. As a broad and overly simplistic categorization of the different stressors commonly experienced by soldiers in Vietnam, we have conceptualized three general dimensions which abstract what were typically emotionally painful, intense, morally conflicting, and profoundly difficult human experiences.

First, we believe that what characterizes the core elements in intrusive imagery in PTSD is the reliving of an emotionally traumatic episode that involved death, injury, pain, and destruction. Therefore, we propose that exposure to *injury and death* is the most important dimension of the various stressors encountered in combat. As Figure 2 indicates, exposure to injury and death includes such experiences as *active* killing of the enemy in firefights, search and destroy missions, aerial assaults, mortar bombing, hand-to-hand combat, and life-death survival situations. Further, intense combat in Vietnam also included the *passive* witnessing of the carnage of war and involved such experiences as *seeing* enemy and American dead, *participating* in the body count of dead enemy, *seeing* civilian casualties and atrocities, *seeing* villages, property, and the earth destroyed by bombs, chemical defoliants and the deliberate torching of hootches, etc.

Second, it is necessary to understand and conceptualize the *environmental* stressors in the Vietnam war. We believe that the central element of the environmental stressors was the *unpredictable* nature of the jungle terrain and the events that occurred within it. Specifically, the *unpredictability* of events extended to: the nature and whereabouts of the enemy; the identity of the enemy in terms of whether they were an ally or Viet Cong; the location of different types of booby traps; the onset of enemy attacks (ambushes, firefights, incoming mortar, sapper attacks, etc.); the repetitive capture and loss of military objectives; the reliability of allied Vietnamese troops and the ecological nature of the jungle itself (e.g., triple canopy, insects, etc.). Moreover, the environmental stressors also included functioning in a difficult terrain, especially for Western soldiers. The geography of Vietnam could be characterized as diverse in nature and ranged from flat rice paddies growing under water to double- and triple-canopy jungle in mountainous areas. No matter where the soldier fought, it was usually hot, wet, rainy, and teeming with insects, rats, and leeches. The "bush" was simply a difficult and often unpleasant place in which to negotiate combat activities.

4) Short-Timer Syndrome

Another dimension of stressors in the Vietnam war we have called the short-timer syndrome. By this we wish to recognize the psychological effects of a 12-13 month tour of duty in a combat unit whose membership was frequently changing since each soldier had a different Date of Expected Return from Overseas Service (DEROS) by which to rotate back home. We believe that this system of rotation, especially when associated with the political controversy which existed over the morality of the war and an inequitable military draft system, led to the development of a survivor mentality in which the primary goal of the tour of duty became that of survival. As such, we believe that many soldiers developed a short-timer syndrome which contributed to the problem of ideological justification for action in combat. Clearly, the awareness of a one-year tour of duty and the search for meaning in the war experiences produced a unique set of psychological stressors for the 19-year old combat veteran.

5) The Homecoming Experience: Social Support Versus Psychological Isolation

As we noted earlier in our discussion of the general model of PTSD the recovery environment is thought to moderate the process of the post-Vietnam adaptation. Figure 2 indicates that we have thought of the homecoming experience as consisting of at least two major phases. The first phase is defined by the *return from the war zone* to the United States. This phase includes becoming a "short-timer" in the field of combat, reaching the DEROS date, leaving Vietnam, outprocessing at a Stateside base, a 20-day leave of absence, and the initial return to a civilian way of life.

The second phase, *the homecoming period,* is operationally defined as the first six months home from the war. During this time, what is important in terms of predicting PTSD is the relative degree of support from significant others and a meaningful community, the opportunity to talk freely about the traumatic experiences of the war, and the social and institutional mechanisms that facilitate a rapid return to normal psychosocial functioning. We believe that if the veteran lacks significant social support, the effects of the trauma may become intensified since the individual is likely to isolate himself and feel alone, lonely, anxious, depressed, and alienated from others whom he perceives as distant and removed from the reality of his inner world of "the 'Nam."

In summary, then, Figure 2 presents a conceptual framework of the major variables affecting the psychological assimilation of the traumatic effects of combat in the Vietnam war. We shall present our hypotheses and the rationale for them after a brief discussion of the divergent theoretical perspectives of the nature of PTSD.

PTSD AMONG SURVIVORS: PRE-MORBID CHARACTER WEAKNESS AND TRANSIENT STRESS REACTION

Until recently, most clinicians have accepted the position derived from psychoanalytical theory that a prolonged stress response to a traumatic event is the result of a premorbid character flaw (Kardiner, 1959). What this position asserts, in effect, is that a *transient stress reaction* is to be expected following a traumatic event. However, within a reasonable period of time, say six months, the healthy ego is fully capable of assimilating the trauma without lasting neurotic symptoms. Thus, according to this theoretical position, based on libido and instinct theory, if the classical symptoms of "traumatic neurosis" appear in a survivor, it is because he or she lacks the necessary ego-strength to deal with the event. This weakness of the ego, then, is presumably due to premorbid fixations in psychosexual development.

In psychoanalytic theory, fixation of libido is usually thought to be caused by repression of instinctual impulses. Therefore, the logic of the position dictates that if there is excessive stimulation from an *external* source (e.g., trauma) it breaks through the "protective shield" of the ego (Lifton, 1980) producing excessive *internal* arousal of instinctual drives which, in turn, leads to repression and the contraction of the ego (Kardiner, 1959) in order to maintain homeostatic psychic functioning. This repression, brought on by the external event and the subsequent release of repressed sexual and aggressive urges, generates a variety of neurotic symptoms. Therefore, if the survivor fails to assimilate the traumatic episode, it is because of a preexisting tendency that predisposed the formation of a "traumatic neurosis."

The pervasiveness and uncritical acceptance of the "transient stress reaction" view of human adaptation to life-threatening events can be documented in three major disasters. First, Lifton (1967) has noted that among the Japanese who survived the atomic bomb at Hiroshima, the hibakusha (atomic disease affected people) were not adequately compensated by the government for their injuries and some of them were relegated to inferior social status as outcasts not fit to live with others in society.

Similarly, Niederland (1964) has documented many cases of holocaust survivors who endured the most dehumanizing experiences imaginable in Nazi concentration camps, only later to be denied restitution for their trauma-related stress symptoms on the grounds that they should have gotten over the experience once their persecution stopped. After working psychotherapeutically with persecution victims, Niederland concluded: "It is unscientific to attribute dogmatically the persistence of abnormal reactions and psychological changes to Anlage constitution, or other innate deficiencies and to ignore the linkage, demonstrated by clinical evidence and research, between traumatization and permanent psychic alterations resulting therefrom" (p. 472).

More recently, the survivors of the flood at Buffalo Creek in 1972 who sued a coal company for negligence in constructing a slag dam which broke and caused massive damage to a 16-mile long valley of communities in West Virginia were viewed as either malingerers or suffering from premorbid character flaws when they became litigants against the coal company for psychiatric damages caused by the trauma of the flood (Gleser, Green, & Winget, 1981). However, careful psychiatric and empirical analysis of the victims revealed that the best predictor of PTSD was the severity of the stressors encountered during the flood and the degree of bereavement experienced by the victims. There was no evidence found for malingering or significant premorbid disposition toward PTSD. On the contrary, the citizens of Buffalo Creek were ordinary, healthy middle-class people before the flood. Afterwards, however, a prolonged stress syndrome was the common pattern and "approximately a third of the sample continued to suffer symptoms five years later as severe as when seen initially" (Gleser et al., 1981, p. 136).

The debate over whether PTSD is the result of premorbid characteristics or the nature of the trauma contains within it a number of implicit theoretical assumptions. On the one hand, the proponents of the "premorbid" view are arguing a *dispositional* model in which the observed post-trauma psychopathology is attributed to person variables, particularly the lack of ego-strength, and to pre-existing personality disorders characterized by maladaptive personality traits such as suspiciousness, aggressive antisocial tendencies, or narcissistic qualities. On the other hand, those who argue that PTSD is the common response to catastrophic stress are favoring a *situational* attributional model in which the anxiety disorder is viewed as a response to the contingencies in the traumatic event. Hence, prolonged stress syndromes may vary in speed of onset, duration, and severity depending on the magnitude and nature of the trauma. In essence, this theoretical position adopts the stance that if the trauma is powerful and intensely overwhelming, perhaps as illustrated by the atomic bomb at Hiroshima and Nazi persecution camps, then all survivors will experience PTSD or other forms of psychopathology to some degree.

Finally, an *interactional* theory of PTSD would necessitate a model which attempts to predict which personological variables interact with specific situational dimensions of the trauma in producing both healthy and pathological outcomes. To the best of our knowledge no such theoretical paradigm exists at this time. In a descriptive way, however, Lifton (1980) has developed psychoformative theory as a theoretical alternative to psychoanalytic theory in an attempt to move beyond the obvious limitations of instinctually based, drive-reduction models of human functioning. In our view Lifton's (1976, 1980) work is noteworthy because it recognizes that catastrophic stress requires a theoretical model of traumatic stress syndromes that explicitly accounts for the extremity of the situations which produce it. Clearly, the immensity of an event such as the atomic bomb at Hiroshima trivializes the average neurotic's strivings to understand unresolved Oedipal problems. That the two experiences are frequently assumed by some clinicians to be equivalent psychological experiences probably points to the primitive and unconscious mechanisms which operate in professional psychotherapists and others who *actively* avoid confrontation with the death experience and its symbolic equivalents.

HYPOTHESES FOR THE PRESENT STUDY

Our research program during the last two years (1980-82) has enabled us to develop the Vietnam Era Stress Inventory (VESI, Wilson & Krauss, 1981) which can be used to assess PTSD in Vietnam veterans (see Method section for a more complete description of the instrument). Through the cooperation of many outreach centers across the country, we have received over 200 VESI's for analysis. These provide a rich data base for hypothesis testing. For the purposes of this paper, we will focus our attention on only four classes of variables in terms of their predictive power of the assessed level of PTSD from the VESI: 1) premorbid personality disorders, specifically paranoid, antisocial, and narcissistic characteristics; 2) combat roles; 3) exposure to stressors in Vietnam; and 4) homecoming experiences. Thus, the general hypotheses for the study are as follows:

Hypothesis 1

There will be a significant positive relationship between the number of combat roles performed, the subjective stress experienced in those roles, the number of weeks in combat in Vietnam, and the severity of PTSD as assessed by the VESI (subscale IV A-VPTSD) Stress Assessment Questionnaire.

Hypothesis 2

There will be a significant positive relationship between the frequency of exposure to specific stressors in Vietnam as assessed by the VESI subscale III-Specific Stressors in Vietnam, and the severity of PTSD as assessed by the VESI Stress Assessment Questionnaire.

Hypothesis 3

There will be a significant positive relationship between a lack of support during the homecoming period from Vietnam and the severity of PTSD as assessed by the VESI Stress Assessment Questionnaire. Specifically, the greater the degree of psychological isolation reported by the veteran, the more the severity of PTSD.

Hypothesis 4

In general, the three premorbid personality disorders assessed by the VESI subscale I-Biography Questionnaire will not be significantly related to PTSD as assessed by the VESI subscale IV A-Stress Assessment Questionnaire. Specifically, it is predicted that these variables will predict significantly less of the measured variance in PTSD than will the combat role factors exposure to stressor factors and homecoming variables.

METHOD

Selection of Subjects

The subjects for this study were 114 combat veteran volunteers who were attending the V.A.'s program Operation Outreach for Vietnam Veterans. Ninety-one percent of the sample was white, 4.4% black, 2.6% American Indian or Alaskan native, and about 1% Asian and 1% Hispanic. Geographically, the sample was distributed regionally according to V.A. criteria as follows: 1.6% were living in the Northeast region, 12.2% in the Atlantic region, 4.4% in the Southeast region, 60.5% in the Great Lakes region, 5.3% in the Plains States region, and 12.2% in the Western region. The sample ranged in age from 27 to 43 years old with a mean age of 33 years. In terms of educational attainment 91.4% were high school graduates, 18.4% graduated from college or trade school, 29.8% had completed some postsecondary education or trade school, and 1.7% had obtained graduate degrees.

The information available on marital status indicated that 34.4% were married and not previously divorced, 16.1% were married but had been previously divorced, 18.3% were divored and single, and 4.3% were currently separated. Eighteen point four percent (18.4%) of the sample failed to answer the question.

The data on military service revealed that 23.7% of the men were drafted and 76.3% enlisted. The distribution of veterans by branch of service indicated that 58.0% were in the Army, 26.9% in the Marines, 9.7% in the Navy, and 5.4% in the Air Force. Eighty-seven point five percent (87.5%) of the sample had honorable discharges, 4.4% a general discharge, 6.3% a medical discharge, and 1.8% had an undesirable discharge.

Analysis of employment status indicated that about 57% of the men were employed, 35% were unemployed, and 7.5% were laid off from their jobs.

Assessment Instruments

The Vietnam Era Stress Inventory (VESI) was developed by Wilson and Krauss in 1980 as an objective, self-report inventory designed to yield different measures of a veteran's psychosocial functioning. The VESI contains six parts. Part I assesses biographical and demographic data, including a retrospective check list on behavioral tendencies which define personality disorders according to the criteria established in DSM-III.

Part II assesses combat experiences in Vietnam and contains several scales designed to measure the number of combat roles performed and their subjective stressfulness in terms of threat, injury, and death as measured by a 5-point Likert scale which operationally defines stress at the first scale point as "None—no real concern over death and injury," and at the fifth scale point as "Extreme—feared might die in the situation." Thus, across the 22 items which define the standard combat roles in the Vietnam war, a score is obtained for the total number of roles performed as well as a total score of how stressful they were evaluated by the veteran. Additionally, the respondent indicated how many weeks he performed these combat roles. Factor analysis performed on the combat role scale has produced three orthogonal factors using the Varimax solution: 1) infantry ground troop; 2) aerial and remote patrol combat duties; and 3) demolition/graves registration. The item loading for these factors is presented later in this section.

Part III of the VESI assesses the frequency with which the soldier was exposed to specific stressors in Vietnam across 46 items scaled in a 5-point Likert format which ranges from "Never—experience did not occur" to "Very often—experience occurred three or more times each week." The items include questions such as "How often did you see enemy wounded; how often did you participate in a body count of enemy dead, etc." Thus, the scale yields a total score indicative of the degree to which the veteran was exposed to a broad range of stressors indigenous to military service in Vietnam. Furthermore, the scale has been factor analyzed and contains three orthogonal factors: 1) exposure to injury and death; 2) lack of personal comforts and jungle terrain; and 3) short-timer syndrome. Separate factor scores can be computed to estimate the severity of exposure to a specific class of stressors.

Part IV of the VESI assesses the symptoms of PTSD and general psychiatric complaints by a 106-item Stress Assessment Questionnaire constructed in a 5-point Likert format which defines the frequency of experiencing the problem. For example, item 7, "Feeling guilt that a buddy was killed in Vietnam and not you," can be answered at scale points 1) "Not at all—problem does not occur," 2) "A little bit—1 to 9 times a month," 3) "Moderately—10 to 14 times a month," 5) "Extreme—21 to 30 times a month." Thus, across the 106 items a total score can be derived as an index of the overall severity of PTSD. Additionally, the scale has been factor analyzed (see *Discussion* below) and yields seven orthogonal factors: 1) depression; 2) physical symptoms, memory impairment; 3) stigmatization, alienation, and cynicism; 4) sensation seeking, authority conflict; 5) anger, rage; 6) intrusive imagery; and 7) intimacy conflict, for which total scores may be assessed and used as indices of the severity of different dimensions of the stress syndrome.

Part V of the VESI contains four sections designed to measure different dimensions of the homecoming experience: (A) DEROS from Vietnam, (B) Homecoming experience during the first six months, (C) Physical symptoms at homecoming, and (D) Organizational membership. Factor analyses of sections B and C have generated four orthogonal factors for each section. For section B the factors are: 1) psychological isolation; 2) drug use: self-medication; 3) exercise/activity; and 4) seeking professional service/counseling. For section C the factors are: 1) anxiety and general somatic complaints; 2) gastrointestinal symptoms; 3) cardiovascular-hypertension; and 4) paresthesia and localized pain.

Finally, Part VI of the VESI assesses post-Vietnam legal difficulties and asks the veteran to indicate whether or not he has been arrested, acquitted, or convicted of any of 19 criminal offenses.

Design. Given the construction of the VESI and the interest in predicting the symptoms of post-traumatic stress disorder in the sample population of Vietnam combat veterans, it was decided to first establish Pearson-product moment correlations between the predictor variables and the measure of PTSD. Second, as a more sophisticated technique, the factors derived from the Varimax solution factor analysis for combat roles, exposure to stressors in Vietnam, and the homecoming experiences were regressed in a step-wise multiple regression procedure onto the seven PTSD factors which composed the dependent variable. Finally, in order to obtain an initial estimate of the best set of predictors of the PTSD factor scores, a step-wise multiple regression analysis was performed on all the variables measured by the VESI.

RESULTS

In order to establish coherence to the research findings, we will first present in Tables 1-7 the results of the factor analysis of the Stress Assessment Questionnaire, from Part IV of the VESI. These tables are presented with the individual item loadings for two reasons. First, the items which make up a factor are interesting theoretically and informative to clinicians. Second, since the VESI is now in widespread use in V.A. hospitals and outreach programs, the results will be of interest to other researchers. After presenting the results of the factor analysis of the PTSD measure, we shall test the hypotheses.

Inspection of Tables 1-7 reveals the results of the factor analysis of the measure of PTSD. The Varimax solution indicated that there were seven orthogonal factors which we have labeled: 1) depression, search for meaning, identity confusion; 2) physical symptoms, memory impairment; 3) stigmatization, alienation, cynicism; 4) sensation seeking, authority conflict; 5) anger, rage; 6) intrusive imagery of Vietnam; and 7) intimacy conflict. The tables indicate the specific item loadings on the factor. Space limitations prevent us from a detailed discussion of the item loading on the factors. However, what is noteworthy is how uniformly these seven factors conform to the defining criteria of PTSD listed in DSM-III of the American Psychiatric Association.

The Relationship of Combat Roles to PTSD Scores

Tables 8-10 show the factors and item loadings for the combat role scale. As would be expected, the items grouped together to define the factor in accordance with the function of the role.

In support of Hypothesis 1, Table 11 indicates that the number of combat roles, the number of weeks in combat in Vietnam, and the subjective report of stress in combat roles are all significantly correlated with the total PTSD score (r's > .20, $p < .05$).

TABLE 1
Factor Analysis of Post-Traumatic Stress Scale-IV A
(PTSD-IV A)
Varimax Solution—7 Factors

Factor 1—Emotional: Depression, Search for Meaning, Identity Confusion

Scale Item	Loading
2. Suicidal thoughts	.40
4. Feeling depressed	.50
8. Feeling like withdrawing from others	.53
16. Feeling numb or nothing inside	.55
17. Feeling that problems are caused by others	.50
18. Fear losing control of your impulses	.48
19. Mistrusting what others say or do	.62
26. Feeling an ability to be close to someone	.47
29. Feeling alienated from other people	.63
30. An inability to talk about the war	.38
31. Experiencing a fear of losing loved ones	.34
35. Feeling unable to express real feeling to others	.57
38. Experiencing problems with your wife or lover	.46
39. Arguing with your wife or lover	.45
40. Problem trusting others for fear something bad happening to you	.54
44. Wife complaining Nam messed up your relationship	.36
46. Feeling that you are no good and worthless	.71
48. Feeling that you have no real goals that matter	.75
49. Feeling that you are different than before Nam	.55
50. Feeling self-conscious as a Vietnam veteran	.55
51. Experiencing self-doubt and uncertainty	.74
52. Feeling that you can't control important events in your life	.70
53. Feeling like you really "died" in Nam and are a walking "shell"	.57
54. Not feeling really satisfied with yourself	.73
55. Not feeling proud of yourself	.71
56. Feeling that you are not a person of worth	.69
57. Feeling that Nam took away your "soul"	.48
58. Feeling that you just can't get a hold on things	.78
59. Feeling like you're still searching in your life	.72
60. Feeling like a failure since leaving military	.66
71. Feeling uneasy in a crowd	.53
72. Experiencing conflicts with co-workers	.31
75. Feeling that life has no meaning	.76
76. Feeling a need to find more purpose in life	.69
88. Feeling not free to make own choices in life	.51
89. Feeling your personal existence is meaningless	.78
90. Feeling you should be achieving something	.73
106. Feeling that nothing matters anymore	.68
% of Variance	17.75

TABLE 2

Factor 2—Physical Symptoms, Memory Impairment, and Drug Use
(PTSD-IV A)

Scale Item	Loading
1. Feeling anxious or nervous	.43
3. Problems of concentration	.50
21. Using alcohol to help you feel better	.29
23. Using military self-defense tactics when under stress	.35
25. Taking prescribed drugs for emotional upset	.35
47. Problems remembering things you should know	.53
73. Legal problems	.43
77. Feeling jumpy when hear sudden noises	.35
84. Feeling need to have weapon near you	.38
91. Headaches	.56
92. Nervousness or shakiness inside	.53
93. Faintness or dizziness	.61
94. Pains in heart or chest	.57
95. Feeling low in energy or slowed down	.63
96. Trembling	.64
97. Poor appetite	.54
98. Heart pounding or racing	.64
99. Nausea or upset stomach	.63
100. Trouble getting your breath	.67
101. Hot or cold spells	.59
102. Numbness or tingling in parts of your body	.61
103. A lump in your throat	.49
104. Feeling weak in parts of your body	.68
105. Awakening in the early morning	.46
% of Variance	11.22

TABLE 3

Factor 3—Stigmatization, Alienation, Cynicism
(PTSD-IV A)

Scale Item	Loading
20. Memories of Nam "pop" into your head	.49
24. War-related thoughts	.58
41. Getting nervous around non-Nam veterans	.45
45. Nam affecting the way you relate to your children	.35
61. Want to "kick some ass" for what happened in Nam	.56
62. Fantasies of retaliation for what happened to you in Nam	.51
63. Feeling alienated from the government	.69
64. Feeling you're being stigmatized for being a Nam vet	.58
65. Feeling cynical about governmental processes	.66
66. Feeling like you lost faith in people after Nam	.53
67. Feeling you were used by the government for serving in Nam	.54
78. Feeling nervous when you hear a helicopter	.39
81. Hard to really believe that Nam (really) happened to you	.49
% of Variance	8.41

TABLE 4

Factor 4—Sensation Seeking, Authority Conflict
(PTSD-IV A)

Scale Item	Loading
22. Using hard drugs to help you feel better	.40
27. Feeling that you treat women like sexual objects	.39
68. Having problems with persons in authority positions	.45
69. Feeling that your work is menial	.56
74. Feeling (like) quitting job because work under your abilities	.52
80. Walking in woods and listening carefully	.35
85. Feeling you drive recklessly	.45
86. Need to engage in dangerous adventures	.61
87. Need to seek out high degrees of "sensation" that are risky	.64
% of Variance	5.25

TABLE 5

Factor 5—Anger, Rage
(PTSD-IV A)

Scale Item	Loading
11. Experiencing anger	.53
12. Experiencing rage	.69
13. Experiencing explosive anger	.75
34. Getting into fights with others	.45
36. "Flying off the handle" when things don't go right	.53
37. Losing your temper and getting out of control	.69
% of Variance	5.22

TABLE 6

Factor 6—Intrusive Imagery of Vietnam
(PTSD-IV A)

Scale Item	Loading
5. Thoughts of a buddy killed in Vietnam	.71
6. Asking self why a buddy killed in Nam and not you	.76
7. Feeling guilt that a buddy was killed and not you	.74
10. Experiencing nightmares of the war	.50
14. Unable to express sadness over lost buddies	.68
15. Getting rid of unpleasant, intrusive Nam thoughts	.53
70. Wish you could do work that would do good for others	.33
79. Searching for ambush spots while driving	.50
82. Vietnam something you still can't accept in your life	.49
83. Vietnam was just one great big nightmare	.47
% of Variance	6.84

TABLE 7

Factor 7—Problems of Intimacy
(PTSD-IV A)

Scale Item	Loading
9. Having problems going to sleep	.37
28. Experiencing sexual problems	.27
32. Feeling like you lost your romantic, sexual sensitivity in Nam	.51
33. Getting into fights or conflicts with loved ones	.48
42. Experiencing problems being close to your mother	.48
43. Experiencing problems being close to your father	.51
% of Variance	4.20

TABLE 8
Factor Analysis of Combat Roles in Vietnam War
Varimax Solution—3 Factors

Combat Roles: Factor 1—Infantry Ground Troop

Scale Item	Loading
1. Forward observation on ground	.47
4. Perimeter guard duty no incoming or sapper fire	.44
5. Perimeter guard duty and receiving incoming mortar/rocket fire/sapper attack	.73
6. Being part of a convoy and receiving enemy fire	.55
7. Being part of unit patrols which encountered anti-personnel weapons	.78
8. Being part of unit patrol which was ambushed	.75
9. Being part of unit patrols which engaged Viet Cong or NVA in firefight	.80
10. Being part of unit patrols which received sniper fire or sapper fire	.86
11. Being part of unit patrols which received incoming mortar fire, artillery, or rockets from enemy	.82
12. Being part of a base camp which received mortar fire, artillery, or rockets from enemy	.40
17. Being a tunnel rat and checking enemy base camps	.38
22. Walking "point man"	.33
% Variance	5.23

TABLE 9

Combat Roles: Factor 2—Aerial and Remote Patrol Combat Duties

Scale Item	Loading
2. Flying reconnaissance observation and taking fire	.74
3. Flying reconnaissance observation and getting shot down	.67
14. Flying helicopter slicks and receiving enemy fire	.70
15. Flying helicopters and not receiving enemy fire	.53
16. Performing LRRP	.46
18. Being a part of a river patrol or gunboat	.49
21. Being a medic in combat	.22
22. Photographer	.54
% Variance	3.19

TABLE 10

Combat Roles: Factor 3—Demolition/Graves Registration

Scale Item	Loading
19. Being a demolitions expert	.53
20. Being assigned to Graves and Registration	.60
22. a. Being a bridge guard	.47
22. b. Being a prisoner of war	.42
22. c. Being part of a Seal Team	.68
% Variance	2.18

TABLE 11
Relation Between Combat Experiences in
Vietnam to Total Post-Traumatic Stress Score

Variable	Correlation with VPTSD Score	p-value
Number Combat roles	.20	.04
Number Weeks in Vietnam	.32	.001
Subjective report of stress in combat roles	.23	.02
Exposure to Stressors in Combat	.49	.0001
Total Vietnam Stress Score	.51	.001

TABLE 12

Correlation Between Number of Weeks in Vietnam, Number of Combat Roles, and Subjective Stress Experienced in Combat Roles to Post-Traumatic Stress Disorder (PTSD) Factors

PTSD Factors (N = 114)	Number Weeks in Vietnam	Number Combat Roles	Subjective Stress in Roles
Depression	.26 **	.11	.14
Physical Symptoms	.30 **	.25 **	.28 **
Stigma/Alien	.24 **	.23 *	.25 **
Sensation Seeking	.25 **	.19 *	.17
Anger	.20 *	.09	.18 *
Intrusive Image	.23 *	.46 ***	.51 ***
Intimacy Conflict	.17	.09	.16

* $p < .05$
** $p < .01$
*** $p < .001$

Table 12 presents a more detailed analysis of the relationship between the number of combat roles, the number of weeks in combat in Vietnam, and the subjective stress in the combat roles to each of the seven PTSD factors. As can be seen by examining Table 12, the number of weeks in combat in Vietnam correlated significantly with all of the PTSD factors (r's = .20 to .30, $p < .05$) except for intimacy conflict. Similarly, the number of combat roles was significantly correlated with four of the PTSD factors (physical symptoms, stigmatization, sensation seeking, and instrusive imagery). As would be expected, the highest correlation is found for intrusive imagery ($r = .46$). On the other hand, depression, anger, and intimacy conflict did not significantly correlate with the number of combat roles. The pattern of results for subjective stress in combat roles is virtually the same as that for the number of combat roles with two exceptions. First, the magnitude of the correlations is slightly higher. Second, subjective stress scores are significantly correlated with the PTSD factor anger/rage.

The Relation of Combat Role Factors and Exposure to Stressors in Vietnam to PTSD Scores

Tables 13-22 summarize the relationship between the three combat factors and the three exposure-to-stressor factors to each of the seven factors of the PTSD scale. Additionally, each table presents the results of the step-wise multiple regression (R^2) analysis of the combat role and

TABLE 13
Factor Analysis of Exposure to Stressors in Vietnam
Varimax—3 Factors

Factor 1: Injury/Death	
Scale Item	Loading
1. How often did you fire your weapon at the enemy?	.79
2. How often did you kill the enemy?	.82
3. How often did you see someone killed?	.80
4. How often did you see enemy wounded?	.70
5. How often did you see our guys wounded?	.56
6. How often did you see dead enemy?	.78
7. How often did you see dead Vietnamese?	.66
8. How often did you see our own dead?	.63
9. How often did you find yourself in a combat situation in which you thought you would never survive?	.56
10. How often were you directly involved as a participant in hurting Vietnamese?	.58
11. How often were you indirectly involved as an observer in killing Vietnamese?	.52
12. In your opinion, how often were you in danger of being killed or wounded in Vietnam?	.57
13. How often were you unable to identify the enemy upon engaging Vietnamese?	.47
14. How often were you adequately briefed of military objectives before participation on maneuvers?	.40
15. How often did you experience frustration over repetitive capture and loss of terrain objectives?	.51
16. How often did tactical briefings coincide with your experiences in operations?	.48
17. How often did you feel that the ARVN were not committed to the defense of South Vietnam?	.33
18. How often did you participate in a body count of enemy dead?	.72
19. In your opinion, how often was the military objective dependent upon the body count?	.34
20. How often did you see our guys wounded by anti-personnel devices (booby traps, trip wires, etc.)?	.58
22. How often did you find yourself in a combat situation in which the enemy attack was unpredictable?	.39
23. How often did you hear statements made by guys with less than 30 days left in-country (short-timers) which mentioned the loss of a buddy while in Vietnam?	.54
32. How often were you bothered by the sight and sound of dying people?	.60
39. How often were you directly involved as a participant in killing Vietnamese?	.67
40. How often were you indirectly involved as an observer in hurting Vietnamese?	.68
44. How often were you directly involved in mutilating bodies of Vietnamese (e.g., cutting off ears, putting heads on sticks, placing bodies in grotesque positions)?	.63
45. How often were you indirectly involved as an observer of the mutilation of bodies of Vietnamese?	.70
% Variance	10.66

TABLE 14
Factor Analysis of Exposure to Stressors in Vietnam

Factor 2: Lack of Personal Comforts	
Scale Item	Loading
21. How often did you not find yourself in a safe area (e.g., Saigon, Unit HQ)?	.19
25. How often were you bothered by bad climate?	.62
26. How often were you bothered by bad food?	.63
27. How often were you bothered by separation from family?	.56
28. How often were you bothered by separation from friends?	.50
31. How often were you bothered by the insects and filth?	.73
33. How often were you bothered by loss of freedom of movement?	.67
34. How often were you bothered by not having any girls or sex for one year?	.55
35. How often were you bothered by lack of privacy?	.68
36. How often were you bothered by fatigue?	.58
37. How often were you bothered by long periods of boredom?	.37
38. How often were you bothered by the threat of disease?	.45
42. How often were you bothered by the threat of injury?	.66
43. How often were you bothered by not counting as an individual?	.43
% Variance	5.21

TABLE 15
Factor Analysis of Exposure to Stressors in Vietnam

Factor 3: Short-Timer Syndrome	
Scale Item	Loading
24. How often did you hear statements made by a guy (short-timers) which indicated he saw himself as a survivor within his unit?	.62
29. In your opinion, how often were you aware of the controversy the Vietnam war was creating in the U.S.?	.64
30. In your opinion, how often were you aware of the controversy the Vietnam war was creating in your home community?	.66
41. How often were you aware that guys with less than 30 days left in Vietnam acted differently because they were survivors who were going home?	.56
% Variance	2.50

TABLE 16

Relationship Between Combat Roles and Stressors in Vietnam to Post-Traumatic Stress Disorder (PTSD) Factor Depression.

Stressor Variable	PTSD—Depression	
Exposure to Stressors in	r	*p-value*
Vietnam—Alone (N = 114)		
S_1 = Injury/Death	.29	.002
S_2 = Lack of Comforts/Jungle	.27	.004
S_3 = Short-timer	.12	NS
Combat Roles-Alone (N = 114)		
C_1 = Infantry	.06	NS
C_2 = Aerial/Remote	.28	.003
C_3 = Demolition/Graves	.11	NS
Stressors plus Combat Roles (N = 88)	R^2	
$S_1 -$ Injury/Death	.23	.01
$S_1 +$ Aerial/Remote (C_2)	.28	.02
$S_1 + C_2 +$ Demolition/Graves $- C_3$	.32	.04
$S_1 + C_2 + C_3 +$ Lack Comforts $- S_2$	.35	.05
$S_1 + C_2 + C_3 + S_2 +$ Short-Timer $- S_3$	.35	.09
All variables	.36	NS

TABLE 17

Relationship Between Combat Roles and Stressors in Vietnam to Post-Traumatic Stress Disorder (PTSD) Factor Physical Symptoms

Stressor Variable	PTSD—Physical Symptoms	
Exposure to Stressors in		
Vietnam—Alone (N = 114)	r	*p-value*
S_1 = Injury/Death	.43	.0001
S_2 = Lack of Comforts/Jungle	.35	.0001
S_3 = Short timer	.10	NS
Combat Roles-Alone (N = 114)		
C_1 = Infantry	.24	.009
C_2 = Aerial-Remote	.23	.01
C_3 = Demolition/Graves	.26	.006
Stressors plus Combat Roles (N = 88)	R^2	
$S_1 -$ Injury/Death	.34	.002
$S_1 +$ Demolition/Graves $- C_3$	.39	.003
$S_1 +$ Aerial/Remote $- C_2$	.44	.005
$S_1 + C_3 + C_2 +$ Short timer $- S_3$	.46	.01
$S_1 + C_3 + C_2 + S_3 +$ Lack of		
Comforts/Jungle $- S_2$	.46	.02
All Variables	.46	.04

TABLE 18

Relationship Between Combat Roles and Stressors in Vietnam to Post-Traumatic Stress Disorder (PTSD) Factor Stigmatization/Alienation

Stressor Variable	PTSD—Stigmatization/Alienation	
Exposure to Stressors in		
Vietnam—Alone (N = 114)	*r*	*p-value*
S_1 – Injury/Death	.43	.0001
S_2 – Lack of Comforts/Jungle	.34	.0002
S_3 – Short-timer	.17	.07
Combat Roles—Alone (N = 114)		
C_1 – Infantry	.17	.07
C_2 – Aerial/Remote	.30	.001
C_3 – Demolition/Graves	.21	.02
Stressors plus Combat Roles (N = 88)	R^2	
S_1 – Injury/Death	.36	.001
S_1 + Short-timer – S_3	.37	.005
S_1 + S_3 + Infantry – C_1	.38	.01
S_1 + S_3 + C_1 + Lack of Comforts/Jungle –		.03
S_2	.39	
S_1 + S_3 + C_1 + Aerial/Remote – C_2	.40	.05
S_1 + S_3 + C_1 + S_2 + C_2 +		.05
Demolition/Graves – C_3	.40	
All Variables	.41	.09

TABLE 19

Relationship Between Combat Roles and Stressors in Vietnam to Post-Traumatic Stress Disorder (PTSD) Factor Sensation Seeking

Stressor Variable	PTSD—Sensation Seeking	
Exposure to Stressors in		
Vietnam—Alone (N = 114)	*r*	*p-value*
S_1 – Injury/Death	.29	.001
S_2 – Lack of Comforts/Jungle	.18	.05
S_3 – Short-timer	.01	NS
Combat Roles—Alone (N = 114)		
C_1 – Infantry	.12	NS
C_2 – Aerial/Remote	.20	.03
C_3 – Demolition/Graves	.13	NS
Stressors plus Combat Roles (N = 88)	R^2	
S_1 – Injury/Death	.10	NS
S_1 + Short-timer – S_3	.23	.05
All Variables	.26	NS

TABLE 20

Relationship Between Combat Roles and Stressors in Vietnam to Post-Traumatic Stress Disorder (PTSD) Factor Anger

Stressor Variable	PTSD—Anger	
Exposure to Stressor in		
Vietnam—Alone (N = 114)	*r*	*p-value*
S_1 − Injury/Death	.37	.0001
S_2 − Lack of Comforts/Jungle	.32	.0006
S_3 − Short-timer	.09	NS
Combat Roles—Alone (N = 114)		
C_1 − Infantry	.09	NS
C_2 − Aerial-Remote	.17	.03
C_3 − Demolition/Graves	.26	.005
Stressors plus Combat Roles (N = 88)	R^2	
S_1 − Injury/Death	.44	.0002
S_1 + Short-timer − S_3	.51	.0003
S_1 + S_3 + Demolition/Graves − C_3	.56	.0003
S_1 + S_3 + C_3 + Infantry − C_1	.58	.0008
S_1 + S_3 + C_3 + C_1 + Aerial/Remote − C_2	.58	.002
All Variables	.58	.006

TABLE 21

Relationship Between Combat Roles and Stressors in Vietnam to Post-Traumatic Stress Disorder (PTSD) Factor Intrusive Imagery

Stressor Variable	PTSD—Intrusive Imagery	
Exposure to Stressors in		
Vietnam—Alone (N = 114)	*r*	*p-value*
S_1 − Injury/Death	.61	.0001
S_2 − Lack of Comforts/Jungle	.39	.0001
S_3 − Short-timer	.16	.08
Combat Roles—Alone (N = 114)		
C_1 − Infantry	.46	.0001
C_2 − Aerial/Remote	.34	.0002
C_3 − Demolition/Graves	.34	.0002
Stressors plus Combat Roles (N = 88)	R^2	
S_1 − Injury/Death	.39	.001
S_1 + Infantry − C_1	.38	.004
S_1 + C_1 + Short-timer − S_3	.39	.01
S_1 + C_1 + S_3 + Lack of Comforts/Jungle − S_2	.39	.01
S_1 + C_1 + S_3 + S_2 + Aerial/Remote − C_2	.39	.06
All Variables	.39	NS

TABLE 22

Relationship Between Combat Roles and Stressors in Vietnam to Post-Traumatic Stress Disorder (PTSD) Factor Problems in Intimacy

Stressor Variable	PTSD—Problems of Intimacy	
Exposure to Stressors in		
Vietnam—Alone (N = 114)	*r*	*p-value*
S_1 − Injury/Death	.18	.05
S_2 − Lack of Comforts/Jungle	.23	.01
S_3 − Short timer	.16	.08
Combat Roles—Alone (N = 114)		
C_1 − Infantry	.13	NS
C_2 − Aerial/Remote	.18	.06
C_3 − Demolition/Graves	.19	.04
Stressors plus Combat Roles (N = 88)	R^2	
S_1 − Injury/Death	.17	.04
S_1 + Aerial/Remote − C_2	.25	.04
S_1 + C_2 + Infantry − C_1	.27	.07
S_1 + C_2 + C_1 + Demolition/Graves − C_3	.28	NS
All other variables	.29	NS

stressor factors as predictor variables to each PTSD factor. First, however, it is necessary to present the results of the factor analysis of Part III of the VESI, exposure to stressors in Vietnam. Since the tables contain a large number of findings we will discuss separately the results for each of the seven PTSD factors.

PTSD factor Depression. In support of Hypothesis 2, the stressor factors "injury/death" and "lack of comforts/jungle" are significantly correlated with the depression dimension of the PTSD scale (r's $> .27$, $p < .004$). The factor "short-timer syndrome" is not significantly associated with depression. Among the combat role factors, only "aerial/remote" is significantly correlated with depression ($r = .28$, $p < .003$). In terms of the multiple regression analysis, the best predictor of the depression variable is the stressor "injury/death" which accounted for 23% of the variance predicted by all six variables (36%).

PTSD factor Physical Symptoms. In support of Hypothesis 2, the stressor factors "injury/death" and "lack of comfort/jungle" are significantly correlated with the physical symptoms factor of the PTSD scale (r's $> .35$, $p < .0001$). Similarly, all three combat role factors are significantly correlated with the physical symptoms dimension of PTSD (r's $> .23$, $p < .01$). The results of the multiple regression analysis indicated that, of the six predictor variables, the best predictor of physical symptoms is the stressor variable "injury/death" which accounted for 34% of the total predicted variance (46%).

PTSD factor Stigmatization/Alienation. In support of Hypothesis 2, all three of the stressor variables are significantly correlated with the factor stigmatization/alienation of the PTSD scale (r's = .17 to .43, $p < .07$). Further, all three combat role factors are significantly correlated with stigmatization (r's = .17 to .30, $p < .07$). The regression analysis indicated that among the six predictor variables, the stressor variable "injury/death" accounted for 36% of the total predicted variance (41%).

PTSD factor Sensation Seeking. In support of Hypothesis 2, the stressor variables "injury/death" and "lack of comforts/jungle" are positively correlated with the sensation-seeking factor of the PTSD scale (r's > .18, $p < .05$). Among the combat role factors, only "aerial/remote" is significantly associated with the PTSD factor (r = .20, $p < .03$).

Interestingly, of the six factors entered into the regression analysis, the best predictors of sensation seeking are the stressor variables "injury/death" and "short-timer syndrome" ($R^2 = .23$, $p < .05$).

PTSD factor Anger. The results of the analysis paralleled those presented above and indicated that the stressor variables "injury/death," "lack of comfort/jungle," and the combat role variables "infantry" and "demolition/graves registration" are significantly correlated with the anger/rage factor of the PTSD scale (r's = .17 to .37, $p < .03$). Further, the results of the regression analysis indicated that the best predictor variable was the stressor "injury/death" ($R^2 = .44$, $p < .0002$).

PTSD factor Intrusive Imagery of Vietnam. The results of the analysis for the intrusive imagery variable are especially interesting since unbidden imagery of the traumatic event constitutes the core feature of post-traumatic stress disorder. In strong support of Hypothesis 2, the stressor variable "injury/death" and "lacks comfort/jungle" are significantly correlated with intrusive imagery (r's = .61 and .39, $p < .0001$). Similarly, as would be expected, all three combat role factors are significantly correlated with the dependent variable (r = .34 to .46, $p < .0002$). Moreover, the regression analysis showed that the stressor variable "injury/death" accounted for all of the predicted variance ($R^2 = .39$, $p < .001$).

PTSD factor Problems of Intimacy. The results of the analysis for this dimension of the PTSD scale conform to those presented above. The stressor variables "injury/death", "lack of comfort/jungle", and the combat role variables "aerial/remote" and "demolition/graves" are all significantly associated with the intimacy conflict factor (r's = .18 to .23,

$p < .06$). Further, the regression analysis indicated that the best predictors among the stressor and combat roles factors are "injury/death" and "aerial/remote" ($R^2 = .25$, $p < .04$).

The Relationship of the Homecoming Experience After Vietnam to PTSD

Hypothesis 3 predicts that the severity of PTSD is significantly associated with the degree to which the veteran felt psychologically isolated during the first six months of the homecoming period. To test the hypothesis, each of the four factors of the homecoming experience was correlated with each of the seven PTSD factors. Tables 23-26 present the results of the item loading derived from Varimax solution for the factors: 1) psychological isolation; 2) drug use: self-medication; 3) exercise/activity; and 4) professional service/counseling.

TABLE 23
Factor Analysis of Homecoming Experience
Varimax—4 Factors

Factor 1: Psychological Isolation	
Scale Item	Loading
1. How often did you feel rejected by family?	.51
2. How often did you feel rejected by friends?	.71
3. How often did you feel rejected by relatives?	.62
4. How often did you feel stigmatized (e.g., baby killer, doper, crazy)?	.78
5. How often did you feel mistrust of authority?	.71
6. How often did you feel angered over being used or exploited for serving in the military?	.65
7. How often did you experience problems with authority figures?	.57
8. How often did you feel you were not appreciated by others for serving your country?	.78
9. How often did you feel like isolating yourself (e.g., continuously staying in a basement, room, or attic)?	.73
10. How often did you feel cynical about political leaders?	.83
11. How often did you feel cynical about war-related decisions by political leaders?	.83
18. How often did you need to use alcohol?	.41
21. How often did you find yourself unable to go to sleep at night?	.58
22. How often did you keep irregular hours?	.54
23. How often did you keep an irregular diet?	.69
% Variance	7.12

TABLE 24
Factor Analysis of Homecoming Experience

Factor 2: Drug Use: Self-Medication

Scale Item	Loading
12. How often did you need to smoke pot (marijuana) after coming home from Vietnam or release from active service?	.73
13. How often did you need to use hallucinogens (LSD, acid, mescaline, etc.)?	.84
14. How often did you need to use hard drugs (heroin, smack, horse, opium)?	.76
15. How often did you need to use amphetamines (speed)?	.66
16. How often did you need to use downers (Darvon, seconal, "soapers," angel dust, barbiturates)?	.77
17. How often did you need to use cocaine?	.80
% Variance	3.97

TABLE 25
Factor Analysis of Homecoming Experience

Factor 3: Exercise/Activity

Scale Item	Loading
19. How often did you exercise regularly (e.g., jogging, swimming, weightlifting)?	.71
20. How often did you worry about your physical health and well-being?	.75
24. How often did you feel like discussing your Vietnam experience?	.65
% Variance	1.98

TABLE 26
Factor Analysis of Homecoming Experience

Factor 4: Professional Service/Counseling

Scale Item	Loading
25. How often did you use the services of the Veterans Administration during homecoming?	.52
26. How often *to date* have you used the services of the Veterans Administration?	.54
27. How often *to date* have you used the services of a private social worker, psychologist, or psychiatrist for war-related personal problems?	.45
28. How often to date have you used the services of the clergy (e.g., minister, priest, rabbi, etc.) for war-related personal problems?	.78
29. How often have you *ever* talked about Vietnam since you came home?	.41
% Variance	2.27

Table 27 shows the relationship between the homecoming variables and the seven factors of the PTSD scale. As predicted in Hypothesis 3, psychological isolation is significantly correlated with all seven of the PTSD factors (r's = .50 to .74, $p < .001$). Furthermore, Table 27 also indicates that drug use and seeking counseling are also significantly correlated with most of the PTSD factors with the exception of intrusive imagery and intimacy conflict. Interestingly, "exercise/activity" is also significantly correlated with physical symptoms, sensation seeking, and intrusive imagery.

The Relationship of Premorbid Personality Disorders to PTSD

To assess the relationship between premorbid personality disorders and post-traumatic stress disorder, we constructed a 42-item scale which listed "problems reported by some veterans as having happened to them before military service." The respondent was simply asked to check those problems which applied to him "prior to military service." Three subscales attempted to measure paranoid, antisocial, and narcissistic personality disorder characteristics. In constructing this retrospective self-report checklist of behavioral tendencies, we used the explicit criteria listed in DSM-III for each subdimension of the personality disorders and converted them into problem statements. Thus, for each person at least four estimates of premorbid tendencies were obtained: three total scores for the personality disorder subscales as well as a total personality disorder score which represents the total number of items checked by the respondent.

TABLE 27

Correlation between Homecoming Variables to Post-Traumatic Stress Disorder Factors

PTSD Factors (N = 114)	HOMECOMING VARIABLE			
	Psych Isolation	Drug Use	Exercise	Seek Counseling
Depression	.65 ***	.20 **	.08	.18 *
Physical Symptoms	.74 ***	.29 ***	.24 **	.39 ***
Stigma/Alien	.71 ***	.19 *	.13	.32 **
Sensation Seeking	.66 ***	.44 ***	.19 *	.21 *
Anger	.58 ***	.25 **	.16	.34 **
Intrusive Image	.59 ***	.17	.19 *	.38 ***
Intimacy Conflict	− 50 ***	.07	.03	.16

* $p < .05$
** $p < .01$
*** $p < .001$

TABLE 28

Correlation Between Premorbid Personality Disorder Characteristics and Post-Traumatic Stress Disorder (PTSD) Factors

| PTSD Factor | Premorbid Personality Disorder Measure | | | |
	Total Anti-Social Score (N = 85)	Total Paranoid Score (N = 75)	Total Narcissistic Score (N = 60)	Total Personality Disorder Score (N = 92)
Depression	.18	.13	.30 *	.19 *
Physical Symptoms	.21 *	.14	.26 *	.28 *
Stigma/Alien	.16	.09	.36 **	.18 *
Sensation Seeking	.26 *	.14	.32 *	.29 *
Anger	.17	.21 *	.24 *	.23 *
Intrusive Image	.17	.04	.31 *	.21 *
Intimacy Conflict	.04	.15	.16 *	.09

* $p < .05$
** $p < .005$

Table 28 presents the results of the analysis and shows, contrary to Hypothesis 4, that there are significant correlations between the premorbid personality disorder measures and the PTSD scale. First, antisocial tendencies are significantly correlated with the PTSD factors physical symptoms and sensation seeking. Second, paranoid traits are significantly associated with the anger factor of the PTSD scale. Interestingly, narcissistic tendencies are significantly correlated with all seven factors of the PTSD scale. Finally, the total personality disorder score was also correlated with all of the PTSD scale factors except intimacy conflict.

In support of Hypothesis 4, however, Table 29 shows the results of the regression analysis and indicates that, overall, the premorbid personality disorder accounted for less than 3.5% of the variance in the seven factors of the PTSD. Specifically, the results showed that paranoid character traits best predicted the PTSD factors depression, stigmatization, and intrusive imagery. Narcissistic traits are the best predictor of the PTSD factors sensation seeking and intimacy conflict.

Since the average age of the combat soldier in the Vietnam war was 19 years, it is necessary to ask why the measure of narcissism showed the strongest pattern of correlation with the PTSD scale. Based on Wilson's (1980) earlier research, we speculated that the narcissism scale might be assessing self-esteem and identity formation since the issue of identity integration is the paramount developmental task during young adulthood (Erikson, 1968). If this logic were correct, we expected that

TABLE 29
Multiple Regression for Premorbid Personality Disorder Characteristics
and Post-Traumatic Stress Disorder (PTSD) Factors

| PTSD Factors | Premorbid Personality Disorder Characteristic Prediction of PTSD | | |
	Variable	R^2	p-value
Depression	High Paranoid	.04	.02
Physical Symptoms	None	—	—
Stigma/Alien	High Paranoid	.03	.04
Sensation Seeking	Low Anti-Social,	.04	.01
	High Narcissism	—	—
Anger	None	—	—
Intrusive Image	High Paranoid	.03	.05
Intimacy Conflict	High Narcissism	.04	.03

the first two items of the narcissism scale should correlate positively with the measure of PTSD since they were constructed to measure narcissitic grandiosity and ideology.

As Table 30 shows, this was indeed the case. Apparently then, the scale items "feeling that you were a person of unusual importance and uniqueness and capable of doing truly great things in life" and "often feeling or thinking that you could achieve unlimited success, power, accomplishment, beauty, and wealth" are tapping concerns that are genuine tasks for the young adult, i.e., to decide who one is in terms of personal identity and setting levels of aspiration for personal goals.

This argument is bolstered by the findings of Wilson and Prabucki (1983) that among a sample of college sophomores, whose mean age was 21 years, the grandiosity and ideology subscales were positively correlated with Constantinople's (1973) measure of positive psychosocial maturity whereas the other three subscales of narcissism were negatively correlated to ego-identity and positive ego development. Thus, these results add support to Wilson's (1980) findings that the stressors of combat in Vietnam may have impacted negatively on the process of identity formation among Vietnam veterans.

Best Predictor Variable of PTSD

As a final analysis we ran a large step-wise multiple regression of all predictor variables on our dependent measure. Table 31 indicates that for each dimension of PTSD measured by the Stress Assessment Scale, the best predictor variable, with exception of intrusive imagery, was

TABLE 30

Correlation Between Premorbid Narcissistic Personality Disorder
Characteristics and Total Post-Traumatic Stress Score

Narcissistic Personality Disorder Characteristic	Total PTSD Score
Grandiosity (N = 33)	.30 *
Ideology (N = 34)	.39 **
Exhibitionism (N = 20)	.34
Indifference (N = 18)	.10
Interpersonal Exploitiveness (N = 20)	.18

* $p < .09$
** $p < .05$

TABLE 31

Multiple Regression Analysis of Best Predictors of Post-Traumatic Stress
Disorder Factors

PTSD Factor (N = 110)	Best Predictor Variable	R^2	F	p-value
Depression	Psychological Isolation (at Homecoming)	.42	78.68	.0001
Physical Symptoms	Psychological Isolation	.56	141.75	.0001
Stigma/Alienation	Psychological Isolation	.50	108.96	.0001
Sensation Seeking	Psychological Isolation	.44	86.34	.0001
Anger, Rage	Psychological Isolation	.33	21.74	.0001
Intrusive Imagery	Injury/Death, Psychological Isolation	.49	55.65	.0001
Intimacy Conflict	Psychological Isolation	.26	23.62	.0001

psychological isolation, which accounted, on the average, for about 43% of the measured variance in PTSD. As would be expected, the regression equation indicated that the combination of injury/death and psychological isolation were the best predictors of intrusive imagery.

DISCUSSION

The results of this study extend the growing body of research on the psychological effects of the Vietnam war on its veterans in several new directions. First, the factor analysis of the Stress Assessment Scale to measure PTSD has identified seven interrelated dimensions of the stress syndrome. The dimensions of PTSD generated by the factor analysis are remarkably similar to clinical descriptions of traumatic neuroses which have been documented among survivors of other disaster situations (e.g., Hiroshima, Nazi persecution, Buffalo Creek Dam disaster, POWs, etc.) and therefore suggest that scale is measuring some of the core features of PTSD.

Second, the findings strongly suggest that in terms of accounting for the measured variance in the severity of PTSD the best predictors of the symptoms of the stress syndrome are knowledge of the frequency of exposure to the stressors indigenous to guerilla warfare in Vietnam, and the degree of psychological isolation experienced by the veteran after returning home from the war. As we will discuss below, it would appear that the *severity* of PTSD is directly associated with the subjective evaluation of combat stress, the number and length of time in combat roles, the frequency of exposure to injury and death, and the psychological *process* of constructing a personal perspective of the meaning and purpose of life-death encounters.

The dimensions of PTSD found in this study (depression, physical symptoms, stigmatization, sensation seeking, anger/rage, intrusive imagery of Vietnam, and intimacy conflict) are both theoretically and clinically meaningful. In terms of theoretical considerations, these seven dimensions of PTSD are clearly connected to the stressors encountered in combat and the post-Vietnam homecoming experiences. In a psychodynamic sense the dimensions make up a syndrome that characterizes the attempts the veteran makes to assimilate the traumatic event into preexisting cognitive schemata and emotional coping styles.

In analyzing the dynamics of PTSD among Vietnam combat veterans, it is necessary to explain how the dimensions of the disorder interrelate in producing the symptoms which define it. To begin, it is instructive to point out that the typical soldier was a 19-year-old young adult who went to the war zone without really knowing why he was there. Perhaps the best characterization would be that the vast majority of combatants were ordinary, naive, decent, youthful, innocent, and well-intentioned Americans doing what they thought they were supposed to do (Caputo, 1977; Webb, 1980; Emerson, 1976; Delvecchio, 1982). And despite the fundamental adequacy of his military training, the typical soldier was not ideologically or emotionally prepared to face the complex and often surreal nature of jungle combat against a resilient, tenacious, resourceful, and determined enemy that had for centuries defeated invaders by sheer willpower and tactical mastery of the environment. As history has documented, the decisive weapon of enemy forces was ultimately ideological conviction rather than material and military superiority. To engage in battle necessitated combat assaults in the enemy's lair which was always ephemeral, hidden, and paradoxically ubiquitous. This, then, was the arena in which the combatant experienced life-death events that now constitute the elements of prolonged stress responses and intrusive recollections of what happened there.

The central issue in terms of understanding and predicting post-traumatic stress syndromes among Vietnam veterans focuses on how the veteran attempts to assimilate the emotionally painful and unbidden images of the trauma and why they might persist for many years. The results of the study indicated among all the independent variables we have used to predict PTSD as measured by the VESI that the single best predictor is the factor "psychological isolation" at homecoming. This finding helps to understand the seven dimensions of the stress syndrome in more precise ways.

First, it is reasonable to speculate that *psychological isolation* means that the veteran feels trapped in the trauma and unable to talk about it with significant others. Consequently, the veteran may have lost a sense of communality (Erikson, 1974) because psychological isolation meant that the network of bonding, support, trust, and mutuality with the larger corpus of society was no longer functional. Simply stated, the psychologically isolated veteran had to come to grips with the residual effects of the Vietnam experience alone. Thus, it is likely that the state of psychological isolation intensified the process of assimilating the trauma by *increasing* the defenses against instrusive imagery and developing coping strategies to minimize, block, or fend off emotionally painful thoughts associated with Vietnam. For example, the memory of buddies killed in action; the awareness of lost innocence, youth, and pre-Vietnam identity; the recognition of the horrors of war and the destruction of Vietnamese villages and their people, etc. typically produce feelings of sadness and some degree of impacted grief (Shatan, 1974). This loss of self, others, innocence, and ideology, especially when coupled with a state of psychological isolation, is likely to cause feelings of depression, helplessness, anxiety, hopelessness, and despair. It is also likely to be asssociated with identity confusion, changes in values, and a search for meaning and purpose in life. As Lifton (1976) has observed, the confrontation with death often leads to a decentering of the self in ways that produce the sense of being disconnected, disintegrated, static, and symbolically dead.

The sense of psychological isolation experienced by Vietnam combat veterans is, of course, a natural consequence in a recovery environment that did not officially or ritually welcome the returning warrior. Indeed, Wilson (1980) has written that the actual homecoming experience of the Vietnam veteran *maximally* exacerbated the residual stresses of combat since there was an absence of social and institutional support mechanisms to facilitate the reentry and recovery process. Furthermore, the controversy over the war as well as their experiences in it led many veterans to feel stigmatized for their actions in Vietnam and cynical about the honesty, integrity, and trustworthiness of authority and political leaders. Partially for this reason, many veterans report fantasies of retaliation (Wilson, 1978) or what Horowitz (1976) has labeled "rage at the source." This inner state of anger may, of course, be expressed in many different forms ranging from episodes of explosive rage and uncontrollable irritability to feelings of impotence at having been a pawn in a war game.

Consistent with other findings on traumatic stress syndromes, the results also indicated that the presence of *physical symptoms* is a component of PTSD among Vietnam veterans. As would be expected from Horowitz's (1976) model, the alternation between the denial and intrusive stages of PTSD corresponds to threshold levels in defensive functioning. Thus, when ego defenses succeed in blocking unconscious thoughts about the trauma, the individual may not be troubled by nightmares or other overt symptoms of the anxiety disorder. However, the internal conflict may then get expressed in a somatic form which, in turn, produces a wide range of physical symptoms.

Perhaps the least understood behavioral style designed to cope with PTSD is that of *sensation seeking* or the seeking out of intense forms of experiences which symbolically recreate the exhilarating aspects of combat. By seeking intensity in life-styles, the individual recreates the subjective, adrenalin-filled emotional experience of "living on the edge" in risky, dangerous, adventurous, challenging, or novel enterprise. In effect, then, these activities enable the veteran to feel subjectively alive, animated, and existentially anchored in "here and now" experiences which counteract feelings of boredom and meaninglessness.

Furthermore, Wilson (1981) has noted that when the veteran seeks intense forms of experience, they are not typically symptomatic because the action-oriented behavioral syndrome is a complex form of repetition compulsion. By behaving in ways psychologically similar to those previously experienced in Vietnam, the veteran unconsciously continues trying to master the trauma by behaving with similar adaptive and cognitive strategies which succeeded in keeping him alive in the war zone. This "survivor mode" of functioning had been strongly reinforced time and time again in the face of the life-death stressors. Paradoxically, it is when the veteran stops functioning in the intense survivor mode that he becomes flooded with intrusive images that are emotionally distressing.

Our results also indicated that *intimacy conflict* is a major dimension of PTSD among Vietnam veterans. As we understand it, the problem of establishing or maintaining intimate relations is associated with other dimensions of the stress syndrome. First, the survivor is often psychically numb and finds it difficult to experience emotions, especially those associated with love, caring, nurturance, and sexuality.

Wilson (1978, 1980) has described the mechanism of purposeful distancing by which the veteran erects a protective shield around himself by maintaining tight controls over the degree of intimacy experienced with significant others. In large measure this protective shield is a security operation which allows the person to control the consequences of social interaction by avoiding unpredictable outcomes that might be painful. For most combat veterans of the Vietnam war, purposeful distancing and the numbing that accompanies it began in response to witnessing injury, death, and dying. Now, however, the psychic numbing, as well as the anger, rage, cynicism, depression, and intrusive images of Vietnam, reactivates this primitive survival mechanism over and over again, causing the individual to control the depth of intimate involvement out of fear of loss of loved ones and intolerable emotional pain. Ultimately, of course, the tendency towards self-estrangement and the inability to fully express and communicate the inner struggle with the Vietnam experience results in tension, confusion, anger, and conflict in attempts at intimacy.

What set of factors best predicts the stress syndrome we have just described? When examining the results there exists strong support for the hypotheses. First, in terms of *combat role dimensions*, the number of weeks in combat, the number of combat roles, and their subjective stressfulness were significantly correlated with most of the dimensions of PTSD. However, there were some interesting differences in the pattern of correlations. Depression was significantly correlated only with the number of weeks in combat. Similarly, anger was significantly related to the number of weeks in combat and subjective stress but was not correlated with the number of combat roles. Apparently, anger and the depressive dimensions of PTSD are related to how long the person performs the combat roles and how stressful they are for him. On the other hand, it is also possible that states of anger and depression are the result of intrusive imagery which was strongly correlated with the number of combat roles (r = .46) and the subjective stress measure (r = .51).

Furthermore, the results also indicated that specific combat roles were significantly correlated with the various factors of the VESI scale. In particular, aerial and remote combat duties (flying in helicopters, etc.)

were significantly associated with all seven dimensions of the PTSD measure. The infantry ground troop and demolition combat role was correlated with the PTSD factors physical symptoms, stigmatization, intrusive imagery, anger, and intimacy conflict. Taken as a composite set of findings, the results clearly indicate, as predicted, that combat role factors are significantly associated with the dimensions of PTSD as assessed by the VESI scales.

As predicted, the results supported Hypothesis 2 that there exists a relationship between exposure to traumatic stressors and the severity of PTSD. As Tables 16-22 show, the best predictor of each factor of PTSD assessed by the Stress Assessment Questionnaire was the stressor variable "injury/death." In terms of the total variance in each PTSD factor accounted for by the three stressor and combat role variables, the variance contributed by "injury/death" was as follows: depression (64%), physical symptoms (74%), stigmatization (88%), sensation seeking (43%), anger (76%), intrusive imagery (100%), and intimacy conflict (59%). Moreover, when the three combat role and stressor variables are regressed onto each dimension of PTSD, the stressor injury/death predicts 29% of the measured variance in the scores.

If exposure to traumatic stressors in combat lays the foundation for potential changes in the personality structure of the survivor, then the recovery environment may determine whether or not the post-trauma adaptation is pathological or positive in nature. In support of Hypothesis 3, the results indicated that the four homecoming variables (psychological isolation, drug use, exercise, and seeking counseling) were all significantly correlated with most of the dimensions of the stress disorder measure. Overall, however, Table 27 reveals that the variable psychological isolation gives a strongly positive correlation with each dimension of the PTSD measure (r's = .50 to .74). Thus, it would seem that the greater the degree of psychological isolation the more severe the symptoms of PTSD.

This argument is bolstered by the findings presented in Table 31 that when *all* items and factor scores from the VESI were regressed onto each factor of PTSD, psychological isolation accounted, on the average, for about 43% of the measured variance in the factors (R^2 = .26 to .56; F's > 23.62, p < .01). Indeed, with the exception of intrusive imagery, psychological isolation emerged as the first predictive variable in the regression equations. Thus, for Vietnam combat veterans it is reasonable to suggest that when a state of psychological isolation exists during the recovery period there is likely to be an intensification of PTSD.

Previous research findings (Helzer, Robbins, Wish, & Hesselbrock,

1979) have indicated that some features of PTSD (e.g., depression) may be due to premorbid personality characteristics rather than the effects of combat. The results of this study suggest a different perspective on the relation of premorbid personal attributes to the development of post-war psychopathology. When analyzing the results shown in Table 28, it would be reasonable to suggest that, as a consequence of combat in Vietnam, premorbid behavioral tendencies were aggravated. For example, the total antisocial score is significantly correlated with the PTSD dimensions of physical symptoms and sensation seeking. These results are quite consistent with the well-established fact that sociopathic persons somatize conflicts and seek high levels of stimulation which are often illegal in nature (Hare, 1970). Similarly, the paranoid score was significantly correlated with anger, a finding consistent with the tendency of paranoid individuals to "attack" against perceived threats in the world. Finally, the table shows that the total narcissism score was significantly correlated with the seven dimensions of the PTSD scale. However, this result raises some intriguing questions.

First, how is it possible that so many men could have been clinically narcissistic at the average age of 19? As recent studies have indicated (Masterson, 1982) the onset of florid pathological narcissism generally occurs when the person is in the 30s and 40s. Thus, it is unlikely that this personality syndrome would manifest itself when the typical soldier was fresh out of high school. However, it is reasonable to conjecture that what may be producing the observed findings are responses to items on the narcissism scale that measure concern with self-esteem and ego-identity. As Table 30 shows, this was the situation since only the narcissistic grandiosity and ideology subscales were significantly correlated with the total PTSD score.

Further, since recent findings have shown that these two subscales are correlated with positive psychosocial development according to Erikson's (1968) schema, it is reasonable to suggest that the combat experience in Vietnam may have intensified and, perhaps, negatively affected the normative developmental task of establishing a coherent and positive sense of personal identity. If this were the case, the veteran would manifest symptoms of identity confusion (role confusion) which would overlap with the defining characteristics of PTSD.

Wilson (1978) has argued that for Vietnam veterans, PTSD can be readily understood from the theoretical perspective of ego-development in which identity confusion results from the traumatic experiences. Clearly, if the stressors of war cause changes in the basic element of ego-identity in terms of values, goals, motives, ideology, and personal aspirations, it thus aggravates a normal developmental process, especially if a state of psychological isolation exists. Perhaps the common outcome of this series of events would be the development of PTSD.

In conclusion, the results of the present study have shown that it is possible to predict the different dimensions of PTSD among Vietnam veterans from a theoretical model that attempts to specify the relevant conceptual variables which are associated with the development of the disorder. In addition, the results provide support for the validity of the VESI as an administered, objective questionnaire which assesses different aspects of the veteran's experiences during the Vietnam war.* In particular, the results indicate that the best pedictors of PTSD as assessed by the VESI are knowledge of combat role factors, including the veteran's subjective evaluation of combat stress; exposure to traumatic situations, especially injury and death; and the degree to which the veteran felt psychologically isolated upon returning home from the war.

REFERENCES

Caputo, P.: *A rumor of war.* New York: Holt, Rinehart & Winston, 1977.
Constantinople, A.: An Eriksonian measure of personality development in college students. *Developmental Psychology, 28*:313-320, 1973.
Delvecchio, J.: *The 13th valley.* New York: Bantam, 1982.
Diagnostic and Statistical Manual (DSM-III). Washington, D.C.: American Psychiatric Association, 1980.
Emerson, G.: *Winners and losers.* New York: Random House, 1976.
Erikson, E.: *Identity, youth and crisis.* New York: W.W. Norton, 1968.
Erikson, K.T.: *Everything in its path.* New York: Simon & Schuster, 1974.
Freud, S.: Inhibitions, symptoms and anxiety. In J. Strachey (Ed.), *Standard edition,* Vol. 20. London: Hogarth, 1959.
Gleser, G.C., Green, B.L., & Winget, C.N.: *Buffalo Creek revisited: Prolonged psychosocial effects of disaster.* New York: Simon & Schuster, 1981.
Green, B.L., Wilson, J.P., & Lindy, J.: A conceptual framework for post-traumatic stress syndromes among survivor groups. In C.R. Figley (Ed.), *Trauma and its wake: The study and treatment of post-traumatic stress disorder.* New York: Brunner/Mazel, 1985.
Hare, R.D.: *Psychopathy: Theory and research.* New York: Wiley, 1970.
Helzer, J.E., Robins, L., Wish, E., & Hesselbrock, M.: Depression in Vietnam and civilian controls. *American Journal of Psychiatry, 136*:526-529, 1979.
Horowitz, M.J.: *Stress response syndromes.* New York: Jason Aronson, 1976.
Horowitz, M.J.: Psychological response to serious life events. In V. Hamilton & D.M. Warburton (Eds.), *Human stress and cognition.* New York: Wiley & Sons, 1979.
Kardiner, A.: Traumatic neuroses of war. In S. Arieti (Ed.), *American handbook of psychiatry, (Vol. I).* New York: Basic Books, 1959.

*Copies of the VESI research instrument may be obtained from Dr. John P. Wilson, Department of Psychology, Cleveland State University, 1983 E. 24th Street, Cleveland, Ohio 44115.

Lifton, R.J.: *Death in life: Survivors of Hiroshima.* New York: Simon & Schuster, 1967.
Lifton, R.J.: *The life of the self.* New York: Simon & Schuster, 1976.
Lifton, R.J.: *The broken connection.* New York: Simon & Schuster, 1980.
Masterson, J.F.: *The narcissistic and borderline disorders.* New York: Brunner/Mazel, 1981.
Niederland, W.G.: Psychiatric disorders among persecution victims. *Journal of Nervous and Mental Disease, 139:*458-474, 1964.
Niederland, W.G.: Clinical observation on the survivor syndrome. In H. Krystal (Ed.), *Massive psychic trauma.* New York: International Universities Press, 1968.
Shatan, C.F.: Through the membrane of reality: "Impacted grief" and perceptual dissonance in Vietnam combat veterans. *Psychiatric Opinion, 3*(II):6-15, Oct. 1974.
Titchener, J., & Kapp, F.T.: Family and character change at Buffalo Creek. *American Journal of Psychiatry, 133:*295-299, 1976.
Webb, J.: *Fields of fire.* New York: Dell, 1978.
Wilson, J.P.: *Identity, ideology and crisis: The Vietnam veteran in transition.* Vol. II., Washington, D.C.: Disabled American Veterans, 1978.
Wilson, J.P.: Conflict, stress and growth: The effects of war on psychosocial development among Vietnam veterans. In C. Figley & S. Leventman (Eds.), *Strangers at home: Vietnam veterans since the war.* New York: Praeger Books, 1980.
Wilson, J.P.: Cognitive control mechanisms in stress response syndromes and their relation to different forms of the disorder. Unpublished manuscript, Cleveland State University, 1981.
Wilson, J.P., & Krauss, G.E.: The Vietnam Stress Inventory. A scale to assess war stress and post-traumatic stress disorder among Vietnam veterans. Cleveland State University, 1981.
Wilson, J.P., & Prabucki, K.: Psychosocial antecedents of narcissistic personality syndrome. *Psychological Reports, 53:*1231-1239, 1983.

9

The Unknown Warriors: Implications of the Experiences of Women in Vietnam

LYNDA M. VAN DEVANTER, R.N.

The "Vietnam Vet"
people instantly conjure
their own picture
in their mind

Is it ever of
a woman?
Huddled . . . somewhere . . .
alone
sleeping

The author wishes to thank Kenneth Harbert, Sarah Haley, John Wilson, Norma Griffiths, Sharon Grant, Gustavo Martinez, and Jenny Schnaier for their editorial and other assistance in the preparation of this chapter.

trying desperately to shut out the world
that shut her out
or
that disappeared
as she reached out to trust it

Is it ever
that vision?
that woman?

Norma J. Griffiths, Cpt., A.N.C., Ret.

BACKGROUND

In 1969, Peter Bourne began chronicling his work with American Viet nam veterans who were experiencing long-term psychological difficulties as a result of their experiences in the war (Bourne, 1969). Since then, major studies have been carried out and reported by some of the finest clinical researchers in the country. These papers and books have contributed significantly to the body of knowledge concerning stress disorders and Vietnam veterans.

There is, however, a population of Vietnam veterans which has been largely ignored by the researchers. This is exemplified by Bourne's (1970) monograph which was entitled *Men, Stress and Vietnam*. In addition, Figley (1978) began the introduction to his text, *Stress Disorders Among Vietnam Veterans*, by writing, "The theme of the present volume is the concept that *the war is not over for thousands of men who served their country during the Vietnam war*" (p. xiii) (his emphasis). John Wilson, Mardi Horowitz, Arthur Egendorf, Robert Lifton, Sarah Haley, and numerous other credentialed researchers who have written about and treated Vietnam veterans have all written and spoken exclusively about men.

The theme of this chapter, then, is the concept that the war is not over for thousands of *women* who served their country during the Vietnam war.

DEMOGRAPHICS AND STATISTICS

You don't remember me, but I remember you. I held your hand when they brought you to the Operating Room while they put you to sleep. Many times I was the only female on the surgical team trying to hide my emotions. (Marron, 1982)

The United States Government has no idea how many women served their country in Vietnam. "Guesstimates" have ranged from 559 to 55,000, and these numbers include only those women who served in the military. The number of women who served in Vietnam with the Red Cross, Agency for International Development (AID), State and Defense Departments, and as Department of the Army Civilians (DAC) will probably never be accounted for, yet it is thought there are thousands of them. The Veterans Administration (1981) has estimated, however, that approximately 193,000 women served in the military during the Vietnam era. According to a report (1982) of the GAO (General Accounting Office of the U.S. Government), the needs of the female veteran population have not been adequately addressed by the Veterans Administration. The literature lacks much evidence of the civilian professional community addressing this issue of women veterans as well.

Yet one current piece of research does address women veterans. That report is entitled "Women Vietnam Veterans and Mental Health Adjustment: A Study of Their Experiences and Post-Traumatic Stress," by Jenny Schnaier (1982). It is an in-depth study which examines readjustment problems of 87 women who served in military medical positions in Vietnam. This landmark study provides an important new perspective on Post-Traumatic Stress Disorder (PTSD) among women veterans.

RESEARCH

Who are these women who served? Where are they now? How are they handling the legacy of their experiences? How have those experiences affected them? What characteristics have they developed which may relate to their experiences? How do they differ from or are they similar to male Vietnam era veterans? Why have they been invisible for so long? Do they have drug and alcohol abuse problems? Have they been able to sustain relationships any better than the men? Have they had employment problems? Are they affected by Agent Orange? Are they using their veterans benefits? What is their education level and how has that been affected by their experiences? How were their experiences affected by their educational level? Are they having physical problems? Do they feel cynical and mistrustful of government and authority? Do they have positive or negative effects from their experiences?

Have they gained anything from the experience? How was their psychosocial development affected?

These questions and more need to be asked and answers need to be sought. Although little has been done in the way of research on these women, the Schnaier study gives us some important insights into who some of them are.

Schnaier's (1982) population consisted of 87 women who had served in Vietnam during the war. All had been in the military, with 90 percent of them having served in the U.S. Army. All had served in medical positions in Vietnam.

The average age of the women in the study was somewhat older than the average age of most men who served in Vietnam. Seventy percent of them were between the ages of 22 and 25, while the average age of the male who served in Vietnam was 19 years. The educational level of the women in this study was also higher than the average educational level of the male soldier. All of the women had completed high school and nearly three quarters of them had completed college or professional school prior to going to Vietnam. In contrast, 21 percent of the soldiers serving in Vietnam had not completed high school (Egendorf et al., 1981). Over 90 percent of the women were white and nearly 75 percent now fall into the age group of 34 to 39. Fewer than half of the women are currently married, and fewer than half have had children. Their average length of tour in Vietnam was 12.6 months. All of the women in the study had received favorable discharges from the military.

The Schnaier (1982) report has limitations since its data are derived from a small sample, and a self-selected one. Nonetheless, some important information has been gained from the study. It provides preliminary evidence that Post-Traumatic Stress Disorder may be applicable to women Vietnam veterans. Women who had experienced high stressors such as continual streams of casualties, mutilated young bodies, and negating of emotions had a correlation with experiencing symptoms of PTSD. There is evidence of continuing mental health distress in the women in this study: 27.6 percent reported having suicidal thoughts between one and nine times per month during the past six months; 19.5 percent reported feeling alienated from other people between 15 and 30 times per month; 19.2 percent reported feeling depressed between 15 and 30 times per month.

Nearly half of the women in the study had sought help for mental health problems, but only 43 percent of those had ever discussed Vietnam. Many of the women reported still having difficulty talking about their Vietnam experiences. Additionally, a significant number of the women indicated a continuing cynicism and mistrust of government agencies.

The Schnaier study attempted to examine both positive and negative aspects of the Vietnam experience. For many of the women there were positive, growthful aspects to the Vietnam experience. In response to the open-ended questions, both personal and professional gains were mentioned, such as recognizing their own strengths and capabilities, appreciation for life, and gaining extraordinary nursing education and experience. A small group, however, reported only negative outcomes, such as learning to hate, becoming more cynical, and learning their own inadequacies. Forty-five percent felt that the Vietnam experience had affected them mostly positively, while 32 percent felt that it had affected them mostly negatively.

The study contains a veritable wealth of information about this population, but possibly one of the most significant things about it is that Schnaier had nearly a 97 percent response rate. Thus, it would seem that the women are eager to examine their experiences, talk about them, understand them and the effects the experiences had on them. In answer to the open-ended questions in the study, many of the women wrote several pages in order to fully express themselves. This was after having answered a written questionnaire of well over 200 items. Clearly, more research is needed in this area.

THE WOMAN'S VIETNAM EXPERIENCE

The nature of the Vietnam war and the experiences of men who participated in it have been documented extensively in the past several years. The highly technological weapons, the confusion of who was friend and who was foe, the lack of commitment to a goal in the war, the absence of unit identification caused by the one-year "short-timer's" tour of duty, and the negative homecoming caused by the unpopularity of the war have all been seen as contributing to the difficult post-Vietnam adjustment of Vietnam veterans. But what of the experience of a woman who went to Vietnam to serve her country? What kinds of jobs did she perform? She couldn't have been in combat, could she? Wasn't she living in air-conditioned luxury in a hotel in Saigon, if she was there at all?

In the past few years, the popular press has begun writing some articles about women who served in Vietnam. Most of those articles, however, concentrated on women who served in medical capacities. Women did serve as nurses, physical therapists, occupational therapists, medics, and in other health care roles. Still other women served as air traffic controllers, aerial reconnaissance photographers, intelligence and language specialists, legal officers, security, supply and administrative personnel. Women in these positions were subjected to the same type of stressors as were men in such jobs.

Because fewer of the women who served in non-medical positions have been heard from, this chapter will of necessity focus more closely on those who served as medical personnel. It should, however, be remembered by clinicians that many other kinds of issues or difficulties may be raised by women who served in those other jobs. It should also be remembered that many of the areas which apply to women who served in medical positions will also apply to men who were medical personnel during the war. The issue of dealing with death and injury by combat veterans has been dealt with by Wilson and Krauss in their recent research on predictors for PTSD in combat veterans (see Chapter 8). The results of their study indicate that exposure to injury and death is one of the best predictors for PTSD. However, limited research can be found which addresses the specific effects of war on medical personnel.

The guerrilla nature of the war's activity meant that no location was safe from attack. There were no front lines in the war. Blank (1979) has written, "There were two kinds of zones in Vietnam, combat zones and non-combat zones. Except the only non-combat zones were on some pacification director's map in the Embassy." One could be blown away by the enemy's mortars and rockets in a bunker, an office, a hospital, or an air traffic control tower. American or allied "friendly fire" maimed and killed as effectively as enemy fire. Helicopters and planes were shot down carrying personnel from one assignment to another. As many as one-fifth of American military deaths in Vietnam were from so-called non-hostile causes (Veterans Administration, 1981).

The war with the country and land was not limited to weapons either. Deaths occurred from typhoid, blackwater fever, malaria, cholera, and hepatitis. Snake bites were sometimes described as "one-step" or "two-step," referring to the distance one could go before dying from the poisonous venom. One could be ripped out of a peaceful sleep by tigers, hungry because their other sources of food had been eliminated by the ecological destruction caused by defoliation of the countryside. The chromosomal difference of women from men did not, unfortunately, provide them with an immunity to such things. The female anopheles mosquito showed no concern for sisterhood before biting women to transmit malaria. Nor did the female or male Viet Cong show partiality to women before lobbing mortars into a compound housing men and women Americans. For those who served in medical facilities, it seemed at times that the red cross on the top of the tent or quonset hut served as nothing more than a good target for the enemy to sight in the crosshairs of its weapons.

On a daily basis, the medical personnel in Vietnam and on the hospital ships off the coast dealt with an unending stream of the bits and pieces of people coming across the tables to be put back together. This kind of stressor could be overwhelming at times. The medevac system in Vietnam was the most highly developed in history. As a result, many casualties could be at a medical station within minutes of being wounded. This same system could bring hundreds of casualties to the facility within hours. Wounds which would have been fatal on the battlefield in previous wars arrived continually. Multiple traumatic amputations, massive abdominal wounds, chest wounds, spinal injuries, disfiguring head and facial wounds, and overwhelming burns were the order of the day.

Because of the maximal casualty load and the minimal supplies, personnel and time, often the triage (sorting) process required deciding who would live and who would die. Making those kinds of choices could create tremendous guilt in the responsible individual, compounding the problem.

Medical personnel, women and men alike, worked long hours under sleep deprivation conditions, sometimes going for days on end without rest. At times, the onslaught of death and destruction would seem unending, and when the influx of fresh casualties slowed, the patients still required care for long periods. Getting the patient through surgery was no guarantee of survival, and death was their constant companion.

The stress of dealing with heavy casualties was not limited to those who served in Vietnam itself. Medical and surgical assignments to Japan, Guam, the Philippines, and even stateside hospitals during the war meant long battles with the injuries of the young combat soldiers. Ronald Glasser's excellent book *365 Days* (1971), recounting his tour of duty as a physician at an American military hospital in Japan, gives a graphic illustration of the difficulties of dealing with the wounded who were evacuated from facilities in Vietnam. Many of the GIs were already addicted to narcotics prescribed in the hospitals in Vietnam, and they could be terribly abusive to medical staff who were trying to wean them from the drugs. While the medical staff in Vietnam had to deal with the wounded for days or weeks after their injuries, the personnel in hospitals outside of Vietnam cared for the soldiers for months on end, doing the tedious reconstruction work which could not be done in Vietnam. Nurses, doctors, and medics in the burn units experienced daily the havoc of war wreaked upon the massively injured burn victims, sometimes for years. The memories they retain are often of infected, bug-ridden, legless, armless, faceless wonders of medical technology.

How could I forget you? The faces you had and the faces you didn't have. Some of you came back so many times to haunt me with your faces blown off. And for some of you there was so little we could do for you. We gave you more skin grafts when what you needed was a whole new face. The despair and hopelessness I felt, I saw in your face and I saw in your eyes. I remember changing your dressings and the roaches that came crawling out of the wounds of your stumps. The roaches were eating you alive and you didn't know it. I tried to hide the roaches from you and stop from vomiting and still provide you with nursing care all at the same time. Yes, those were difficult days, for me too. And I remember your screams when they had to amputate your legs. I had compassion for you and cared about your recovery. I held your hand then, too. After the surgery was over, I cleaned the blood up in the Operating Room and then had to carry your amputated leg to the laboratory and prepare the room quickly for the next case, all day and sometimes all night. There were so many of you. There were days when I felt haunted from the constant stress of taking care of so many of you. Don't tell me women don't know anything about war because we weren't out on the "front lines." I had battle fatigue, too. From those grueling years in surgery; it was a war zone there, believe me. There were days when the stress and strain and blood and guts almost had to equal what you experience. (Marron, 1982)

THE HOMECOMING

Coming home from the war is a theme which has been repeatedly discussed in the literature on Vietnam veterans. Figley & Leventman (1980) especially addressed this aspect of the veteran's experience. For many veterans, the culture shock of arrival in Vietnam was comparable only to the culture shock upon returning home.

When I got out of the Army four years ago, I came home with some of the same problems you did. Alcohol, antisocial behavior, and isolation from family and friends. I had a hard time holding

down a job, too. I also had to change occupations—I couldn't go
back to surgery. Like you I was misunderstood by society, too. No
one took my military service seriously either because I was a
woman. So in one way it was easier for me than for you to quietly
hide out when I got home. Then a year ago I came down with a
severe depression and anxiety and was hospitalized. I was exhausted and suffered fatigue—and I still never talked about my
experiences in the military. . . . The scars are still there and they're
deep. (Marron, 1982)

Thoughts of home, "back in the world," as it was called by most,
were probably the most prevalent mental images for those who served
in Vietnam. The plaintive lyrics of "The Green, Green Grass of Home"
could be heard from firebase to landing zone to hospital to supply hut.
Gustavo Martinez (1983) has said that the psychological expectations
before coming home helped the veteran to survive the war experience.
Where the war created disequilibrium within the individual, dreams of
friends, family, football, and Saturdays at the park helped restore the
balance.

Coming home from the war turned out to be a devastating experience,
however, for many Vietnam veterans. Much has been written in the
popular and professional press about the negative reception accorded
the returning soldier. Americans on both sides of the controversy about
the war found in the veteran an available scapegoat upon which to vent
their anger at the war. The veterans "were viewed by many as suspect,
tainted, dangerous, undisciplined, inferior" (Figley & Leventman, 1980).

Vietnam veterans found themsevles *persona non grata* on the campuses,
in the job market, at the Veterans Administration facilities, even in the
local posts of many veteran's organizations. They frequently heard from
their older comrades, the veterans of earlier wars, "You lost your war."
The media particularly portrayed the Vietnam veteran as an unstable,
drug-crazed killer, a walking time bomb ready to explode upon the
slightest provocation.

It would not be surprising, then, to note that the returning veteran
was stopped short by this reaction. There was an immediate shattering
of those psychological expectations that Martinez spoke of, and it was
difficult for the veteran to regain equilibrium. Many found their veteran
status a stigma rather than a source of pride. Few joined the traditional
veterans organizations. Many looked upon the Veterans Administration
and other government agencies with suspicion and mistrust. The inadequate GI bill and hostility on the campuses made it difficult for the
veteran to return to school.

For the returning woman veteran, that disequilibrium also continued. She not only faced those general accusations heaped upon many of the men, but also her moral virtue was called into question. Many were called prostitutes or lesbians. Some of the traditional veterans organizations would not permit women to be full members, succumbing only recently to court decisions requiring women veterans to be allowed to join. To be shunned by society was bad; to be shunned by fellow veterans added insult to injury. More than half of the women in the Schnaier (1982) study felt stigmatized for being a Vietnam veteran who is a woman.

The year after Vietnam appears to have been difficult in many ways for the women. Of those sampled in the Schnaier (1982) study, almost 60 percent experienced emotional numbing during the first year. More than half felt hyperalertness, and were easily startled. Nearly 45 percent experienced flashbacks and intrusive thoughts of war experiences. A significant number felt cynical and mistrustful of government and authority. Many felt confusion in their value systems and felt ideological changes. Over a third had difficulty in establishing or maintaining intimate relationships. Many could not talk about their war experiences.

Women had difficulty getting medical care and other benefits from the Veterans Administration, according to the GAO report (1982). This certainly did not serve to increase the ability of the women to trust government agencies. The college campuses weren't a much more friendly location for women than for men veterans. According to one woman, "I was back in the U.S. one year when the Army sent me to the University of Pennsylvania for my bachelor of science degree in nursing. I didn't dare wear my uniform or tell people that I was an Army nurse or that I had served in Vietnam. My professors were taking digs at the military establishment. It was a time of campus unrest and the war was unpopular. Coming home and going into a school situation right away was one of the hardest things about being in Vietnam" (Shellabarger, 1981).

One area which might have been easier for women who were medical professionals in Vietnam was that of employment after returning from the war. Most of them had a good career to return to, and many have said that they plunged right into heavy intensive care types of medicine. For others, like the writer of the letter at the beginning of this section, it was more difficult to do that. Some felt so exhausted by the war and all the death and dying, that they simply couldn't continue in their previous specialties. Not enough is known about the women who served in other capacities to indicate what their employment experiences might have been after returning home. This is an area which bears examining.

Many women have indicated that they just felt generally very different from their old selves and from their families and friends when they returned. Most had been in positions of responsibility in Vietnam. There was great intensity in their work and friendships. When they returned home, there was something of a letdown. One day they were making life and death decisions in a war zone, the next day they were hearing "a neighbor complaining how all the guppies in the fish tank were dying" (McGinley-Schneider, 1981). Another woman said, "We'd been living and breathing the war and it was a shock to come home and find out that life went on. . . The newspapers weren't filled with war news. There were the comics and Miss America as usual" (Balsley, 1981).

THERAPEUTIC ISSUES

The Best Act in Pleiku, No One Under 18 Admitted

I kissed a Negro, trying to breathe life back into him.
When I was a child—back in the world—
the drinking fountains said, "White Only."
His cold mouth tasted of dirt and marijuana.
He died and I put away the things of a child.

Once upon a time there was a handsome, blonde soldier.
I grabbed at flesh
combing out bits of shrapnel and bits of bone
with bare fingers.

A virgin undressed men, touched them,
raped them in public.
By the time I bedded a man
who didn't smell like mud and burned flesh
He made love and I made jokes.

Sharon M. Grant, 1Lt., A.N.C., Ret.

Little has been studied or written about treatment issues for the women who served. The only information which is available at this time is anecdotal information from women whom this author has counseled or corresponded with, as well as the research information in the Schnaier

(1982) study. In addition, this author has gained anecdotal information from some of the few professionals who have treated women. Finally, some of the women are beginning to write about their own experiences. Several issues seem to be repeated by the women.

The primary issue for most of the women from whom we have heard at the Vietnam Veterans of America (VVA) Women Veterans Project is the memories they must live with of the brutally maimed casualties they cared for. They often write or speak of particular soldiers or Vietnamese civilians they treated, and who recur in memories and dreams frequently. They talk of the tears they never shed during the war. Some speak of inability to cry or express emotion still today, while others speak of an inability to stop crying now. There is often an expression of a sense of lost youth or innocence. They write of their inability to find anything in life now which matches the intensity of the experience then. They talk of anger and rages which frighten them and their families. There are depressions, sometimes repeated over the years. They speak of feeling numb, alone, isolated and anxious. Some report sleep disturbances, insomnia, nightmares. For most, there seems to be a sense of unfinished business about Vietnam. And for many there is amnesia for much of their experiences in the war.

Often, they express a fear of and difficulty with asking for help. The fear is for their professional reputations if anyone finds out that they have problems arising from the war experience. The difficulty is that many of them have always perceived of themselves as helpers and caregivers, and they have trouble with asking for help for themselves. Often, in the experience of counselors who have dealt with these women, they have a tendency to become the helper, even in a therapeutic situation as a client. Those who were medical professionals often have high levels of denial, saying Vietnam did not do anything to them, but being on the verge of tears all the while they are saying so.

The women have spoken of the fear for their lives that they had to suppress during rocket attacks, because they had to shield their patients. Many had close friends who were injured and/or killed, and they felt they could not grieve for them because so many others still remained to be cared for. Some of them ignored their own safety completely in order to protect patients, and now find themselves fearful of simple everyday activities like driving on a freeway.

For most of them, the Vietnam experience was an overwhelming culture shock. The terrain, the heat, the rains, the insects, the association with people of different races, colors and eye shapes, and the incredible destruction being wreaked around them continuously combined to create confusion, physical and emotional exhaustion, and enormous internal changes over a very short period of time.

They speak of the intense closeness established with friends they made there, but ironically, there often could be a distancing element to those friendships. Always, there was the awareness that the friends would not be around for long, whether they were transferred, killed, wounded, or simply went "back to the world" at the end of their one year tour of duty. As one woman wrote, "I remember spending a year closely with people—people who I grew closer to than anyone before or since. I learned to buffer my closeness to people, to appreciate them, but never depend upon or grow close to them—because one thing I do remember is that they disappeared from my life—some physically—some only emotionally and it all hurt—constantly saying good-bye—sometimes just as they boarded a chopper on the long way to home—and sometimes as their vacant eyes stared up at me as I zipped up the last few inches of that rubber bag" (confidential personal communication, 1982). Many of these women say that they still feel they are doing the "approach-avoidance rag" with friends and family. They speak of being afraid to trust people, of feeling that nothing is forever, and that anything can be gone in an instant.

> I went home to a lonely apartment and started drinking to kill the pain I had in caring for you. That hurt me even more. After awhile I didn't feel anything and fooled myself and thought I was coping better. But the alcohol was slowly taking its deadly toll on me. (Marron, 1982)

There has been little reported in the area of drug or alcohol abuse. What has been said by those who speak of it, however, is that they hid it carefully, and would have denied it had they been asked. Again, they have fear of their professional lives being damaged by revealing such information, and they fear the stigma of being an alcoholic or a drug abuser. Some say they use it to help them sleep or to ward off nightmares. Some are afraid to admit it even to themselves. There is a serious lack of good data in this area, and it needs to be studied carefully.

Some of the women have reported that their first sexual experiences occurred in Vietnam. This raises a significant question. What might be the long-range effects upon a person whose early sexual experiences have occurred under such traumatic conditions? It might be thought that the early sexual experiences of the young men serving in Vietnam also occurred during the war. Yet there does not seem to be any literature which addresses this issue. Sarah Haley, however, in personal communication, has reported on one male Vietnam veteran client who continues to experience ejaculatory dysfunction following his Vietnam experience.

In this case, the veteran and another soldier were in the same room with prostitutes when a rocket attack began. A rocket landed on the hootch just as the veteran was reaching climax, and both his friend and the second prostitute were killed immediately. The veteran and his prostitute were uninjured. His present orgasmic dysfunction takes the form of increasing anxiety as he approaches climax, frequently diving for cover at the point of ejaculation. This has the further effect of anticipatory performance anxiety, with intermittent episodes of impotence (Haley, 1983).

Is it not likely that the horror surrounding such early sexual experiences would have an impact on the individual's eventual adjustment as a human being and as a sexual being? The psychic numbing which has generally been recognized as an outcome of the war experience would seem to translate to sexual numbing as well. The last lines of the poem at the beginning of this section illustrate this idea.

> By the time I bedded a man
> who didn't smell like mud and burned flesh
> He made love and I made jokes.

It would seem that along with this psychic/sexual numbing and the associated loss of ability to achieve intimacy in a relationship would be the loss of the ability for powerful sexual exchanges. One woman described the experience of making love during a rocket attack, just after returning from doing surgery on a long stretch of casualties, as "Kafkaesque."

The dichotomy is that while trying to exclude emotion and fear during the attacks and firefights around them, they had to maintain an external attitude of giving and caring to the wounded—to such a degree that many of them express the feeling now that they were, at that time, "about 'given' out." They write of a need to reconnect with their own and another's humanity in the midst of the insanity of the war. At the same time, there was also a distancing to that connection, just as there often was in other friendships during the war.

Because of regulations prohibiting "fraternizing" between officers and enlisted personnel, frequently the only man with whom a woman officer in Vietnam could associate was a married doctor or pilot. She always had in the back of her mind that the man would return to his wife soon. In addition, it was always possible that a pilot could be shot down and wounded or killed. Some women ignored the regulations about not associating with enlisted men, but for them there was the additional fear of being discovered and facing punishment for disobeying the regulations. There was confusion and anger for some, coupled with the overriding need to be close to someone "who didn't smell like mud and burned flesh." Considering all of this, it would not be surprising to find that some women might have difficulty expressing genuine emotion and sexuality without feeling numbing and fear.

> I was always afraid
> before,
> that when I pulled down the covers
> all I would see was
> gaping holes
> and blood.
> And I never
> pulled someone's hair
> for fear it would be in my hand,
> with the scalp and skull attached.
>
> Now I explore your body
> telling you that I'm counting the hairs
> but really,
> I'm caressing the curves and dents
> and softness,
> Proving to myself
> that the horror isn't there. . .
> on your body
> under the covers.

Norma J. Griffiths, Cpt., A.N.C., Ret.

Some women have reported varying levels of sexual dysfunction in their present lives, sometimes having no interest in sex at all, sometimes having intense interest in the beginning of a relationship but finding that interest dwindling to practically nothing in a short time, even if the relationship continued. However, many of the women have not reported such difficulties. All of these reports must be seen as anecdotal in nature, and this discussion should not be construed to be suggestive of valid evidence of sexual difficulties in women who served in the war. It is, however, an important area which bears consideration by clinicians and researchers.

> The Army trained me well for the surgical team to help take care of your war-torn bodies, but they didn't train me for that "other war." The one we had. When you turned on me. You turned on me with your unrelenting sexual harassment and assaults. You battered me. I met you on Army post after Army post. Some of you were black and some of you were white but you were all male. Maybe you were frustrated from the war or maybe the Army trained you that way, I don't know. There were days when I felt terrorized by the psychological warfare going on between us. Then there was the added unrelenting stress of working in surgery all those long days and nights. I'm still damaged. The Army never recognized that war either. I felt trapped. I tried to ignore the harassment and hoped you'd leave me alone. I felt so powerless to cope with being a woman in a man's army. There was nowhere to turn for help with a male chain of command. I tried, though. . . I thought if I worked hard, you'd stop your harassment. The Army never trained me to fight back either—only to save your life. So I was at a terrible disadvantage and not prepared for your ruthless attacks. I was stunned and felt helpless. I was devastated. I drank more. I isolated myself. My problems got worse. (Marron, 1982)

A few women have reported sexual harassment and assaults which occurred during their service. Some of these women say that it killed all interest in sex for them. Some of them have said that they remain very angry about the attacks, but have attempted to overcome the anger and establish new relationships. A few women have reported that they now avoid relationships with men altogether. Some have since opted for homosexual relationships. It would seem that the closest analogy here would be with rape victims, since the nature of the experiences are similar. It is important to note that the majority of women have not spoken of such harassment. Many of the women, especially those who were medical officers, have said that they always perceived respect from the men. But for enlisted women especially, sexual harassment may be an issue which should be explored in a therapeutic setting.

There may be problems for some women in the area of gender identity. After spending at least a year in fatigues and combat boots, in a combat situation, surrounded mostly by men, it would not be surprising to note that it may have been difficult for some women to feel "feminine." Many of the characteristics they have of strength and survival and competence are seen in our society as "masculine." Integrating those things with the female side of themselves may be an issue.

Some women have said that they feel a stigma about being a female veteran. They have been accused of going into the military only because they were prostitutes or they were lesbians or they were looking for a husband. They may have felt that their whole contribution in Vietnam or in the military was reduced to an identity which was based on their sexuality. There is a feeling expressed by some that they are unrecognized, uncredited, and disrespected.

A few women have sought counseling. Some have gone to the Veterans Administration's Operation Outreach Vet Centers, some to private therapists. In private therapy situations, often the counselor never asked about the possibility of traumatic experiences such as the war, and many of the women did not volunteer that information, feeling that, "It was so long ago, it can't be Vietnam that's making me feel like this." In Vet Centers, sometimes they got help and sometimes not. If the counselors were aware of and sensitive to women who served, then the women might get help. Sometimes they went into Vet Centers with the excuse that they wanted to help, when they really needed it themselves. If that happened, they could end up worse than when they went in because they took on even more pain of other veterans before having resolved their own. In some Vet Centers, the counselors just didn't have an awareness of women. According to the GAO report, ". . . vet centers vary in their awareness of female veterans' needs . . ." and ". . . female veterans still encounter negative reactions from some V.A. staff and veterans" (1982).

Reports have been made in the past few years of male Vietnam veterans experiencing Post-Traumatic Stress Disorder (PTSD) who were misdiagnosed earlier as schizophrenic, borderline personalities, paranoid personalities, etc. (Van Putten & Emory, 1973; Goodwin, 1980; Nash & Walker, 1981). Some women who have sought counseling for symptoms of PTSD have also been subjected to misdiagnosis and mistreatment. They have been labeled neurotic, depressive, and worse. One woman, diagnosed by the military and the V.A. as "schizophrenic, schizo-affective type, considerable," was subjected to several years in and out of psychiatric institutions. She was treated approximately 45 times with electro-convulsive therapy (ECT), maintained on psychotropic and antidepressant drugs, and barely survived several suicide attempts which required her being in Intensive Care on respirators for considerable periods. In the clinical record of her psychiatric evaluation by the military, there is noted only that she had four years active duty.

There is notation of her Vietnam service, yet she had served as a triage nurse for a year in Vietnam. She had never been questioned about her military history, and when she began having depressions, nightmares, and flashbacks, no one asked her what she was seeing or hearing or smelling. She was simply hospitalized, medicated, and shocked. This woman has, in recent years, begun to receive counseling by a V.A. therapist familiar with PTSD, and a Vet Center counselor. She has improved dramatically, is off all medications, has begun writing about her feelings and experiences in Vietnam and since, and has begun to establish a permanent relationship with a man. Her most troubling feelings now are anger and the inability to remember. The ECT left her with amnesia for significant periods.

Rage and anger are possibly some of the most frequently reported emotions from the women we have been in contact with. For many counselors, this can be difficult to deal with. Women in our society are generally expected to control such emotions, and it can frighten or alienate or distance a therapist who does not expect such fury from a woman. Anger is common with male Vietnam veterans, and therapists have learned to understand and deal with it. The same should hold true for women veterans.

Most of the issues discussed in this section have been symptoms which the therapist familiar with PTSD in male Vietnam veterans will recognize. There may be other things which have not been recognized yet, since so little research has been done on women veterans, but hopefully, more studies will be undertaken in the near and distant future.

COUNSELING AND THERAPEUTIC INTERVENTION

After all these years I'm just now starting to cry. I've cried for days. And I'm starting to feel again. I'm hoping that maybe I'll recover from the emotional trauma I held inside me for so long from all those years of taking care of you and all that abuse that women have to put up with in the Army that seems built into the system.

I recovered from the alcoholism but I desperately need psychiatric care for a full recovery. I tried to get help at the V.A. but they don't have programs for women—and I'm a service-connected veteran too! I'm worried that if I don't get the help I need and soon, I may lose a fine job that I value very much.

After serving in the armed forces for so many years, and helping to save and mend so many lives, now I need help and there is no place for me to go for help. And I am angry.

The V.A. and the American people need to know that women need help, too. We've been silent too long. We count, too, after all, we volunteered our services and took time out of our lives to help save other lives and to serve our country, too. (Marron, 1982)

Judy Marron, the writer of "A Woman Vet Speaks" (1982) quoted just above and throughout this chapter, took her own life by leaping from the Golden Gate Bridge in San Francisco. For her and for other women veterans who have sought suicide, sometimes successfully, sometimes not, the need for counseling can be critical. For many other women, it can improve the quality of their lives and that of their families and friends.

But how does one handle therapeutic intervention with female veterans? Schnaier (1982) has indicated in her research a caution that "mental health professionals [should] not . . . treat or view female Vietnam veterans exactly like male veterans when conducting research or in counseling" (p. 81). Experience of professionals who are trying to do outreach to women veterans, as well as written and verbal communication from the women themselves, indicates that it is very difficult to find them, and even more difficult to get them to talk about their experiences. One woman, interviewed by a reporter for the *Los Angeles Times* (1981), exemplifies this problem.

She has been talking for almost an hour. Still no mention of the horror of what she was seeing in Emergency. How did that affect her?

She recoils from the question flinching, shutting her eyes tightly, shaking her head.

The tears fight through anyhow. She does not give in to them, saying instead, "No. I don't want to talk about that. I can't. I don't ever talk about that."

What are good approaches to assist the female veteran in achieving catharsis? How can the therapist elicit information? Does the therapist teach or interact?

Martinez (1983) has suggested that the female veteran may be analogous to the culturally and ethnically oriented veteran who has difficulty in releasing emotion. There is a need for some minority veterans, particularly Hispanics and Native Americans, to be in control, to be responsible to others and for others, to fulfill obligations to others, and to appear strong. Female veterans seem to exhibit some of these same characteristics.

It should be remembered that the memories of Vietnam and its pain and horrors have been suppressed by these veterans for many years. If and when they seek therapy or counseling, it may be very difficult to get them to talk about the Vietnam experience. Harbert (1983) has noted that a carefully detailed history of the war experiences is essential, though "it may be difficult to elicit because of the veteran's past experiences in trying to talk about it—often with the medical or mental health community. Also they may not connect their current problems with the stress of their war experiences." He also suggests that the history must explore events prior to the Vietnam experience, as well as the homecoming, and events in the intervening years which may affect the veteran now. Obviously, this history is important, but contained within the history are events which have been carefully held in. The therapist should not assume that the woman is going to walk through the door and spill it all in a short time. It will take time for the client to establish enough trust in the therapist to open up.

Using an educational approach may be a way around this problem. During early sessions it may be helpful for the therapist to use some tools such as audiovisual aids, films, books, etc., to open up the subject. This could serve two purposes. First, the feelings which have been suppressed for so long may surface for the client without her being under pressure to bring it up herself. It may help her to disengage from her own experiences in order to encounter feelings about others' experiences. Second, it gives time for the client and therapist to learn something about each other, to begin the process of establishing a trusting relationship. This may work also in a group process; in the beginning when everyone is a bit nervous, no one is placed in the "hot seat." There can be classes on the Vietnam experience, nightmares, flashbacks, etc. What follows in response to the teaching phase would hopefully assist the veterans to begin channeling toward themselves. It may be helpful to have the veteran write about some particular experiences and then discuss what she has written in the therapeutic setting.

Women who have been placed in all-male rap groups have said that they got something out of the group experience. However, most have said that they felt that they needed to have another woman veteran to relate to as well. There has been limited experience with all-female rap groups, notably by therapists Rose Sandecki (1982) and Janet Ott and Julia Stroud (1982). They report very positive outcome to having groups of all women veterans. However, it may be difficult to locate enough women veterans to establish a women's group. It might be suggested that groups of medical personnel who served in Vietnam be tried. Again, many of the experiences of men who served in medical positions may be somewhat similar to those of women who served in those positions.

Harbert (1983) suggests a program of group therapy which covers four main phases:

1) The Vietnam experience itself.
2) Coming home.
3) The individual's relationships with significant others outside the therapeutic group.
4) Plans for the future.

Structuring a program in such a manner allows the clients to progress from the initial pain of the war experience, through the lasting effects of the war on the clients, and on to looking forward. This is only one possibility out of many which can be tried. Most important is to assure that the veteran has the opportunity in a safe and supportive environment to deal with the Vietnam experience and its legacy.

CONCLUSION

Although there is little solid research data available, anecdotal information and counseling experience of some therapists indicates that some women Vietnam veterans may be experiencing lasting mental health effects from the war. Some of these effects may be positive, some negative, but it is important for the caring therapist to recognize that women also served in Vietnam. War is a benchmark experience for anyone, be it man, woman, or child. The individual is left with lasting imprints which remain and need to be sorted out.

This chapter is designed to acquaint the therapist with a population of Vietnam veterans who have generally been missed. Women, too, gave of themselves, gave their lives and limbs, and, as Billy Joel put it, "left their childhood on every acre" (1982). Hopefully, therapists will begin to address the problems of those women for whom the war still rages on.

REFERENCES

Balsley, S., in "Wartime Experiences Change Nurses' Lives," by Smith, Marcia, in *Dallas Times Herald*, Dallas, Texas, January 25, 1981.

Blank, A.S.: 1st Training Conference Papers. Vietnam Veterans—Operation Outreach, U.S. Veterans Administration, St. Louis, Missouri, Sept. 24-28, 1979.

Bourne, P.G. (Ed.): *The psychology and physiology of stress*. New York: Academic Press, 1969.

Bourne, P.G.: *Men, stress and Vietnam*. Boston: Little, Brown, 1970.

Egendorf, A., Kadushin, C., Laufer, R.F., Rothbart, G., & Sloan, L.: *Legacies of Vietnam: Comparative adjustment of veterans and their peers*. Center for Policy Research, Inc. (House Committee Print No. 14). Washington, D.C.: U.S. Government Printing Office, 1981.

Figley, C.R.: *Stress disorders among Vietnam veterans*. New York: Brunner/Mazel, 1978.

Figley, C.R., & Leventman, S.: *Strangers at home: Vietnam veterans since the war*. New York: Praeger Publishers, 1980.

General Accounting Office of the United States Government.: *Actions needed to insure that female veterans have equal access to VA benefits* (GAO/HRD-82-98), September 24, 1982.

Glasser, R.: *365 Days*. New York: Bantam, 1971.

Goodwin, J.: The etiology of combat-related post-traumatic stress disorders. In T. Williams (Ed.), *Post-traumatic stress disorders of the Vietnam veteran*. Cincinnati, OH: Disabled American Veterans, 1980.

Haley, S.: Personal communication, February, 1983.

Harbert, K.: Delayed stress syndromes in Vietnam veterans. *Physician Assistant*, 7(1), 1983.

Hendrix, K.: Women Vietnam vets seeking peace of mind. *Los Angeles Times*, Los Angeles, CA, January 11, 1981.

Joel, B.: Goodnight, Saigon. In *The nylon curtain*. New York: Columbia Records, CBS Inc., 1982.

Marron, J.: A woman veteran speaks. *The Veteran, 12*(4), 1982.

Martinez, G.: Personal communication, January, 1983. Assistant Director for Program Management, Readjustment Counseling Service, U.S. Veterans Administration, Central Office, Washington, D.C.

McGinley-Schneider, C.: Women Vietnam vets seeking peace of mind. *Los Angeles Times*, Los Angeles, CA, January 11, 1981.

Nash, J.L., & Walker, J.I.: Stress disorders in Vietnam Returnees: The problem continues. Case report. *Military Medicine*, 146, August 1981.

Ott, J., & Stroud, J.: Personal communication, 1982. Consulting Counselor, Seattle, Washington Vet Center, VA Readjustment Counseling Service. Private Therapists, Seattle, Washington.

Sandecki, R.: Personal communication, 1982. Team Leader, Concord, California Vet Center, VA Readjustment Counseling Service.

Schnaier, J.A.: Women Vietnam veterans and mental health adjustment: A study of their experiences and post-traumatic stress. Master's Thesis submitted at University of Maryland, College Park, Maryland, 1982. Presented at National Conference on Post-Vietnam Stress Syndrome, Kings Mill, Ohio, October, 1982.

Shellabarger, C.: Wartime experiences change nurses' lives. *Dallas Times Herald*, Dallas, TX, January 25, 1981.

Van Putten, T., & Emory, W.H.: Traumatic neurosis in Vietnam returnees: A forgotten diagnosis? *Archives of General Psychiatry*, 29:695-698, 1973.

Veterans Administration. *Data on Vietnam era veterans*. Office of Controller, Reports and Statistics Service, September, 1981.

Wilson, J.P., & Krauss, G.E.: Predicting post-traumatic stress syndromes among Vietnam veterans. Presented at the 25th Neuropsychiatric Institute, VA Medical Center, Coatesville, PA, October 25, 1982.

The Black Vietnam Veteran: His Representational World in Post-Traumatic Stress Disorders

ERWIN RANDOLPH PARSON, Ph.D.

African-American veterans who served their country in Vietnam and now experience significant emotional turmoil and readjustment conflicts pose an extremely complicated challenge to the clinician. This complexity is due to the interaction of their African heritage and the sociopsychological experience as Black American, in addition to which they are plagued with intrusions of Vietnam. A recent large scale epidemiological research study revealed that 70 percent of Black Vietnam veterans who served in heavy combat suffer from post-traumatic stress disorder (PTSD) today. This study also found that in general 40 percent of Black veterans are stressed compared with 20 percent of the White veterans (Kadushin, Boulanger, & Martin, 1981. This chapter will focus on the inner world of ideas, feelings, and responses of the Black Vietnam warrior who suffers from this disorder.

The bi-cultural nature of Black veterans' identity and the sociopsychic derivatives of racism, as well as their post-Vietnam traumatic states, converge to form the Black veteran's *representational world*. Actually, the Black Vietnam veteran is a product of a conglomeration of social, intrapsychic, interpersonal, experiential, and historico-cultural forces, as well as of the sociopolitical system of the 1960s. This chapter is divided into four parts: 1) Post-Traumatic Stress Disorders: Symptoms and Inner Experience; 2) The Nature of Psychic Representations; 3) Overview of Pertinent Psychotherapy Research; and 4) Treatment Considerations.

POST-TRAUMATIC STRESS DISORDERS: SYMPTOMS AND INNER EXPERIENCE

It is important that clinicians avoid the pitfall of viewing stress disorders as the basic focus of their interventions. The notion that we treat problems, rather than persons with problems, must be strictly avoided in working with any person suffering from psychic trauma. It is always the *person* who is treated. PTSD is a new diagnostic entity for an old problem. It is a *biosomatopsychic* disorder in response to catastrophic events. In DSM-I, published in 1951, the disorder was named "gross stress reaction," and in DSM-II in 1968 the term "transient situational disturbances" was used. Today, in reference to the adverse effects of combat action, this disorder has been variously termed "post-Vietnam syndrome" (Shatan, 1972); "delayed stress reaction" (Figley, 1978); "post-Vietnam traumatic states" (Parson, 1983a); and "post-combat stress response syndrome" (Haley, 1978). In reference to the survivors of the Holocaust, the disorder has been called "post-concentration camp syndrome" (Rosenman, 1956); and "survivor's syndrome" (Krystal, 1968); while in the context of sexual assault the term "rape trauma syndrome" (Forman, 1980) is used. Specific criteria for the PTSD diagnosis in DSM-III are: 1) Existence of a recognizable stressor that would cause distress in anyone; 2) Reexperiencing of the trauma; 3) Numbing of responsiveness; and 4) Other specific symptoms.

The symptoms of PTSD are conceptualized as two basic types of psychological processes. These are: 1) *Automatic incursive phenomena* (Parson, 1983a); and 2) *Reactive numbing of the self*. Automatic incursive experiences often begin as adaptive responses, but later may evolve into maladaptive mental and interpersonal processes involving a variety of cognitive, affective, experiential, and behavioral elements, triggered by internal ideation or environmental stimuli. These incursive elements are repetitive-ruminative ideas, images, and affects that plunge the veteran survivor into a reliving of the original traumatic, inciting event. During *incursive* experiences, the person's on-going conscious awareness is intruded upon by painful memories, frightening nightmares, disquieting and recurrent dream phenomena. *Autonomic physiological reactions* (e.g., the "startle response") represent somatically-programmed intrusions. These intrusive-repetitive experiences force the survivor into passivity, and link him in an almost helpless manner to the original trauma (Parson, 1983a). Attendant hyperalertness and somatic problems, as well as attending and concentration deficits, are aspects of the symptomatic picture of traumatized individuals.

Memory Function in Traumatic States

In trauma, the ego works to reactivate or *actualize* the "buried" traumatic memories and associated ideas and affects as an essential part of "working through" the traumatic experience. Memory formation and function are central elements in traumatic reactions to stressful experiences. In what this author has referred to as the *dilemma of memory*, the survivor persists in a paradoxically painful psychic situation: He is doomed to repeat symptomatically what he would rather *forget*, on the one hand, and he is doomed to reexperience the strong emotions that accompany these memories, if he chooses to *remember*, on the other.

Problematic memory functions in traumatic states are due to poorly structured registration (of the event). Inadequate structuring of memory traces occurs when the stressful event happened so suddenly, or produced such chronic strain, that adequate, well-structured registrations were unattainable. Lipin (1963) refers to poorly structured registration (of the traumatic event) as "replica productions," and believes (as do Freud and others) that their repetitive nature attempts to master the "unbridled" affects and tension states which originally attended these painful memories. Inadequately structured memory traces may reach fuller organization through the repetitiveness of intrusive ideas and emotions. Regressive techniques (Brende, 1983; Parson, 1983a) often restore these traces, thus bringing painful events into greater awareness and movement toward resolution.

Reactive Numbing of the Self

This set of symptoms derive from psychic, interpersonal and somatic reactions to the inner subjective experience of intense, *deregulated* anxiety over a sense of vulnerability to anticipated incursions of troublesome ideas and affects. Thus, *reactive numbing* represents an array of defenses to protect the survivor against guilt, depression, and anxiety. However, due to their deregulated nature, they are regressive, primitive, and hence, ineffectual. This set of symptoms is a defense against reactivation of latent intrusive phenomena. They ward off the ravages of anxiety, fear, and tension states precipitated by recurrent, intrusive ideas and affects.

Symptoms of *reactive numbing* affect psychic, interpersonal, and experiential aspects of the self. They also afflict the bodily self, and the biosomatopsychic problem of insomnia which is a cardinal defensive system against reactivation and intrusion. These symptoms of defensive numbing involve an interpersonal retreat into an isolationist adaptation, and so represent regression in levels of object relations. The consequences of this regression in object relations are observed in the survivor's immature, passive-receptive interpersonal style, irritability, and relative incapacity to fully benefit from interpersonal relationships. This often sets up a rather difficult paradox in that human contacts normally alleviate such symptoms; however, such contacts are now avoided ("interpersonal contact dilemma") by the veteran-survivor.

Generally the inner experience in the PTSD state is marked by a sense of internal crumbling, deadness, chaos, existential malaise and pain, fragmentation, perpetual *Sturm und Drang*, self-strangeness and self-dullness, passivity, hopelessness, powerlessness, and incapacity in dealing with either intrusion or numbing, panic and loss of control (Parson, 1983b).

THE NATURE OF PSYCHIC REPRESENTATIONS

Defining "Representational World"

The human psyche evolves primarily through the infant and young child's interaction with people, beginning with primary human caretakers (i.e., mother, father, siblings, and close relatives, or surrogates), and later with the larger world of persons. During the course of development, the "primal psychophysiological self" (Jacobson, 1964) of the infant and later young child is subjected to a universe of diverse impressions that are organized by the young ego into *representations*. The term "representation" refers to "an enduring schema" (Moore and Fine, 1968), which for Klein (1976) is an active organization of past experiences which always operates in any behavior or response.

Prior to Jacobson's (1964) use of the concept of "representation," it was widely held in psychoanalysis that severely disturbed patients (especially persons with schizophrenia) were unable to form (therapeutically necessary) transferences to their therapists, making them unlikely candidates not only for psychoanalysis, but also for successful psychotherapy. Thus, Jacobson's new concept of "representation" provided a novel and useful paradigmatic shift in that narcissism could now be understood as the libidinal cathexis not of the ego itself, but of a property of the ego—namely, the mental representations regarding the self ("self-representation"). This formulation made it possible to now understand schizophrenic persons as capable of forming transferences since the entire ego was not totally "swallowed up" in regression, but was capable of responding to reality.

As a repository of impressions and images structured by one's interaction with self and world (especially the world of people), mental representations go beyond mere replication of actual external events; they form the basis for an inner world of *private experience,* of *private meaning.* Jacobson points out that the concept of representation distinguishes self and other *as experienced* from self and other *in reality* (Blanck & Blanck, 1974). Along these lines, Triana (1983) states that representations "succinctly defined. . . " refer to "the symbolic evocation of absent realities" (p. 8), which promote inner personal realities and personal experience. This means, essentially, that inner experience of the self is private and personal and may thus differ from externally-constructed evaluations and judgments of the object world.

Psychic representations are composed, moreover, of control and affective components at varying developmental levels—ranging from simple, concrete, primitive, id-laden ones to more mature, differentiated and complex ones typical of symbolic thought (Fraiberg, 1969). They involve unconscious, preconscious, and conscious motivations that may vary from time to time, under the sway of differing internal and external challenges and conflicts. They are thus variable in their organization and control functions, as well as in their distortion and realistic aspects. Geller, Behrends, and Hartley (1982) write that:

> Mental representations, whether concrete or abstract, have great variability with regard to their ease of evocation, affective tone, the sensory modalities which they call into play, and the vividness, intensity, and duration with which they are experienced. Some representations are experienced spontaneously, as if one is merely a spectator of the event rather than its author. Others are actively evoked and are therefore felt to be intentional or purposeful. . . .

Individuals can use or react to mental representations with or without the conscious experience of their meaning or experience. (p. 124)

In his "phenomenology of self-experience," Klein (1976) notes that experience becomes recorded in a cognitive schema which reconstructs human inner events and serves the purpose of regulating inner process. The "representational world" (Sandler & Rosenblatt, 1962), then, refers to the subjective universe of inner impressions and images that underlie and motivate all meaningful behavior.

The representational world is articulated during the course of psychological, biological, and ethnocultural development and adaptation. The person's attitudes, perceptions, values, etc. are organized in terms of representations, which, as structures of enduring schema, regulate conscious and unconscious experience, and shape adaptation.

Self-Representations and Object-Representations

The "representational world" is comprised of a galaxy of impressions and images that had been constructed during the course of personal development in relation to the world of human beings and life-events. These images are organized internally into two distinct (though related) classes of representations: *self-representations* and *object-representations*. Self-representations are structured internal patterns of ideas and affects about one's self and about one's self interacting with others. Moore and Fine (1968) view self-representation as a structure which

includes enduring representations of all the experienced bodily states, all the experienced drives and affects which the *individual has consciously perceived in himself* at different times *in reaction to himself and to the outer world.* Together with object representations it provides the material for all the ego's adaptive and defensive functions. (p. 88, *italics added*)

Object-representations refer to enduring internal patterns of ideas and affects about one's total experience of other persons in the external environment, beginning in infancy and proceeding through the various stages of the life cycle. Like self-representations,

Object representations are an evolving developmental process. New levels of object representation are achieved as the result of a consolidation . . . of each developmental sequence. . . . At each

of these levels object representations become less literal and direct
and more abstract and symbolic. Impairments in the development
of object representation can occur at each of these levels, and each
can have an important role in the potential vulnerability (to psychopathology). (p. 151)

Black Self- and Object-Representations

The biological birth and psychological birth of the human infant do
not occur at the same moment (Mahler, Pine & Bergman, 1975). Psychological birth occurs relatively slowly, and its unfolding involves gradual intrapsychic and biogenetic shifts in the context of a total human
relationship (within the *infant-mother matrix*). The psyche of the Black
infant and child develops along the same basic *developmental lines* (Anna
Freud, 1963) as in most White children. Like the White infant, the Black
infant acquires self-images in accordance with pleasurable and unpleasurable experiences with the maternal one (the "primary environment"),
concomitantly with the acquisition of object-images (i.e., psychological
impressions of the infant's interaction with persons in the environment,
primarily the mother).

During the first three months of life, the Black infant lives an *autistic*,
somatopsychic existence. However, as the infant's "primal psychophysiological self" (Jacobson, 1964) matures with the aid of a competent
"mother holding the situation," facilitated by her own psychobiologic
state of *primary maternal preoccupation* (Winnicott, 1975), the infant's
evolving psychological birth ushers in the second phase of mental development called *symbiosis* (Mahler, 1968), beginning around the third
month of life. In this phase, the mother is now cathected as self and
object images are fused. It's a time, additionally, when psyche and soma,
inside and outside, drive and object, or self and other are undifferen-
tiated, and the mother allows her infant the opportunity for *illusion*.
Illusion, according to Winnicott (1975), develops by the mother's providing "something more or less in the right place and at the right time"
(p. 223). "Memory islands" (Mahler & Gosliner, 1955) become slowly
established, and a dim awareness that needs are being gratified by a
person outside the young child begins around this time as well.

Engrams of "good" and "bad" experiences are established early in the
infant; maturational trends emerge, memory traces activate self and object images (which later become representations) in the context of loving
(pleasurable) and frustrating (unpleasurable) experiences with others.
The infant-mother mutuality or fit need not be perfect; however, ade-

quate mental development and social competency do depend on at least "good-enough" mothering (Winnicott, 1953) that provides a *facilitating environment* and promotes the unfolding of the child's innate *biosociopsychic* development. The young psyche "represents" internally its experience with primary caretakers.

Assuming the *infant-environment matrix* had been sustaining and confirming of the infant's being by the mother's "almost 100 percent adaptation" (Winnicott, 1975), the *differentiation* phase begins. During this phase of development, self- and object-images begin to differentiate; and, as a crucial developmental achievement, along with the differentiation of the body image, differentiation is a product of optimal emotional symbiotic nurturance. Again, like any other child, the Black child is capable of making accommodations for the non-perfect adaptational shortcomings of the mothering one (or surrogate), especially if she is "good-enough." Winnicott (1971) writes,

> *The ordinary good mother is good enough.* If she is good enough the infant becomes able to allow for her deficiencies by mental activity . . . The mental activity of the infant turns a good enough environment into a perfect environment . . . turns relative failures of adaptation into adaptive success. What relieves the mother from her need to be near-perfect is the infant's understanding. (p. 245)

The next phase of the *separation-individuation* process, as discussed by Mahler, et. al. (1975), is the *practicing* phase, marked by intense self-interest, pride, and self-absorption in mastering his new found reality of increased upright physical autonomy, motor development, visual acuity, and emerging capacity to regulate his bodily self in space. Thus, upright locomotion, increased perception and the "love affair with the world" (Greenacre, 1957) brings the Black child into full contact with the world of colors, people, and things. By 12 to 15 months, the Black child, like any other child, is able to discriminate among many colors (Staples, 1933), to include his own skin color, his mother's, and the skin color of other persons. From 18 to 24 months, the period Mahler calls "rapprochement," the young child expresses ambivalent feelings devolving on concerns of proximity and distance from his mother. Unlike the practicing child, the rapprochement child is fearful of separation and anxious over losing the mother. It is noteworthy that at each developmental phase, the Black child may be vulnerable to the ill effects of poverty, malnutrition, and other untoward effects of racism.

It is this author's opinion that the practicing and rapprochement phases mark the emergence of the Black child's *cultural representational world*, with fairly well differentiated self- and object-representations. By 36 months, the Black child is fully aware of his skin color and its cultural, social, and psychological meanings. As Kenneth Clark (1963) amply demonstrated in his famous race identity research project, all children learn social, racial, and religious attitudes and prejudices from a very young age. They also ". . . learn, first, what color they are and, secondly, what color is best."

Marjorie McDonald (1970) has conducted an excellent study, integrating psychoanalytic and social psychological principles to describe the complex processes in the establishment of ego identity in young children in the context of skin color. She presents three-, four-, and five-year-olds of African-American, Indian, Oriental, and Caucasian cultures, and discusses their reactions to skin color and their "skin color anxiety." The shaping of the Black child's representational world integrates aspects of his social environment, which shapes his identity. Black self- and object-representations, then, are *bi-cultural* in nature—that is, they are composed of both African cultural elements *and* Euro-American cultural elements. The implications of a bi-cultural psychic orientation and the implied strain on the Black child's ego and synthetic functions have tremendous implications for healthy adaptation and psychopathological accommodations in Black Americans.

PROPERTIES OF BLACK SELF-IDENTITY

African and White American values often clash intrapsychically. This basic incompatibility creates a different and unique set of ego challenges and psychological syntheses, which pressure the integrative functions of the ego into pulling together a composite whole (identity) that offers ontogenetic continuity and inner stability. The incompatible nature of African and White American psychic structures produces an identity and representational world that is qualitatively different than either 1) African, 2) American alone, or 3) in situations in which the bi-cultural elements happen to be compatible or congruent. The following Table portrays the essential differences in African and White American cultures.

The integrative task of bringing these basically inconsonant psychic elements and values into an harmonious, well-functioning, and sustaining identity system is extremely difficult, but with good early experiences in a protective family system (to include extended and adopted

TABLE 1
Black American Bi-Cultural Value System

African Culture	Euro-American Culture
1. TIME PERSPECTIVES	
Circular; emphasis on the past (*Zannini*) and present (*Sasa*)	Linear; emphasis on distant *future*; planning
2. CONCEPT OF SELF	
Psychological, physical, social, and spiritual well-being are dependent on the *community*; affiliation; unity	Psychological, physical, social, and spiritual well-being are dependent upon the *individual*; self-reliance; independence
3. OWNERSHIP	
Possession belongs to community; sociocentric; focus is on the *non-material*	Possession belongs to the individual; individuo-centric; focus on the *material*
4. AUTHORITY	
Obedience to authority; respect for the aged—indispensable to the young	Question and challenge authority; the aged is dispensable
5. CHILD REARING	
Depend on extended family—kinship	Socialization based primarily in the early years on the parents, especially the mother

family members), integration of both African and American elements may result in a flexible self-identity, and may conceivably facilitate dialectical ego states. Thus, such flexibility may make it possible for the Black person to transcend social and economic oppression, while being enabled to move with relative freedom between inner and outer reality, between drive and object, between primary- and secondary-process thinking, and generally among id, ego, and superego derivatives. It is this author's belief that these ego-discordant elements may produce significant ego strength in Black Americans, providing the family has succeeded in adequately protecting and sustaining the young evolving self from the ill effects of racism and its many derivatives (poverty, malnutrition, self-hate, etc.).

In addition to *bi-culturality*, the Black psyche has to contend with the vicissitudes of racism. Racism produces what Elaine Pinderhughes (1982) has referred to as the "Victim System." She describes the victim system as one that

> threatens self-esteem and reinforces problematic responses in communities, families, and individuals. (The *victim system*) works as follows: Barriers to opportunity and education limit the chance for achievement, employment, and attainment of skills. This limitation

can, in turn, lead to poverty or stress in relationships, which interferes with adequate performance of family roles. Strains in family
roles cause problems in individual growth and development and
limit the opportunity of families to meet their own needs or to
organize to improve their communities. Communities limited in
resources (jobs, education, housing, etc.) are unable to support
families properly, and the community all too often becomes itself
an active disorganizing influence, a breeder of crime, and a source
of even more powerlessness. (p. 109)

The influence of the victim system upon the Black person's psychological
development is probably potentially more detrimental to his well-being
than the bi-cultural strain sustained by the ego in establishing the identity system. The Black person's representational world, then, is comprised of self- and object-representations organized around: 1) The
Individual Mode (ontogenetic experiences); 2) The African Mode; 3) The
Euro-American Mode; and 4) The Survivor Mode. The "Survivor Mode"
describes the personal, social, and existential plight of many Black
Americans whose struggles are geared toward overcoming the victim
system by *outliving* it through surviving. To maintain *survivor functioning*
requires a great quantum of mental energy. Hiding one's true feelings
from others by a non-self-disclosing personal policy, and maintaining
a "pan-suspicious attitude" (Parson, 1984a) toward the world, are all
aspects of the Black Survivor Mode.

   In addition to stress-related symptomatology from Vietnam, like most
Americans of African heritage, the Black Vietnam veteran has adopted
the Survivor Mode from a very young age, in order to overcome the
forces that make him "believe that white is good, that black is bad; that
white is strong, that black is weak; that white is intelligent, that black
is stupid; that white is moral, that black is immoral; that white is beautiful, that black is ugly . . ." (Comer, 1972, p. 140). These images of the
Survivor Mode represent an integral part of the self- and object-representations of Black Americans. The Black representational world appears
to have been disproportionately influenced by the Survivor Mode (compared to African and Euro-American Modes), whose negative, and destructive images are propagated by social science, as the following
exemplifies (Parson, 1975, p. 6):

   Thus, so-called "scientific" literature portrays the Black person as
   hopelessly suffering from the indelible "mark of oppression,"
   short-sightedness, severe psychopathology, and cultural deprivation (Kardiner and Ovesey, 1951); as belonging to a "culture of

poverty" that creates in Blacks a "poverty of culture" (Lewis, 1966); as using "deleterious" language (Houston, 1971); as lacking in initiative, motivation, and self-control (Hunt, 1971); and as belonging to a family environment characterized by a "tangle of pathology" (Moynihan, 1965). Additionally, the negative aspects of the Black representational world also include the images perpetuated by "social science" that African-Americans are disadvantaged (Hellmuth, 1967); inferior in genetic and intellectual endowment (Jensen, 1969); and other such generalizations existing today in scientific and professional circles in this country and abroad. These assumptions about Black life and experience lay at the heart of "scientific racism." (Thomas and Sillen, 1972)

POST-TRAUMATIC STRESS DISORDERS AND THE BLACK VETERAN'S REPRESENTATIONAL WORLD

The Case of Sam

Sam is a Black veteran of the Vietnam war. He had served in Vietnam during the 1968 Tet counter-offensive and had killed several VC. He had been immersed in this profoundly terrorizing milieu for several months of fighting. His presenting symptoms were: restlessness, irritability, fear, anxiety, interpersonal isolation, rage, distrust of authority persons, suicidal ideation, sleeplessness, some dreams, flashback experiences, and profound guilt (due to his taking personal responsibility for his killing Vietnamese). Sam's night terror experiences involved large spikes and daggers chasing after him and the faces of Vietnamese children and parents whom he had killed in battle. His flashback experience included heaps of dead bodies he had seen while in Vietnam.

Sam had left Vietnam some 12 years before, and had made a reasonable adjustment to civilian life. His symptoms began when the American hostages held in Iran returned to the United States. At the initial interview, he had left his job, divorced his wife, abandoned his children, retreated from interpersonal contacts with friends, lost interest in hobbies, and became generally constricted in his affective, cognitive, and behavioral functioning.

Sam was the youngest of six children and grew up in a Southern town. He fondly remembers the many times he spent listening to his grandmother and great grandmother on the back porch telling stories about slavery and survival; beatings and lynchings of Blacks in the South; intense fear and distrust of Whites; the nobility of the Black character, the will to live against great odds, and the common bond between non-European peoples. From very early Sam had been influenced by the *intergenerational transmission* of stress-determined images of slavery, racism, and its many social and psychological derivatives.

While in Vietnam, Sam often remembered the teaching of his past—of the close and common affinity between African-Americans and Third World peoples—and today talks about his guilt and rage over having harmed and killed Vietnamese people. He believes that his intense guilt, inner fears and current anxieties are related to his inability to come to terms with "my terrible past." His intense fears of losing his children, and seeing them in his nightmares as Vietnamese, he believes are linked to his guilt.

The *Legacies of Vietnam* (LOV) study (Kadushin, Boulanger, & Martin, 1981) found that 70 percent of Black veterans in heavy combat in Vietnam suffer stress disorders today; and that, in general, 40 percent of Black veterans compared to 20 percent of White veterans are stressed today. The study also showed that, whereas being in heavy combat was the most critical factor in soldiers succumbing to stress reactions in general, for Black veterans merely having been *in* Vietnam was sufficiently psychotoxic to induce stress reactions and disorders. In partial explanation of these phenomena, this author invokes the concepts of *impacted stress* and the *"gook"-identification. Impacted stress* refers to the assumption that, added to the stresses of the theater of war, many Black soldiers in Vietnam had brought with them "cumulative stress" from psychic and social origins, related to exclusion, poverty, and cultural "pan-suspiciousness." *"Gook"-identification* refers to *"the conscious and unconscious emotional identification with the devalued, maligned, abused, and helpless aspects of the Vietnamese, by the Black soldier"* (Parson, 1983b, in press).

Thus, Black soldiers brought the effects of their sociopolitical past to Vietnam ("impacted stress"), which facilitated their identifying with the plight of the Vietnamese ("gook"-identification). For many Black veterans today, this identification represents a condensation of psychohistorical images and images of Vietnam. Impacted stress and identification with the Vietnamese would tend to make the adaptation to war problematic and make Black soldiers susceptible to post-combat reactions and disorders, due to their heightened *ambivalence* (marked by conflict between service to country and harming and killing people very much like themselves). For the Black soldier, killing the Vietnamese was the psychological equivalent of killing a part of his psychological and spiritual life. This was an essential aspect of Sam's post-war themes in his treatment.

The Black veteran's representational world perhaps can be described in terms of *survivorship*. The Black veteran is a "triple survivor" (Parson, 1984b). He thus survives: 1) the social and psychic "push-and-pull, tug-of-war" intrinsic to a bi-cultural identity system; 2) the imprint of being descendant of African slaves and the ubiquitous impact of racism; and 3) the imprint of combat trauma in Vietnam and the repatriation.

Vietnam-Generated Survivor Images

For many Black veterans, having served in Vietnam was the beginning of a postwar existence of painful experiences, especially guilt. Like most survivors of catastrophe, the Black veteran suffers from the *death imprint* (Lifton, 1982) and its various equivalents—depressive affect, drug-use, and other destructive behavior, and perpetual existential pain—which interfere with his living. Intrusion experiences for many Black veterans reinforce their sense of powerlessness, passivity and the persistence of low self-esteem. However, as Lifton (1982) points out, surviving "is likely to be associated not only with pain but also with value . . . [of having] 'been there and returned' " (p. 1015). The Black veteran must be encouraged to ponder, identify, and claim the self-esteem-building satisfaction related to having survived in Vietnam and in America.

Intergenerational Transmission of Survivor Images

Black families transmit their experiences from one generation to another by story-telling, a very important aspect of Black culture referred to as the *oral tradition*. Black Americans have used oral means of communicating the history of their people in the West. Storytelling, rather than the written word, still continues to be the preferred mode of intergenerational transmission of Black people's feelings, ideas, philosophies, tragedies, comedies, survival, and triumph. The advantage of Br'er Rabbit, the tales of "Uncle Remus," are among the many well-known adventures, tales, and Black humor. Through these stories the young 1) accrue a sense of continuity with the past; 2) learn the value society accords them; and 3) become aware of the suffering of their forebears at the hand of society. These images of slavery are encoded and internalized into the ego, and become a part of the representational world. These transmission processes are similar to those reported in second-generation survivors of the Holocaust (Epstein, 1982), and other types of transmission experiences (Winnicott, 1975). Sam often spoke of the nature of these encoded imageries, and the stress they generated in his life. The Black veteran can also derive strength and purpose from his having survived as a Black American. The following overview of psychotherapy research and its implications for the Black veteran further elucidates the nature of his representational world.

OVERVIEW OF PERTINENT PSYCHOTHERAPY RESEARCH

Psychotherapy research with minority and low-income patients has yielded findings pertinent to the Black Vietnam veteran, discussed under the following headings: 1) *Expectational Variables;* 2) *Patient Variables;* 3) *Therapist Variables;* 4) *Therapist-Patient Similarity;* 5) *Process Variables;* and 6) *Outcome Variables.*

Expectational Variables

Expectation on the part of *both* therapist and patient correlate highly with psychotherapy outcome (Goldstein, 1973). Most working class and minority clients expect the therapist to be directive, active, and advice-giving, and they prefer to engage in therapy for short periods of time. They expect the treatment process to be goal-directed, focused, and concrete, rather than reflective and abstract. The therapist must either meet or alter the patient's expectations.

Patient Variables

The Hollingshead and Redlich (1958) study, more recently confirmed by Lorion (1978), showed that psychotherapy is used chiefly by and recommended to the middle class, while lower class individuals are offered the somatic therapies. Recent studies, however, have changed this view of Black and working class clients and psychotherapy.

Clinicians and researchers lacking in transcultural sophistication believe that the client should be young, attractive, verbal, intelligent, and successful (the YAVIS syndrome) in order to benefit from psychotherapy. Thus, patients who are homely, old, unsuccessful, nonverbal, and dumb (the HOUND syndrome) are given chemotherapy and, at best, a few talking sessions. Lower class and minority clients have been regarded as being intrinsically unsuitable for psychotherapy. The client is "blamed for not having what it takes." This blame-the-victim psychology abounds in the mental health industry. Along these lines Parson (1981) writes,

It is thus the original conceptualization or theory that is flawed or deficient, not the patient having some intrinsic defect that has to be overcome. Theories of personality and of general psychological development, in order to be useful, must incorporate a truly unbiased, realistic view that considers the patient's values, norms, unique perceptions and problems, adaptation capabilities, their historical background and current life-circumstances. Moreover, theories of therapy can be efficacious in alleviating mental distress in minority persons only when these factors are appreciated, understood, and considered important to the conceptualization of the presenting problems and to the course of treatment. (p. 12)

Therapist Variables

For the most part, therapists and counselors are YAVIS people (Schofield, 1964). Thus, Black clients often experience their therapist at sharp variance with themselves; they are described by white researchers as HOUND people or QUOID people (quiet, ugly, old, indigent, and dissimilar culturally) (Sundberg, 1981). In fact, a recent study by Acosta (1980) with Blacks, Hispanics, and low-income Whites at an outpatient clinic found that premature termination was related to these patients' negative reactions for their therapists. Howard and Orlinsky (1972) show, however, that most therapists come from lower middle-class families. As *achieved* elites, who themselves were culturally marginal, these therapists may be able to work effectively with Black veterans who themselves are viewed by society as culturally marginal. It seems generally accepted that the personal qualities and actions of the therapist's engagement, contact, empathy, and rapport determine therapy outcome.

Therapist-Patient Similarity

Research in the area of therapist-patient similarity has not produced conclusive findings. However, it has been shown that Black patients do better with a Black therapist (Harrison, 1975). Additionally, sex and socioeconomic status variables were found to be important considerations in similarity research (Parloff et al., 1978). Vail (1978) found that opposite-sex therapist correlated highest with remaining in therapy.

Process Variables

There are a number of factors that have been found to enhance or limit the efficacy of psychotherapy with the Black of low-income patients. One of these factors is the bi-cultural "fit" or mutuality between therapist and patient. Since the therapeutic process is an interactive mutuality (hence, "intercultural") consisting of ethnocultural, cognitive, affective, and behavioral elements, therapy process variables must take into account not one, but both participants in the treatment dyad. Successful treatment with the Black veteran is contingent upon this mutuality. A therapist's negative feelings about race differences and Vietnam veterans will erect formidable anti-therapeutic barriers. Critical process variables that positively influence the patient are the therapist's expertness, social attractiveness (i.e., social acceptability), and trustworthiness (Merluzzi et al., 1977; Schmidt & Strong, 1977; Spiegel, 1976).

To the Black veteran, what is most important in his treatment is whether or not the professional can understand the contents of his representational world, and relate to him as a full person, as a person in his own right—not merely a product of social phenomena.

Outcome Variables

The psychotherapy research studies on outcome address either patient variables or therapist variables or both. General findings on outcome as it pertains to the patient suggest that severity of psychological problems and symptoms, degree of ego strength, level of expectancy, and consistent motivation all correlate with outcome. For the therapist, relationship skills and professional experiences are also consistently correlated with outcome. It is also noteworthy that issues of class and ethnocultural differences correlated highly with unsatisfactory termination (Sue, 1981).

INTEGRATION OF RESEARCH FINDINGS AND THE BLACK VETERAN'S REPRESENTATIONAL WORLD

The implications of recent psychotherapy/counseling research for the Black veteran are summarized with the following:

1) The Black Vietnam veteran brings his own psychological and social reality to treatment. Thus, his representational world must be understood by the provider.
2) Traditional approaches to therapy are not congruent with the cultural (Black) and experiential (Vietnam) needs of the Black Vietnam veteran, especially in the early phases of the treatment.

3) The Black Vietnam veteran's expectancy in therapy is for problem-solving oriented advice and goal-directed interventions, rather than an "insight-gleaning," reflective therapy.
4) The veteran's perception of his needs may differ substantially from the therapist's views, based on differing cultural values and divergent representational worlds.
5) Black Vietnam veterans are able to benefit from psychotherapy when these services are offered by a therapist who is *transculturally* and *transexperientially* competent (Parson, 1984b).
6) If a Black or White Vietnam veteran therapist or counselor is not available to the Black Vietnam veteran, a woman therapist of either race may be the next choice.
7) Most Black Vietnam veterans would seem to prefer a Black therapist. However, a White therapist from a culturally marginal background may also be successful with this population of clients.

TREATMENT CONSIDERATIONS

An understanding of the veteran's representational world can lead to more culturally sensitive interventions. Thus, when the Black Vietnam veteran seeks services for his mental woes, the therapist should be aware of his expectations, his needs, and his culture. The therapist or counselor must thus: 1) meet or alter the veteran's expectations; 2) study and understand the Vietnam experience and the toxic mental effects of guerrilla warfare on the adolescent ego structure; 3) become aware of ethnocultural characteristics of African-Americans, and how to evaluate these as they unfold in assessment and in the therapeutic arena. The clinician must become aware, additionally, of the potential for destructive countertransference-based emotional entanglements with the Black veteran, due to conscious and preconscious Vietnamism* and unconscious racism.

For the most part, Black veterans expect services that are direct, practical, active, and short-term. Such requirements do not reduce the level of sophistication of the treatment, as some believe. Because the veteran may not know what he is to expect from therapy, nor what the treatment experience demands of him, a *pre-therapy* phase in working with Black

---

*Vietnamism refers to predujicial attitudes and behaviors toward persons who served in Vietnam.

Vietnam veterans is recommended in orienting the veteran to the treatment process. It is recommended that psychotherapy with minority and low-income patients should be in time-limited segments of six or less sessions per therapy contract (Acosta, Yamamoto, & Evans, 1982). A written contract clearly outlining mutual expectations understood and agreed upon by both veteran and therapist helps the veteran: 1) assume more responsibility for his treatment; 2) experience a sense of control over the treatment situation while offering ego-bolstering assurance that he is capable of taking charge of his own life.

The therapist must show interest and concern for the veteran and reduce the impediments to treatment by listening transculturally and intervening *actively*. During the initial phase, perhaps the best way to show the Black veteran that "things can happen" in his life is by facilitating the fulfillment of his immediate, concrete needs. The therapist may thus decide, based on understanding of the veteran's needs and representational world, to assist him in securing V.A. benefits and services, legal assistance, food stamps, employment, etc.

This focus can take place concurrently with the exploration of emotional conflicts related to Vietnam and to his current and pre-service life and experiences. The Black veteran should be encouraged to explore his emotional reactions to Vietnam. He needs specific therapeutic support in: 1) making sense of his general war involvement and actions; 2) reexperiencing heretofore unacknowledged and unavailable feelings about Vietnam; 3) getting in touch with his possible "gook"-identifications (with the Vietnamese) and related guilt; 4) expressing feelings about racism at home, in the military, and in Vietnam; 5) feeling self-empowered to live and to be worthy of living (developing sound and lasting self-esteem); 6) becoming acquainted with the totality of his emotional life; 7) handling intrusion; and 8) integrating fragmented aspects of the self—pre-service, Vietnam, and post-Vietnam experiences and dynamics—into a cohesive self-organization.

In exploring the Black veteran's emotional conflicts, his self- and object-representations will come into focus. Being Black, being post-traumatically stressed, and being despised and rejected by one's country will converge in the treatment in a complex manner. The "enduring schema" of the Black veteran's inner world operates in all behavior and reactions. This means that if the therapist is to understand the Black veteran from *within*—i.e., from the center of his phenomenology and self-experience—he must strive to understand how the veteran "represents" the various individual, social, ethnocultural, experiential, and familial elements that occur in the treatment setting. Understanding the veteran in terms of his own inner life (rather than in terms of erroneous albeit well-intentioned biased clinical and social formulations) has the potential of forestalling misalliances and intractable countertransference problems that occur when basic misunderstanding of the Black veteran's communications and style of adaptation prevails. As is true of other patients, the veteran's representational world may not be congruent with external reality. In fact, it often diverges from familial and societal values and psychological criteria for health and illness. Thus, though Sam might be said to be suffering from survivor guilt, an understanding of how he *represented* aspects of his interpersonal environment in Vietnam vis-à-vis the Vietnamese people may lead to a different conclusion. Sam's guilt originated from his taking personal responsibility (Smith, 1982) for killing Vietnamese persons and destroying their land. Sam's guilt, like other emotions and behaviors, may contain condensations of self- and object-representations about early personal experiences and dynamics as well.

Understanding the veteran's representational world involves a knowledge of his healthy adaptation as well as his pathological accommodations. The concept of *"cross sectional analysis"* of the representational world is useful in discovering the *meaning* the veteran gives to a particular behavior. This is the meaning that ultimately counts, first and foremost, for it is out of this meaning that the therapeutic work acquires its mandate for intervention. The representational world—its ontogenetic, sociocultural, psychohistorical, and experiential self-elements—in post-traumatic stress disorders is fraught with intense fears and deep anxieties over the possible "return of the disassociated" (intrusion). Splitting, denial, projection, and psychic numbing are used as coping and defensive measures.

As in treating any group of survivors, the therapist should maintain a *non-intrusive* posture—that is, the therapist's interventions must be sensitively worded and attuned to the pain and narcissistic vulnerability survivors feel after their ordeal. Understanding the Black veteran's inner world, as in the case of Sam, reveals an interaction of variables from a variety of sources, including psychohistorical images of slavery, images of Vietnam, and his post-service life (particularly his inability to handle his rage), care for his children, his projected guilt, and punishment-seeking and self-destructive behaviors.

Ultimately, the treatment of the Black Vietnam veteran must empower the veteran with a sense of worthiness and competency in the world and engage him in a useful therapeutic experience that assists in turning the scars of trauma into the stars of hope and life.

REFERENCES

Acosta, F.X.: Self-described reasons for premature termination of psychotherapy by Mexican-American, Black-American and Anglo-American patients. *Psychological Reports,* 47:435-443, 1980.

Acosta, F.X., Yamamoto, J., & Evans, L.: *Effective psychotherapy for low-income and minority patients.* New York: Plenum, 1982.

Blanck, G., & Blanck, R.: *Ego psychology: Theory and practice.* New York: Columbia University Press, 1974.

Brende, J.O.: A psychodynamic view of character pathology in combat veterans. *Bulletin of the Menninger Clinic,* 47:193-216, 1983.

Clark, K.: *Prejudice and your child.* (2nd ed.). (p. 17). Boston: Beacon Press, 1963.

Comer, J.: *Beyond black and white.* New York: New York Times Book Co., 1972.

Diagnostic and Statistical Manual of Mental Disorders (1st ed.). Washington, D.C.: American Psychiatric Association, 1952.

Diagnostic and Statistical Manual of Mental Disorders (2nd ed.). Washington, D.C.: American Psychiatric Association, 1968.

Diagnostic and Statistical Manual of Mental Disorders (3rd ed.). Washington, D.C.: American Psychiatric Association, 1980.

Epstein, A.W.: Mental phenomena across generations: The holocaust. *American Journal of the Academy of Psychoanalysis,* 10:565-570. 1982.

Figley, C.R. (Ed.): *Stress disorders among Vietnam veterans.* New York: Brunner/Mazel, 1978.

Forman, B.D.: Psychotherapy with rape victims. *Psychotherapy: Theory, Research, and Practice, 17*(3), 1980.

Fraiberg, S.: Libidinal object constancy and mental representation. *Psychoanalytic study of the child:* Vol. 14. (pp. 9-47). New York: International Universities Press, 1969.

Freud, A.: The concept of development lines. *Psychoanalytic study of the child:* Vol. 18. New York: International Universities Press, 1963.

Geller, J., Behrends, R., & Hartley, D.: Images of the psychotherapist: A theoretical and methodological perspective. *Imagination, cognition, and personality:* Vol. 1. (pp. 123-146). New York: International Universities Press, 1982.

Goldstein, A.: *Structured learning therapy: Toward a psychotherapy for the poor.* New York: Academic Press, 1973.

Greenacre, P.: The childhood of the artist: Libidinal phase development and giftedness. In *The psychoanalytic study of the child:* Vol. 12. New York: International Universities Press, 1957.

Haley, S.: When the patient reports atrocities. *Archives of General Psychiatry, 30*:191-196, 1975.

Haley, S.: Treatment implications of post-combat stress response syndrome for mental health professionals. In Figley, C.R. (Ed.), *Stress disorders among Vietnam veterans.* New York: Brunner/Mazel, 1978.

Harrison, I.: Race as a counselor-client variable in counseling and psychotherapy: A review of the research. *The Counseling Psychologist, 5*:124-133, 1975.

Hellmuth, J.: *Disadvantaged child:* Vol. 1. New York: Brunner/Mazel, 1967.

Hollingshead, A., & Redlich, F.C.: *Social class and mental illness: A community study.* New York: John Wiley & Sons, 1958.

Houston, S.: A re-examination of some assumptions about language of the disadvantaged child. *Child Development, 41*:13-38, 1971.

Howard, K. & Orlinsky, D.: Psychotherapeutic processes. *Annual Review of Psychology, 23*:615-668, 1972.

Hunt, J.: Parent and child centers: Their basis in the behavioral and educational sciences. *American Journal of Orthopsychiatry, 41*:13-48, 1971.

Jacobson, E.: *The self and the object world.* New York: International Universities Press, 1964.

Jensen, A.: How much can we boost IQ and scholastic achievement? *Harvard Educational Review, 39*:1-123, 1969.

Kadushin, C., Boulanger, G., & Martin, J.: Some causes, consequences and naturally-occurring support systems. *Legacies of Vietnam: Comparative adjustment of veterans and their peers*: Vol. 4. Washington, D.C.: Government Printing Office, 1981.

Kardiner, A., & Ovesey, L.: *The mark of oppression*. New York: Norton, 1951.

Klein, G.S.: *Psychoanalytic theory*. New York: International Universities Press, 1976.

Krystal, H.: *Massive psychic trauma*. New York: International Universities Press, 1968.

Lewis, O.: The culture of poverty. *Scientific American, 215*:19-25, 1966.

Lifton, R.J.: The psychology of the survivor and the death imprint. *Psychiatric Annals, 12*(11):1011-1017, 1020, 1982.

Lipin, T.: The repetition compulsion and "maturational" drive-representatives. *International Journal of Psychoanalysis, 44*:389-406, 1963.

Lorion, R.P.. Research on psychotherapy and behavior change with the disadvantaged: Past, present and future directions. In S.L. Garfield and A.E. Bergin (Eds.), *Handbook of psychotherapy and behavior change: An empirical analysis* (2nd ed.). New York: Wiley, 1978.

Mahler, M.: *On human symbiosis and the vicissitudes of individuation. Infantile psychosis*: Vol. I. New York: International Universities Press, 1968.

Mahler, M., & Gosliner, B.: *On symbiotic child psychosis: Genetic, dynamic and restitutive*. (pp. 195-212). New York: International Universities Press, 1955.

Mahler, M., Pine, F., & Bergman, A.: *The psychological birth of the human infant*. New York: Basic Books, 1975.

McDonald, M.: *Not by the color of their skins*. New York: International Universities Press, 1970.

Merluzzi, T., Merluzzi, B., & Kaul, T.: Counselor race and power base: The effects on attitude and behavior. *Journal of Counseling Psychology, 24*:430-436, 1977.

Moore, B., & Fine, B.: *A glossary of psychoanalytic terms and concepts*. New York: American Psychoanalytic Association, 1968.

Moynihan, D.P.: Employment, income and the ordeal of the Negro family. *Daedalus*, pp. 745-770, 1965.

Parloff, M., Waskow, I., & Wolfe, B.: Research on therapist variables in relation to outcome. In S. Garfield, & A. Bergen (Eds.), *Psychotherapy and behavior change*. New York: Wiley, 1978.

Parson, E.R.: *The Interethnic Dasein: Some comments on the Daseinanalytic treatment of the black patient and the phenomena of awareness and responsibility*. Unpublished paper, 1975.

Parson, E.R.: In the interest of mental health care of minority and poor patients. *New York Society of Clinical Psychologists Newsletter*, Fall, pp. 7-12, 1981.

Parson, E.R.: The reparation of the self: Clinical and theoretical dimensions in the treatment of Vietnam combat veterans. *Journal of Contemporary Psychotherapy, 14*(1):4-56, 1984(a).

Parson, E.R.: The intercultural setting: Encountering the readjustment needs of black Americans who served in Vietnam. In press, 1984(b).

Pinderhughes, E.: The Afro-American family and the victim system. In M. McGoldrick, J. Pearce, & J. Giordano (Eds.), *Ethnicity and family therapy*. New York: The Guilford Press, 1982.

Rosenman, S.: The paradox of guilt in disaster victim populations. *Psychiatric Quarterly Supplement, 30*:181-222, 1956.

Sandler, J., & Rosenblatt, B.: The concept of the representational world. *The psychoanalytic study of the child*: Vol. 17. (pp. 128-145). New York: International Universities Press, 1962.

Schmidt, L., & Strong, S.: Attractiveness and influence in counseling. *Journal of Consulting Psychology, 18*:348-351, 1977.

Schofield, W.: *Psychotherapy: The purchase of friendship*. Englewood, N.J.: Prentis Hall, 1964.

Shatan, C.: Post-Vietnam syndrome. *The New York Times*, p. 35, May 6, 1972.

Smith, J.R.: Personal responsibility in traumatic stress reactions. *Psychiatric Annals,* 21:1021-1030, 1982.

Spiegel, S.: Expertness, similarity, and perceived counselor competence. *Journal of Consulting Psychology,* 23:436-441, 1976.

Staples, R.: The response of infants to color. *Journal of Experimental Psychology,* 15:119-141, 1933.

Sue, D.W.: *Counseling the cross-culturally different.* New York: Wiley, 1981.

Sundberg, N.D.: Cross-cultural counseling and psychotherapy: A research overview. In A.J. Marsella, & P.B. Pedersen (Eds.), *Crosscultural counseling and psychotherapy.* New York: Basic Books, 1981.

Thomas, A., & Sillen, S.: *Racism and psychiatry.* New York: Brunner/Mazel, 1972.

Triana, R.: The representational world of combat in Vietnam veterans. Unpublished dissertation, Smith College, 1983.

Vail, A.: Factors influencing lower class black patients remaining in treatment. *Journal of Consulting and Clinical Psychology,* 46:341, 1978.

Winnicott, C.: Fear of breakdown. *International Journal of Psychoanalysis,* 61:351-357, 1980.

Winnicott, D.W.: Transitional objects and transitional phenomena. In D.W. Winnicott, *Playing and reality.* London: Tavistock, 1971.

Winnicott, D.W.: *Through pediatrics to psychoanalysis.* (p. 245). New York: Basic Books, 1975.

CHAPTER

11

The Use of Hypnosis in Post-Traumatic Conditions

JOEL OSLER BRENDE, M.D.

The survivors of traumatic events frequently possess lasting and emotionally distressing post-traumatic symptoms. These include symptom complexes of intrusive traumatic memories, emotions, and imagery alternating with amnesia, denial, and emotional numbing—the latter symptom complex representing the attempt "to forget" (Horowitz, 1976). Yet therapists have long recognized that a survivor cannot truly forget a traumatic experience without first remembering it and making "possible its integration into the structure of the present personality" (Reiff & Scheerer, 1959 p. 41).

"REHEARSING" THE PAST

The "rehearsal" of the past is a common experience in everyone's life. Its importance is based not only on the need to relive and master a previously traumatic situation but to have access to one's own previous life experiences, which is necessary for a sense of identity and continuity with the past (Reiff & Scheerer, 1959). However, persons suffering from the post-traumatic symptoms of amnesia and hypermnesia (Horowitz, 1976) lack such continuity.

Historically, the loss of memory has been described as symptomatic of hysteria, believed caused by sexually traumatic events (Ellenberger, 1970; Veith, 1977). In fact, Breuer & Freud (1893) conceptualized the presence of "hypnoid" or altered states of consciousness taking place in association with traumatic events which provided emotional amnesia for persons with hysteria. Lifton (1979) has suggested that "hypnoid states" are forms of post-traumatic "psychic numbing" which keep traumatic memories from conscious recall, similar to the "over-control—under-control" phenomenon of denial vs. intrusion of traumatic memories (Horowitz, 1976). These seemingly protective "hypnoid" states prevent conscious "rehearsal" of the past from occurring and thereby interfere with resolution of post-traumatic symptoms since they perpetuate a condition of intrapsychic "splitting" (Shapiro, 1965).

As each group of post-traumatic symptom complexes remains separated or "split" from one another, the resulting intrapsychic instability gives rise to repetitive reenactments of traumatic experiences which are unconscious and potentially "uncontrollable" attempts to achieve resolution of the intrapsychic "split". Thus, reenactments are behavioral ways of rehearsing the past in order ". . . to restore an earlier state of things, (by creating) a bondage to the past, and . . . in repeating, past and present are merged" (Sedler (1983); ". . . by experiencing again and again what once had to be gone through in the trauma . . . (so that) . . . control may slowly be regained" (Fenichel, 1945).

HYPNOSIS AND ABREACTION

Achieving resolution of the internal psychic split through "rehearsal" and abreaction of past traumatic experiences is one of the important therapeutic goals of hypnotic age regression. It is not surprising, then, that hypnosis has been a primary treatment for post-traumatic conditions, particularly hysteria, dating back to before the 20th century (Janet, 1887, 1889, 1907; Ellenberger, 1970). For example, Breuer & Freud (1893) successfully applied the standard hypnotic technique of that time by inducing an abreaction and re-enactment of a past traumatic experience in their patient, Anna O.

Hypnotic treatment thus had as its primary focus the facilitation of abreaction. The benefits of which have been described by Jung (1954) as follows:

  (a) . . . Abreaction . . . the dramatic rehearsal of the traumatic moment, (is) emotional recapitulation in the waking or in the hypnotic state (and) often has a beneficial therapeutic effect. We all know that a man feels a compelling need to recount a vivid experience again and again until it has lost its affective value. . . . (p. 131-132)

(b) . . . Abreaction is . . . an attempt to reintegrate the autonomous (traumatic) complex, to incorporate it gradually into the conscious mind as an accepted content, by living the traumatic situation over and over again, once or repeatedly. (p. 132)

Abreaction has been the commonly used term for an hypnotically induced reexperience of a traumatic event. The word revivification has also been used (Erickson & Kubie, 1941) to describe this reexperience. Abreactions and revivifications have usually been associated with formal hypnotic trance induction but they may occur spontaneously during therapy or a hypnotic session, even without formal age regression (Gill, 1948). An abreaction or revivification is most likely to promote improvement in a patient's functioning when he can maintain awareness of the revivification experience, while simultaneously maintaining awareness of the present time and of the therapist's presence (Gill, 1948; Weitzenhoffer, 1955).

Jung (1954) also used abreaction during hypnotic treatment, but gave new recognition to the power of the therapeutic relationship, which he described as follows:

The rehearsal of the traumatic moment is able to integrate the neurotic dissociation only when the conscious personality of the patient is so far reinforced by his relationship to the doctor that he can consciously bring the autonomous complex under the control of his will. . . . The mere rehearsal of the experience does not itself possess a curative effect: the experience must be rehearsed in the presence of the doctor . . . the intervention of the doctor is absolutely necessary. (The patient's) conscious mind finds in the doctor a moral support against the unmanageable effect of his traumatic complex. No longer does he stand alone in his battle with these elemental powers, but someone whom he trusts reaches out a hand, lending him moral strength to combat the tyranny of uncontrolled emotion. In this way, the integrative powers of his conscious mind are reinforced until he is able once more to bring the rebellious affect under control. . . . (pp. 132-133)

In spite of the fact that hypnosis and abreaction were often successfully used, permanent cures were infrequent. At times, the hypnotic induc-

tion merely reproduced the hysterical condition. Charcot reportedly reproduced hysterical symptoms using hypnotic trance induction
(Ellenberger, 1970). Lifton (1979) has referred to Breuer & Freud who
found that hypnosis reproduced the intrapsychic splitting found in hysteria:

> . . . the various kinds of hypnoid states in hysteria share with
> one another and with hypnosis, namely the ideas which emerge
> in them are very intense but are cut off from associative commu-
> nication with the rest of the content of consciousness. (p. 201)

Freud used hypnosis for a number of years in his treatment of hysteria,
but eventually concluded after 1895 that his patients' hypnotically induced reenactments and emotional catharses did little more than temporarily alleviate post-traumatic symptoms. Furthermore he suspected
that these reenactments were likely contaminated by exaggerated fears,
fabrications, or even wishful fantasies. Freud's disillusionment with hypnosis led him to discontinue its use. He consequently abandoned abreactive treatment in favor of free association, creating an "anti-hypnosis"
climate which appeared to bias all those who followed him.

HYPNOSIS AND PSYCHOANALYSIS

Although Freud concluded that hypnosis was an ineffective treatment,
he appeared to be influenced by his years of experience as a hypnotherapist to realize that there was a therapeutic quality to the patient's
altered state of consciousness. It is not surprising then that he incorporated this knowledge into his psychoanalytic technique which he did
in a very creative way. Freud began to instruct his patients in his newly
developed technique of *free association*. The patient was instructed to lie
down and relax mentally with the therapist behind and out of view. He
was told that he would soon note an ability to talk freely about any idea,
daydream or thought that might enter his mind. The choice of subject
matter was immaterial and left entirely up to the patient. He would note
that as he related things, various ideas would occur to him which he
would feel inclined to put aside for certain criticisms, but he was to
verbally express whatever was going through his mind. The patient was
to imagine and act as if he were sitting at the window of a railway car,
relating to someone behind him the changing views he might see outside
the window (Freud, 1913, p. 135).

Freud's movement away from hypnotic abreaction as a treatment was enhanced by the development of psychoanalytic theory which rested heavily on the concept of tripartite mind—id, ego, and super-ego—bisected by conscious and unconscious components which were separated by the boundary of "repression." It was believed that repression was an important ego defense which prevented intrusive noxious ideas and emotions from entering consciousness. Anna Freud (1946) described the detrimental effects of bypassing this repressive barrier with hypnosis:

> . . . Hypnosis was a means of getting rid of (the noxious experience) temporarily. (The ego) tolerated the intruder only so long as it was itself under the influence of the physician who had induced hypnosis. Then it revolted and began a new struggle to defend itself against the . . . id which had been forced upon it, and so the laboriously achieved therapeutic success was vitiated. Thus it came about that the greatest triumph of hypnotic technique—the complete elimination of the ego during the period of investigation—proved prejudicial to permanent results and disillusionment as to the value of the technique set in. (p. 12)

Freud also realized the burden upon the hypnotherapist who was placed in the position of breaking through this repressive barrier through hypnotic suggestion, discussed by Sedler (1983): ". . . by means of my psychical work I had to overcome a psychical force in the patients which was opposed to the pathogenic ideas becoming conscious. . . ." (Freud, 1895, p. 268).

Freud came to realize that the patient should be responsible for his own recovery and developed a technique, which he called the "working through" process, that would be partially separate from the responsibility of the therapist. With this concept, he departed even further from the traditional use of the hypnotist's suggestion as a primary treatment: ". . . the doctor has nothing else to do than to wait and let things take their course. . . ." (Freud, 1914, p. 155).

Thus, in emphasizing this departure from hypnotic treatment, he defined working through as ". . . that part of the work which effects the greatest changes in the patient and which distinguishes analytic treatment from any kind of treatment by suggestion" (Freud, 1914, p. 155-156).

Sedler (1983), in an article about Freud's concept of working through, has referred to Fenichel's (1945) definition as primarily interpretive and educational, partly involving the framework of the therapeutic transference, and extending beyond ". . . a single operation resulting in a single act of abreaction; it is, rather, a chronic process of working through, which shows the patient again and again the same conflicts and his usual way of reacting to them, but from new angles and in new connections. . . . (This systematic) and consistent interpretive work . . . can be described as educating the patient to produce continually less distorted derivatives until his fundamental instinctual conflicts are recognizable" (p. 31).

PSYCHOTHERAPY AND ABREACTION IN WORLD WAR II COMBATANTS

Although the use of hypnotic abreactive treatment lost favor within the psychoanalytic movement, attempts were subsequently made to combine psychoanalytic principles with hypnosis for the treatment of post-traumatic symptoms in war combatants. For example, Grinker & Spiegel (1945) have reported treating combat-related symptoms with abreactive techniques as well as with individual and group psychotherapy for World War II combatants, described as follows:

> 1) Establishment of doctor-patient relationship (transference).
> 2) Support, and gratification of the patient's weakened and regressed ego by means of tenderness . . . attentive interest . . . and identification with the therapist's strength.
> 3) Release and uncovering of isolated, repressed and suppressed emotions, memories and conflicts (ABREACTION). (p. 373)

They described seven additional treatment concepts, including the following recollection and desensitization technique:

> Desensitization from the memories of the anxiety-producing situations (can be achieved) by repetitive recounting of traumatic experiences, as the therapist helps the dependent ego to discriminate between past danger and present safety, and between the world of reality and inner anxieties. (p. 374)

Their treatment approach included a type of working through which they have described as follows:

> After the abreaction has been started and the patient has come out of his narcosis, he is forced to review the material in a conscious state. However, this is not always necessary, for insight may be reached and learning established by the unconscious ego. Con-

scious verbalizations are not always necessary to indicate therapeutic benefits. . . . (p. 279)

Watkin's (1949) treatment of World War II combatants also involved the use of psychotherapy with a hypnotic approach to achieve abreaction, which he has reported (1971) as follows:

a)The reaction is indicated only in neurotic and not in psychotic or prepsychotic personalities.

b) Cathartic abreactions should enlist the total personality.

c) The released material must be interpreted and integrated. (Watkins, 1980, p. 102)

OTHER ABREACTIVE AND REGRESSIVE TECHNIQUES

Drug-induced abreactions, developed during and after the Second World War (Grinker & Spiefel, 1945), have been referred to as an effective uncovering technique for the treatment of combat veterans. In reviewing the use of Amytal interviews, Perry & Jacobs (1982) called them preferable uncovering techniques in acute traumatic conditions: "Amytal frees up a highly defended traumatic experience and aids in reintegration of dissociated ideas and affects. It provides a pharmacological cushion that allows exploration and a lowering of defenses against the anxiety-provoking recollection of trauma" (p. 556).

Reports have also been published of Amytal interviews being excessively intrusive. Klein (1945), for example, expressed his concern about "forced" abreactions on World War II combatants, suggesting instead that the therapist's reassurance and verbal support were more important:

At first an attempt was made . . . to use the method . . . described as narcosynthesis . . . but it was given up and found to have no advantage over adequate sedation. . . . Indeed, in many of the patients it was felt to be detrimental to (their) early recovery. What these men wanted most was not to be reminded of their grievous ordeal or horrifying experiences but rather to be permitted the healing . . . of merciful forgetfulness. . . . The so-called "abreaction" is a neat term implying an analogy of draining off disturbing emotional states . . . but was found to be poorly founded. (pp. 39-40)

Grinker and Spiegel (1945) emphasized a positive transference and permissive interview techniques as a means of avoiding such intrusiveness with Pentothal induced abreactions: "No patient is given pentothal treatment without adequate preliminary interviews, until a good grasp is obtained of the factual material regarding combat and past life, or until a good transference relationship has been established by the physician" (p. 392).

However, the authors emphasized a free association style of interview as a means of cutting through resistence, while omitting questions prompted by the interviewer's personal needs and curiosity, described as follows:

> . . . resistances occur under pentothal as well as in the conscious state and the therapist must put the patient under pressure to overcome them. Psychiatrists accustomed to the method of free association, and not disturbed by silences, have no difficulty in following this method. (p. 391)

Amytal interviews have also been reported as useful in the treatment of Vietnam veterans with post-traumatic symptoms. Yet abreaction alone has usually been insufficient. Recognizing the need for ego integration of abreacted material, Perry & Jacobs suggested psychotherapy following Amytal induced abreactions while Maoz & Pincus (1979) recommended concomitant group therapy for patients who had Amytal interviews. Similarly, other authors (Cavenar & Nash, 1976) have used videotaped reviews by patient and therapist to facilitate ego integration of chemically induced abreacted traumatic experiences.

NON-CHEMICAL ABREACTIVE TECHNIQUES

Non-chemical means have often been preferred for achieving "adaptive regressions" (Fromm, 1977), including affective recollections, abreactions, and revivifications of traumatic experiences during treatment of combat veterans. Such experiences have been referred to as "healing recapitulations" (Figley, 1978) and "integrative regressions" wherein the patient has the opportunity for "psychic growth, recovery, or renewal . . . (and can) temporarily 'let go' of defenses against past memories or archaic images within the unconscious (and face) memories and images directly (may) . . . progress to higher levels of psychic functioning" (Brende & McCann, 1984).

Although such experiences have commonly been associated with hypnotic age regression, some authors have preferred other therapeutic modalities to achieve the same purpose believing them to be less likely to intrude upon ego autonomy. Thus, the supportive milieu of "Rap group therapy" has been found to facilitate "therapeutic revivifications" (Brende & Benedict, 1980). A sensitive therapist can help a patient reexperience a sensation—particularly imagery—which may subsequently evoke an affective recollection or even revivification of traumatic experiences. For example, Brende & McCann (1984) have reported an example of a therapist asking a patient to recall detailed imagery of a past traumatic event and, in so doing, evoking the patient's vivid affective recollections.

The author has had other patients with similar experiences. For instance, during treatment of a veteran who had been unable to recall the details of a man being shot and killed in a hotel room, the patient was asked to describe the situation in the context of current reality: "Let yourself be there as if it were taking place now. What do you see?" The patient responded to that question by pausing and spontaneously achieving a trance-like state without further suggestions. Then he began to describe the emotionally charged details of seeing the man being killed.

In a similar therapeutic situation, a depressed and obviously disabled Vietnam veteran was observed during his first therapeutic session. He was asked by the therapist to describe how he had come to suffer amputations of two of his extremities. As the patient began to talk about it unemotionally and abstractly, the therapist focused on recreating the details of the event, as follows:

> Th: Describe what happened to you. Can you see it?
> Pt: Yeah, I can still see it.

He then began to revivify and abreact his experience of being blown into the air by a rocket, losing his arm and leg and nearly dying when shot by an enemy soldier in Vietnam.

Eisenhart (1977) remembered his own personal reliving of a combat experience and found it to be an essential component of the healing process. He described it as occurring during psychotherapy without the use of hypnosis and with only a suggestion that he reexperience the olfactory sensation:

> For four or five years after Vietnam, a specific intrusive image kept recurring. The image was that of a very badly dismembered man that I had seen. He had been shot, burned, blown wide open

with his guts hanging out, and he stank something fierce. The image recurred continually and triggered affective responses. During therapy I was asked to remember the smell. To remember it vividly and to relive the experience in the present tense. I saw the image and smelled that stink once again. I was told to go further into the image and assume the posture of the dead man. As I was doing this, I came in touch with my fears of emasculation. The individual had been shot and burned in the groin and I had blocked the image. . . . (pp. 3-4)

HYPNOSIS AND POST-TRAUMATIC STRESS DISORDER IN VIETNAM VETERANS

There have been occasional reports of hypnotherapy being used successfully for the treatment of PTSD in Vietnam veterans. Balson & Dempster (1980) used a psychodynamically oriented treatment process for Vietnam veterans lasting 6-9 months which included several hypnotically induced abreactive sessions. Spiegel (1981) has written about his use of hypnosis with Vietnam combat veterans, finding it particularly helpful in resolving traumatic grief experiences by facilitating recollection of not only the death trauma but also a positive memory of the grieved comrade:

. . . the intensification of memory and the emotion which surrounds it in hypnosis can be used as part of the process of doing grief work. The trance state provides a structured intensification of memory which becomes the setting for repeating and working through, or putting into perspective painful memories and experiences. . . . (p. 35)

Brende and Benedict (1980), in their report of successful hypnotherapy of a Vietnam veteran, used hypnosis in different ways: a) as a supportive technique when the patient required help to control anxiety; b) as an uncovering technique when he was amnestic for important events; c) as an abreactive technique when symptomatic; and d) as an integrative technique.

Differentiating between these varied uses of hypnosis is dependent on the quality of the therapeutic relationship and follows to some extent the hypnotherapist's understanding of the patient's ego strength, character defenses, phase of treatment and the therapeutic goal at the time. The following examples will illustrate these different applications of hypnotic treatment in survivors of trauma.

Hypnosis as a Supportive Technique

Parson (1981) has described the use of hypnosis and relaxation techniques during the first phase of therapy when patients suffer from considerable anxiety. Fairbank et al. (1981) have found that relaxation is an effective treatment for reducing frequency of post-traumatic startle reactions. Brende & McCann (1984) give accounts of using therapeutic techniques during early phases of therapy which would promote "regression in the service of the ego" rather than a dis-integrative regression. Similarly, Brende & Benedict (1980) have reported their use of hypnosis in the treatment of a Vietnam veteran during the initial phase of psychotherapy for controlling anxiety and target symptoms. His improvement with supportive hypnotic techniques was enhanced by his learning self-hypnotic and meditative techniques as well.

In addition to its initial value in relieving specific target symptoms, hypnosis can also be useful as a means for building trust. For example, the following hypnotic suggestions were used during a session six months after the beginning of combined group and individual psychotherapy with a Vietnam veteran who had significant character pathology and suffered from chronic, severe shoulder and back pain:

> I would like to have you relax and imagine that I and the other veterans in your therapy group are all helping you with the burden that you are carrying. It's been there ever since you've returned from Vietnam and has contributed to all the pain that you are feeling in your back and shoulders. Imagine that we are right here with you now, helping you hold up the burden. As you let us share that burden with you, it will be easier for you in the future to talk about what is bothering you and to share your feelings with us.

Following this session, the veteran temporarily experienced relief from pain, but more importantly felt increased support from his therapist and fellow group members. It also became easier for him to talk about emotionally charged combat experiences and, within a short time during one of the group therapy sessions, he was able to grieve the loss of buddies who had died in Vietnam.

Hypnosis as an Uncovering Technique

Following an initial supportive phase of therapy, a patient may gain control over his most severe target symptoms and be amenable to "opening up". Parson (1981) has characterized the therapist's task during this time as being able to "gently crack the shell with which the vet has surrounded himself." Hypnotic techniques can be used for this purpose.

In the previously described case (Brende & Benedict, 1980), the patient's continuing use of self-hypnosis and meditation was soon associated with recollections of war-related experiences, for which he had been amnestic. This use of meditation as an "opening-up" process has been described by Carrington & Ephron (1979) as facilitating psychotherapy. The patient's recalled war memories were important and provided information which enabled the therapist to understand the nature of his combat experiences. However, within a few weeks, the opening-up process became excessive due to the lifting of repressive barriers over traumatic memories. He began to have disturbing symptoms similar to what has previously been described in some borderline patients who use meditation or biofeedback training excessively (Brende & Rinsley, 1979; Glueck & Stroebel, 1975).

Thus, within a few weeks, the patient ". . . began to be flooded with feelings of guilt about combat deaths for which he felt responsible. . . . The flooding of consciousness with such material interfered with effective concentration . . . (and) he began to feel increasingly guilt-ridden about having killed civilians . . . and (about) feelings of guilt related to his emerging rage. . . . He began to feel like a 'bomb' that could explode at any time and which he was unable to defuse" (p. 36).

Because the patient could not tolerate this influx of traumatic memories, hypnosis and meditation were discontinued in favor of supportive psychotherapy for the remainder of the first phase of his treatment. He was subsequently able to gain considerable relief from guilt feelings, stabilize his life situation, and establish a trusting therapeutic alliance. The initial phase of therapy thus provided him a sense of self-control and trust in the therapist.

Hypnosis as an Abreactive Technique

The value of abreaction is contingent upon the degree of symptom reduction following the procedure as described earlier. Among those factors related to success is the therapeutic rapport, capable of allowing an "integrative regression" (Brende & McCann, 1984). While the goal of abreaction is usually to facilitate an emotional discharge, Watkins (1980) has encouraged a "silent abreaction" for patients who need to discharge anger.

Parson (1981) has also described this phase of therapy as the "in vivo affective revival phase" during which time treatment facilitates "a controlled regressive pathway to the traumatic experience . . . possible (when) the veteran (can) withstand the possible 'fragmenting' effects of uncontrolled regressive ego activity in response to the ego-lulling impact of meditation, relaxation, and hypnotherapy" (p. 35).

To facilitate an abreaction, the hypnotherapist is frequently permissive in his approach, utilizing the "affect-bridge" technique (Watkins, 1971), described as follows: This is a method "wherein the patient is regressed over a bridge of common emotion to the earlier situation rather than over a 'cognitive bridge,' such as is generally employed in the free associations of traditional analytic therapy. That is feelings, and not thoughts, serve as the associative links from present to past" (Watkins 1980, p. 103).

Abreaction is generally considered to be most effective when used during a later phase in the treatment of Vietnam veterans whose traumatic experiences occurred many years earlier. On the other hand, the treatment of acute combat reactions in war combatants has frequently involved hypnotic abreaction early in the treatment process. For example, Moses et al. (1976) have described their treatment of combat reactions in Israeli soldiers, including "abreaction as a means—not as an end in itself—by encouraging the soldier to experience his feelings and to reconstruct the hours or days of combat, together with the therapist and in direct contact with him."

In another example of hypnosis being used immediately following a traumatic experience, the author previously reported a case (Brende, 1982) of a hospital employee nearly killed by a patient. He suffered from nightmares, startle reactions, and fear of returning to work. The use of hypnotic abreaction four weeks after the trauma resulted in his control of these symptoms and return to work.

As an exception to the concept that abreaction is primarily effective during the immediate post-traumatic period. Godfrey (1983) has described using hypnotic abreactive therapy in a Second World War Veteran nearly 40 years after his traumatic experience. After two sessions which included "working through" the meaning of repressed guilt feelings which were abreacted, his repeated nightmares ceased recurring. During the treatment of the Vietnam veteran previously discussed (Brende & Benedict, 1980), hypnotic abreactive techniques were used during a second therapeutic phase nine months after therapy had begun and lasted five months. This phase of the treatment was prompted by the veteran's increased target symptoms in the form of nightmares and physical symptoms, evidence of the presence of a hidden "victim identification" (Brende, 1983). The veteran's abreactions, occurring several times over a period of five months, were characterized by the emergence of traumatic memories, the details and emotional impact of which had not been expressed previously. The content of the memories were "victim" related, i.e., persons being killed and his own near-death experience.

Victim Identification

The presence of a "victim identification" as well as an "identification with the aggressor" is commonplace in survivors of trauma (Brende, 1983; Brende & McCann, 1984; Shatan, 1974; Moses, 1978; Moses et al., 1976). This identification results from witnessing or being responsible for the death or killing of others and becomes "split-off" from conscious awareness. The manifestation of the hidden identification becomes apparent primarily in the form of self-destructive dreams, behaviors, and physical symptoms. As an example, Moses (1978) found that soldiers with combat reactions frequently had physical symptoms: "Soldiers with combat reactions showed many more vegetative disturbances, considerably more regression . . . (and) a deeper, more extensive type of repression . . . (and) . . . more marked, deeper, longer-lasting resistance to talking about the details of their battle experiences" (p. 358).

The presence of the victim identification in the veteran whose case has been described previously (Brende & Benedict, 1980) was evoked during the hypnotic abreactions occurring during the second phase of therapy. During these sessions, the patient spontaneously relived several different traumatic war experiences. During the first session, he relived an event which took place in Vietnam in 1966, and began to shake and tremble out of fear during the revivification of ". . . a surprise attack when he experienced fear of an enemy tank which appeared on the verge of running over him" (p. 37).

This evoked the emergence ". . . of somatic accompaniments, i.e. generalized tremulousness and a delayed feeling of pain in his leg which had been injured during the battle" (p. 37), further evidence of the presence of the victim identification described earlier. "The theme of the second hypnotic session, three weeks later, was abandonment and betrayal. During this session he revealed feelings of vulnerability as he felt unsupported by his military superiors and . . . (later) his fear of being abandoned in the hospital. . . ." (p. 37).

During the posthypnotic follow-up session, this same patient described his feelings of rage which emerged to cover up his helplessness.

As part of the process of "working through" the content of the previously abreacted experiences, he began to describe guilt-related memories of accidently killing innocent civilians. Further use of hypnosis was curtailed for a month until he developed a resurgence of victim related nightmares. Hypnotic abreaction then uncovered the first experience of killing and the emergence of guilt and grief.

Hypnotic Abreaction as an Integrative Technique

When the goal of treatment includes the integration of "split-off" aspects of the self, i.e., part-identities linked to traumatic events, it is often facilitated by hypnotic age regression and abreaction. For example, in the previously described case, hypnotherapy had eventually exposed not only a "victim identification" but also an identity split between "killer-self" and "protective-self" (Brende, 1983), as follows:

> He (had) suppressed his prior value system and slipped into the role of a "killer." He . . . had come to get pleasure out of killing so that he had come close to accepting a job as a "hit man". . . . The evolving change in his identity had led him into an identity "split" between the "killer" and the healthy, protective "leader," both of which had been idealized by his peers. Ultimately, the "killer" part came into direct conflict with the protective part . . . (and) he developed serious problems, including at least one dissociative episode when it was reported by a friend who had observed him . . . killing Viet Cong soldiers and laughing hysterically, although having complete amnesia for that episode at a later time. (Brende & Benedict, 1980, p. 38)

The final hypnotic session was useful in the process of integrating the patient's split-off identifications involving not only the "killer-self" but also the "victim-self." This occurred in the process of abreacting and revivifying a final battle wherein he was nearly killed, and in the process, he became "aware of his dissociated helpless and aggressive feelings. After each revivification of the experience of being shot, he was able to reexperience the components of the original occurrence which consisted of . . . (being wounded, reliving the fear, reliving the absence of pain, experiencing the grief of expecting to die, and finally) . . . "experiencing being rescued by his friends. The hypnotic age regression and revivification of the final battle with (the therapist's help) and the memory of the suppport of his peers, enabled him to integrate the different painful components of the experience that had been dissociated by feelings of guilt and shame" (pp. 38-39), and find meaning in his own survival. Thus, the veteran integrated dissociated aspects of himself linked to fear, dehumanization, killing, guilt, grief, through an abreaction and revivification of traumatic events, including his own experience of nearly being killed; first through hypnotic abreactions and revivifications and second by "working through" these memories between each of the hypnotic sessions.

DISCUSSION

Vietnam veterans, particularly those with anti-social or borderline traits (Brende, 1983), are often not amenable to personality integration via abreaction alone but require concomitant and lengthy psychotherapy, including the confrontation of resistance in the form of character traits. The previously described hypnotic techniques of support, uncovering, abreaction, and integration can be used for specific purposes during different treatment phases. It is particularly important that a period of stabilization precedes uncovering or abreactive hypnosis.

Furthermore, it is important to be aware that a poorly timed hypnotic intervention may be ineffective and precipitate increased resistance or a disintegrative regression (Brende & McCann, 1984), particularly if the patient displays omnipotent character traits and unstable ego boundaries (Brende & McCann, 1984). As an example, a Vietnam veteran with narcissistic character traits and symptoms of dissociated aggressive outbursts and flashbacks experienced hallucinated frightening images while hypnotized one and a half years after the onset of psychotherapy. In another Vietnam veteran with longstanding character pathology, age regression and revivification of combat-related betrayal and abandonment experiences were followed by symptoms of aggressive outbursts a week later.

The need for hypnotic intervention can be ascertained in various ways. Veterans requiring stabilization and support during early phases of treatment need hypnotic techniques which accomplish that purpose. During later phases of the treatment process, hypnosis can be useful to uncover traumatic experiences. Specific target symptoms indicate when the use of hypnosis is appropriate. These may consist of neurological symptoms, pain or destructive dreams, and suggest the presence of hidden victim and aggressor related identifications. The therapeutic task is thus hypnotic revivification of victim and aggressor related events and the expression of fear, guilt, and grief. In this way, victim and aggressor identifications can be successfully integrated into the self.

REFERENCES

Balson, P.M., & Dempster, C.R.: Treatment of war neuroses from Vietnam. *Comprehensive Psychiatry*, 21:167-175, 1980.

Blanck, R., & Blanck, G.: *Ego psychology: Theory and practice*. New York: Columbia University Press, 1974.

Brende, J.O.: Electrodermal responses in post-traumatic syndromes: A pilot study of cerebral hemisphere functioning in Vietnam veterans. *Journal of Nervous and Mental Disease, 170*:352-361, 1982.

Brende, J.O.: A psychodynamic view of character pathology in combat veterans. *Bulletin of the Menninger Clinic, 47*:193-216, 1983.

Brende, J.O., & Benedict, B.D.: The Vietnam combat delayed stress response syndrome: Hypnotherapy of "dissociative symptoms." *The American Journal of Clinical Hypnosis, 23*:34-40, 1980.

Brende, J.O., & McCann, I.L.: Regressive experience in Vietnam veterans: Their relationship to war, post-traumatic symptoms and recovery. *Journal of Contemporary Psychiatry, 14*:57-75, 1984.

Brende, J.O., & Rinsley, D.: Borderline disorder, altered states of consciousness and glossolalia. *Journal of the American Academy of Psychoanalysis, 7*:165-188, 1979.

Breuer, J., & Freud, S. (1893): *Studies of Hysteria*. I: On physical mechanisms of hysterical phenomena: Preliminary communication. In J. Strachey (Ed.), *Standard Edition*, Vol. 2. London: Hogarth Press, 1957.

Carrington, P., & Ephron, H.S. Using meditation with psychotherapy. In J.L. Fusshage & P. Olsen (Eds.), *Healing: Implications for psychotherapy*. New York: Human Sciences Press, 1979.

Cavenar, J.O., & Nash, J.L.: The effects of combat on the normal personality: War neurosis in Vietnam returnees. *Comprehensive Psychiatry, 17*:647-653, 1976.

Eisenhart, R.W.: Flower of the dragon: An example of applied humanistic psychology. *Journal of Humanistic Psychology, 17*:3-23, 1977.

Ellenberger, H.E.: *The discovery of the unconscious*. New York: Basic Books, 1970.

Erickson, M.H., & Kubie, L.S.: Successful treatment of case of acute hysterical depression by return under hypnosis to critical phase of childhood. *Psychoanalytic Quarterly, 10*:583-699, 1941.

Fairbank, J.A., DeGood, D.E., & Jenkins, C.W.: Behavioral treatment of a persistent post-traumatic startle response. *Journal of Behavior Therapy and Experimental Psychiatry, 12*:321-324, 1981.

Fenichel, O.: *Psychoanalytic theory of neurosis*. New York: W.W. Norton, 1945, pp. 117-128.

Figley, C.R.: Psychological adjustment among Vietnam veterans: an overview of the research. In C.R. Figley (Ed.), *Stress disorders among Vietnam veterans*. New York: Brunner/Mazel, 1978.

Freud, A.: *The ego and the mechanisms of defense*. New York: International University Press, 1946.

Freud, S. (1895): The psychotherapy of hysteria. In J. Strachey (Ed.), *Standard edition*, Vol. 2. London: Hogarth, 1955.

Freud, S. (1913): On beginning the treatment. In J. Strachey (Ed.), *Standard edition*, Vol. 12. London: Hogarth, 1958.

Freud, S. (1914): Remembering, repeating and working-through. In J. Strachey (Ed.), *Standard edition*, Vol. 12. London: Hogarth, 1958.

Fromm, E.: An ego psychological theory of altered states of consciousness. *International Journal of Clinical and Experimental Hypnosis, 15*:372-387, 1977.

Gill, M.M.: Spontaneous regression on the induction of hypnosis. *Bulletin of the Menninger Clinic, 12*:41-48, 1948.

Glueck, V.C., & Stroebel, C.F.: Biofeedback and meditation in the treatment of psychiatric illness. *Comprehensive Psychiatry, 16*:303-321, 1975.

Godfrey, K.: Personal communication, V.A. Medical Center, Topeka, KS, 1983.

Grinker, R.R., & Spiegel, J.P.: Men under stress. Philadelphia: Blakiston Co., 1945.
Horowitz, M.J.: Stress response syndromes. New York: Aronson, 1976.
Janet, P.: L'anesthesia systématique et la dissociation de phénoménon psychologique. Rev. Philosoph., 23:449-472, 1887.
Janet, P.: L'automatisme psychologique. Paris: Alcan, 1889.
Janet, P.: The major symptoms of hysteria. New York: Macmillan, 1907.
Jung, C.J.: Therapeutic value of abreaction, (from) The practice of psychotherapy. In Collected papers, Part II, Vol. 16. New York: Pantheon Books, 1954.
Klein, E.: Acute psychiatric war casualties. Journal of Nervous and Mental Disease, 107:25-42, 1945.
Lifton, R.J.: The broken connection. New York: Simon & Schuster, 1979.
Maoz, B., & Pincus, C.: The therapeutic dialogue in narco-analytic treatments. Psychotherapy: Theory, Research and Practice, 16:91-99, 1979.
Moses, R.: Adult psychic trauma: The question of early predisposition and some detailed mechanisms. International Journal of Psycho-analysis, 59:353-363, 1978.
Moses, R., Bargal, D., Calev, J., et al.: A rear unit for the treatment of combat reactions in the wake of the Yom Kippur War. Psychiatry, 39:153-162, 1976.
Parson, E.R.: The reparation of the self: Clinical and theoretical dimensions in the treatment of Vietnam combat veterans. Presented at Queens Psychiatric Grand Rounds, April 10, 1981.
Perry, J.C., & Jacobs, D.: Overview: Clinical applications of the amytal interview in psychiatric emergency settings. American Journal of Psychiatry, 139(5):552-559, 1982.
Reiff, R., & Scheerer, M.: Memory and hypnotic age regression. New York: International Universities Press, 1959.
Sedler, M.J.: Freud's concept of working through. The Psychoanalytic Quarterly, 52:73-98, 1983.
Shapiro, D.: Neurotic styles. New York: Basic Books, 1965.
Shatan, C.F.: Through the membrane of reality: "Impacted grief" and perceptual dissonance in Vietnam combat veterans. Psychiatric Opinion, 11:6-15, 1974.
Spiegel, D.: Vietnam grief work using hypnosis. The American Journal of Clinical Hypnosis, 24:33-40, 1981.
Veith, I.: Four thousand years of hysteria. In M.J. Horowitz (Ed.), Hysterical personality. New York: Aronson, 1977.
Watkins, J.G.: Hypnotherapy of war neuroses. New York: Ronald, 1949.
Watkins, J.G.: The affect bridge. International Journal of Clinical and Experimental Hypnosis, 19:21-27, 1971.
Watkins, H.H.: The silent abreaction. International Journal of Clinical and Experimental Hypnosis, 28:101-111, 1980.
Weitzenhoffer, A.M.: General techniques of hypnotism. New York: Wiley, 1953.

CHAPTER

12

Hypnotherapy of Post-Traumatic Stress Disorder in Combat Veterans from WW II and Vietnam

STEVEN M. SILVER, Ph.D., and

WILLIAM E. KELLY, M.D.

PART I: VIETNAM VETERANS WITH PTSD
TREATED WITH THE AID OF HYPNOSIS

As has been shown in earlier chapters in this volume, Vietnam War
veterans are prime candidates for PTSD. Besides the well documented
trauma of the war itself, there was the additional factor of the return to

---

This chapter will focus on cases of PTSD, from two widely differing theaters of combat,
separated in time by over a quarter of a century and from wars with totally different
outcomes. Techniques of hypnotherapy, the underlying psychodynamics, and the methods of successful resolution of PTSD are extensively illustrated. Also similarities and
differences in the two types of war experience are reviewed and discussed.

The first section on Vietnam veterans is by Dr. Silver. The second section on World
War II veterans is by Dr. Kelly.

a society indifferent and even hostile to the participants of that war. This societal reaction served to deny catharsis and encouraged the burying of combat-related reactions. The veterans of this war found themselves, when not ignored, regarded as outlaws or victims by their nation; no amnesty was offered, no colored ribbons were worn for them. The social and personal imperatives to deny and suppress were great.

The experience of Vietnam veterans both in Asia and in America requires the therapist utilizing hypnosis to be aware of two interrelated issues. The first, of course, is the importance of the therapeutic relationship. While this is a basic consideration in all hypnotic work, it is particularly important when working with Vietnam veterans whose estrangement from society has increased their sensitivity to the attitudes of others. This issue comes into sharp focus, as Haley (1974) has noted, when the horrors many of these veterans have endured begin to surface.

The second major critical issue is that of control. Again, this is often a concern when doing hypnosis, but with Vietnam veterans the issue is particularly acute. The therapeutic relationship may serve as an ontogenetic microcosm for the struggle to reestablish and assert control by the veteran over her or his life. Vietnam veterans, whether male or female, were placed in positions in which they often had enormous responsibility and authority of literally a life and death nature. Paradoxically, while on one level they had enormous power, on another they were apparently helpless. One Vietnam veteran nurse found that conducting triage decisions of life and death, deciding who would receive medical care and who would not, was her daily routine. Despite this apparent power, she was well aware she could do nothing to stop or even reduce the flow of shattered and ripped bodies onto her hospital ship.

The same level-metalevel conflict of power and powerlessness existed for virtually all who were caught up in the maelstrom. Hypnosis, as it is often popularly perceived, offers an arena for struggle for control. An approach often found effective is to present the hypnotic procedure as a self-controlled activity, with the therapist serving as a commentator and advisor.

Hypnosis, it is suggested to the veteran, is simply a portion of the broad band of human consciousness and is a state of focused attention accessible to virtually anyone, once he or she becomes familiar with the technique. Repeatedly stressed is that ultimate control rests in the person being hypnotized. This calls for relatively nondirective approaches which tend to follow the individual and which use less potentially confrontive techniques, such as metaphor. Continually emphasized is the point that hypnosis is an effort on the part of two people—therapist and patient—to achieve the desired goals. This is not to say that a directive, confrontive approach cannot be successful; it can be and has been. However, fewer problems of resistance are aroused when using a collaborative approach.

Perhaps the most valuable use for hypnosis is the uncovering of repressed material, both of historical events and their associated emotive content. Often significant is the denial and repression of the related affect. In such instances, the experience has not been integrated and accepted but is, in effect, being kept at arm's length. As the veteran reports no particularly acute emotions associated with the events, both the veteran and his or her therapist are led to look elsewhere for the symptom source.

Hypnosis as a method of uncovering repressed material has several advantages over the utilization of drugs, such as sodium amytal. First, the medical requirements and problems are less—no anesthesiologist need be present and there is no concern with drug side effects or interactions. Second, as noted by Leahy & Martin (1967), hypnosis can surface material related to combat even 20 years after the event. Third, hypnosis permits a finer control of how and which material will be brought back into consciousness.

Case 1

A case example illustrates this point. A 35-year-old male veteran, married with two children, was seen as an outpatient. Having served in Vietnam in 1970, he reported no particularly severe symptoms until the Summer of 1981. He began to experience sleep disturbances and nightmares. He found it increasingly difficult to be involved with his family and steadily withdrew from contact with his small network of friends. During the course of the second session, he reported an incident from the war which he could not get out of his thoughts and which had repeatedly been the subject of his nightmares. He had watched Vietnamese soliders torture an old man and two boys, aged eight and ten. He could not recall the name of the other American who was present, nor could he remember what took place after watching a hand holding a bayonet stab the old man. The nightmares had begun the summer his two boys reached ages eight and ten, indicating, as Haley (1978) has suggested, that family events might serve as "triggers" for delayed responses to stress.

Under trance, it was learned he had had no control over the events; it was a situation of Vietnamese killing Vietnamese. He and the other American, a medic, were forced to stand by and helplessly watch. When the soldiers were done, the old man was dead but the two boys were left alive in horrible agony with "their entrails strung out in the dust," in the veteran's words while in the trance. The medic told him there was nothing which could be done for either boy and suggested killing them to put them out of their agony, which he did with a single shot into each child's head.

During the trance state, it was suggested that he was viewing the incident as an "instant replay" from a videotape machine and therefore could speed up, slow, or stop the action to match his ability to handle it. It was also suggested that he would remember that amount of the incident which he could handle now; the rest would come back as he was able to handle it.

When he came out of trance, he reported that he could remember the torturing of three people in more detail, including seeing the Vietnamese soldier who did the stabbing. No other memories were reported. He was told not to be alarmed if more details came back before the next session since the suggestion had been given that they would come back as he felt able to handle them and he could trust his mind's judgment in this regard.

He returned the following week and reported that the entire incident had come back while he was alone with his wife. He had cried and she had been very supportive. He was seen four more times and hypnosis was used to provide ego-strengthening and tension-reduction suggestions. Nightmares and other sleep disturbances ceased and self-report and reports from his wife indicated that he had ceased his isolation from his family and friends. A follow-up at eight months confirmed the cessation of PTSD symptoms.

One of the problems with suppressed memories is the difficulty caused by the unresolved possibility that mistakes might have been made. Where this is not the case, hypnosis is useful as it brings forth the actual circumstances, as shown in the following example.

Case 2

A 34-year-old veteran was seen on an inpatient basis. His treatment team agreed that a diagnosis of PTSD was warranted based on symptoms reported and displayed, including a "flashback" which took place on an admissions ward in response to the sound of thunder.

During the course of the initial interview, he reported extreme feelings of guilt for an incident which had taken place in Vietnam. While he was leading a platoon of 21 men, his unit had been ambushed and cut off. For eight hours they were isolated as the enemy tried to overrun them. Of the combat action he could only recall bits; the major conscious memory was eventually walking down off the hill with only seven men of the original 21. Without recalling any specifics, he was afraid that he had made errors while commanding the platoon which had resulted in the wounding and killing of his men. His guilt, then, was for errors he assumed he had committed.

Under trance, again using the videotape imagery, he reviewed the entire combat action in an objective time of 45 minutes. It was suggested that he observe himself and evaluate his tactical performance in the context of the events. That is, he was told, "See how well you did, based on what you knew and could do at the time." It was also suggested that the entire incident was now on tape and accessible to him any time he wished to review it.

Once out of trance, he reported that he could remember the entire combat action. He discovered he had committed no serious errors and had done as well as could be expected under the circumstances.

Obviously, uncovering suppressed material entails the possibility that it may confirm the individual's fear that he or she erred. Nonetheless, hypnotic uncovering of this material is important and a useful technique. The usefulness comes from the ability of the therapist to control the amount of material which is brought out from the trance into conscious memory. This permits adequate preparation to be made for especially powerful material. The importance lies in, first, the therapeutic efficacy of clearly identifying the source of the trauma and, second, the usefulness of hypnosis in providing ego-enhancing suggestions which enable the individual to accept and deal with these life experiences. Indeed, as Reiser (1982) has noted, simply being able to clearly recall traumatic events is useful in the reduction of symptom severity. An example of this follows.

Case 3

A 36-year-old male inpatient Vietnam veteran had led a patrol of seven men. As members of one of the first units sent into Vietnam, all the men knew each other quite well and had worked together for almost a year. All the men in the patrol were within

30 days of leaving Vietnam and a reunion already had been planned. On the return leg of the patrol, the patient had the choice of two routes. After only brief consideration of the fact that the patrol had passed through a Viet Cong controlled village on the outbound leg and thereby probably had alerted any enemy military forces in the area, he chose the shortest way back through the same village. While crossing a canal his patrol was ambushed. He himself was severely wounded by a grenade—the other members of the patrol were all either killed or wounded.

Most of this information was available consciously, with the exception of the basis for his decision to take the riskier route. He suspected he had simply been in a hurry. Therefore, when a trance was induced, two suggestions were made. First, as in the earlier example, he was instructed to examine the total context of his decision-making situation—the drain on his judgment brought about by exhaustion and stress of 11 months of combat, the desire to respond to the wishes of his friends to return to basecamp as soon as possible, and so on. The second suggestion was that, as an experienced adult now 15 years older than that young sergeant he was in Vietnam, he had certainly come to understand things better than that sergeant could and, being older and wiser, he could probably be much more forgiving of the sergeant for a single lapse in judgment than the sergeant could be of himself; indeed, it was clearly his role, as the older and more experienced man, to help the sergeant come to terms with the sad events of 15 years ago.

Immediately following this session there was a noticeable improvement in the veteran's morale—his severe depression lifted and his nightmares began to decrease in both severity and frequency. A sense of humor emerged and he began to involve himself more with the other ward residents. After discharge, a 12-month follow-up indicated that he had continued to do well.

Obviously, hypnosis can be used for purposes other than uncovering repressed material and ego strengthening. Specific symptoms and problems, such as grief, anxiety, tension reduction, and other problems, can be addressed directly (Brende & Benedict, 1980; Spiegel, 1981). Often, for example, hypnosis has been found to be useful in tension reduction and as an approach in dealing with sleeping difficulties. In these areas, Vietnam veterans with PTSD are quite similar to others having the same problems.

One possibly unique usage of hypnosis in the area of PTSD may be in its potential as a diagnostic tool. Five veterans received hypnosis while inpatients. Three were tentatively diagnosed as having PTSD (one diagnosis at the time was unclear; the last veteran was suspected of malingering). All presented themselves as combat veterans of Vietnam. Seen individually, each veteran, once trance was induced, was instructed to go back in time to "the critical time" in his life, with no other specification given. This was not a procedure used because of any desire to conduct an experiment. Rather, it was a reflection of the relative unfamiliarity of the therapist with hypnosis and was viewed as a cautious approach. The three veterans diagnosed as having PTSD did go back to events in Vietnam. The patient with the unclear diagnosis went back to his adolescent period and was later diagnosed as suffering from a schizoaffective disorder. The patient suspected of malingering also went back to childhood. It was later learned that this veteran had never served in Vietnam and had repeatedly falsified much of his history.

Obviously, this was not any kind of controlled study and is offered solely for its implications for those interested in conducting research with hypnosis and PTSD.

More and better defined research might be aimed at ascertaining the effectiveness of hypnosis when integrated with other treatment approaches, such as desensitization and flooding, which would appear to be relevant in the treatment of anxiety related disorders such as PTSD.

In summary, hypnosis has shown itself to be an effective treatment approach for both inpatient and outpatient settings for Vietnam War veterans having PTSD when appropriate consideration is made of the particular factors associated with this population.

PART II: HYPNOTHERAPY OF DELAYED
STRESS RESPONSE IN A WW II COMBAT
VETERAN MANIFESTED AS RECURRENT
EPISODES OF AMNESIA

During the summer of 1947 a 23-year-old recruiting sergeant sought treatment at a regional army hospital with the chief complaint of four distinct episodes of "loss of memory." The episodes had lasted for up to one or two days with a spontaneous return of memory usually upon awakening in the morning from an apparently normal night's sleep. His memory for events prior to the onset of these amnestic episodes was quite clear and he could discern no unusual precipitating factors. He had questioned his acquaintances as to his activities and behavior during two of these amnestic periods and they had reported no apparent abnormalities of behavior. However, the fact that he could not recall events during these periods worried him as he feared some form of irresponsible behavior might have occurred. He complained of no other symptoms and actually felt quite pleased with his current status as a recruiting sergeant. He had been assigned to his hometown, was provided a military vehicle for his personal use, and received per-diem pay which was considerably higher than if he were on a regular duty assignment.

A careful review of his past medical history was essentially unrevealing except for one episode during combat when a shell had burst close beside him, following which he had no memory for a period of several hours. There was no previous history suggestive of epilepsy nor was there any family history of this disorder. The differential diagnosis seemed to rest between an atypical post-traumatic (brain injured) seizure disorder and a combat neurosis. He was therefore admitted for further studies.

A complete physical and systems review was essentially negative. A routine neurological exam, an electroencephalogram, and skull X-rays were also unrevealing. A careful psychiatric history revealed nothing particularly abnormal in his pre-morbid developmental history. The question still remained, was his episode of amnesia during combat a typical post-concussion retrograde amnesia or was it psychogenic in origin? Psychological studies revealed a normal I.Q., no evidence of psychosis, and an hysterical profile on the MMPI (Minnesota Multiphasic Inventory).

The essential points in his developmental history are that he was the eldest of two boys, that his father was a farmer, who also drove the local school bus. His mother was a housewife. There were no unusual problems in the relationship between the parents or between the parents and the two children. However, he admitted that there was a great deal of conflict with his younger brother and that they fought with each other quite frequently. He was an average student, graduated from high school, had never had a serious girl friend. All developmental milestones were achieved at the usual age and the family history was negative for mental illness.

A careful review of events immediately prior to and immediately following each of the four amnestic episodes was undertaken, looking for any common triggering events that might help in understanding the underlying psychodynamics.

The first episode took place during the American advance through Northern France and into Germany in the spring of 1945. As a squad leader in the infantry, he had command of a unit of eight infantrymen. During one of their advances the Germans began shelling their position, and as the squad leader he gave orders to his men to scatter and take cover. He then jumped into the nearest foxhole. At the same time one of the squad members jumped in with him. Our patient, as the squad leader, turned to the other soldier saying, "You know you are not supposed to be in the same foxhole with me. We are supposed to spread out. Go find your own foxhole!" The other soldier demurred noting the intense shelling going on overhead. "Is that an order?" he asked. "Yes, that's an order" was the reply. The other soldier jumped out looking for another place to take cover and had gone only a few paces when he was shot and killed.

When the shelling had quieted down and stopped, he and his squad gathered about their fallen buddy. Just then the lieutenant came along and asked how that had happened. When the circumstances had been explained to him, the lieutenant replied, "You shouldn't have done that!" A moment later another shell exploded near by and our patient had no further memory of events until three hours later when he came to around 5:00 P M. resting in a trench, dug in for the night with the remainder of his men. Their location was three miles ahead of where he had last recalled being. Obviously he had participated in the fighting but could not recall any of the circumstances during those three hours. The rest of his period of service was served without event but still without recall of that three-hour period of combat.

It was not until a year and a half later that he again had his second episode of amnesia. The war had been won, he had returned to a hero's welcome as had his buddies and he had reenlisted largely as a result of the promise of a job as a recruiting sergeant, a position he very much desired. On this occasion he was on assignment as the recruiting sergeant in his hometown, apparently performing his work in a quite satisfactory manner when he went to see the movie "Ernie Pyle." Again he had a loss of memory, this time lasting for an entire day. He woke normally the morning of the second day with no memory of any of the events following the movie. He recalled going to the movie but not leaving it. His careful indirect questioning of his associates revealed nothing out of the way in his behavior during this period. He remained mystified and troubled but told no one of the amnesia.

The third episode occurred a few months later, beginning one day as he was driving past a local factory. He noticed a crowd had gathered at the entrance and stopped to find out what had happened. He was informed that someone had been shot. Again for no apparent reason, he had no further memory until the following day.

On the fourth occasion, a short time later, he had gone on leave to a nearby metropolitan area where he had entered a bar, gotten drunk, and returned to his hotel room. The next thing he recalls was coming to in jail the next day. He was told that he had barricaded the door to his room, had begun yelling and throwing things and would let no one in his room. The police were called and the door pushed open and he was taken to jail charged with being drunk and disorderly. He was told that during the time of the disturbance he had acted as though he were fighting the Germans again. He paid his fines and was released but felt his condition was clearly getting out of control and this was his reason for seeking treatment.

In view of the negative neurological survey and the apparently normal functioning during the amnestic periods, some sort of a dissociative reaction was assumed to be operative and it was decided to approach the problem by a combination of the technique of narcosynthesis as described by Horsley (1946) and the techniques of hypnotherapy as outlined by Wolberg (1945) to prevent untoward reactions to premature return of memories and feelings.

This type of therapy of PTSD, or combat neurosis as it was called then, was quite widely used with quite a good success during WWII. The result was a form of therapy that combined the intravenous use of a barbiturate to induce a state of increased suggestibility during which a hypnotic trance was induced with regression to the period of the trauma. Under strong hypnotic suggestion, the memory of the traumatic incident was recovered. This was followed by a period of "revivification" or "abreaction" during which the patient reexperienced, under hypnotic control, the incident and the accompanying emotional reactions. When the events of the traumatic incident had been fully recalled and the accompanying emotions reexperienced under hypnosis, it was then suggested that when the patient felt ready and able to recall the traumatic events and emotions without hypnosis he would do so.

The nature of the procedure was carefully explained to the patient and he readily agreed. A well diluted solution was prepared, consisting of one gram of sodium amytal in 20 cubic cc. of distilled sterile water, to prevent irritation and consequent thrombosis of the veins. The solution was injected intravenously, very slowly at a rate of one cubic centimeter per minute until a very slight slurring of the speech was noted. This is a very critical end point and must be carefully observed to avoid placing the patient into a drug-induced stupor from which he cannot be aroused sufficiently to cooperate with the procedure. This point occurred after twelve cubic cc. (0.6 grams) of sodium amytal had been injected. The needle was removed and a standard hypnotic trance was then induced with the repeated suggestion that he was sinking into an ever deeper sleep during which he would eventually be able to remember the events that up to now he had been unable to recall.

After about 15 minutes the suggestion was made that he was now in a deep state of sleep in which he could recall the events clearly. He was then asked if he could recall them and his answer was affirmative. It was then suggested that he allow his mind to drift back to that day in combat when one of his men had been killed and shortly thereafter when he himself had been subjected to a bomb blast. All the known events from that episode were repeated in recreating the original setting, along with a suggestion that he would now be able to recall all the rest of the events and that he would relive them in his mind exactly as they had happened and that he would tell me everything as it was happening.

He immediately began to relive this war experience and all the events that had transpired during the formerly unremembered three-hour incident. He not only recalled the incident of the death of the other soldier, but the incident of the bomb blast that he suffered following which he developed amnesia. He clearly recalled being knocked down by the blast but scrambling to his feet, with a clear recall of a consuming rage toward the German soldiers, the "Krauts," whom he held responsible for killing his combat buddy (referred to for the first time as his "closest friend") and trying to kill him as well.

Immediately it was apparent that no period of unconsciousness or even confusion had been created by the bomb blast he had experienced and also that he had very close emotional ties to the soldier who had been killed. He recalled all the events of the next three hours of close combat during which his unit advanced three miles. Many people were being killed. He specifically recalled one incident as they advanced through a forest and meeting sniper fire from up in the trees. He was able to locate and shoot down one sniper, only to be horrified upon discovering that it was a beautiful blond young woman. This only increased his rage to think that he had been reduced to killing women. When the advance was finally called to a halt and the troops had dug in for the night, in the relative calm and quiet of the moment his ability to remember events returned.

What feelings and memories had he found so threatening that he had to repress them? Under hypnosis, he knew and he revealed them. It was his overwhelming guilt over the death of his best friend and his incredible rage at the enemy who, he felt, were responsible for what had happened. He was given a strong hypnotic suggestion that he would not remember these events when he awoke but that we would return to them at a later hypnotic session and explore them further. This was done to prevent re-repression before all the amnestic material had been brought out and abreacted and worked through. In addition it was suggested that he would awaken refreshed and free from anxiety.

In a similar fashion the other three episodes were explored. What was revealed was the following: During the second episode when he went to see the Ernie Pyle movie, a true story of a journalist who joined the soldiers in combat and was himself killed, he began ruminating about the episode during which his combat buddy had been killed and about his own feelings of guilt over having caused it. His feelings and thoughts preoccupied his mind for the entire day until he was finally able to repress them the next day. Obviously the only way he could get rid of these unpleasant feelings was to re-repress them, hence the amnesia.

The third episode when he drove to a local factory and stopped to see why the crowd had gathered reminded him that he was told that some-one had murdered his *brother*. The part about the brother had not been mentioned before the hypnotic trance had been induced. Again he began to ruminate about the original combat event with the death of his combat buddy. And again he was only able to relieve himself of the tormenting feelings of guilt and rage by re-repressing them, with still another period of amnesia.

The fourth episode was the most profound reaction, one that took place while his normal controls were lost through the effects of alcohol intoxication. It seems that the repressed events of combat were recalled and reenacted while he was alone in his hotel room, an experience that could easily have been mistaken for a psychotic episode. Certainly he had lost contact with the external environment and was acting out some internalized experience. But what was he acting out? Was it a fantasy such as one finds in a psychotic or was he living out a recollection of a real life experience? Due to the confused state of mind created by the alcohol, his recollection of this event was not as clear as it was for the other occasions but it was clear enough to be able to conclude that what was being reenacted was a real life experience and not a fantasy. This fact was crucial to the decision whether or not it would be safe to continue his treatment with hypnotherapy. It would be quite dangerous to at-tempt the treatment of a borderline psychotic with hypnotherapy. It was decided to continue his treatment.

Treatment continued with a switch over to the hypnotic approach entirely after the first few sessions and no further use of the sodium amytal was made. The events of the amnestic periods were gone over several times until the memory of these events had been fully recovered. It seemed apparent that it was the original traumatic event during combat that was at the center of this man's problem. All the other episodes were due to some chance event having triggered the recollection of this nuclear event. Attention was then devoted to the abreaction of this event while still under hypnosis.

Sessions were held twice weekly lasting for 30 to 45 minutes. He was urged to relive the experience, holding nothing back as to memories or feelings during the reexperiencing of these events, and he was to verbalize his experiences so the therapist could share it with him. Therapeutic intervention took the form of reminding him that, as frightening as the reliving of the event might seem, he did not need to fear it since the therapist would be with him and would see that no harm came to him. Questions of unrealistic guilt were discussed and misinterpretations of events were corrected much as in everyday psychotherapy except it was all under hypnosis with the suggestion that he would not recall it until told to do so.

After six sessions, some with two or more repetitions of the reliving of the traumatic event, it was felt that enough "abreaction" and ventilation had occurred so that he would soon be able to accept and handle in consciousness the much revivified and worked-over material. It was then suggested that when he felt ready to handle it he would be able to recall the heretofore amnestic events, as well as what had transpired under hypnosis. He did not immediately achieve recall and the reenactment procedures, under hypnosis, continued, each time with the suggestion that recovery of these events would occur when he felt able to handle it.

One incident which occurred during these reenactments under hypnosis needs to be mentioned. At one point he inexplicably became highly upset and antagonistic toward the nurse in charge of his ward. Initially he had related to her quite warmly. She was known to be a pleasant and considerate person and his reaction was clearly inappropriate. Under hypnosis he was able to bring out the fact that she resembled the female sniper who had tried to kill him and his buddies and whom he had in turn shot and killed. This episode illustrates the potential for acting out the strong feelings being reactivated under hypnotherapy.

Toward the end of the fourth week of treatment, he asked if he might be allowed a weekend pass to visit with his family. Sensing that within the security of familiar surroundings and in the protective company of his family, he might experience a return of the now only lightly repressed material, the physician granted the pass. He was given a mild sedative to take with him with instructions that should he feel upset he should take the medication and return to the hospital immediately.

Just as had been expected, or perhaps subtly suggested, he returned

Sunday evening, having experienced a return of all the memories that afternoon while at home. He had dutifully taken his medication and caught the next bus for the three-hour ride to the hospital. Therapy then focused on several abreactions while he was fully conscious, with a re-discussion of the inappropriate feelings of guilt, etc. It was then brought to his attention that while up till this point he had never discussed his combat experiences with anyone, he now had an excellent opportunity to begin to learn how to share these experiences with others—and that there were others in the hospital who had undergone similar upsetting experiences while in combat and who would understand and be inter-ested in hearing about them. He was told that anytime he should feel his anxieties mounting, he should find someone to share his combat experiences with and thus learn to express and discuss his feelings with others.

This he did over the next week, at the end of which he reported that while sharing his experiences did help to relieve his inner tensions and anxieties, he had now shared his experience with every available indi-vidual to the point that they were no longer interested in hearing about them.

At this point it was realized that all the unlocking of the repressions of the combat experience and the subsequent periods of amnesia had not adequately relieved his inner tensions and anxieties and therefore there must be something more in the unconscious to be brought forth, perhaps something from an earlier period of his life. What could it be? Although there was little to go on, he had given a few clues. He had said that his combat buddy and he were very close friends, so close in fact that on a few occasions he had unintentionally called him by his brother's name. So, he had identified his buddy with his brother, one toward whom he had experienced ambivalent feelings. And had he not said that he and his brother had fought all the time while growing up? Quite so, and didn't his third amnesic period begin right after being told that "Someone had killed his brother?" Obviously there was more un-conscious material to come relating to the relationship of his brother. But how closely this material paralleled that of the events of the traumatic combat experience was totally unanticipated.

The patient was again placed under hypnosis and regressed back to his pre-military days, searching for some event or events that had a bearing on his present difficulties. The information was not long in coming forth. He readily recounted an event that occurred when he was 11. As he had reported, he and his brother often fought about one thing or another. Such forms of sibling rivalry are more often the rule than the exception. But this particular event had serious traumatic implications. On this occasion he and his brother had been arguing and fussing over some trivial matter when in a fit of rage he had picked his brother up and thrown him to the ground with such force that he had rendered him unconscious. Just at this point his father had come along, reprimanded him for what he had done, quickly picked his brother up, put him in the back seat of the car, and rushed off to the hospital. Our patient was convinced at the time that he had killed his brother and was overcome with guilt and foreboding.

As he was to learn later, his brother recovered consciousness a few minutes after starting to the hospital and although he seemed to be all right, his father thought it would be best to continue on to the hospital and have him checked over. Since they lived a considerable distance from the hospital, it took some time before this could be accomplished. Three hours later his father and his brother returned and our patient was enormously relieved to see his brother alive and well and no worse for the experience. He put the occasion out of his mind but never again physically fought with his brother.

Note here the parallel between the events of combat and his earlier childhood experience. He had, so far as he then knew, killed his brother, just as he had later killed his best friend whom he so strongly identified with his brother. His father had upbraided him for his actions just as the lieutenant had blamed him for the death of his combat buddy. And for three hours he had felt like his brother's murderer. The time interval during which he thought he had killed his brother was the same as that in which he experienced amnesia following the death of his combat buddy. Clearly, the experience at age 11 had been the nuclear conflict and not the combat experience. But in the first experience his fears had not been realized. He could easily dismiss the experience from his mind with no fear of little reminders triggering off his guilt, for he had no reason to feel guilty. But in the second episode his fears had been realized. His surrogate brother had been killed and he felt responsible. Here little reminders did trigger off unbearable feelings of guilt and anger.

The earlier traumatic experience was recalled, relived, and abreacted, and his guilt allayed by the realization that sibling rivalry is quite normal and customary and that what happened was clearly a simple accident. He had no trouble in reexamining the experience of an 11-year-old adolescent with the understanding of a 23-year-old adult and coming to a less disturbing conclusion as to his responsibility.

Now it had all become clear to the patient and to his therapist. He had abreacted the childhood incident and brought it into consciousness and had integrated it with the later experiences. It seemed necessary only to see if he could now remain comfortable without having to talk to others for a week or two; if so he could be discharged.

While waiting to see if he would remain symptom-free, he reported a dream which took place in a childhood setting. He and his mother were passengers in a school bus being driven by his father. The patient didn't like the way his father was driving so he told his father to stop and let him drive the bus, which he did. This appeared to be a clear, uncomplicated Oedipal dream. He was taking over control from his father. He would conduct his own affairs and those of the family from now on. This seemed to indicate that therapy had extended down to the level of the Oedipal conflict. But was it necessary to probe more deeply into this man's unconscious? After all, didn't everyone have an Oedipal conflict? Only in cases where the Oedipal conflict caused trouble was it necessary to probe this deeply. In this case, probing at this level did not seem necessary.

The transference implications of this dream were not recognized at the time but the message now seems clear enough. It was time to move aside and let the patient take charge of his life again. And this was done. The patient was discharged after six weeks of hospitalization. It was estimated that his treatement had required about 30 hours of his therapist's time. He now appeared to be symptom-free. Not a bad result for the amount of time involved. He was told to return in three months or sooner if symptoms recurred. His three-month follow-up visit found him still symptom-free, as did his six-month follow-up. Subsequently, his therapist was transferred to another post although he was still accessible to the patient if needed. Nothing further was ever heard from the patient and it is presumed that he had secured a permanent therapeutic result.

DISCUSSION

While this case illustrates with unusual clarity the genesis, the underlying dynamics, and the therapeutic process with the technique of hypnotherapy, one should not assume that a similar result can be obtained in all cases. In fact, success of this type is more the exception than the rule. First, this is a case of amnesia. Amnesia and hysteria have long been recognized as quite susceptible to hypnotic intervention, unlike other types of neurosis. Secondly, this case was carefully screened with appropriate neurological studies and psychological testing to rule out organicity and psychotic features. Thirdly, this patient was susceptible to deep hypnosis, something which many patients are unable to achieve.

Moreover, this patient was hospitalized for the entire period of treatment so that his emotional reactions could be monitored at all times, with adequate emotional support and hypnotic interventions. The tendency to act out the strong emotions being stirred up by his therapy were demonstrated by his reaction to the ward nurse who subconsciously reminded him of the female German sniper. Only within a hospital setting with frequent and intimate contact with his therapist could such acting out be controlled and incorporated into his therapy.

Also, great care was taken to retain all memories and emotions at the unconscious level until the traumatic experiences had been thoroughly and repeatedly abreacted and a systematic process of interpretation and desensitization undertaken. The return to the consciousness of the repressed memories and emotions was delayed until the patient felt himself capable of handling them. The final step of abreacting and reviewing the entire experience while he was in a fully conscious state was accomplished. And finally, his treatment was conducted by a therapist who was quite familiar with the dynamics of the unconscious and the techniques of hypnotherapy.

It should be pointed out that this same therapist has not always had such gratifyingly successful results with other cases approached by the same techniques. His experience upon returning to civilian life and attempting to treat his patients by similar techniques was the same as that of many other physicians who returned to a nonmilitary practice and found that the procedures so successful in military service were of little value in a civilian setting.

Many explanations for this have been advanced. One significant factor would seem to be the military hospital setting where protective controls against acting out while in treatment could be established. However, what seems to be of major significance is the fact that most combat neuroses of that era seem to have been of the single trauma type in which the individual's defenses were suddenly and completely overwhelmed. This is in contrast to most civilian neuroses which are due to less intense but repetitive attacks upon the defenses until the individual's ability to cope is gradually eroded away. Not that the latter type cannot occur in a military setting just as the cataclysmic, single episode type can occur in civilian life. But up until the Vietnam era the erosive type was rare in the military while the cataclysmic type is rare in civilian life.

Another factor that is clearly illustrated by this case is the importance of the pre-trauma conflict or the so called "childhood trauma." Everyone has had some trauma during the impressionable years of pre-adult life. For some children the trauma had been more severe than for others. Yet not every childhood trauma results in neurotic symptoms. As Saul (1947) has suggested, everyone has his Achilles heel, which if hit upon hard enough and often enough, will result in his undoing. It is the adult trauma, striking an already sensitized area of the protecting ego structures, that brings forth the regression into neurotic defensive symptomatology. Many who work with PTSD patients minimize the preexisting intrapsychic conflict, perhaps for fear that it implies preexisting ego weakness, which might obscure the legal issues of responsibility and compensation. However, it is not that the preexisting childhood trauma and conflicts are the cause of the neurotic symptoms but that they shape the pattern of the response to the adult combat-related trauma.

In most cases it takes an overwhelming adult trauma to reactivate childhood traumas, most of which have been adequately sealed over and buttressed with defenses. When the emotional pressures engendered by the adult trauma reach overwhelming proportions it is quite understandable that the defenses of the sealed-over childhood trauma might be the first to let go. But it is the abnormal and overwhelming power of the adult trauma and not the well healed and sealed over scars from childhood that are the true cause of the neurotic response. When excessive pressure develops in a boiler, is it the first rivet to let go that is the cause of the explosion? Obviously it is the abnormal pressure that is the cause. Had the pressure remained at normal levels, the boiler would have functioned satisfactorily. Only where preexisting neurotic symptomatology exists could it be reasonably said that the childhood trauma is the cause. Still, this does not mean that the childhood trauma should be ignored. In the case described, recovery did not occur until the childhood components of the neurotic symptoms were also dealt with. Yet he had had no neurotic symptoms before being overwhelmed by the traumatic combat experience. His psychic structure had served him quite well until overwhelmed by the emotional pressures engendered by the trauma of combat.

Something should be said about the hazards of hypnotherapy even in the hands of experienced therapists. It is interesting that many therapists who have utilized hypnotherapy, sometimes with great success, in time seem to use it less and less, switching to other methods of treatment. Freud himself began with hypnotherapy, later switching to free association. He gave as his reasons that many people were not susceptible to hypnosis and that equally good results could be obtained by other methods (1958). Yet hypnotherapy can sometimes achieve remarkable success in a relatively short period of time—in this case, for example, six weeks instead of several years of psychoanalysis. So why is hypnotherapy not used more frequently? Perhaps it has to do with the dangers of acting out. The same therapist who successfully treated the case just presented gave up the use of hypnosis after numerous instances of unexpected acting out. After several patients who broke treatment in the midst of trying to work through some very traumatic material, two others who while out of contact with their therapist experienced several hours of reliving of the original traumatic experience with loss of reality contact, and several others who experienced serious untoward outcomes, hypnotherapy was put aside.

This is not to say that hypnosis should not be used, but it should be realized that there are risks involved, sometimes quite serious risks. Perhaps it is because hypnotherapy has the potential for laying bare the undefended unconscious through the bypassing of ego defenses. Without the defense there is the danger of either acting out or regression to even more primitive and damaging neurotic defenses. Even a skilled operator has difficulty in correctly determining the location and strength of the unconscious emotions and their defenses when employing hypnotherapy. This is what makes hypnotherapy so potentially hazardous.

Perhaps one of the main values of hypnotherapy is that it so clearly demonstrates the fact that there really is an unconscious part of the mind and that there are mechanisms that operate to protect the individual from its awareness. As a teaching tool and a learning process, it has no equal. Its use gives conviction about the principles of psychodynamics and enhances the understanding of them. It is perhaps the gateway to the understanding of the unconscious. But as a therapeutic method, it has its risks and should be undertaken only after a careful selection of patients by an experienced and knowledgeable therapist under circumstances where adequate controls against acting out can be instituted.

CONCLUSIONS

Both authors are experienced therapists and both are quite familiar with the treatment of PTSD. However, the first author's exposure to PTSD in the veteran population has been largely confined to PTSD in the Vietnam veteran, while the second author's exposure was limited to the WW II experience. There are striking similarities among the two experiences and some striking differences.

One of the similarities between the Vietnam and the WWII veteran groups is that the stress reaction is delayed in both. Why is the reaction to the stress delayed? If the traumatic experience overwhelms the defenses, why do some individuals immediately develop symptoms while for others the symptoms come on only after a period of delay, often after a period of five or ten years or even longer? Could this be on the same basis as that described by Freud (1958) as the "return of the repressed" in which earlier represed material comes to awareness in midlife or later? Or could there be a limit to how much one can successfully retain under repression without the old being displaced by the new? Or is it that current circumstances reactivate repressed emotions and thoughts, bringing them closer to the surface? Why do some people seem to be able to successfully repress indefinitely while others are subjected to the discomfort of repeated confrontations with undesired thoughts and emotions? While the scope of this chapter does not permit the discussion of these issues, they are addressed elsewhere in this volume. Let it suffice to say that examples of delayed response to stress are found in substantial numbers in both the WWII and the Vietnam veteran groups.

However, the severity and possibly the frequency of PTSD appear greater among the Vietnam veteran population. An exact determination of these facts is made difficult by the simple fact that the diagnosis of PTSD did not exist until precisely defined by the DSM-III in 1980. Nevertheless there is some support for this assumption from research and clinical impression. Comparative research involving Vietnam and Korean war veterans (Thienes-Hontos, Watson, & Kucala, 1982) found the severity of PTSD greater in the Vietnam veteran group. An informal review of the clinical experience of the two authors of this chapter supports the impression that PTSD is not only more severe in the Vietnam veteran group but also more frequent when compared to the WWII veteran group.

Perhaps this dissimilarity can be explained by the very significant differences in the WWII and Vietnam experience. As noted before, most of the WWII PTSD cases resulted from single episodes of traumatic experience. This was because most of the WWII experience was spent behind relatively well defined lines of defense. Sentries were posted and one could at times relax and sleep in relative security. Although fighting was intense when it occurred, it was circumscribed and fairly predictable. In contrast, the Vietnam guerrilla warfare was quite different. There were relatively few and poorly defined lines of territorial control. One never knew when or from where attacks might come. Serious threat to life was a 24-hour-a-day occurrence. One could never distinguish with assurance between friendly Vietnamese supporting troops, enemy troops, and innocent uninvolved civilians. Everyone was a potential enemy, even women and children. It was a war with people from a totally different culture. Attitudes toward human life seemed totally different from that of the typical American. In addition, there was the uncertain support of their own command, with military decisions often giving way to those made by politicians trying to conduct a "limited war."

But most disturbing of all was the divided attitude at home about the "morality" of the war. There were indeed many factors that induced a sense of purposelessness to the war effort. Survival became the primary goal of the soldier. The threat to survival was an omnipresent danger that greatly heightened the stress of the Vietnam experience. It should be no surprise that the proportion of Vietnam veterans suffering from PTSD greatly exceeded that of WWII veterans.

Another significant difference is that a greater proportion of PTSD victims from the Vietnam experience were of the multiple trauma type, in contrast to the single trauma type from the WWII experience. This is of special significance because it has a direct bearing on treatment. PTSD of the single trauma type is more circumscribed and the pathology relatively easy to distinguish from normal mental functioning. The less cataclysmic erosive multiple trauma type is so blended with the experience of everyday living that it is much more difficult to dissect out and deal with therapeutically. This may be why WWII PTSD seems to have been so readily responsive to narcosynthesis, whereas the Vietnam multiple trauma PTSD responded better to the storefront rap group approach.

Another new factor was the negative attitude of society to the returning Vietnam veteran that led to a *voluntary* attempt to cover up the combat experiences, a form of *suppression,* if you will, whereas WWII experience was quite supportive of the returning veteran and suppression was less likely to occur. However, those WWII veterans who had been subjected to the cataclysmic single episode type of trauma developed an *immediate involuntary* forgetting, or repression, of the experience. Not that cataclysmic traumas did not also occur in the Vietnam experience but when they did occur they were in a setting of continuous multiple small traumas as well. *Many Vietnam veterans suffer from both types of PTSD.*

There is a significant difference in how Dr. Kelly treated his patient and the way Dr. Silver handled his patients. Dr. Kelly utilized the combined narcosynthesis-hypnotherapy approach almost entirely, guided by a classical psychoanalytic model of mental functioning. Dr. Silver employed a more flexible type of desensitization therapy, utilizing hypnosis only infrequently, sometimes to overcome resistance and memory blocks, but more frequently to promote relaxation and the control of anxiety. Each therapist seems to have intuitively adapted his treatment approach to the needs of his patient. This may very well indicate that the method of approach must be different for the two types of PTSD.

Both therapists used hypnosis to facilitate recall, to control anxiety and for bringing out buried emotions, although one gets the impression that the depth of the hypnosis was lighter and the strength of the transference was much reduced with Dr. Silver's patients. Both utilized the support of other veterans in their treatment. But one directed his therapeutic efforts almost entirely to the exposure of the unconscious, according to the classical psychoanalytic model of mental functioning, while the other depended more on a behavioral model, with a significant dependence on group-support techniques. These differences in approach probably reflect the need for the therapist to adapt his treatment methods to the type of problem being dealt with.

This leads to our last and perhaps major conclusion, namely that the presence of periods of amnesia for even a small part of the traumatic experience is a very significant marker for PTSD, where repression (involuntary forgetting) exists. It may be that this type requires a more intensive uncovering type of therapy and even a resort to hypnotherapy on occasion.

It is hoped that the reader has absorbed some of the enthusiasm and enlightenment that these two therapists have experienced in sharing their treatment experiences with one another. A large generation gap, with rare exceptions, exists between the veterans of WWII and Vietnam. The same if often true of their therapists. By bridging the gap, both therapists have arrived at a clearer understanding of the similarities and differences between the WWII and Vietnam experiences as they affect the character of post-traumatic stress responses and the types of treatment appropriate to each. By breaking down this communication gap, the authors hope they have brought new insights into PTSD and have tried to share them with you, the reader.

REFERENCES

Brende, J.O., & Benedict, B.D.: The Vietnam combat delayed stress syndrome: Hypno-therapy of "dissociative symptoms." *American Journal of Clinical Hypnosis,* 23:34-40, 1980.

Brenman, M., & Gill, M.: *Hypnotherapy.* New York: International Universities Press, 1947.

Diagnostic and statistical manual of mental disorders, 3rd ed. Washington, D.C.: American Psychiatric Association, 1980.

Freud, S. (1913): On psycho-analysis. In J. Strachey (Ed.), *Standard edition,* Vol. 12. London: Hogarth, 1958, p. 208.

Haley, S.A.: When the patient reports atrocities: Specific treatment consideration of the Vietnam veteran. *Archives of General Psychiatry,* 30:191-196, 1974.

Haley, S.A.: Treatment implications of post-combat stress response syndromes for mental health professionals. In C.R. Figley (Ed.), *Stress disorders among Vietnam veterans.* New York: Brunner/Mazel, 1978.

Horsley, J.S.: *Narco-analysis.* New York & London: Oxford Medical Publications, 1946.

Leahy, M.R., & Martin, I.C.: Successful hypnotic abreaction after 20 years. *British Journal of Psychiatry,* 113, 383-385, 1967.

Reiser, M.: Erickson and law enforcement: Investigative hypnosis. In J.K. Zeig (Ed.), *Ericksonian approaches to hypnosis and psychotherapy.* New York: Brunner/Mazel, 1982.

Saul, L.: *Emotional maturity.* Philadelphia: J.B. Lippencott, 1947.

Spiegel, D.: Vietnam grief work using hypnosis. *American Journal of Clinical Hypnosis,* 24:33-40, 1981.

Thienes-Hontos, P., Watson, C.G., & Kucala, T.: Stress-disorder symptoms in Vietnam and Korean War veterans. *Journal of Consulting and Clinical Psychology,* 50, 558-561, 1982.

Wolberg, L.R.: *Hypnoanalysis.* New York: Grune & Stratton, 1945.

Wolberg, L.R.: *Medical hypnosis,* Vol. I & II. New York: Grune and Stratton, 1948.

CHAPTER

13

Establishing a Post-Traumatic Stress Disorder Inpatient Program

W. PETER SAX, M.D.

For reasons deep within man's heart, the discovery and forgetting of the bloodless wounds of war recur throughout history. Certainly, from the early days of enduring communities we have accounts of the purification of warriors returning from combat (Schwartz, 1982). Shakespeare provides an unmistakable description of PTSD in the words of Hotspur's troubled wife:

> O my good lord, why are you thus alone?
> For what offence have I this fortnight been
> A banish'd woman from my Harry's bed?
> Tell me sweet lord, what is't that takes from thee
> Thy stomach, pleasure, and thy golden sleep?
> Why dost thou bend thine eyes upon the earth,
> And start so often when thou sitt'st alone?
> Why hast thou lost the fresh blood in thy cheeks
> And given my treasures and my rights of thee
> To thick-eyed musing, and curst melancholy?

234

In thy faint slumbers I by thee have watch'd,
And heard thee murmur tales of iron wars,
Speak terms of manage to thy bounding steed,
Cry, "Courage! to the field!" And thou hast talk'd
Of sallies and retires, of trenches, tents,
Of palisadoes, frontiers, parapets,
Of basilisks, of cannon, culverin,
Of prisoners' ransom, and of soldiers slain,
And all the currents of a heady fight.
Thy spirit within thee hath been so at war,
And thus hath so bestirr'd thee in thy sleep,
That beads of sweat have stood upon thy brow
Like bubbles in a late-disturbed stream;
And in thy face strange motions have appear'd,
Such as we see when men restrain their breath,
On some great sudden hest. O what portents are these?
Some heavy business hath my lord in hand,
And I must know it. Else he loves me not.

King Henry the Fourth, First Part (Act II, Scene 3)

In our own century America's wars have noted these psychic wounds with names of "shell shock," "combat fatigue," "zombie reaction," "combat neurosis," and "post-Vietnam syndrome."

Industrial accidents (particularly in the hazardous trades), train wrecks, fires, disasters at sea, automobile and airplane carnage, rape and heinous physical assault share with combat in the etiology of what used to be called "traumatic neuroses." They also share an equally long history of strongly divided opinions and judgments about these perplexing handicaps.

Trimble (1981) recounts the early history of efforts to understand these troubles and to distinguish them from invention and malingering (p. 1). He includes an account of the experience of author Charles Dickens and his change of conviction about the topic after suffering a train accident (p. 27).

Division of opinion has long been expected between legal and medical observers, frequently bolstered by adversarial involvement. However, within the "pure world of healers and helpers," one also finds an abundance of equally strong beliefs and disbeliefs regarding traumatic phenomena, their causes, mechanisms, and prognosis. These varied positions are an integral part of the historical perspective. Education, medical experience, even considerable exposure to police and military experience are no predictors of how the thus enlightened observer will perceive persons subjected to overwhelming events, either immediately or in the long run.

My own exposure to these interesting attitudes about traumatic neuroses began in medical school with a case history of an oil tanker seaman whose ship burned and sank with considerable loss of life. The lecturer described the patient's symptoms and noted that persons in hazardous trades often lost their sense of magical protection (necessarily developed in such work) whenever they experienced a major accident. The case description ended with the prognostic statement: "Most of these men never go back to work again, not only in their former occupation but anywhere." Discussion of long-term management and rehabilitation was notably lacking. Although the loss, the chronicity, and the challenge to remedy the impairments and relieve distress were no less than in diabetes, tuberculosis, or compound fracture of the femur, still they remained almost totally unaddressed. On the other hand, it was the prevalance of combat fatigue in World War II and its often spectacularly successful management through the sophistication of hypnosis or narcosynthesis demonstrating the power and reality of the unconscious that motivated a flood of young physicians to enter the field of psychiatry in the late 1940s and early 1950s.

I had seen few traumatic neuroses in my practice prior to joining the Veterans Administration in 1976, where assignment to an admission ward allowed me to see many acute and chronically exacerbating patients.

A small but steady flow of Vietnam war veterans among these admissions had already established their reputation with the staff as irritable, demanding, and likely to leave the hospital as soon as possible according to their own ideas. Their diagnoses ran the gamut from depression and alcohol and/or drug abuse to sociopathy and atypical schizophrenia. In retrospect, some of these diagnoses were accurate, some only described major presenting behavior, and many were misdiagnoses, totally missing the underlying traumatic component of the illness.

The would-be helper soon learns the necessity of listening to the veteran state his distress in his own terms without leaping to premature diagnostic conclusions, facile reassurance, or reductive explanations. In this manner, feeling components evolve, leading to the inevitable development of an interpersonal field of meaning between the distressed veteran and the helper.

Once a good therapeutic alliance has been established, the deeper disturbing thoughts and feelings are brought to the fore and discussed. Intense long-standing anger is common, and so long as one does not challenge its validity, control remains remarkably good. There is an ease with naming and blaming government and society but this is usually accompanied by an acceptance of responsibility to solve at least some of the problems themselves. In the few instances where control has been lost, anger has been directed against property or at themselves. The therapeutic spin-off is an awareness that anger produces a sense of autonomy and power which anxiety does not. The fact that anger keeps personal distance at a more comfortable level is easily recognized, and is accepted by many vets as "not really the primary problem." While anger remains a significant though secondary problem, it is as frightening to the patient as it is to others. In contrast to the stereotypes and worries of some staff members, particularly those who do not work directly with Vietnam veterans, there is the fact that there have been no assaults on any staff member in the year and a half we have been working with this program (which is true of no other ward in the hospital).

What is less obvious than anger and less readily available, though deeply important for patients and critical for staff rapport with them, is *grief*, usually profound and persistent. Most often it relates to lost comrades and lost beliefs about themselves and/or society. Though usually hidden and offered with great caution, grief and anguish have so far been invariable. The chaplains of this medical center have noticed it as a regular companion to memories of acts of omission and commission, frequently screened by tough denial. "Hardly a day goes by now that I don't see at least one of the Vietnam veterans who is asking ultimate questions about the morality (or immorality) of the Vietnam conflict! My first experience with one of these cases was as a chaplain at a college in Tennessee in 1969-70" (Kaylor, 1982).

I recall one physical giant of a man, described as "unmanageable," sent to this institution from a Philadelphia prison where he had been for eight months. In one brief session our social worker and I met with him and his family. The family showed us letters and newspaper clippings documenting that the patient had been an outstanding scholar and athlete, and had been so constructively active in a difficult center city community that he had been written up in the newspapers. His family had letters from teachers and administrators remarking upon his ability and promise. He had forgone college scholarship offers to "do his duty for his country" and had enlisted in the Marines. He served a tour of combat duty in Vietnam and "returned home changed." He was not able to cope beyond self-care at home, and his increasingly exaggerated defensiveness finally resulted in his incarceration.

During the course of this meeting, the social worker and I were quietly engulfed by the massive tragedy of these losses and later ventured to acknowledge the surprising degree of pain and grief which each of us had personally felt in witnessing it. Neither his family nor our staff were able to keep him from leaving as soon as he felt ready, but the image and recall of that experience will remain for years. In my opinion, the degree of comfort with one's own evoked responses to another's intense anger and deep grief is critical to avoiding significant observer distortion, even rejection of the patient's problem.

By 1980 our increased awareness of the problems of Vietnam veterans, an increased interest in the literature, and the advent of the Diagnostic Statistical Manual (DSM-III) prompted several interested staff members to bring this active area of need to the attention of the Chief of Staff to see how our Medical Center could best address it. At that time a handful of V.A. Medical Centers across the country were initiating "homegrown" programs for Vietnam veterans. The motivation included interest in the condition, therapeutic efficacy, and public pressure, most notably from this cohort of veterans themselves.

The Chief of Staff appointed a committee to address the problem as promptly and expertly as possible and to advise as to program needs. This committee included a psychiatrist, a psychologist, a social worker, a clinical nurse who had been active with these patients, a physician from the Rehabilitation Medicine Service (a former medical school dean with wide experience in imaginative care, teaching, and planning), and one of the chaplains interested in these patients. To this core committee another psychologist (a former career Army man with combat in three wars, including Vietnam) several physicians, chaplains, pharmacologists, and from time to time occasional veterans were asked to join the meetings on an ad hoc basis. The committee met monthly, the frequency decreasing as the program took shape.

Within a few months after the committee had been organized, we had developed a considerable awareness of the problem, a sense of its emerging visibility and extensiveness, and some experience in identifying persons suffering predominantly from PTSD, as well as those who had admixtures of other psychiatric and characterological problems. A once-a-week evening group was opened to Vietnam veterans from all of the wards so long as they were not so disturbed as to preclude managing themselves in a gathering. At these meetings we hoped to address the problems of an estimated 20 to 40 Vietnam veterans in our hospital at any given time, many of whom were on substance abuse units. These group meetings were well received and exciting. They also stirred memories and feelings, some of which were anxiety-laden and resulted in defensive responses such as irregular attendance and focus on the external, and/or on bureaucratic problems to a point that those ready to work on the more personal aspects of their war experiences were discouraged.

In October 1981, a program for PTSD was officially established at our medical center "to assess and provide psychotherapeutic and psychopharmocological treatment for veterans with post-traumatic stress disorder" . . . "to assist hospital staff by direct service, consultive services, and by the development and delivery of educational programs for professional and other veteran focused groups and by research activities" in PTSD and related issues. The multidisciplinary committee for this purpose consisted of a psychiatrist, a psychologist, a clinical nurse, a social worker, a rehabilitation medicine service physician, and a chaplain, with options to call in other professionals on the hospital staff for consultation as needed.

Medical Administrative Services sought to identify all Vietnam era veterans and to provide the names of those actually having served in Southeast Asia to the program coordinator (the psychiatrist). Committee members were asked to address both inpatient and outpatient problems. Pressure to consider establishing a specific inhospital unit made up of Vietnam veterans continued to be voiced by those in the hospital and by veteran-concerned organizations in the community. Some feared that exclusive Vietnam grouping might promote the already existing isolation and exclusiveness of the group. However, the committee finally opted for the positive aspects of peer support which builds strength and has growth potential far in excess of the feared regression and static élitism. Early and repeated observations of this valuable support action in acute crises amongst the spontaneous groupings have continued to confirm the rightness of this choice.

V.A. policy states that patients are not to be treated by social or historical groupings but by their clinical and/or diagnostic condition. Therefore, a unit built around the diagnosis of PTSD regardless of historical time or type of stressor is possible. Indeed it has been our belief that the presence of persons with the same disorder from varied stressors could be a factor stimulating a vision of commonality in society generally. Unfortunately, the opportunity to test this idea has fallen through on three or more occasions due to disqualifying factors appearing in these other candidates for admission to the PTSD unit; as a result, the actual persons on our present unit are in fact uniformly Vietnam combat veterans.

All veterans who had served in Southeast Asia during the Vietnam era were to be evaluated for PTSD and for possible exposure to herbicides or other chemical contamination, receiving a basic physical examination and routine laboratory studies. The latter part of the evaluation was the standard physical survey for all admissions. Alertness to chloracne, unusual health and neurological problems, tumors, and deformed offspring comprised the special physical health features specifically looked for. In practice, the bulk of the evaluation consisted of identifying PTSD in pure, mixed, or modified forms.

Of the program team at that time, only the psychologist was appointed fulltime. The other team members had clinical responsibilities occupying fully half their time elsewhere. In consequence, the hopes and expectations of these first proposals proved too ambitious to be fully or even satisfactorily achieved. Educational efforts were extensive and informative for the educators as well as for those targeted for benefit. It is notable here that experience offers constant informational input and provides questions for the sturdiest and most enduring of assumptions.

Betweeen October 1981 and October 1982, an effort was made to offer twice weekly group therapy programs for all inhospital PTSD veterans. The mixed ward groups consisted of those with essentially pure PTSD and those with mixed diagnoses (some still psychotic and some grossly manipulative patients). This made for uneven and difficult groups, often polarized as to agenda and aims. Unfortunately, this often caused those with an acitve motivation for working through their PTSD problems to withdraw and drop out in silent disappointment or disgust. It was also noted that a therapeutic approach favoring revelation of buried pain before reliable support is in place tends to churn the group membership, thus losing many individuals who then resume their former withdraw-and-wait status. In retrospect, a structured, supportive, even didactic group model is preferable for those who for whatever reason are not able to actively address the problem with professional help and peer support.

To this early phase of the program (which consisted of consultations, a scattering of therapeutic victories, and education), the response by the outreach programs and by individual veterans was one of appreciation and optimism. At the same time, numerous instances of unsubstantiated cries of "favoritism," along with sharp criticism and embittered rumor, appeared. Most of this reaction came from veterans who hoped for magical solutions (including instant cure, undoing, denial, and restitution of a world which never was). Equally often these negative responses came from those for whom this limited effort was experienced as an irritant, mocking, face-saving, neither real nor a symbol of hope.

During this time it is also important to recognize that other professionals, on one admission ward in particular, were moving to meet the needs of their PTSD patients, with notably informed sensitivity, ingenuity, and dedication. This program also featured individual and group therapy and a particular focus of approach on guilt feelings, along with an innovative involvement of the chaplains and the family. This is mentioned to support spontaneous approaches to this very numerous patient population, and to discourage the notion that their care is the exclusive property of any élite team. It is important to disavow that patients have only one possible trail to escape the doom of chronic suffering and impaired function.

In new country the first traffic is likely to travel different trails; despite our road building, the road is not large and the existence of other trails is appreciated, though their ultimate blending into an established thoroughfare often figures in the dreams of all parties counting upon it.

In late 1981 the Coatesville Veterans Administration Medical Center administration, consistent with an ever-present concern for patient needs, practicality, and recurrent veteran requests, proposed the utilization of an unused 12-bed wing of the women's ward to launch an inpatient PTSD program. This opened in January, 1982, and was designed to be an open ward, accepting persons who are abstinent of drugs and alcohol, not cognitively or affectively disturbed, and capable of living with minimal nursing supervision.

The 12 beds were distributed through five rooms on the distinctly separate wing: a single, two doubles, a three-bed, and a four-bed room, and a toilet. Shower facilities were shared with an adjacent locked ward (alcohol program) for men. A day room and laundry facilities were shared with the women's ward (29 patients on the far side of the day room and the nurses' station). The men were appealed to as a competent nonpsychotic group to be alert for unauthorized strangers coming to the floor and to be generally protective of the women patients. Mainly this went fairly well, although the sharing of facilities (television, radio, refrigerator, ping pong, and pool table) caused some friction and a need in both populations for rules about territory, noise, conflict management, and socializing. All patients able to do so were expected to eat in a central hospital dining room in another building.

In view of the history of some of our patients losing their temper and punching holes in doors and walls, it was hoped we could duplicate an earlier ward experience and set up a heavy punching bag to work off aggressive feelings. However, the structure of the building baffled this effort. Actually the PTSD population appeared to have less need of this than anticipated. While the admitting ward had experienced frequent broken, lacerated and bruised hands, X-rays, etc., which the punching bag markedly reduced, among our PTSD patients battered hands seldom materialized.

Once the program was in operation, we found that several issues took a different turn than we had expected. The most evident of these was the passive resistance and verbalized annoyance at being asked to engage in shop and educational activities. Even though the choice of "details" at the hospital is considerable, several men with previous machine shop and woodworking experience did not attend more than one or two times after making their selection, citing the controlled atmosphere (designed to promote participation by the more cognitively damaged patient) as uncongenial. This was common but not invariable and appeared to be related to deep fears of becoming chronic V.A. patients and to extreme sensitivity to any authority which is not both earned (by their standards) and clearly appropriate to the immediate situation. Just as at work prior to hospitalization, so on details, many interpersonal events were too reminiscent of previous experiences associated with being placed in severe danger by others' incompetence in combat. The feeling responses were automatic and distressing; the controls were almost always unobtrusive and effective—avoidance and reduction of the stimulus.

One overall feature of the program has been the veterans' insistence, variously expressed, on shaping their treatment to fit their individual progress and their requirements for becoming effective in their communities again. Thus, procedures which in effect only fill time, which seem arbitrary or unfair with no clear useful outcome, and which are not honestly explainable—all receive little respect, but occasionally the veteran's suggestions offer a useful alternative.

Our rules are fairly basic: The standard V.A. rules regarding alcohol, drugs, weapons, violence, and generally unacceptable social behavior are enforced. In our particular setting, infractions of rules do not result in automatic discharge but are dealt with in terms of the patients' and group capacity to use the incident for growth and learning. In cases where the patient is not ready to use the program or is being destructive of it, he is discharged or transferred.

We have learned to handle acute psychological (in contrast to behavior) loss of control in a different-than-usual manner through an early experience of one patient's becoming psychotic and threatening in his panic. Because a show of force and seemingly arbitrary medical decisions can be sharply evocative of patient group defensiveness and cause instant combat team readiness and loyalty to the disturbed individual, we decided, together with the patients present at that episode, that when it becomes necessary to remove a resident to a more secure psychiatric setting the decision will be made by the PTSD unit staff, or on evenings and weekends, by the nurse in charge of the unit. The decision would be shared with the unit leaders (their elected officers), together with information about how the patient is going to be approached, why the move is necessary, how it is desired for the other residents to function, how the hospital psychiatric emergency team is going to function, and how the unit staff will be in charge of the transfer. Working this through has been valuable in preventing confrontational and escalating styles of interaction between hospital staff and the unit residents which are always disheartening and destructive for everyone concerned.

The weekly program of the unit consists of: daily 8:30 A.M. community meetings with residents and staff, chaired by the residents who have a rotation of elected officials every two weeks—president, vice-president, ward monitor and ward detail man (this meeting covers the events of the past 24 hours, or weekend, as well as future appointments and activities, and affords a time for questions and clarifications, usually lasting about 15 minutes); group therapy from 9:00 to 10:30 A.M., Monday, Wednesday, and Friday (more recently increased to Monday through Friday); desensitizing groups on Tuesday and Thursday; staffing Wednesday, 10:30 to 12:00 A.M.; cooking class for fun and self-reliance, Monday and Tuesday 11:00 A.M. to 1:00 P.M.; patient education and history of the Vietnam war, Wednesday 1:00 to 2:00 P.M. and sometimes also on Thursday 1:00 to 2:00 P.M. Patient education usually involves videotapes. Also included are topics on medicine, psychology, life, job finding, etc. and the staff is expected to work together to keep these regular events from overlapping with individual therapy sessions, medical, dental, podiatry, and biofeedback appointments, as well as recreational or paid details, workouts and games in the gym or on the playing fields.

This is an active (mid to late 30s) population needful of medical attention; among 13 resident patients (as of April 1983) we have three patients with diabetes requiring insulin, four patients receiving medication for hypertension, two with angina pectoris, three with actively painful combat wounds, and two with tumors of the sinuses. This is a somewhat larger distribution of physical pathology than usual, but, aside from the sinus tumors and the angina, is not unusual. Insomnia and nightmares of greater or lesser severity are almost universal. Social, legal, and family problems are extremely common, as are problems with employment. Many are in the process of asking for a decision on service-connected disability.

Possibly the most critical aspect of the organization of our inpatient unit is the selection of who will be brought together to bring about this important period of change and development in their lives. This pertains equally to staff and patients, for it has long been observed that certain mixes in school, in service units, and in business enterprises are "magic," while others are pedestrian or disastrous. Ideas of selection are presented below, but it must be kept in mind that the actual interaction is what determines the nature of the experience, its aliveness, and its capacity to promote more effective visions and practices.

We find that the capacity of the staff to make rapid shifts of assumptions or paradigms is limited and not to be attained by simple rote memorizing, shamming, or public relations gimmickry. Thus, we want staff who come well motivated and with an active interest in our residents and their problems; people who are anticipating some growth and change from their experience; individuals who can endure the absence of quick answers and tidy intellectual frames, and who can use rules to establish common ground, not hiding places. For we have found that the professional caretaker who is unwilling to make these adjustments will serve as no alternate model, will not generate trust, and will not afford any genuine receptive support for the major moves the veteran seeks. The veteran will protect his impacted experiences and his dignity from any attempt to sell his hard-won knowledge for a smile-button normalcy or for any gloss-over quick fix which denies the lessons of the Vietnam experience and the sacrifices of comrades lost and crippled.

In turn, we speak of the veterans who are the most likely to benefit from such a program as those who present clearly diagnosable PTSD with an absense of major mood and thought disorders and ego-dystonic behavioral dyscontrol responses and who have a capacity to see substance abuse as ultimately destructive to themselves. PTSD veterans whose substance abuse is most clearly a self-medication with ultimately unacceptable side effects have been found to be good candidates for successful treatment, sometimes even after a decade or more of dependency and/or abuse. We find that those who have a need to talk or to find a means to talk about their distress and to find meaning in it are well motivated and focused. The acceptance of the final ownership of the problem and the responsibility for its actual management are positive signs, whatever the presenting stage of development.

On the other hand, those who are relentlessly dedicated to blaming others or who are preoccupied with revenge, justification searches, or a persistent need to astonish or derive narcissistic nourishment from their experience are not available for help. They are in major danger of "buying" or romanticizing their problems and accepting them as a meaningful way of life rather than as an interference wasting their humanity and uniqueness. True thought and affect disorders, even in remission, pose a high-risk group. In our experience, exacerbation has too often been inflamed and reprecipitated by the focus on areas where these major defenses have been evoked before. Just as in their original breakdown, they are not amenable to management within an open ward, communal setting.

In addition to attempting to screen admissions, we have, after several months' experience, established that a person admitted to the unit is on probationary status for the first month while we become better acquainted. This makes it less traumatic to all concerned if we find we have admitted someone unable to use this particular program and requiring transfer to another treatment unit. Scales, tests, and such predictive devices so far have not been perfected, though one of our team (Silver, 1983) is currently engaged in establishing to what extent the Minnesota Multiphasic Inventory can contribute to subtle differentiations.

Of the treatment modalities, one of the most critical is the milieu of the peer group. This should function for maximal healing and growth and each member is encouraged to continue with other veteran groups well beyond the period of hospitalization. This latter aspect is consolidating in its effect in the same way that many therapists have seen individuals attain familiarity and control of their problems, both during and following treatment, by the informal helping of others. It can serve significantly to help the patient in making his own decisions and establishing a pattern of self-maintenance. This contrasts with the often mentioned idea that helping others is "only" a displacement and avoidance of one's own conflicts and emotions.

Group therapy affords a chance to try new areas of risk with peer support, to explore and expand interpersonal relationships, manage hazardous interpersonal relationships, and to be exposed to examples of these moves in others. Recognition of the importance of and respect for working through of group resistances is established.

Individual therapy is conducted by the psychiatrist, the psychologist, a nurse specialist with training in psychotherapy, and a social worker who is also trained in family therapy. The styles and techniques range from hypnosis (training in self-hypnosis with cooperative explorations of key painful memories) to interviews enriched by gestalt therapy and psychoanalytic understanding in an effort to assist the veteran in making actual changes in his disturbed responses to key trouble-producing situations. At base is the need to find and drain the psychological abcess that lies beneath the manifest material.

Some phenomena of note are: 1) that development for these young soldiers who went to war while still in the midst of establishing adult identities is in some ways arrested, yet in other ways is vastly accelerated so that the development of a sense of seriousness, of questions about death and life's meaning appear frequently. These awarenesses are usually not encountered until at least middle age; 2) that ego constriction and frozen invariable patterns of imagination are relatively common in these young soliders and contribute to the helplessly constricted visions of depression; 3) that addictive behavior is vastly enhanced, offering as it does an avoidance of the active burden of choosing in a world unalterably devoid of positive affirmations; 4) that there is evidence of an emotional state existing as a conditioned response and not built on internalized representational and symbolized conflicts.

The use of medicines is problematic—partly because of the ease of shifting to medical sedatives (benzodiazepines in particular) which do much the same job as street sedatives. At base, the excavation of buried and avoided overwhelming experience and meanings is the key to reexperiencing psychological integrity. To an extent medication can serve as a function-enabling umbrella under which to define otherwise unbearable interpersonal experiences, but the danger exists of its subversion to evasion and postponement, as well as of its use to calm staff anxiety. As Gitlow (1983) states, all of these substances are sedatives, which some persons find socially and reasonably enabling but with ultimately life-threatening side effects which usually drain any possibility of meaningful existence from the picture.

Aside from medical problems and psychosomatic symptoms needing treatment for control of morbidity, there exist problems of physiological disorder, minimal brain damage, subictal seizures, and altered states of physiology and consciousness which medical treatment can only partially modify in the effort to remove their disorganizing and masking effects. Tricyclic antidepressants (doxepin, imipramine, amitriptyline) for specific endogenous depression and phenelzine (Nardil) for some of the dysthymic disorders, nightmares, and intrusive memories can surely be useful. Ibuprofen (Motrin) and propranolol (Inderal) have limited use in our experience. Occasionally, in persons suspected of covert cyclothymic disorder and in moody people, some of whom have been using substances of abuse in response to mood changes, lithium carbonate has been found to be helpful.

In a larger sense it would be unfortunate if PTSD could be swept away by packageable FDA-approved technological brooms, blessed by their "proper" associations (as whiskey and dope are not), and insulating this war's civilians and its veterans from the pain of an overall reintegration to new wholeness, for the Vietnam war remains to be digested by the whole community.

In the beginning of our unit we took Philip Caputo's statement as a guiding philosophy:

> If America wants its Vietnam veterans to be cleansed, if it wants them to come home, it must give them genuine compassion, dignity, and respect; compassion for having been misused, dignity for having answered the call to arms and doing their duty as they saw it, respect for having had the courage and tenacity to survive.
>
> But if American society is to give its forgotten warriors the respect they deserve, those warriors have to learn to respect themselves first. They cannot . . . wallow in self-pity, carry on passionate love affairs with their own self-destructive guilt. They have to see themselves as survivors, not as victims, for the victim . . . is the man who says "I can't," the survivor the man who says "I can." (Caputo, 1982, p. 274)

Yet, with even our modest experience with this inpatient unit, it is becoming increasingly evident that this encounter between a returning army and its society is not so much the lancing of an abscess by the physician as it is a vast and dynamic process for a nation. The healing dialogue is not only between the two but perhaps even more within each of the participants themselves, each being enriched, exercised, and challenged by the input of the other until the mending is not just "back to" before but, in fact, stronger than before as a result of gaining true wisdom through integration of his experiences.

REFERENCES

Caputo, P.: The unreturning army. *Playboy*, January 1982, p. 274.

Gitlow, S.E.: Alcoholism, the primary disease concept (audiotape). *Audio Digest Psychiatry*, *12*(12):June 1983.

Kaylor, W.: Personal communication, 1982.

Schwartz, H.J.: "Fear of the dead": The role of the social structure in the rehabilitation of combat veteran. Paper presented at Coatesville VAMC, PA, 1982.

Silver, S.M.: Personal communication, 1983.

Trimble, M.R.: *Post-traumatic neurosis: From railway spine to whiplash*. New York: John Wiley & Sons, 1st ref. p. 1; 2nd ref. p. 27, 1981.

CHAPTER

14

Management and Implementation of Nursing Care for the Post-Traumatic Stress Disorder Patient

GERTRUDE C. WOODS, R.N., THOMAS A. SHERWOOD, R.N., and ROSE MARIE THOMPSON, R.N.

The Vietnam veteran suffering with post-traumatic stress disorder (PTSD) has presented a new challenge to the medical profession. This challenge has had an even greater impact on the nursing staff who are charged with the implementation of nursing care. Most psychiatric nurses are well versed and quite competent in implementing care in traditional psychiatric conditions, i.e., functional psychosis, addictions, etc. However, the care of the Vietnam veteran is quite different, frequently presenting a baffling problem to the nurse. In addition to problems normally encountered with combat participants, the nurse must also deal with problems specifically related to PTSD which are more severe and more complex.

At a time when many Vietnam veterans were emerging from adolescence, they were being sent to fight a war that many Americans did not condone. When the young soldier did return home, idealism had turned to disenchantment (Goodwin, 1980). Unlike World War II veterans, Vietnam veterans were not received in the U.S. as heroes, but instead "returned in defeat and witnessed antiwar marches and protests" (Williams, 1980). Jackson (1982) has written:

> Many Vietnam soldiers, during combat or following their return home, experienced traumatic disillusionment with the military establishment, with the policies that were carried out in Vietnam, and with their society's values, and attitudes toward its returning heroes. (p. 229)

Thus many Vietnam veterans found themselves estranged from a society in which they did not have a sense of belonging. Jackson also writes:

> . . . The disparity between the adolescent's inner life and the reality of the chaotic and irrational combat world in which he found himself was so great that he was unable to integrate the experience either cognitively or verbally. Expansion and growth were inhibited. . . . The difficulties this group of Vietnam veterans experience may, in part, be related to being fixed in an adolescent phase of moral development. . .•. (p. 228)

The above factors underlie many of the behaviors that have been described by nurses (Furey, 1982; Adams 1982; Huppenbauer, 1982), i.e., demanding, hostile, withdrawn, opposed to rules and regulations of ward routine and, in general, difficult to care for. This behavior not infrequently brings about feelings of anger and helplessness on the part of the nurse.

The purpose of this chapter is to identify factors affecting the nurse-patient relationship and to give some guidelines that are relevant in implementing the care of the PTSD patient. Much of the material is based on the authors' experience of working with an inpatient PTSD program in a large Veterans Administration Psychiatric Center.

FACTORS AFFECTING THE NURSE-PATIENT RELATIONSHIP

The Nurse

Attitudes: The nurse in an inpatient PTSD unit must have the personal resources and inner strength to accept continual challenge to her flexibility and nursing skills. She must be able to confront her own feelings about aggression, killing, and death on a daily basis and to endure the pain and sense of vulnerability which accompany this process. Some nurses who are not oriented to the complexity of PTSD may tend to see the Vietnam veteran only externally, i.e., physically able to "get a job, support a family" and in general, "fall in line with society." Whether this is a self-defensive mechanism or a lack of insight into human behavior, the result is that the nurse who perceives only on an external level will not see the sadness, the fear and terror, the shattered self-concept and ideals, the loneliness, the guilt for living, and the need to feel someone cares, which is locked inside the veteran.

High level communication skills (empathetic listening, using "I" statements, tactfulness, demonstrating a sensitive awareness of individual differences) are also essential to a nurse's success in building a trusting relationship. The Vietnam veteran, reflecting his generation, is more articulate, more demanding, more politically aware and active than older veterans with more traditional backgrounds. He requires an explanation for all that he experiences in his milieu. In responding to that challenge directly and without defensiveness, the nurse helps develop a feeling of trust in the treatment process. The nurse who relies upon compliance with rules backed by threats of disciplinary action or security forces will be quickly frozen out of the therapeutic alliance.

Education: It is important that the nurse read all she can about the war in Southeast Asia. Much of the literature regarding the war focuses on vivid descriptions of the conditions which the veteran was subjected to and the aftermath, both social and psychological (Resing, 1982; Figley & Levantman, 1980; Goodwin, 1980). Goodwin (pp. 3-10) gives a vivid and impassioned description of the Vietnam war, the conflicts it created in moral values, and the ambiguities which predisposed the combatant to the post-traumatic stress disorder. Shatan (1978) has focused on the emotional aftermath of combat and presents some theoretical considerations about how this predisposes one to stress.

From the theory and accounts in the literature, two important criteria for therapy emerge: the need for an accurate diagnosis and a specific milieu of care. Throughout the literature it is emphasized that diagnoses be based on certain criteria and symptomatology as listed in DSM-III (1980). It is most important that nurses recognize these symptoms of PTSD and not confuse them with indications of other forms of mental illness, such as functional psychosis, addictions, and sociopathy. PTSD is a reaction to extreme stress frequently encountered by combat Veterans in Southeast Asia (Goodwin, 1980).

There is much in the literature pertaining to research in specific milieus designed to treat the PTSD patient (Williams, 1980; Shatan, 1974; Figley, 1978). However, Egendorf (1982) reports there is little research on clinical outcome. There is a paucity of literature written by nurses regarding interventions in the care of the PTSD patient (Furey, 1982; Adams, 1982; Huppenbauer, 1982; Resing, 1982). Like Furey (1982), the authors agree on the importance of the nurse becoming knowledgeable about the Vietnam conflict and its emotional consequences. In turn, this may increase the nurse's sensitivity to what the veteran is feeling.

Educational Qualifications and Skills: Educational qualifications beyond nursing school are helpful but the willingness to become educated through inservices, continuing education classes, and experience in crisis intervention, individual, group, and family therapy is essential. PTSD is on the leading edge of psychiatry and new information is constantly becoming available. The nurse utilizes herself as a role model, teaching interpersonal skills to patients whose own skills have become rusty or lost through separations from family and friends. There are some veterans who may refuse to engage in other than superficial conversation with the nurse, especially if she is female. In some cases, these are the same clients who are having difficulty relating to other women in their lives. Adams (1982) describes incidents in the inpatient program when the female staff members are subjected to derogatory remarks (p. 1705). Williams (1980) and Shatan (1978) have described the warrior role that the combatant tends to play, i.e., an exaggerated masculine self-image wherein women are seen in stereotyped sex roles.

Haley (1978) has found in her experience of working with Vietnam combat veterans that some stress responses may be precipitated by closeness to women, especially when coupled with the responsibilities of marriage, a wife's pregnancy, or the birth of a child. She further states that veterans who have fought and killed women and children often find it impossible to make a smooth transition to the role of husband, protector, and father (Haley, 1978). This feeling may extend to women in general, with the result that the veteran has a shattered male self-image. If the nurse can assist the patient in working through this treatment issue, then the therapeutic alliance can continue.

We have found that there are times when being female has its advantages; sometimes the male veteran will express his grief when talking to the female therapist. It has been reported that some women therapists have been successful with Vietnam veterans where male therapists have been ineffectual. This is related to the fact that the women were able to deal with issues of intimacy and emotions more quickly than a male therapist (Williams, 1980, p. 33).

The Patient

Unlike WW II veterans who returned home to a hero's welcome, the Vietnam veteran returned home feeling defeated and witnessing antiwar projects and marches (Goodwin, 1980). There was little or no time for readjustment. Some men had to make the transition from the rice paddies of Vietnam to home within 36 hours! For many, the intensity of guerrilla warfare was simply locked within as they attempted to make an abrupt adjustment. Shatan (1978) and Wilson (1978) have described the veteran's rotation home as having the appearance of being asymptomatic largely during the first year. However, the veteran soon began to notice that the America he had known before did not appear the same to him. Consequently, fantasies he previously had were just that—fantasies (Goodwin, 1980). When symptoms, such as intensive thoughts of combat, nightmares, feeling of alienation and rage began to emerge, the Vietnam veteran sought treatment, usually in various V.A. Hospitals. According to Goodwin, (1980):

> Treatment from the V.A. was very difficult to obtain. The veteran began to feel depressed, mistrustful, cynical, and restless. He experienced problems with sleep and with his temper. Strangely, he became somewhat obsessed with his combat experiences in Vietnam. He would also begin to question why he survived when others did not. . . . (p.10)

The veteran seeking admission to our program has usually had previous treatment in a substance abuse program, Veterans Outreach Center, or an outpatient clinic. His request for admission is prompted by a life management crisis such as difficulty with his spouse, divorce, job loss, legal difficulties related to substance abuse, aggression in the community, or a vagrant life-style. A suicide attempt may have preceded his admission. The clinical picture the veteran presents on arrival is usually one of overall depression. Goodwin (1980, p.11) states that many Vietnam combat veterans have been continuously depressed since Vietnam. Along with the depression is a feeling of worthlessness, numbness, grieving for buddies who were killed in combat, and a sense of helplessness. Consistently, the veteran will express the feeling that this is "my last chance to get it together." The veteran cannot define or explain what will happen if this treatment program is not successful.

Although the patient will state that he needs to be in the program, some veterans are quite difficult to engage in the treatment process. There are various reasons for this, some of which are related to the psychodynamics of delayed stress disorder, particularly in the case of the Vietnam veteran. The patient may already feel that he has been used and scapegoated by the U.S. Government (Goodwin, 1980; Williams, 1980), and he sees the V.A. as an extension of that government, i.e., it is not to be trusted. This distrust extends to rules and regulations. Some patients may refuse to attend therapeutic acitivities, sleep most of the day, which sometimes is prompted by nightmares much of the night, and experience feelings of worthlessness, difficulties with spouses, difficulties in expressing their hostility toward the nurse who is attempting to follow rules. A similar clinical picture has been described by Lipkin, et al. (1982) who outline four types of PTSD:

1) Those manifested primarily as specific psychological symptoms.
2) Those detectable mainly through a major alteration in life course.
3) Those evident because of difficulties in relating to others.
4) Those where there had been a profound destruction of concepts of self and reality, with many different external manifestations. (p.910)

The Case of Dan

The following case demonstrates both the typical presenting situation on an inpatient unit and the scope of clinical knowledge the nursing staff must have.

Dan, 34 years old, married, and questionably employed, is a Vietnam veteran suffering from PTSD. He and his fellow patients (with the same diagnosis) are housed on a ward in a large northeast Veterans Administration Medical Center, one of several such wards recently set up throughout the nation. He had been receiving counseling at a nearby Operation Outreach Vet Center and was sporadically attending an Alcoholics Anonymous (A.A.) group. The psychologist in the Vet Center had recommended that he enter the V.A. Medical Center for substance abuse treatment and then enter the PTSD program. His wife had threatened to leave him if he did not follow the advice of the psychologist.

When Dan entered the PTSD program, he had completed a six-week program for substance abuse; thus, he was oriented to the hospital. He stated that he was glad to be here and showed some understanding of the term PTSD, stating that no one could tell him what was wrong with him five years ago. He stated that he'd had seven jobs within the past 10 years and had lost almost all of them due to alcohol abuse and inability to concentrate. He had held his current job for the past year but it was questionable whether or not that job would be available after his discharge because of his poor work record. For the past five years, he had slept an average of three hours per night, with frequent nightmares when he did sleep, often causing him to awaken in a cold sweat.

Dan stated that he had no friends. Although his family seemed supportive, he felt isolated from them and was unable to share his feelings with them or show any affection toward them. He stated that no one wanted to hear about his combat experience; therefore, he had denied that he was ever involved in the actual fighting until encouraged to talk about it at the Vet Center. Dan avoided watching war combat stories on TV for fear that it would reactivate his traumatic memories of the war. He stated that on some days, especially when it was excessively hot or rainy, he continuously had intrusive thoughts about his experiences in Vietnam, sometimes causing him to imagine himself back in the combat zone. He admitted that he had a gun in the house and had at times considered using it on himself. He spent some of his time marveling at his wonderful wife, stating that he did not deserve her.

Dan's personal history showed that he was the youngest of four siblings from a middle class family, was an average student in high school, and had no particular goals formulated at the time of enlistment. His father had been in World War II and often reminisced about his experiences. In 1965 at the age of 17, and before completing high school, Dan volunteered for the military out of a sense of patriotism because "it was the right thing to do."

As a patrol leader, Dan was involved in intensive combat throughout his 12-month tour in Vietnam. In one of his encounters, all but two of his patrol were killed by the enemy. In another experience, a Vietnamese family had befriended his troop. However, it was later found that some of the people in this Vietnamese village were sabotaging American troops. The CO then ordered that the entire village be demolished. Dan, as a member of the troop, was forced to carry out these orders. One of the persons he shot, a Vietnamese woman, was approximately four feet from where he stood. When Dan returned to the U.S., the nation was experiencing the peak of the war protest activities. Some young men were openly burning their draft cards and some were fleeing to Canada. Dan avoided talking about his experiences in the war and pretty soon was even denying that he had been there. Yet on the surface he appeared to be readjusting satisfactorily within the community.

At the age of 24, Dan married a school teacher, bought a house, and began working as a construction worker. Six years after military duty, he began to have intrusive thoughts about his war experiences. He began having a drink or two to banish these thoughts. Also, at this time his wife was moving up the education ladder and putting pressure on Dan to obtain his GED (Graduate Equivalency Diploma). Dan began to increase his alcohol consumption to blot out the pressure and the increase in nightmares. Consequently, he missed much time at work and after a while he was fired.

Dan began to isolate himself and drank more and more. There were other jobs which were soon lost. One night, Dan's wife found him in the backyard, dressed in military garb and digging a trench while yelling wildly, "The enemy are coming." Dan was hospitalized for a short while and released. There were other episodes as he became increasingly depressed, isolated, and more dependent on alcohol. At this point, one of his brothers insisted that he seek help at the Veterans Outreach Center.

After counseling at the Veterans Outreach Center and treatment in a substance abuse program, Dan was admitted to the PTSD program. After some time in the program, Dan began to share some of his feelings with the group. In individual sessions it soon became obvious that Dan was more depressed than previously recognized. As he spoke of his personal experiences, invariably he cried while stating his feelings of worthlessness because he let his buddies down. He had tremendous guilt regarding the destruction of Vietnamese villages in which he had participated. This was compounded by the bitterness he felt about not winning the war, especially when his father could brag that "they" did win. He was also bitter about the U.S. Government denying him any monetary compensation for his psychological disabilities while at the same time considering the Iranian hostages as heroes.

Dan had ambivalent feelings toward his wife which he was reluctant to expound upon. On one hand he was angry with her for not understanding his problems and making demands on him, yet on the other hand, he loved and depended on her. Basically his feelings of unworthiness were related to his overwhelming feeling of guilt. Dan's wife appeared to be supportive of him when she visited. However, she frequently reminded him of the money he had squandered and other examples of unproductive behavior in the past. She refused to attend a support group for wives, stating that she had already heard enough.

During Dan's tenure in the PTSD program, the ward received a distress telephone call from another part of the hospital stating, "Those Vietnam guys are causing trouble again!" Some of the staff immediately ran to the scene. There they found that one of the PTSD patients had suddenly become angry over a minor incident. Security personnel had been called. As a policeman approached, representing authority, the patient, overcome with his unresolved rage, lunged toward the officer but was restrained by his fellow patients. This was one of several crises where intervention had been necessary.

Gradually, during Dan's four months in the PTSD program, he made significant improvements. During his last month in the program, contact was established with his last employer for the purpose of acquainting him with PTSD and establishing the feasibility of Dan returning to work. Dan did return to work at his last place of employment and is attending a group therapy on an outpatient basis.

Assessment and Planning

The preceding case has been reported to illustrate the effects of PTSD. In case after case, each veteran suffering from PTSD has reported similar symptoms. In Dan's case, as with all of our patients, a history of his experiences was obtained. It is very important that the history be perceived by the veteran as thorough, in order to gain his assistance in the assessement and planning of his treatment. Those patients who have medicated themselves to the point of abuse (like Dan) may have their symptoms masked. Thus, the nurse may not see the underlying PTSD symptoms in the initial assessment if she does not have a broad knowledge of PTSD. Haley (1974) notes that because of lack of knowledge or avoidance/denial, many mental health workers will take an elaborate history but avoid asking the veteran about his Vietnam experience. One cannot begin to assess the impact of the experience on him unless one takes a history (p. 260). Dr. W. Peter Sax, coordinator of our program, has developed a history-taking format which is used by our staff. The questions must be specific and include the following:

1) *Pre-military experiences:* What were his relations with family and others? What were his ambitions? What activities was he involved in? What was his general health, etc.?
2) *Work history:* This would include the veteran's employment experience before and after military service. There should be a detailed account of the work experience, interpersonal relationships at work, his work capacity, the number of jobs he has had, his current employment or reason for unemployment.
3) *Military history:* This would include branch of service, units, and location. It should also include dates, military training and occupational specialty, a detailed account of personal experience (which may include a traumatic or life-threatening situation), and the veteran's reaction. This area should also describe the area of combat and casualties, injuries sustained by the veteran and his buddies.
4) *The onset and severity of presenting symptoms:* Were the present symptoms first experienced during the military or after discharge? What are the times, duration, and frequency of the symptoms? According to the DSM-III (1980), the diagnostic criteria should include a stressor, which evokes significant symptoms of distress.
5) *The experience of the veteran since his military duty:* This would include friends and family relationships, outlook, steps to alleviate symptoms, and the reasons for seeking help. If possible, additional information from other sources should be obtained to verify the veteran's preceptions.

In assessing Dan's history, the following problems emerged:

1) A history of alcohol abuse—related to attempts to alleviate symptoms (patient's last drink was eight weeks prior to inpatient PTSD program).
2) Depression most of the time—related to a number of actual life events that produced a feeling of hopelessness.
3) Feelings of worthlessness (low self-esteem)—related to feelings of failure.
4) Survivor's guilt—related to losing buddies in combat while he survived.

5) Unresolved grief—related to inability to grieve the loss of his buddies.
6) Inability to concentrate—related to intrusive thoughts about Vietnam.
7) Unresolved rage and anger—related to many aspects of the political nature of the war.
8) Frequent nightmares—related to experience in combat.
9) Unfulfilled desire to obtain his GED—related to inability to study effectively.
10) Obesity—related to poor nutrition.
11) Unresolved marital conflict—related to feelings of isolation and withdrawal.
12) Need to verify employment and explore options.
13) An old back injury for which he received service compensation.

In planning Dan's treatment, a three-part thrust was adopted: 1) reduction of the PTSD symptomatology; 2) guidance in resolving his life management crisis; and 3) assistance in making viable discharge plans. In our time-limited program (4 months), a team member was assigned as a primary therapist to provide individual therapy and oversee treatment throughout his hospitalization. His treatment plan included the following: the social worker contacting his employer for the purpose of resolving the job crisis; therapy; participation in group therapy; the therapeutic community; desensitization; biofeedback; physical therapy; life management skills class (cooking). It was also planned that Dan should attend educational therapy for the purpose of assisting him toward his GED.

A physical examination showed that Dan was quite obese and had hypertension. A plan was made for Dan to meet with the dietitian to arrange a reduction diet and patient education regarding nutritious low-calorie foods. Dan's blood pressure and diet would be monitored by the nursing staff. The nursing staff would also utilize certain strategies aimed toward reducing symptomatology as well as overseeing nursing care in general. The nurse must remember that the trauma was real; thus, the treatment must focus on the symptoms resulting from the veteran's reactions to stresses (Ewalt & Crawford, 1981). This means an atmosphere whereby the patient can, in addition to other gains, increase his sense of self-worth and awareness of choices and responsibility.

In an inpatient PTSD program, the effectiveness of the treatment depends heavily on the therapeutic milieu. The therapeutic milieu includes all that is in the patient's environment, and is geared toward fostering the patient's rehabilitation (APA, 1969). This includes the treatment team, the treatment program, the attitude of the staff, the environment, nursing interventions, and specific therapies. In implementing care for Dan and other PTSD patients, the following issues were addressed. We do not suggest that everything works in fine tune or that every endeavor has been a success. However, the authors wish to share their experiences, along with some theoretical considerations.

THE THERAPEUTIC MILIEU

The Treatment Team

The nurse's function on a PTSD treatment team is the same as that on a general psychiatric team. She collaborates with those in other disciplines by sharing information, providing consistency, and securing cooperation in devising an effective treatment plan (Kreigh & Perko, 1983). However, there is an immense difference in the type of patient being treated on a general psychiatric unit and that on a PTSD unit. Generally speaking, the patient on a general psychiatric unit is seen as either passively psychotic or acting out in response to delusions, hallucinations, or other thought disturbances. The patient on a PTSD unit is not psychotic and is acutely aware of his surroundings. Thus, he can be coherently and actively demanding, raise moral and ethical issues, and challenge every treatment decision.

These behaviors, combined with the patient's painful combat experiences with which the staff must deal, create the most intense countertransferences the authors have ever experienced. We have had to examine our own personal vulnerability and question long-held values. The nurses' knowledge and professionalism are challenged continuously. The issues that the veteran raises forces the nurse to reexamine personal feelings and previously held philosophies. Haley (1974) notes that working with PTSD patients is difficult for the therapist (team member) for three reasons:

1) Confrontation with one's own personal vulnerability to catastrophe.
2) The challenge to one's moral attitudes about aggression and killing.
3) The fear of the intensity of the countertransference and transference. (p.265)

Countertransference is a continuous threat to the treatment team members. Williams (1980) writes, "It is difficult to achieve the necessary clinical detachment because these men raise moral and political questions for the mental health professions" (p.27). The gruesome stories they tell are painful to hear. However, the team member has to be careful that treatment decisions are not based on unconscious emotional reaction to the patient. Haley (1978) writes that the team member (or therapist) "must continually monitor and confront his reactions to the patient's experiences" (p.265).

One issue with which the team on a PTSD unit is most likely to be confronted and that has a heavy impact on nursing is the veteran's attitude toward women (Haley, 1974; Adams, 1982). Female staff on a PTSD unit may find themselves treated very differently from the men. Men are less likely to be the targets of verbal abuse and are more strongly welcomed as therapists. Women frequently find themselves perceived in a stereotyped sexual role. This may be related to the fact that many of the patients have a poor self-image. Thus, the veteran tends to compensate by projecting an exaggerated masculine self-image which he hopes the female will view as seductive or intimidating (Williams, 1980). As Adams (1982) points out, women may respond to these pressures by choosing to assume a passive role.

Some treatment decisions may bring out unresolved feelings about women in the male staff. Adams (1982) found in their inpatient PTSD unit that when the female staff were subjected to demeaning sexual comments, the male staff appeared unsupportive and began resisting having female therapists in their groups. When and if this occurs, one of the female's workable options is to confront, validate, and work toward resolving these issues. The male staff member who rejects stereotyped sex roles is seen as a healthy role model for the veteran who has experienced distancing and alienation from significant women in his life.

Another important function of the treatment team is to extend their knowledge and experience of the PTSD patient beyond the unit to the hospital community and the community at large. This means that the team has the responsibility to educate and to act as an advocate for the PTSD veteran. Education can be extended to include hospital employees, dietary service, physical, recreational and occupational therapy, security, and other areas who come in contact with the PTSD patient but have little knowledge of the behavioral manifestations. The authors are frequently called upon to give inservices to nurses on other units. In addition, as the public consciousness continues to be raised regarding the Vietnam war and the veterans suffering from PTSD, team members are called upon more and more to educate the public.

Advocacy should be an integral part of the assignment of each team member on the PTSD unit. Kreigh and Perko (1983) have defined advocacy as:

> . . . an attitude of support which safeguards the rights and integrity of the patient. It demands that the nurse expand the health concept of doing unto a person for his own good to include standing up for the good of the patient. . . . (p.215)

Advocacy, in the broadest sense of the word, means that the nurse (and the team member) must fight for the rights of the patient. The nurse performs this responsibility by becoming informed on social and legislative issues affecting the veteran. Thus, she provides the patient with information he needs in order to make logical decisions. In addition to information, the nurse provides the reassurance and care that the veteran so desperately needs in making the step back into American life.

Environmental Considerations

Ideally, the Vietnam veteran in treatment for PTSD should be housed in a unit with other Vietnam veterans for obvious reasons: He needs to have a peer group with which to identify; he needs to know that there are others with similar sypmtoms; and he needs social interactions with others. The PTSD patient needs to feel that he has a measure of personal freedom within the environment. He needs to participate with the treatment team in setting up ward rules that they both can abide by. The ward community can then be seen as "government of the people, by the people, for the people." The ward becomes a microcosm of society whereby the patient can learn to develop social interactions and responsibilities.

In our program, a system of self-government was set up through a Therapeutic Community. It has been observed and noted throughout the literature that Vietnam veterans seek out each other; thus this characteristic was utilized in a therapeutic sense. In this system, the patients assist in writing the rules, monitor each other in adhering to the rules, uphold each other when one begins to fall, assist in setting up disciplinary actions, learn to have genuine concern for each other, and, if necessary, point out the staff's inefficiencies. For example, Dan had a strong sense of organization, having been a sergeant in the military. Thus, he was voted to be the community (unit) president. Dan was accustomed to making hard-and-fast rules, and in general felt, "People should abide by the rules, no matter what." The staff saw this as overreaction of the superego but tactfully let the patient group handle this therapeutic issue. The patients themselves rebelled against Dan's hard-and-fast rules. The patients focused on Dan's attempt to see the staff as authority figures who had to be obeyed. The patients' impact on Dan had a far greater therapeutic effect than the staff might have had. Dan slowly learned that it is O.K. to question rules you don't agree with and that most rules can be amended or revised.

We had previously thought that the PTSD unit should be housed separately from other units. In our program, because of insufficient space, the PTSD unit and the women's unit are housed on the same ward. The units are at opposite ends of the ward and the nursing staff, which is in the middle, is responsible for both units. Each unit has its own separate activity. This setting sometimes poses strategic difficulties for the nurse who is attempting to provide care for both groups. There are times when the nurse may be supplying care to acutely psychotic female patients. On the other end of the ward, the depressed PTSD patients, who have never learned how to reach out, may be withdrawing more and more.

However, there are some advantages in this setting. The interactions between the men and women can be seen as having therapeutic values. There are times when brief interactions with the women have brought about stress responses in the men which served as the catalyst for abreaction. Sometimes the PTSD patients have shown much support and empathy for what the female patients are experiencing.

Ideally, the PTSD unit should be structured in such a way that adequate space is provided for semiprivate rooms, a place to sit and rap, and a place that provides some quiet time. Semiprivate rooms are especially helpful when sleep disturbances are involved. There should be an adequate visiting room where family visits can be fairly private and a recreation space for activities such as billiards, table tennis, etc. Somewhere on the ward there should be a punching bag or a boxing mattress with which the patient can release some pent-up tension.

The staff may find that everyday items in the environment will set off stress responses in the PTSD patients—for example, nurses with uniforms and employees with oriental eyes. Many patients have told us that uniforms represent authority and oriental eyes remind them of Vietnamese women. Most V.A. hospital settings have both nurses wearing uniforms and oriental employees. This is reality. The nurse can assist the veteran in adjusting to that reality by helping him to explore the validity and appropriateness of "here and now" feelings. This approach has worked effectively in our program where we do have an oriental employee and some of the registered nurses do wear uniforms.

The inpatient PTSD program is not an oasis within the hospital setting. Hence the patient is brought into contact with others outside of his immediate environment—in the dining room, the gym, etc. The importance of educating others within the hospital environment has been discussed. However, learning how to cope with indifferent attitudes and with interactions with others should be an ongoing part of the therapeutic process and incorporated into the environment of the PTSD patient. New patterns of behavior can be practiced along with the other rehabilitative aspects of the treatment of the PTSD patient.

NURSING INTERVENTIONS

The nursing interventions discussed in this chapter are based largely upon the experience of the authors while assigned to the PTSD inpatient unit.

Ward Organization

A self-governing therapeutic community was taken as the organizational model to be followed. It was reasoned that men who are distrustful, cynical, and alienated would be more likely to be willing to follow program rules if they helped to make them. The rules reflect medical center policies and expectations and provide a moderate degree of structure with which to meet program needs. A ward that is too loosely structured can become chaotic, and when it is too highly structured, attention is focused on the environment instead of on therapeutic issues. In a highly structured unit, nursing would be forced into a policing role and this is clearly counterproductive when working with Vietnam veterans.

As each new group of patients are admitted and coalesce into a working group, they demonstrate their togetherness by revising ward rules closer to their collective thinking of how they should be. Staff also feel a need to revise the rules and handle disciplinary matters together. This provides a natural opportunity for patient resocialization. It should be noted that although patients help to write the rules, this does not necessarily assure compliance.

The nursing approach to the patient is nonauthoritarian, nonjudgmental, and accepting. This is the only approach that will consistently elicit cooperation from the majority of patients. Adult-to-adult transactions are encouraged. The patient's right to refuse is respected.

This is not an easy approach to maintain. As noted above, the veteran alienated from authority does not follow rules well, accept prescribed treatment, or even come regularly for medication. The nurse's professional values may be threatened by this behavior. The nurse has to recognize consciously that she has a need to control patients (motivated by a desire to protect their well-being) and consciously relinquish it so that she becomes comfortable with this approach. Problems with veterans should be handled directly. "Is something wrong?" "You seem angry. Is there a problem?" Essentially, the nurse needs to be open, direct, appropriately self-disclosing, warm and nonauthoritarian. "A real person" (Haley, 1974, pp. 191-196).

Administration of Medication

Administration of medication is an area in which the nurse finds it difficult to relinquish control. Her professional values are involved and it is difficult not to harry the patient who is missing half of his medication every day. Recognizing that the patient does have the right to refuse may help the nurse to be accepting of the patient's behavior. If a patient is late for a medication but within an allowable time frame, medication should be given in an accepting, nonjudgmental way. If the patient is too late for the nurse to give him the medication, that is explained and he can be referred to the physician again. The emphasis is on the nonauthoritarian, nonjudgmental approach. Documentation in these cases is important, as is follow-up with the physician for proper resolution.

Medications given at 8:00 A.M. and 8:00 P.M. are taken more consistently. Sometimes the physician will choose to give medications, which are usually given in several doses during the day, at these times instead, i.e., twice daily instead of four times daily.

Because of substance abuse histories and inconsistent behaviors, the patient may be a poor candidate for self-medication. When this is the case, self-medication is usually limited to self-applied creams and selected items like antacids.

Generally, the most frequently ordered medications are the tricyclics for depression and Dalmane as necessary for sleep. Phenothiazines (Thorazine and Stelazine) or benzodiazapines (Valium) are the next most frequently ordered medications, but they are given only for short periods of time.

Dan, because he was clinically depressed, did receive the tricyclic Imipramine along with Dalmane for sleep. A daily vitamin supplement was ordered because Dan had been placed on a reducing diet.

A patient history of chronic, long-term alcohol abuse and depression such as Dan's should alert the nurse to observe closely for evidence of alcohol use and drug-seeking behaviors.

Substance Abuse

Substance abuse is a major management problem for the nursing staff on a PTSD unit. Virtually all the PTSD patients admitted to the unit have had a history of substance abuse. Criteria for admission to the PTSD unit require the veteran to have been free of drugs and/or alcohol for at least 30 days before admission. Nevertheless, one-third of the veterans who are admitted are discharged or transferred before completing the four-month-long program for repeated instances of drug or alcohol use.

Medications administered to the veteran may accentuate the effects of the substance being used, with potentially tragic results. The nursing staff must be vigilant in observing for alcohol and drug use. Procedures that are used rather uniformly in medical centers may have a deterrent effect. These include frequent ward searches and supervised collection of drug urines and breathalyzer tests after all passes, off-station trips, and randomly during the day. Disciplinary action whenever substance use is found may be helpful. However, restrictions or refusing weekend passes may stimulate the desire for alcohol because of the loneliness, boredom, and inactivity experienced over the weekend. Voluntary service, or a combination of voluntary service and restrictions, is sometimes a more successful way of handling discipline. Patient education and Alcoholics Anonymous groups are helpful.

Patients recognize that substances brought onto the unit are enormously tempting to others who are abstaining. Consequently, the ward rules now specifically state that any patient bringing alcohol or drugs onto the ward will be discharged from the program. The intense loyalty the veterans develop toward each other has regularly prevented them from indicating their buddies in previous incidents. Whether this rule will survive must be tested.

Sleeping Disturbance, Hyperalertness, Flashbacks

Dan was unable to sleep more than three consecutive hours at a time for a period of several years. His sleep was disturbed by frightening dreams and nightmares. Sometimes he cried out and on several occasions had struck his wife during these episodes. His fear and sense of vulnerability during the eight hours were such that he kept a loaded gun under his bed at home. Fearing for her own safety, his wife rarely slept with him in the master bedroom. He frequently became stressed by and exhibited startle reaction to loud noises. He had experienced several flashbacks.

Managing patient sleep disturbances and related sypmtoms such as Dan's requires the staff to monitor and be aware of the noise that is made while performing nursing duties. At night, quiet shoes or slippers should be worn by the staff. Bath towels placed over the tops of the sleeping room doors will permit them to be opened and closed quietly. Patients need the freedom to sleep where and in whatever way they are comfortable. If the patient needs to sleep sitting up in a chair, then a chair should be provided. The patient who falls asleep on the dayroom couch should be left to sleep there. Nursing staff are cautioned not to shine flashlights in patients' faces when making breathing checks. This can stimulate nightmares, flashbacks, and rage reactions.

Patients who need to have the radio playing softly can be given roommates with the same need who are untroubled by that sound. Others who need quiet can be grouped together. Sometimes the use of earplugs proves helpful to the individual veteran. Veterans who cannot fall asleep before dawn are permitted to sleep as late as ward routine will allow. Napping during the day is essential for some. The dayroom is open throughout the night and veterans are encouraged to use it freely. There they can watch television, listen to the stereo, read, or use craft kits and art supplies to help them through the night. Registered nurses on the night tour must be available for frequent periods of one-to-one intervention, and assignments should reflect this. Important therapeutic gains can be made at night.

It is essential that evening and weekend staff coming on duty receive regular communication about the veteran's treatment so appropriate interventions can be made. The advice to stay a distance away from the veteran when he has to be awakened or when he is experiencing nightmares is valid. Veterans will occasionally strike out at those times. Staff are advised to call the patient's name softly. A loud, shrill or harsh sounding voice awakening them is reported to be very stressful and occasionally rage reactions are elicited.

Loud or unusual noises, whenever they occur and especially at night, need to be explained to the veterans in the vicinity. During the night, after loud and unusual noises, the staff should circulate through the sleeping areas to give reassurance if it is needed. Behavioral techniques like relaxation training are useful in reducing hyperalertness responses.

Flashbacks are traumatic reenactments of the original stressful situation. Patients report experiencing flashbacks without anyone else around them, patients or staff, being aware that this is happening. Flashbacks sufficient to disorient the veteran, causing him to exhibit bizarre behavior, may respond to reorientation and reassurance by staff members. This is done by calling him by name, explaining where he is, and reassuring him that he is safe.

Anger, Aggression, Violence

At the time of the admission, Dan appeared sad, depressed, withdrawn, and passive; yet he gave a history of rage reactions so violent and out of control that he had on occasion attacked strangers in bars with no apparent provocation. His rageful outbursts at home resulted in physical attacks upon his wife and other family members. His wife was so frightened of him that she was considering terminating their marriage. He, too, was frightened by his rage and violent behavior but could not control it. Goodwin (1980) has written that "this behavior (violence) generally frightens the veteran, leading many to question their sanity; they are horrified at their behavior. However, regardless of their afterthoughts, the rage reactions occur with frightening frequency" (p.12).

In the inpatient setting, rage reactions are triggered by small incidents or petty inconveniences; the rage reaction is out of proportion to the cause. Many of these rage reactions happen in the dining room at the medical center. Analyzing these incidents together with the patients involved to assist them in developing better coping skills reveals that the trigger is often a negative interaction between the patient and dietary personnel. For example, in the dining room the noise level is very high, and patients crowd into lines and wait to take their turn at the serving table. The men are usually quite hungry. Unfortunately, the Vietnam veterans are frequently made anxious by noise and crowds. Just at this point, dietary personnel may refuse the patient a second helping or may tell him that he must return to the ward to get his diet card. It isn't the action that triggers the rage. It is the tone of voice used, the body language exhibited, and the attitude that rules must be rigidly enforced that elicit the rage reaction.

Treating the patient in a direct, accepting, nonjudgmental way reduces this kind of a rage response. Interpersonal reactions can be confronted assertively and directly, e.g., "Is something wrong?" "You look angry. Is there a problem?" Dialoguing about the actions that took place and the feelings that were aroused by those actions help the patient understand the dynamics. Understanding what will trigger his rage helps the veteran to cope with it. Ventilating his feelings reduces his internal tension and makes a wrathful explosion less likely. Clear, straightforward explanations about procedures and ward routine reduce their power to annoy the patient.

Injury and threats of injuring personnel cannot be accepted on the unit. This is especially important on a unit that is open and does not have facilities to protect patients and personnel from another's aggression. Immediate discharge or transfer is the rule. However, it needs to be pointed out that on this unit no physical aggression has ever been directed toward unit personnel. This is in contrast to other psychiatric units in this hospital where physical acting out involving other people and personnel has at times occurred. Courtesy is consistently extended and is expected in return. Verbal outbursts almost always are followed by an apology and an explanation for the loss of control. An attitude of openness throughout the program reduces the impetus for acting out. Procedures are explained. Medical jargon is avoided. Questions are answered knowledgeably or referred to someone who can do so.

Anger vented on property is different. Putting his fist through the wall instead of into a person may be a therapeutic gain. "It does not help the Vietnam veteran to get uptight about a door getting kicked, a chair banged against the wall, a broken coffee mug, or whatever. That kind of thing usually shows such an enormous climb toward civilization from the level of violence which characterized daily life in the Vietnam war that it merits . . . congratulations" (Blank, 1983, p.5).

Nursing staff using the nonauthoritarian nonjudgmental approach do not usually stimulate conflict. The veteran is making his own choice and is openly offered opportunities to ventilate his irritations. When conflict appears to be developing, the nurse and patient are advised to break off contact courteously and drop the issue until tempers have had an opportunity to cool. Serious issues are raised in the community for discussion and resolution. It is advisable to avoid bringing outsiders such as security forces onto the unit unless nursing personnel on the ward have control of how they will act and react with the patients.

A situation involving Dan gives an example of a well-handled aggressive incident. Dan had been withdrawn and tense for several days. He was not open to attempts at intervention and he was becoming increasingly irritated by the petty inconveniences of ward routine. One day, while the nurse was administering medication in the PTSD hallway, Dan jumped up, picked up his chair and threw it against the wall so hard that it broke. He went into his room and slammed the door. The nurse and a couple of patients ("buddies") asked if he needed to talk and if they could be helpful. He said, "No," pushed the door open and retrieved a couple of pieces of the broken chair, returned to his room and again slammed the door. The patients returned to playing cards, while the staff removed the remaining pieces of the chair. The floor nurse got a tranquilizer tablet and returned to Dan's room. She told Dan she had some medication for him. He opened the door, took the medication and slammed the door again. An hour later Dan came out, sat down in a chair near the men playing cards and smoked a cigarette. One said, "You O.K., Dan?" Dan nodded his head, yes. The incident was over.

Depression, Withdrawal, Detachment

Usually the PTSD patient on being admitted to the unit is clinically depressed and withdrawn. Dan's depression was associated with long-standing feelings of isolation, disillusionment, alienation, and helplessness. All these feelings were exacerbated by life management crises involving a threatened job loss and divorce. Frequently, the veteran will isolate himself, sit on the periphery of the group, and watch TV or sleep. Dan's depression would sometimes escalate when he found himself unable to concentrate on studying for the GED. In situations like this, the nurse needs to approach the patient frequently and sit beside him. Some words should be spoken such as "I saw you sitting here, and I would like to join you for a few minutes." In this way the nurse conveys to the patient that she is aware of him and is concerned. At a later time the veteran may be able to express some positive feedback about her support for him during his depression. However, nursing staff must depend primarily upon observation of the veteran's reactions and his overall response to treatment rather than patient feedback to assess the effectiveness of their interactions with the patient.

The nurse must remember that the depressed patient is susceptible to returning to substance abuse, which may have been his primary coping response in the past. Coupled with this is the ever-present possibility of suicidal preoccupation. Patients who show more than a mild depression should promptly be given the medication ordered for that purpose by their physician. Other approaches that have been effective involve eliciting cooperation of the other patients to monitor their buddy and assist in encouraging his involvement in activities.

Among the most difficult symptoms the nurse must deal with is the patient who has become very detached and estranged. Many veterans at first will evidence estrangement for a short period of time, but as their trust in the therapeutic alliance grows, they move away from this position. In the more serious cases, the veteran typically stays constantly in bed. He refuses to participate in any activities. Frequently, he will state that nothing in life has any meaning. When the level of estrangement is very high, the patient finds that being on a PTSD unit intensifies his sense of anxiety. He may compare being on the ward to being in a combat troop in Vietnam. He may develop many somatic complaints. The basis for his behavior is an intense feeling of impending disaster; thus, he finds it difficult to concentrate on developing meaningful relationships.

After the veteran has refused to get up for several days, the staff may find themselves becoming angry and alienated towards the patient. A specific behavioral contract may be utilized here; i.e., the patient must attend therapy sessions and get up for meals; other than these, he may sleep, if he wishes. The physician may prescribe for both depression and anxiety. The nurse must maintain close communication with the patient by being there as needed without forcing the issue.

Other Considerations

There are many additional symptoms of PTSD of which the nurse must be aware, such as unresolved grief, disillusionments, inability to concentrate, intrusive thoughts, feelings of guilt for living, etc. These may not be apparent as management problems on the ward. However, these symptoms may underlie behavior which will be manifested in less obvious ways. They may become issues in the patient's therapy in which the nurse participates. The nurse's observations of these hidden symptoms can be very helpful at team discussions of the patient's therapy. As is frequently stated in the literature, the veteran is difficult to treat. He comes to treatment with an attitude of suspicion, cynicism, and mistrust. He is anxious, depressed, angry, sad, deeply wounded, helpless, hopeless, and yet paradoxically helpful and certainly challenging as he approaches the staff with, "This is my last chance. I've got to make it here."

The key to managing the Vietnam veteran lies in Haley's (1974) statement "Establishment of a therapeutic alliance for this group of patients is the treatment rather than the facilitator of the treatment. It is critical that in every sense the therapist be 'for real'; a 'real person' respectful of the veterans' strength and concerned about but not 'put off' by their psychopathology" (p.195).

SUMMARY

Approaches to the implementation of nursing care of Vietnam veterans suffering from PTSD have been presented. Although one may have many credentials, be knowledgeable about theory, and possess much expertise in psychiatric care, not everyone is able to work with the PTSD patient. However, for those nurses who are willing to examine pain and suffering in the moral sense and can examine their own inner feelings, the challenge can be most rewarding. The following guidelines will assist the nurse in her effectiveness in managing and caring for the PTSD patient in an inpatient unit:

1) *Read*—Become informed about the Vietnam conflict, the aftermath, and the psychodynamics of PTSD. Know the symptoms of PTSD as outlined in DSM-III (1980). Learn about the areas and provinces where U.S. military were fighting in S.E. Asia.
2) *Listen*—Hear and demonstrate that you are interested in what the patient has to say. Ask questions. When the patient begins to feel that you are interested, he will begin to share bits and pieces about his combat experience. Combat veterans tend to talk military jargon. Ask him to explain terminology.
3) *Be objective*—Don't tend to judge the veteran for his actions in combat. Examine your own feelings about war and killing. Imagine yourself in a life-threatening situation—kill or be killed.
4) *Become educationally prepared*—If you do not have education/experience in psychotherapy (group, individual, marital, etc.) and crisis intervention, seek continuing education and develop all available educational resources.
5) *Approach*—We have found that a nonauthoritative, adult approach is most effective. Keep in mind that any derogatory remarks aimed at the nurse are only a covering veneer for the anguish the patient feels inside. The nurse has to assume a straightforward, honest stance and assist the patient in working through any male-female issues.

6) *Assessment*—Take a thorough history of all of the patient's experiences. Ask him about his experiences in Vietnam, where stationed, his assignment, and any traumatic experiences. Find out about his life before Vietnam and problems encountered since military duty. This includes jobs, coping mechanisms, interpersonal relationships, and presenting symptoms. Find out what is his presenting stressor (usually related to his traumatic experiences). When possible, a staff member who is a Vietnam veteran should be present for the intake or be easily accessible for consultation.

7) *Therapeutic milieu*—The patient needs to feel secure. The milieu includes the physical surroundings, the treatment team, attitudes and therapies. Make every attempt to establish a treatment alliance with your fellow treatment team members. Keep the communication lines open. Working with such demanding and emotionally demanding patients frequently precipitates burnout among the staff members. The possibility of disturbing countertransferences is a constant threat. The nurse has to keep this in mind and take steps in replenishing herself—mutual support, a short vacation, etc. Establish ground rules that both staff and patients can abide by. Keep in mind that the only rules made in stone are those made many years ago on Mount Sinai. Other rules can be amended or adjusted.

8) *Be prepared with procedures and methods of care to meet his problems*—Follow through with any promises that you make. Frequently, things do not go as planned, especially in institutions. When this occurs, explain to the veteran and provide a rationale for a change of plans. Involve him in activities that he enjoys (or used to enjoy) and in which he can excel. The nurse quite often may have to initiate the activity. If possible, the nurse should initially accompany the patient and become involved in the activity, which should not require a high degree of concentration. It might be bowling, baseball, basketball, etc. Pay attention to the patient's somatic complaints. Sometimes such complaints can indicate serious physical conditions.

9) *Be his friend*—Demonstrate your concern by being fair, honest, and real. This also means letting the veteran know that you, as a human being, are capable of emotions.

10) *Be an advocate*—Learn about the various veteran organizations. Be informed about legislation regarding veteran affairs. Give the patient any information he needs in making logical deci-

sions concerning his discharge planning. Educate the community and other employees regarding PTSD. Stand up for the rights of the patient.

We are continually learning different approaches. We do know that the major thrust for implementation of care for the PTSD patient is to heal the wounds and assist him in returning home.

REFERENCES

Adams, M.F.: PTSD: An inpatient treatment unit. *American Journal of Nursing, 82*(11):1704-1705, 1982.

American Psychiatric Association: *Diagnostic and statistical manual of mental disorders, 3rd ed.* (DSM-III). Washington, D.C.: American Psychiatric Association, 1980.

American Psychiatric Association: *American psychiatric glossary, 3rd ed.* Washington, D.C.: American Psychiatric Association, 1969.

Blank, A.S.: Anger and Violence in Vietnam Veterans. Unpublished paper presented at V.A. Northeast Regional Medical Educational Center at Northport, L.I., August 2, 1983.

Egendorf, A.: The postwar healing of Vietnam veterans: Recent research. *Hospital & Community Psychiatry, 33*(11):904, 1982.

Ewalt, J.R., & Crawford, D.: Post-traumatic stress syndrome. In J.H. Masserman (Ed.), *Current psychiatric therapies.* New York: Grune & Stratton, 1981.

Figley, C.R. (Ed.): *Stress disorders among Vietnam veterans: Theory, research and treatment.* New York: Brunner/Mazel, 1978.

Figley, C.R., & Levantman, S. (Eds.): *Strangers at home: Vietnam veterans since the war.* New York: Praeger, 1980.

Furey, J.A.: For some, the war rages on. *American Journal of Nursing, 82*(11):1695-1698, 1982.

Goodwin, J.: The etiology of combat-related post-traumatic stress disorders. In R. Williams (Ed.), *Post-traumatic stress disorders of the Vietnam veteran.* Cincinnati: D.A.V., 1980.

Haley, S.A.: Treatment Implications of post-combat stress response syndromes for mental health professionals. In C.R. Figley (Ed.), *Stress disorders among Vietnam veterans: Theory, research and treatment.* New York: Brunner/Mazel, 1978, pp. 255-267.

Haley, S.A.: When the patient reports atrocities. *Archives of General Psychiatry, 30*:191-196, 1974.

Huppenbauer, S.L.: PTSD a portrait of the problem. *American Journal of Nursing, 82*(11):1699-1703, 1982.

Jackson, H.C.: Moral nihilism: Developmental arrest as a sequela to combat stress. In S. Feinstein, & P.L. Giovacchini (Eds.), *Adolescent Psychiatry, 10,* 228-238, 1982.

Kreigh, H.L., & Perko, J.E.: *Psychiatric and mental health nursing: A commitment to care and concern, 2nd ed.* Reston, VA: Reston Publishing Co., 1983.

Lipkin, J.O., Blank, A.S., Parson, E.R., & Smith, J.: Vietnam veterans and post-traumatic stress disorder. *Hospital & Community Psychiatry, 33*(11):910, 1982.

Resing, M.: Mental health problems of Vietnam veterans. *Journal of Psychiatric Nursing & Mental Health Services, 20*(9):41-43, 1982.

Shatan, C.F.: Through the membrane of reality: "Impacted grief" and perceptual dissonance in Vietnam combat veterans. *Psychiatric Opinion, 2*(6):6-14, 1974.

Shatan, C.F.: Stress disorders among Vietnam veterans: The emotional content of combat continues. In C.F. Figley (Ed.), *Stress disorders among Vietnam veterans: Theory, research and treatment.* New York: Brunner/Mazel, 1978.

Williams, T.: Therapeutic alliance and goal setting in the treatment of Vietnam veterans. In R. Williams (Ed.), *Post-traumatic stress disorders of the Vietnam veteran.* Cincinnati: D.A.V., 1980.

Wilson, J.P.: *Identity, ideology and crisis: The Vietnam veteran in transition,* Parts I & II. Cleveland: Cleveland State University Press, 1978.

15

An Approach to Treatment of Post-Traumatic Stress Disorder

WILLIAM D. RACEK, Ph.D.

Post-traumatic stress disorders have been treated for a number of years at "Outreach Clinics." In many ways this has been a successful method of containment of the disorder. We have been led to believe that it has been successful in moderating or removing the symptoms which have kept the veteran from living a "normal life." There seems to be little doubt that this presumption has been accurate, if one is to judge by the relatively small number of requests for hospitalization. During recent years, however, and particularly in the last year, there seems to be an increase in requests for hospitalizations for this disability. One of the unfortunate aspects of PTSD is that for many health care professionals it is not an acceptable diagnosis. Another is that the veteran himself often does not know why he is suffering.

Diagnostic and Statistical Manual III quite thoroughly describes the symptoms and, if only by inference, the causes. There seem to be some indications of fallibility in the interpretation of what is known as a "recognizable stressor." The consensus seems to be that the more recognizable the stressor, the more certainty there is of the diagnosis. Most who diagnose PTSD accept the concept that the disorder can be present only in those who have encountered extremely hazardous and violent enemy contact for extended periods. Based on experience, this does not appear to be entirely true. One contact with gross stress may cause equally as virulent a reaction as a number of stressful events over a period of months.

Emerging gradually from many contacts with veterans of the Vietnam episode appears to be the remarkable similarity among those who are diagnosed PTSD. Most have an average or greater than average I.Q. They appear to come from the middle or upper middle strata of American society, have had a religious background, and a great sense of moral values. They seem for the most part to come from the more élite and highly trained military units (U.S. Marine Corps, Airborne Army Units, "Recondo Army" forces). This may suggest that military training prior to combat may have some effect on these veterans. It is also apparent that the veteran who had PTSD distrusts and tends to withdraw from others who have not shared the Vietnam experience. It is almost as though this is an "élite club" which "feeds" on the horror of the war, whose "members" are only comfortable in the company of other "members."

It is this latter aspect which makes it difficult for a "non-member" therapist to be of assistance. This is not an impossible aspect to overcome, but does present obstacles. While the PTSD veteran is willing, to a moderate degree, to discuss his experience with other veterans individually or in groups, there are, it seems to me, many reservations which prevent full disclosure of the more traumatic episodes even in the "club" setting and present great difficulties outside the "club" with "non-members."

It appears, also, that coping behavior is a factor frequently overlooked. Withdrawal, listed in DSM-III, seems to be one method of coping. If the veteran is distressed, he tends to withdraw from everyone, in many cases leading a reclusive, almost hermit-like existence, alone even among members of his own family. The veteran often attempts to self-medicate. The incidence of illicit drugs or alcohol seems to be high and often causes further dissociation from family and friends. Another dangerous and occasionally fatal method of coping with their symptoms is the inordinate emphasis which they place on the possession of firearms and which they are very reluctant to part with even when recognizing the danger to themselves and others.

It is relatively easy to fall into the trap of establishing an inpatient program for PTSD. To some degree, this seems to be necessary if we are to believe the current statistics which indicate that great numbers of these veterans require hospitalization. However, a four-, five- or even six-month wait to enter these programs is not unusual. In some cases, veterans waiting for these programs are held on acute psychiatric wards pending admission to these programs. This suggests two approaches. The first and most apparent is to expand current PTSD programs. The second is to provide pre-therapy treatment to the veterans who are waiting to enter programs. The more economical way to approach this aspect seems to be to expand the treatment capabilities of the existing "outreach" clinics.

What follows below is not a treatment "program." It is a series of interventions which have been shown to be needed in the majority of cases for the successful treatment of PTSD. Success herein is defined as being symptom-free at the time of discharge. While the memories of the Vietnam conflict are always there in the minds of the patient, success is achieved when symptoms have been largely, if not totally, eliminated. The only remaining deficiency is the possibility of a return to maladaptive coping behavior when faced with stress, even if that stress if not related to PTSD.

DIAGNOSIS

This aspect of treatment presents a number of problems. One referred to previously is the tendency to look for the patient who has had the most frequent, most stressful, and longest exposure to the "recognizable stressor." The judgment of "recognizable stressor" is a very important and difficult one to make. A veteran who has had limited field experience and what would appear (as compared to other stressors) as a minor short duration stress is often rejected for admission to the PTSD program and assigned another diagnosis or discharged from the hospital. Some programs use the services of other PTSD-diagnosed patients to "sit in" on the initial interviews to assist in diagnosis. This may be a viable way to approach diagnosis, but the "member of the club" aspect is an ever-present danger when using other PTSD patients.

Another hindrance to diagnosis would appear to be learned response. Veterans who have frequented outreach clinics have, through association, learned what is desirable and acceptable as a "recognizable stressor" and have also learned a great deal about the symptom of the disorder.

It has become increasingly important that the professional who makes the diagnosis have an extensive knowledge of combat stress. It is also desirable to have input from wives, parents, employers, and significant others. It seems apparent that the combat record of the veteran should be made available to the diagnostician. Although there has been some experimentation with psychological testing, at this point the use of these tests does not appear to present a definitive basis for diagnosis.

DSM-III

To the sophisticated and discriminating diagnostician the outline of symptoms in DSM-III seems to be accurate and the validity of self-reporting is readily determined by close attention to the descriptions of the symptoms and the affect of the patient when presenting his symptoms. Additionally these can be confirmed by contact with persons who had a prior or presently close relationship with the veteran.

In many patients, it becomes apparent during the diagnostic procedures or therapy that there is evidence of sociopathy. There is a caveat indicated in a too hasty acceptance of sociopathic tendencies. It is apparent to the knowledgeable therapist that these tendencies may be related to the non-acceptance of the veteran by society after the war. This appears to be frequently the case. Only input from associates of the veteran prior to the Vietnam experience can be relied upon to address this problem. It is not inconceivable that what the therapist views as borderline or sociopathic behavior is a learned response to rejection over a period of years. However, even the confirmed presence of character disorders should not necessarily preclude treatment.

TREATMENT

The reader is reminded that what follows has not been subject to research but is based solely on the treatment of approximately 25 veterans diagnosed as having PTSD. These patients were assigned to an acute admissions ward for any one of a number of reasons. Some were treatment failures from the PTSD program at this hospital. In most cases these veterans were untreatable because of repeated reliance on their habitual method of coping (alcohol or illicit drugs). Some were behavioral problems, some were received from Substance Abuse Treatment Units, and some were directly admitted to the ward. There were a few who were diagnosed as having an endogenous depression and were nonresponsive to standard and experimental drug treatment. A small number of these veterans had an underlying psychosis (manic depressive in two cases).

After completion of treatment, the majority of cases treated were either symptom-free or having symptoms reduced to proportions where they could be controlled by psychotropic medication. Unfortunately there has been no long-term follow-up on these patients. In only two cases, however, have patients been readmitted to this ward. In the first case, the patient reported no symptoms of PTSD. However, it was apparent that once the PTSD was treated, a manic depressive disorder had emerged. In the second case, the patient reported his symptoms much relieved but still present. He elected to leave hospital treatment because of pressing family problems (loss of his children because financial and personal problems prevented his spouse from providing adequate care). At this time, "success" in treatment (symptom-free or within tolerable limits) is estimated at between 70 to 80 percent.

What follows is a series of modalities of treatment which have been used for the majority of patients following diagnosis. The reader should not presume that these are listed in order of their importance, the sequence of their application, or their degree of importance to patient care. In this respect the treatment is tailored to the individual patient's need. However, in a general way these treatments apply to most patients.

In the initial session, after the diagnosis has been determined, the structure of the program is explained to the patient. The return to their previous inappropriate coping behavior is forbidden and the patient is informed that an infraction of this rule will be cause for termination of treatment. Motivation to participate in treatment is assured by the patient's adherence to this rule. This has been widely discussed with various veteran's organizations, including the Vietnam Veterans of America, who agree that this aspect is essential if progress is to be made.

It seems desirable that during treatment "the least medicine is the best medicine." The stress of PTSD therapy may require medicine to relieve anxiety and/or depression for some patients. Also p.r.n. (when necessary) medication may be required after particularly stressful sessions in order to prevent a return to their former coping behavior. In most cases the requirement of medication seems to diminish gradually after a certain number of sessions.

In the initial session, the patient is informed that there will be considerable stress and in all probability an increase in symptoms. Complete honesty with the therapist is emphasized. An analogy is made between a physical and psychic wound. If a physical wound is untreated, it becomes infected and must be cleaned and properly dressed before healing can take place. A psychic wound is similar in that it often goes untreated because the wound is not apparent. A form of psychic infection sets in and the wound must be cleaned before healing can take place. This requires removal of the (psychic) scab and probing which results in pain and stress.

Provided with this information the patient is asked to "think over" the requirements of the treatment process and return the next day with his decision to accept or reject treatment. Only two patients have rejected treatment. One was a WW II veteran who stated that he remembered only parts of his combat experiences but did not want to accept drug-induced interviews or hypnosis to recover these memories. The other, a Vietnam era veteran, refused on the grounds that while the combat episodes were providing considerable stress and disruption of his life, he was "afraid to get into psychotherapy."

The establishment of a therapeutic relationship has been easier for the author because of his previous combat experience. It permits at best an "honorary membership or associate membership in the club." It also permits understanding of the military jargon and slang terms used by veterans which allows for a greater degree of perception of the meaning of the patients' verbal productions and a deeper appreciation of the emotional impact of combat-related activities.

It is during the second session that procedures are established. The patient is asked if he prefers to discuss his trauma in a chronological way, that is from basic training to discharge, or if his preference is to approach the problem by bringing up episodes which cause him the greatest stress. The majority of patients want to discuss their single most stressful episode. The unsophisticated therapist would probably accept this disclosure as being indeed the one which causes the greatest stress. In all cases treated so far, later sessions reveal that while the episode initially discussed is quite probably among those which provide much stress, it is not the most stressful. This is probably the patient's way of testing the therapist. As the individual therapy sessions progress they almost always return to the chronological approach.

During all of the therapy sessions, the therapist must avoid the acceptance of an overwhelming rush of material. It is important that the information be released in such a way that closure or partial closure is reached at the end of each session. Closure in PTSD therapy requires that the patient explore with the help of the therapist the action itself, its emotional impact and all of the possible alternative courses of action raised by the patient. In all cases, effort must be made to permit the patient to explore the episode for what it was and if possible accept a different way of perceiving the action.

It is very useful for the therapist to encourage his patient to discuss his combat stress in the first person, singular (i.e. "I did. . . ," "I felt. . . ," etc.). Experience has led to the conclusion that escape into plurality such as "my outfit," "my squad," etc. are nonproductive and allow the veteran to depersonalize an episode which he has already accepted as personal but which causes him pain from which he now attempts to dissociate himself. Depersonalization leads to a mere discussion of war stories and tends to lead to nonproductive, albeit temporary, relief in therapy sessions, but without lasting therapeutic benefit.

Chaplaincy Input

While frequently overloaded, this is an important aspect of treatment. In WW II, it was often stated, "There are no atheists in foxholes." This generalization, like many, is usually true. Experience on this ward has indicated that most of the veterans have a religious affiliation of some type. Some are deeply involved, some moderately so, and some only to a slight degree. None have claimed to be atheists and only one stated that he was agnostic. Prior to the recognition that the Chaplaincy should be an important part of PTSD therapy, the most difficult issue to resolve was guilt adherent to actions taken to survive, and survivor guilt (because the individual felt unworthy to survive the war).

Regardless of how shallow or deep the veteran's religious convictions are, it appears to be very productive to provide access to a chaplain early in treatment. The discussion with the chaplain can be general and confined to the concept of guilt vs. sorrow, or it may be in depth as regards the veteran's concept of sin and religious morality. Whatever the approach used by the chaplain, the feelings of guilt have been expressed and when this is accomplished, one of the major barriers to therapy is reduced. In many cases, this is the "opening wedge" to real and honest exposure of the problem to the therapist.

Rehabilitation Medical Service

Functioning in a therapeutic activity is an important aspect of the patient's recovery. Preferably, the activity selected should be something which engages his interest and requires creative thought. Occupational therapy has proven to be very effective in doing this. The nature of the activity should be changed periodically so that the patient's focus is on the work being performed and not on thoughts of Vietnam combat experiences. Activities such as raking leaves or messenger and escort details should be avoided because rote activity and long waiting periods permit the patient's mind to dwell on Vietnam combat issues. Occupational therapy promotes an atmosphere of learning and creativity. However, being left on a single assignment in O.T. for long periods of time creates a sense of frustration and/or a regression into obsessive-compulsive behavior. The therapist who works in this milieu has a very important contribution to make. The primary therapist must rely on the judgment and skill of the occupational therapist to gain and sustain the patient's interest in this modality of his treatment.

Physical Exercise

This, too, is an important aspect of treatment. Patients who cannot or will not engage in physical activities have a greater tendency to brood about Vietnam issues and other matters. They are inclined to sit apart from others for long periods of time. Occasionally, they drop off to sleep which prevents them from establishing regular sleep patterns at night. Many of these patients regularly seek sleeping medication. Exercise is also an important factor in the reduction of stress after psychotherapy. Some patients report a reduction of stress through jogging immediately after a therapy session.

Anxiety

Recently, the Rehabilitation Medicine Service has established a biofeedback laboratory which is reported to be attempting to relieve some of the stress experienced by these patients. Deep muscle relaxation with imagery could produce some beneficial effects. However, care should be exercised in selecting an image which does not promote stress (for example, woods or beaches may have stressful connotations since they may stimulate memories of combat in these locations).

Family Involvement

The importance of involving the family in the patient's treatment deserves considerable attention. This or any other connection with the real world becomes increasingly important as therapy progresses. The veteran's only contact of therapeutic importance to him usually has been other veterans who understand the problem. The guilt and shame (frequently without cause) deter the veteran from discussing Vietnam with anyone other than his comrades who served in the same war.

All types of family therapy are important and should include the extended family where possible. If the veteran is married and there are children (frequently the case), his family has suffered deprivation of a husband/father, financial deprivation, avoidance of other family members, the sight of drunken or drug-induced episodes, and occasionally physical abuse with bewilderment over their plight. Most frequently the immediate family has no conception of the nature of the problems which cause the veteran to behave in these ways which are destructive to the family.

Despite these hardships, many marriages have remained at least partially intact over a period of years. If the patient is to be rehabilitated, the family's perceptions of his behavior must be changed. In most cases it seems advisable, with the veteran's permission, to provide the family members with an understanding of the trauma-induced neurosis, its causes (the stressor), the symptoms, and the maladaptive coping behavior. In the interests of maintaining a therapeutic alliance with the veteran, this first family session must be discussed prior to bringing the family to the hospital. It is very important at this stage that the issue of confidentiality be stressed. A generalized discussion of the disorder, with a review of the symptoms outlined in DSM-III, generally suffices. The issue of self medication and maladaptive coping behavior should be discussed.

In most cases, the mere recitation of these facts brings an emotional response from the entire family. Tears of pity and relief are frequent. In two cases, wives, between tears, have stated, "My God, all of these years he has been suffering and never told me." "I thought he was just another drunk." This initial effort is generally effective in supplying an emotional support system outside of the hospital.

As family sessions progress, however, other problems begin to emerge. The wife's suffering during protracted periods, coupled with her efforts to keep the family together emotionally and financially, have caused considerable stress. This was forcibly brought to attention in one of the initial PTSD family therapy sessions, when the wife, in tears, complained bitterly that her husband was receiving treatment and obviously feeling better but her feelings over a period of 8 to 10 years were unresolved. It is still very apparent that wives, as well as some of the children, require individual therapy. This is particularly true of the sons and daughters who are teenagers. Their view of family life is for the most part based on maternal authority and emotional support. There is an almost unbelievable desire to assist the veteran. One family (father, mother, sister, and brother-in-law) commuted from Puerto Rico for family sessions. Another family (mother and sister) have been coming from the state of Maine.

As family therapy evolves, it sometimes becomes necessary to involve the veteran's family as well as the spouse's family. These two groups are frequently at odds with each other over the veteran's suffering. The wife is frequently hesitant to discuss the veteran's problems with her family and is often blamed by the veteran's family, or at least felt to be partially to blame, for the veteran's condition. As these different groups begin to become more knowledgeable about the veteran's plight, an increasingly strong outside support system is set in place.

Neighbors and employers who were formerly supportive of the veteran may have become estranged because of his erratic and often self-destructive behavior. In many cases, after one or two sessions with the veteran, the perceptions of these people also change for the better. Neighbors see him as a more worthwhile person, and employers as worthy of employment.

Family therapy in the extended family modality is occasionally difficult and causes problems for the therapist. Just as with some professionals in the field of mental health, there are skeptics in society at large. Still, in most cases one can reasonably hope for a qualified support, or at least a "wait and see" attitude. Even the latter is usually an improvement for the veteran. If done correctly, this therapy permits him to have a better self-image and a feeling of being *a part* of society rather than *apart* from society.

As noted above, the teenage children seem to be the most difficult members of the family to address. Lacking paternal support and somewhat scornful and ashamed of the veteran's behavior, they become resistant to the father's reentry into the family. This disruptive influence is difficult to overcome. The patient, frequently eager to become a father in the true sense of the word, tends to rush into the family circle, only to be rebuffed by the children or his spouse who do not accept his perception of his parental role. Changing these perceptions takes time and patience on the part of the therapist. This aspect of family rejection has been noted with alcoholics as well. The family tends to become suspicious, resentful and rejecting of the parent who formerly abdicated, but who now wants to resume his role in the family.

Vocational Counseling/Veteran's Organizations

Toward the end of the therapy, quite frequently there is an onset of depression which is related to but not necessarily a part of PTSD therapy. In most cases it has been apparent that the veteran's vocational efforts have been sporadic and on a downward trend as to type and value. This may require vocational counseling aimed toward academic schooling, vocational training/retraining, or actual job placement. The usual organizations are quite effective within their means. The V.A. provides for veterans whose disability is judged to be connected with the service. The State-operated Office of Vocational Rehabilitation provides an effective resource as well. Veteran organizations are another possible resource which so far has not been explored sufficiently. It is supposed that a part of their role could be, at the very least, to represent rehabilitated veterans in a favorable light to prospective employers.

CASE HISTORY

The following is a case history of treatment for PTSD which seems to illustrate to some degree the points covered so far.

Mr. P. is a 41-year-old male whose father is an American of German origin and his mother is Hispanic. He has one female sibling who is two years older than he. The patient's sister is married and has two children. The patient's family and his sister are quite affluent. The patient's father, prior to his retirement, held a responsible and rather high position in government despite the lack of a formal education in his early maturity. The father later attained a master's degree in engineering. The patient's sister, a college graduate, owns and manages three businesses. The entire family is staunchly Roman Catholic and quite strict in the practice of that religion. During his later years, the patient's father became addicted to alcohol and is now an alcoholic who refuses treatment. There is no other history of psychiatric illness in the patient's family.

Mr. P. is married and resides with his wife and four children. His wife is 38 years old and is a college graduate. The children include a son (age 18) who is a college student, a daughter (age 16) who is a high school student, a son (age 13) who is about to enter high school, and a daughter (age 6) who is in first grade.

Diagnosis: Upon his arrival on the ward, it was determined that the patient has been diagnosed as having PTSD and receiving a service-connected disability pension (100%) for PTSD and injuries sustained in combat. Psychological testing and physical evaluations were done which confirmed the disabilities. There was little room for doubt in regard to the "stressor" (discussed later in this chapter) or the symptoms which were apparent and observed during the course of treatment.

Military History: The patient entered the service in 1964 and was discharged honorably in 1969. He was commissioned a 2nd Lieutenant as a result of ROTC training in college. When he left the service, it was with the rank of Captain. He was reluctant to leave the military but was forced to do so because of injuries sustained in combat. During the course of his service he became a fixed-wing and helicopter pilot. He was highly decorated and among his decorations are the Distinguished Service Medal, Distinguished Flying Medal, and the Air Medal with 21 oak leaf clusters.

The veteran was in Vietnam from 1966 to 1967 (13 months). During combat he was shot down twice and several of his helicopter crew members were wounded or killed. As a pilot, the veteran flew not only his own missions, but accepted (volunteered) for the more hazardous missions given to his unit. As a helicopter gunship pilot, he frequently acted, on his own initiative, in a medical evacuation role ("dust off missions").

The patient related one mission which he found particularly stressful. During the course of providing support for ground troops, he attracted fire from an automatic weapon and started to "hunt down" the source of fire. The fire from his gunship had been effective in dispersing the enemy except for this one automatic weapon which continued to fire at the helicopter. He was able to locate the enemy soldier and quite literally hunted him down through the brush and limited ground cover. This enemy soldier was particularly stubborn and brave. Eventually, the soldier was severely wounded. The veteran landed in the vicinity and, leaving his crew with the ship, located the wounded enemy soldier, who as a last act of defiance fired his single remaining round of ammunition at the patient. Mr. P. captured this soldier and returned him to the rear area, where he found out that the enemy soldier had not only been freshly wounded by fire from the gunship but had a former wound which had gangrene.

A search of the soldier revealed that he was carrying a picture of his wife and family. This seemed to have a profound effect on Mr. P. He wept when he discussed the incident and felt severe guilt. The wounded soldier died shortly after the helicopter landed. There were numerous other incidents, some which would seem more stressful but this single incident seemed to predominate. The thoughts expressed by the veteran seemed to indicate feelings of anger, hatred, respect, and empathy for this enemy who chose to fight a helicopter rather than hide.

Toward the end of his tour in Vietnam the veteran received a back injury from a second helicopter crash which precluded further flying. Mr. P. opted for discharge rather than to resume his military career as a ground officer, which would have been possible at the time.

Family Therapy: Family therapy was initiated after the patient had been on the ward for two weeks. The initial session was with his wife and children. It seemed obvious that the family had lost the ability to communicate with one another and were puzzled by the father's drinking problem which by that time had reached unmanageable proportions. In addition, he would periodically leave the family for periods of time occasionally lasting as long as two weeks. Prior to his hospitalization, he remained in his room drinking for weeks at a time, only leaving the room when the family was asleep. The family made frequent attempts to reestablish ties with Mr. P., who would not respond. This resulted in the family's acceptance of guilt. In addition to losing contact with Mr. P., they had started to lose contact with one another. A "ripple" effect became apparent. The patient's parents and sister withdrew, as did his in-laws. The family avoided any contact with either Mr. P.'s family or Mrs. P.'s family. This gradually extended to the neighbors and the few remaining friends the family had left.

The initial effort at therapy was to inform the family that the patient was not an alcoholic nor was he psychotic. After several sessions with the immediate family, they became quite supportive. The larger family was gradually included in these sessions, as were several neighbors. Once an understanding of this illness was promoted, the reaction was excellent. The patient's father, mother, and sister commuted by air frequently to attend these sessions.

Individual Family Therapy: As family therapy progressed, the patient's wife in an explosive episode stated, "Yes, I can see him (Mr. P.) getting better but what about me? I'm still suffering." At this point the wife entered individual therapy which continued weekly for 9 sessions. Later the older son and daughter received individual therapy.

Auxiliary Therapy: As regards Mr. P., the chaplain's assistance was necessary to help the patient come to terms with his feelings of guilt. This was most productive and allowed for an earlier therapeutic entry into stressful combat episodes than might otherwise have been possible.

Occupational therapy involving creative activities was very helpful in providing a distraction from intrusive thoughts and promoting feelings of self-worth. Physical exercise was a necessary addition and helped the patient regain some self-confidence; as it proceeded, it was helpful in promoting restful sleep.

Deep muscle relaxation was attempted with marginal results.

However, biofeedback proved a very useful treatment modality by easing feelings of tension and hyperalertness. Corrective therapy was also used to good effect in assisting the patient with control of back pain (residual from the helicopter crash injury). A back brace was later provided, which was helpful.

Toward the end of the patient's hospitalization, vocational issues were addressed, first through vocational counseling and later in exploring the possibilities which would tend to minimize stress and avoid aggravation of the back injury. The patient's vocational history had formerly been quite good. His educational background included a master's degree in engineering and a baccalaureate degree in business administration. This history, while initially good, was later characterized by a downward spiral in terms of types of employment and length of employment. Prior to hospitalization, the veteran had been unemployed for three years and had no hope of ever getting employment.

Present Status: Mr. P. was released from the Medical Center after 11 months of treatment. The first five months of his treatment had been spent on a psychiatric ward where problems relating to his alcoholism, establishing his correct diagnosis as PTSD, and determining his pension status were dealt with. He was then transferred to another unit where the last six months were devoted to the treatment of his primary diagnosis of PTSD.

At the present time the patient is a functioning member of the family and the community. He is currently receiving "on-the-job training" and functioning at a relatively high level as he prepares to take a civil service position as a GS 10 step 4 (grade level). The position requires a significant degree of engineering and management skill.

There has been no return of symptoms related to PTSD and the prognosis for complete recovery and a return to full-time employment within a few months seems good to excellent. I am presently following this patient in outpatient therapy on a weekly basis and expect that continued treatment will be necessary for approximately one additional year.

If one considers the base-line of this patient and his family at the point of admission the degree of recovery achieved seems excellent. Up to this point, 10 patients have been treated in a similar way and so far our efforts have provided good results in eight out of the 10 cases. The treatment outlined in this discussion has the potential for being developed into a "program" which with some modifications could reasonably be expected to be successful for other patients with similar problems. It has the advantage of being applicable within a standard psychiatric

ward setting without the necessity of establishing a special PTSD treatment unit. Also, it permits greater flexibility of treatment approach since
the treatment program can be "individualized" to each patient's particular needs. By maintaining both a unit approach and the above described
individualized approach, we hope eventually to be able to determine
which patients will do best in the PTSD treatment unit and which will
do best outside the unit.

SUMMARY

In providing adequate treatment of PTSD, the therapist must consider
that treatment for the disorder may, and in fact often does, relieve the
symptoms or in many cases even eradicate them. This does not repair
or in any way alter the circumstances which the veteran faces upon
discharge unless the disruption and often total disorganization of his life
are addressed. Lacking this complete treatment, the veteran's symptoms
of PTSD do not seem to recur but the former neurotic coping behavior
begins again at some later date when he is faced with the other stresses
which have not been addressed.

The financial aspects of PTSD are a continuing problem, with review
boards' reluctance to accept PTSD as a viable disability related to the
stress of warfare. The wounds these veterans have received do not
manifest themselves in loss of limbs, sight, or hearing, but are equally
disabling. These psychological wounds are frequently viewed more as
weakness and degeneracy. Frequently, we hear, "I was in Vietnam and
have made a success of my life. Why can't he?"

This is not a valid statement. Many who have suffered severe physical
trauma in combat recover and become successful. Many men who served
their country well in Vietnam were not affected or were removed from
the horror of war. The men who seek treatment in the V.A. Medical
Centers are the walking wounded, the difference being that their
wounds are not apparent to the untrained and disbelieving eye. The
war in Vietnam was an unpopular war. It was abruptly brought to an
inglorious and unsatisfactory conclusion. There were few heros, even
fewer parades, and no monuments, save those erected by the veterans
of this war or their families. The government of the United States still
seeks futilely for a final accounting of the missing in action and prisoners
of war.

The men we are trying to help in our V.A. hospitals are of a generation
which should be experiencing their most productive years. It has only

been recently that PTSD has been officially recognized. If we do not now bring all of our talents and considerable capabilities to bear on this condition, we will not be, in the words of Abraham Lincoln, "binding up the nation's wounds."

APPENDIX A

A Suggested Reading List on Vietnam Veterans and Post-Traumatic Stress Disorder

CHAPLAIN RAY W. STUBBE

Adams, C.P., & McCloskey, J.: Twice born men. In A.B. Tulipan, C.L. Attneave, & E. Kingstone (Eds.), *Beyond the walls*. University, AL: University of Alabama Press, 1974.

Addlestone, D.: Legal issues facing mentally distressed veternas. Taped presentation at the National Conference on the Treatment of Post-Vietnam Stress Syndrome. Datyon, Ohio: Human Resource Initiatives, 1982.

Adelaja, C.: Patterns of psychiatric illness in the Nigerian army. *Military Medicine, 141*: 323-326, May 1976.

Adler, A.: Neuropsychiatric complications in victims of Boston's Coconut Grove disaster. *Journal of the American Medical Association, 123*: 1098-1101, 1943.

Adler, A.: Two different types of post-traumatic neurosis. *American Journal of Psychiatry, 102*:237-240, 1945.

Adler, B.: *Letters from Vietnam*. New York: Dutton, 1977.

Agus, C.: Some Vets can't leave Vietnam behind. *The Milwaukee Journal*, June 10, 1984, Life Style section, pp. 1, 2, 5.

Alarcon, R.D., Dickinson, W.A., & Dohn, H.H.: Flashback phenomena, clinical and diagnostic dilemmas. *Journal of Nervous and Mental Disease, 170*(4):217-223, 1982.

Allerton, W.S.: Psychiatric casualties in Vietnam. *Roche Medical Image and Commentary*, Oct. 1970, 27-29; in V.A., *Viet Vet*, pp. III-54-59, 1972.

Amdur, M.J., & Harrow, M.: Conscience and depressive disorders. *British Journal of Psychiatry, 120*:259-264, 1972.

American Psychiatric Association. *Diagnostic and statistical manual of mental disorders* (3rd ed.) (DSM-III). Washington, D.C.: American Psychiatric Association, 1980, pp. 236-238.

Amter, J.A.: *Vietnam verdict: A citizen's history*. New York: Continuum, 1982.

Andersen, R.S. (ed.): *Neuropsychiatry in World War II*, Vol. I. Washington, D.C.: Office of the Surgeon General, 1966.

Andersen, R.S.: Operation Homecoming: Psychological observations of repatriated Vietnam prisoners of war. *Psychiatry, 38*:65-74, 1975.

293

Anonymous: Dividend from Vietnam. *Time*, October 10, 1969, pp. 60-61.
Anonymous: Survey probes causes and manifestations of Post-Vietnam Syndrome (PVS) suffered by significant number of returning Vietnam veterans. *New York Times*, August 21, 1972, 1:2.
Anonymous: The war that won't go away. *Newsweek*, April 17, 1972.
Anonymous: Forgotten warriors: America's Vietnam era veterans. *DAV Magazine*, January 1980, pp. 8-12.
Anonymous: Pleading post-traumatic stress disorder: Novel defense for Viet vets. *Time*, May 26, 1980, p. 59.
Anonymous: Aftermath for Vietnam combat veterans. *Science News*, April 11, 1981, p. 236.
Anonymous: The war came home. *Time*, April 6, 1981, p. 17.
Anonymous: Vietnam vets fighting for their rights. *Time*, July 13, 1981, p. 2, 18-25.
Anonymous: A Vietnam vet's toughest battle. *Newsweek*, July, 1983, p. 18.
Apostle, D.T.: The unconscious defense as applied to post-traumatic stress disorder in a Vietnam veteran. *Bulletin of the American Academy of Psychiatry and Law, 8*(3), 1980.
Archibald, H.C., Long, D.M., Miller, C., & Tuddenham, R.D.: Gross stress reaction in combat—A 15-year follow-up. *American Journal of Psychiatry, 119*:317-322, October 1962.
Archibald, H.C., & Tuddenham, R.D.: Persistent stress reaction after combat: A 20-year follow-up. *Archives of General Psychiatry, 12*:475-481, May 1965.
Artiss, K.L.: Human behavior under stress—From combat to social psychiatry. *Military Medicine, 128*:1011-1015, October 1963.
Askevold, F.: War sailor syndrome. *Psychotherapy and Psychosomatics, 27*:133-138, 1976.
Atkeson, B.M., Calhoun, K.S., Resick, P.A., & Ellis, E.M.: Victims of rape: Repeated assessment of depressive symptoms. *Journal of Consulting and Clinical Psychology, 50*(1):96-102, 1982.
Atkinson, R.M., Henderson, R.G., Sparr, L.F., & Deale, S.: Assessment of Vietnam veterans for post-traumatic stress disorder in Veterans Administration disability claims. *American Journal of Psychiatry, 139*(9): 1118-1121, 1982.
Atkinson, R.M., Sparr, L.F., Sheff, A.G., White, R.A.F., & Fitzsimmons, J.T.: Diagnosis of Posttraumatic Stress Disorder in Vietnam veterans: Preliminary findings. *American Journal of Psychiatry, 141*(5):694-696, 1984.
Auerbach, A., Scheflen, N., & Scholz, C.: A Questionnaire survey of the post-traumatic syndrome. *Diseases of the Nervous System, 28*:110, 1967.
Aufhauser, M.C.: Guilt and guilt feeling: Power and the limits of power. *Ethics, 85*(4):288-297, 1975.
Ayres, B.D.: The Vietnam veteran: Silent, perplexed, unnoticed. *New York Times*, Nov. 8, 1970, pp. 1, 32; in V.A., *Viet Vet*, pp. IV-5-11, 1972.
Bachman, J.G., & Jennings, M.K.: The impact of Vietnam on trust in government. *Journal of Social Issues, 31*(4):141-155, 1975.
Baer, G. (photographer), & Howell-Koehler, N. (ed.): *Vietnam: The battle comes home*. Dobbs Ferry, NY: Morgan and Morgan, 1984.
Bailey, J.E.: The differential diagnosis of PTSD and anti-social personality disorder. Taped presentation at the Second National Conference on the Treatment of Post-Traumatic Stress Disorder, Dayton, Ohio: Human Resource Initiatives, 1983.
Bailey, J.E.: Special patient populations: Some factors in the treatment of delayed stress in Vietnam era veterans. Unpublished article.
Baker, M.: *Nam*. New York: William Morrow & Co., 1981.
Balson, P.M., & Dempster, C.R.: Treatment of war neurosis from Vietnam. *Comprehensive Psychiatry, 21*(2):167-175, 1980.
Barocas, H.A., & Barocas, C.B.: Manifestations of concentration camp effects on the second generation. *American Journal of Psychiatry, 130*(7):820-821, 1973.
Barrett, J.E. (Ed.): *Stress and mental disorder*. New York: Raven Press, 1979.
Barry, J. (Ed.): *Peace is our profession: Poems and passages of war protest*. Montclair, NJ: East River Anthology, 1981.

Barry, J., & Ehrhart, W.D. (Eds.): *Demilitarized zones: Veterans after Vietnam.* Perkasie, PA: East River Anthology, 1976.

Barton, B.S.: Post traumatic stress disorder as an insanity defense for Vietnam veterans. *Criminal Law Seminar,* March 4, 1981.

Baum, A., Gatchel, R.J., & Schaeffer, M.A.: Emotional, behavioral, and physiological effects of chronic stress at Three Mile Island. *Journal of Consulting and Clinical Psychology,* 51(4):565-572, 1983.

Beck, A.T.: *Depression: Causes and treatment.* Philadelphia: University of Pennsylvania Press, 1967.

Beck, A.T.: *The diagnosis and management of depression.* Philadelphia: University of Pennsylvania Press, 1967.

Beck, A.T., Ward, C.H., Mendelson, M., Mock, J., & Erbaugh, J.: An inventory for measuring depression. *Archives of General Psychiatry,* 561-571, 1961.

Beebe, G.W., & DeBakey, M.E.: *Battle casualties.* Springfield, IL: Charles C Thomas, 1952.

Bentel, O.J., & Smith, D.E.: Drug abuse in combat: The crisis of drugs and addiction among American troops in Vietnam. *Journal of Psychedelic Drugs,* 4:23-30, 1971.

Berger, D.: The survivor syndrome: A problem of nosology and treatment. *American Journal of Psychotherapy,* 31:238-251, 1977.

Berkowitz, M.: Themes in treatment of Vietnam veterans. In T. Williams (Ed.), *Post-traumatic stress disorders of the Vietnam veteran.* Cincinnati, OH: Disabled American.

Berman, S., Price, S., & Gusman, F.: An inpatient program for Vietnam combat veterans in a Veterans Administration hospital. *Hospital and Community Psychiatry,* 33(11):919-922, 1982.

Bettelheim, B.: Individual and mass behavior in extreme situations. *Journal of Abnormal and Social Psychology,* 38, 1943.

Bettelheim, B.: *The informed heart.* Glencoe: Free Press, 1960.

Bey, D.R.: Division psychiatry in Vietnam. *American Journal of Psychiatry,* 127(?):228-232, 1970.

Bey, D.R.: Change of command in combat: A locus of stress. *American Journal of Psychiatry,* 129:698-702, 1972.

Bey, D.R., & Zecchinelli, V.A.: Marijuana as a coping device in Vietnam. *Military Medicine,* 136:448-450, 1971.

Bingaman, D.: Client assessment of Operation Outreach. Taped presentation at the National Conference on the Treatment of Post-Vietnam Stress Syndrome, Dayton, Ohio: Human Resource Initiatives, 1982.

Bitzer, R.: Caught in the middle: Mentally disabled veterans and the Veterans Administration. In C.R. Figley (Ed.), *Strangers at home: Vietnam veterans since the war.* New York: Praeger Publications, 1980.

Bizzell, D.L.: Results of the eight year psychiatric follow-up among former prisoners of war and their matched comparisons. Taped presentation at the National Conference on the Treatment of Post-Vietnam Stress Syndrome, Dayton, Ohio: Human Resource Initiatives, 1982.

Black, F.W.: Personality characteristics of Vietnam veterans identified as heroin abusers. *American Journal of Psychiatry,* 132(7):748-749, 1975.

Black, S., Owens, K.L., & Wolff, R.P.: Patterns of drug use: A study of 5,482 subjects. In V.A., *Viet Vet,* pp. III-65-69, 1972.

Blanchard, E.B.: Physiological assessment of post-Vietnam stress syndrome. Taped presentation at the National Conference on the Treatment of Post-Vietnam Stress Syndrome, Dayton, Ohio: Human Resource Initiatives, 1982.

Blanchard, E.B., Kolb, L.C., Pallmeyer, T.P., & Gerardi, R.J.: The development of a psychophysiological assessment procedure for post-traumatic stress disorders in Vietnam veterans. *Psychiatric Quarterly,* in press.

Blanchard, E.B., Kolb, L.C., Pallmeyer, T.P., & Gerardi, R.B.: A psychophysiological study of post-traumatic stress disorder in Vietnam veterans. *Psychiatric Quarterly,* 54(4):220-

229, 1983.

Blanford, R.: Sexual dysfunction and the Vietnam veteran. Taped presentation at the National Conference on the Treatment of Post-Vietnam Stress Syndrome, Dayton, Ohio: Human Resource Initiatives, 1982.

Blank, A.S.: 1st Training Conference Papers, Vietnam Veterans—Operation Outreach, St. Louis, Missouri, Sep 24-28, 1979; in *Resource Manual*, Pt. 2.

Blank, A.S.: The unconscious flashback to the war in Vietnam: Veterans clinical mystery, legal defense, and community problem. Paper presented at the annual meeting of the American Psychological Association, Montreal, Quebec, Canada, 1-5 Sept. 1980; revised July, 1981.

Blank, A.S.: Stresses of war: The example of Vietnam. In L. Goldberger & S. Breznitz (Eds.), *Handbook of stress*. New York: Free Press/Macmillan, 1981.

Blank, A.S.: Apocalypse terminable and interminable: Operation Outreach for Vietnam veterans. *Hospital and Community Psychiatry, 33*(11):913-918, 1982.

Bloch, H.: Army clinical psychiatry in the combat zone—1967-1968. *American Journal of Psychiatry, 126*(3):289-298, 1969.

Bloch, H.S.: The psychological adjustment of normal people during a year's tour in Vietnam. *Psychiatric Quarterly, 44*:613-627, 1970; in V.A., *Viet Vet*, Pt. 3.

Blum, M.D., Kelly, E.M., Meyer, M. Carlson, C.R., & Hodson, W.L.: An assessment of the treatment needs of Vietnam-era veterans. *Hospital and Community Psychiatry, 35*(7):691-696, 1984.

Bobbitt, R.: Growing pains in the evaluation and treatment of post-traumatic stress disorder among Vietnam veterans. Taped presentation at the National Conference on the Treatment of Post-Vietnam Stress Syndrome, Dayton, Ohio: Human Resource Initiatives, 1982.

Bond, T.C.: The why of fragging. *American Journal of Psychiatry, 133*(11):1328-1331, 1976.

Borchard, D.C.: Self-actualization in Vietnam veteran and nonveteran male college students (Doctoral Dissertation, George Washington University, 1976). *Dissertation Abstracts International, 37*:4975A, 1977.

Boriskin, J.A.: Group therapy process from an objective relations perspective. Taped presentation at the National Conference on the Treatment of Post-Vietnam Stress Syndrome, Dayton, Ohio: Human Resource Initiatives, 1982.

Borus, J.F.: Reentry: I. Adjustment issues facing the Vietnam returnee. *Archives of General Psychiatry, 28*:501-506, 1973.

Borus, J.F.: Reentry: II. "Making it" back in the States. *American Journal of Psychiatry, 130*(8):850-854, 1973.

Borus, J.F.: Reentry: III. Facilitating healthy readjustment in Vietnam veterans. *Psychiatry, 36*(4):428-439, 1973.

Borus, J.F.: Incidence of maladjustment in Vietnam returnees. *Archives of General Psychiatry, 30*:554-557, 1974.

Boscarino, J.: Current drug involvement among Vietnam and non-Vietnam veterans

Bourne, P.G.: The Vietnam veteran. In V.A., *Viet Vet*, pp. IV-83-86, 1972.

Bourne, P.G.: 17-OHCS levels in combat: Special forces "A" team under threat of attack. *Archives of General Psychiatry, 19*:135-140, 1968.

Bourne, P.G. (ed.): *The psychology and physiology of stress*. New York: Academic Press, 1969.

Bourne, P.G.: *Men, stress and Vietnam*. Boston: Little, Brown, 1970.

Bourne, P.G.: Military psychiatry and the Vietnam experience. *American Journal of Psychiatry, 127*:481-488, 1970.

Bourne, P.G.: The Vietnam veteran: Psychosocial casualties. *Psychiatry in Medicine, 3*:23-27, 1972.

Bourne, P.G.: The Vietnam veteran. In V.A., *Viet Vet*, pp. IV-83-86, 1972.

Bourne, P.G., Rose, R.M., & Mason, J.W.: Urinary 17-OHCS Levels: Data on seven helicopter ambulance medics in combat. *Archives of General Psychiatry, 17*:104-110, 1967.

Bourne, P.G., & San, N.D.: A comparative study of neuropsychiatric casualties in the

United States Army and the Army of the Republic of Vietnam. *Military Medicine,* 132:904-909, 1967.

Bowlby, J.: *Attachment and loss: Value, attachment.* London: Hogarth Press, 1969.

Boyd, J.: Treatment of PTSD in Vietnam-era veterans in rural settings: Obstacles and innovations. Taped presentation at the Second National Conference on the Treatment of Post-Traumatic Stress Disorder, Dayton, Ohio: Human Resource Initiatives, 1983.

Braatz, G.A., & Lumry, G.K.: The young veteran as a psychiatric patient. *Military Medicine,* 134(12):1434-1439, 1969.

Braatz, G.A., Lumry, G.K., & Wright, M.S.: The young veteran as a psychiatric patient in three eras of conflict. *Military Medicine,* 136:455-457, 1971.

Braceland, F.J.: Psychiatry and the returning veteran. *Mental Hygiene,* 30:33-46, 1946.

Braceland, F.J.: Forgotten men. *Psychiatric Annals,* 12(11):975-976, 1982.

Brady, D., & Rappoport, L.: Violence and Vietnam: A comparison between attitudes of civilians and veterans. *Human Relations,* 26:735-752, 1973.

Braverman, M.: Validity of psychotraumatic reactions. *Journal of Forensic Sciences,* 22(3):654-662, 1977.

Braverman, M.: Onset of psychotraumatic reactions. *Journal of Forensic Sciences,* 25(4), 1980.

Braverman, M., & Hacker, F.J.: Post-traumatic hyperirritability. *Psychoanalytic Review,* 55(4):601, 1968-1969.

Brende, J.O.: The character pathology of Vietnam combat veterans: Hypervigilance and aggressive outbursts. Paper in V.A., *Resource Manual,* Pt. 1.

Brende, J.O.: Combined individual and group therapy for Vietnam veterans. *International Journal of Group Psychotherapy,* 31(3):367-378, 1981; in V.A., *Resource Manual,* Pt. 6.

Brende, J.O.: Electrodermal responses in post-traumatic syndromes: A pilot study of cerebral hemisphere functioning in Vietnam veterans. Taped presentation at the National Conference on the Treatment of Post-Vietnam Stress Syndrome, Dayton, Ohio: Human Resource Initiatives, 1982.

Brende, J.O., & Benedict, B.D.: The Vietnam combat delayed stress syndrome: Hypnotherapy of "dissociative symptoms." *American Journal of Clinical Hypnosis,* 23(1):34-40, 1980.

Brewin, R.: TV's newest villain: The Vietnam veteran. *TV Guide,* July 19, 1975, pp. 4-8.

Brill, N., Beebe, G., & Gilbert: *A follow-up study of war neuroses.* V.A. Medical Monograph, National Research Council, Jan. 1955.

Brill, N.Q., & Beebe, G.W.: A follow-up study of war neuroses. V.A. Medical Monograph, Washington, D.C.: U.S. Veterans Administration, 1956.

Brooks, J.S.: The therapeutic effects of transcendental meditation on post-Vietnam stress disorder. Taped presentation at the National Conference on the Treatment of Post-Vietnam Stress Syndrome, Dayton, Ohio: Human Resource Initiatives, 1982.

Brown, H., Schoenthal, R., & Katz, B.: A comprehensive multifaceted treatment program for Vietnam veterans suffering from post-traumatic stress disorder and their spouses in a community mental health center. Taped presentation at the National Conference on the Treatment of Post-Vietnam Stress Syndrome, Dayton, Ohio: Human Resource Initiatives, 1982.

Broyles, W.J.: Remembering a war we want to forget. *Newsweek,* November 22, 1982, p. 82.

Bruns, L.: *Die Traumatischen Neurosen.* Wien, 1901.

Bryan, C.D.: *Friendly fire.* New York: Putnam, 1976.

Buber, M.: Guilt and guilt feelings. *Psychiatry,* 20:114-129, 1957.

Buckley, C.: Viet guilt: Were the real prisoners of war the young Americans who never left home? *Esquire,* 68-72, September 1983.

Bunting, J.: *The lionheads.* New York: Braziller, 1972.

Burgess, A.W., & Holstrum, L.L.: The rape trauma syndrome. *American Journal of Psychiatry,* 131(9):981-986, 1974.

Burkle, F.M., Jr.: Coping with stress under conditions of disaster and refugee care. *Military*

Medicine, 148(10):800-803, 1983.

Burstein, A.: Treatment of post-traumatic stress disorder with imipramine. *Psychosomatics*, 25(9):681-687, 1984.

Buss, A.M., & Durkee, A.: An inventory for assessing different kinds of hostility. *Journal of Consulting Psychology*, 21:343-349, 1957.

Buttinger, J.: *Vietnam: The unforgettable tragedy*. New York: Horizon, 1977.

Caplan, G.: "Statement," in V.A., *Viet Vet*, pp. IV-18-28, 1972.

Caplan, N., & Nelson, S.: On being useful: The nature and consequences of psychological research on social problems. *American Psychologist*, 28:199-211, 1973.

Caputo, P.: *A rumor of war*. New York: Holt, Rinehart & Winston, 1977.

Caputo, P.: The unreturning army. *Playboy*, January, 1982, p. 274.

Carden, N.L., & Schramel, D.J.: Observations of conversion reaction seen in troops involved in the Vietnam conflict. *American Journal of Psychiatry*, 123(1):21-31, 1966.

Carr, R.L.: A comparison of self-concept and expectations concerning control between Vietnam-era veterans and nonveterans (Doctoral Dissertation, St. Louis University, 1973). *Dissertation Abstracts International*, 34:4730A-4731A, 1974.

Carroll, E.: Stress-disorder symptoms in Vietnam and Korean war veterans: A commentary on Thienes-Hontos, Watson, and Kucala. *Journal of Consulting and Clinical Psychology*, 51(4):616-618, 1983.

Cassidy, J.: *A station in the delta*. New York: Scribner's, 1979.

Castelli, J.: Society and the Vietnam veteran. *Catholic World*, 212:184-188, June 1971; in V.A., *Viet Vet*, pp. IV-11-15, 1972.

Cavenar, J.O., Jr., & Nash, J.L.: The effects of combat on the normal personality: War neurosis in Vietnam returnees. *Comprehensive Psychiatry*, 17(5):647-653, 1976; in V.A., *Resource Manual*, Pt. 3.

Cavenar, J.C., & Spaulding, J.G.: Delayed psychiatric casualties from the Vietnam conflict. *Newsletter for Research in Mental Health and Behavioral Sciences*, 18(3):8-12, 1976; in V.A., *Resource Manual*, Pt. 1.

Cellucci, A.J., & Lawrence, P.S.: The efficacy of systematic desensitization in reducing nightmares. *Journal of Behavior Therapy and Experimental Psychiatry*, 9:109-114, 1978.

Center for Policy Research. *The adjustment of Vietnam era veterans to civilian life*, New York, 1979.

Center for Policy Research. Vietnam era research project: Preliminary report. New York: Center for Policy Research, 1980.

Chamberlain, B.C.: The psychological aftermath of disaster. *Journal of Clinical Psychiatry*, 41(7):238-244, 1980.

Chodoff, P.: Late effects of concentration camp syndrome. *Archives of General Psychiatry*, 8:323-333, 1963.

Chodoff, P.: Psychotherapy of the survivor. In J. Dinsdale (Ed.), *Survivors, victims, and perpetrators*. Washington, D.C.: Hemisphere, 1980, pp. 205-218.

Chodoff, P., Friedman, S.B., & Hamburg, D.A.: Stress, defenses, and coping behavior: Observations in parents of children with malignant disease. *American Journal of Psychiatry*, 120:743-749, 1964.

Christenson, R.M., Walker, J.I., Ross, D.R., & Maltbie, A.A.: Reactivation of traumatic conflicts. *American Journal of Psychiatry*, 138(7):984-985, 1981.

Cleland, M.: *Strong at the broken places*. Lincoln, VA: Chosen Books, 1980.

Cleland, M.: Vietnam veterans respond to vet center teams. *Vanguard*, September 1980, pp. 1, 4-5.

Cobb, S.: Social support as a moderator of life stress. *Psychosomatic Medicine*, 38(5):300-314, 1976.

Cochrane, R., & Robertson, A.: The life events inventory: A measure of the relative severity of psychosocial stressors. *Journal of Psychosomatic Research*, 17:135-139, 1972.

Colbach, E.M., & Parrish, M.D.: Army mental health activities in Vietnam: 1965-1970. *Bulletin of the Menninger Clinic*, 34:332-342, 1970; In V.A., *Viet Vet*, pp. III-36-41, 1972.

Colbach, E.M.: Psychiatric criteria for compassionate reassignment in the army. *American Journal of Psychiatry, 127*(4):508-510, 1970.

Cooper, P.: 10 years later. *VFW, 70*(1):24-27, 1983.

Corcoran, J.F.T.: The concentration camp syndrome and USAF Vietnam prisoners of war. *Psychiatric Annals, 12*(11):991-994, 1982.

Corson, W.R.: *The betrayal.* New York: Norton, 1968.

Corson, W.R.: Advice and dissent: America's tretment of Vietnam vets. *Time,* July 13, 1981, p. 23.

Cottrell, L.S.: The aftermath of hostilities. In S.A. Stouffer et al., *The American soldier: Combat and its aftermath,* Vol. 2. Princeton: Princeton University Press, 1949.

Dancey, T.E.: Treatment in the absence of pensioning for psychoneurotic veterans. *American Journal of Psychiatry,* 107:347-349, 1950.

Danieli, Y.: Families of survivors of the Nazi holocaust. In C. Spielberger, I. Sarason, & N. Milgram (Eds.), *Stress and anxiety,* Vol. 8. Washington, D.C.: Hemisphere, 1982, pp. 405-421.

Dasberg, H.: Belonging and loneliness in relation to mental breakdown in battle (with some remarks on treatment). *Israel Annals of Psychiatry and Related Disciplines,* 14:307-321, 1976.

Dean, A., & Lin, N.: The stress-buffering role of social support. *The Journal of Nervous and Mental Disease, 165*(6):403-417, 1977.

Deaton, J.E., Berg, S.W., Richlin, M., & Litrownik, A.J.: Coping activities in solitary confinement of U.S. Navy POWs in Vietnam. *Journal of Applied Social Psychology,* 7:239-257, 1977.

DeFazio, V.J.: The Vietnam era veteran: Psychological problems. *Journal of Contemporary Psychotherapy,* 7:9 15, 1975.

DeFazio, V.J., Rustin, S., & Diamond, A.: Symptom development in Vietnam era veterans. *American Journal of Orthopsychiatry, 45*(1):158 163, 1975.

Del Veccio, J.M.: *The thirteenth valley.* New York: Bantam, 1982.

Derogatis, L.R., Lipman, R.S., & Covi, L.: The SCL-90: An outpatient psychiatric rating scale. *Psychopharmacological Bulletin,* 9:13-28, 1973.

Devine, P.E.: The conscious acceptance of guilt in the necessary murder. *Ethics, 89*(3):221-239, 1979.

Dickman, H.R., & Pearson, H.J.: Younger veterans—Older veterans: A comparison of perceptions of hospital treatment, problem areas and needs. In V.A., *Viet Vet,* pp. IV-106-112, 1972.

Diggory, J.C., & Rothman, D.Z.: Values destroyed by death. *Journal of Abnormal and Social Psychology,* 63:205-210, 1961.

DiMascio, A., Shader, R., & Harmatz, J.: Psychotropic drugs and induced hostility. *Psychosomatics, 10:*47-50, 1969.

Dobbs, D., & Wilson, W.P.: Observations on the persistence of war neurosis. *Diseases of the Nervous System, 21:*686-691, December 1960.

Dohrenwend, B.S., & Dohrenwend, B.P.: *Stressful life events: Their nature and effects.* New York: Wiley, 1974.

Domash, M., & Sparr, L.P.: Post-traumatic stress disorder masquerading as paranoid schizophrenia. *Military Medicine,* in press.

Dor-Shav, N.K.: On the long-range effects of concentration camp internment on Nazi Victims: 25 years later. *Journal of Consulting and Clinical Psychology,* 46:1-11, 1978.

Doyle, D.: Vietnam veterans and the corrections systems. Taped presentation at the National Conference on the Treatment of Post-Vietnam Stress Syndrome, Dayton, Ohio: Human Resource Initiatives, 1982.

Dowling, J.J.: Psychological aspects of the year in Vietnam. *USARV Medical Bulletin,* 2:45-48, May/June 1967.

Dunner, F., Copeland, P., Edwards, W., Shaw, D., & Mally-Olson, P.: An evaluation of the clinical efficacy of alprazolan (Xanax) in Vietnam veterans with PTSD. Taped presentation at the Second National Conference on the Treatment of Post-Traumatic Stress Disorder, Dayton, Ohio: Human Resource Initiatives, 1983.

Durkheim, E.: *Suicide*. Glencoe, IL: Free Press, 1951.

Durlak, J.A.: Measurement of the fear of death: An examination of some existing scales. *Journal of Clinical Psychology, 28*:545-547, 1972.

Eaton, W.W.: Life events, social supports, and psychiatric symptoms: A re-analysis of the New Haven data. *Journal of Health and Social Behavior, 19*(2):230-234, 1978.

Edwards, G.: Psychiatric aspects of civilian disasters. *British Medical Journal,* 1:944-947, 1976.

Egendorf, A.: The ones who came back. *New York Times,* September, 1972.

Egendorf, A.: You don't have to be crazy to be a vet. *Penthouse, April, 1974.*

Egendorf, A.: Vietnam veteran rap groups and themes of post-war life. *Journal of Social Issues, 31*(4):111-124, 1975.

Egendorf, A.: One Vietnam veteran: A study of continuity and change. *Dissertation Abstracts International, 38*(4):1877-8b, 1978.

Egendorf, A.: Psychotherapy with Vietnam veterans. In C.R. Figley; (Ed.), *Stress Disorders among Vietnam veterans.* New York: Brunner/Mazel, 1978.

Egendorf, A.: Human development and ultimate reality: The perceptual grounds for transformation. In T. Tulku, R. Moon, & G.S. Randall (Eds.), *Dimensions of thought: Current explorations in time, space and knowledge,* Vol. 2. Berkeley, CA: Dharma Press, 1980.

Egendorf, A.: Statement on behalf of the Association for the Advancement of Psychology and the American Psychological Association. In U.S. Senate, *Hearings of the Committee on Veterans Affairs, 96th Congress, May 21, 1980.* Washington, D.C.: U.S. Government Printing Office, 1980.

Egendorf, A.: Vietnam goes on. *New York Times,* May 26, 1981.

Egendorf, A.: The postwar healing of Vietnam veterans: Recent research. *Hospital and Community Psychiatry, 33*(11):901-908, 1982.

Egendorf, A.: Veterans and the legacy of Vietnam. In Z. Rubin, & E.G. McNeil (Eds.), *The psychology of being human.* New York: Harper & Row, 1982.

Egendorf, A., Kadushin, C., Laufer, R.S., Rothbart, G., & Sloan, L.: *Legacies of Vietnam: Comparative adjustment of veterans and their peers, a study conducted for the Veterans Administration,* March 1981. House Committee Print No. 14, 97th Congress, 1st Session, March 9, 1981.

Eisenhart, R.W.: You can't hack it little girl: A discussion of the covert psychological agenda of modern combat training. *Journal of Social Issues, 31*(4):13-23, 1975.

Eisenhart, R.W.: Flower of the dragon: An example of applied humanistic psychology. *Journal of Humanistic Psychology, 17*:3-24, 1977.

Eitinger, L.: Psychosomatic problems of concentration camp survivors. *Journal of Psychosomatic Research, 13*:183, 1969.

Elmore, T.M.: The development of a scale to measure anomia and its implications for counseling psychology. Proceedings of the *73rd Annual Convention of the American Psychological Association* (summary), 1965, pp. 359-360.

Emerson, G.: *Winners and losers: Battles, retreats, gains, losses and ruins from a long war.* New York: Random House, 1977.

Enzie, R.F., Sawyer, R.N., & Montgomery, F.A.: Manifest anxiety of Vietnam returnees and undergraduates. *Psychological Reports, 33*:446, Oct. 1973.

Erickson, K.T.: Loss of communality at Buffalo Creek. *American Journal of Psychiatry, 133*(3):302-305, March 1976.

Erikson, E.H.: *Identity, youth and crisis.* New York: W.W. Norton, 1968.

Erikson, E.H.: *The life-cycle completed.* New York: W.W. Norton, 1982.

Erlinder, C.P.: Legal problems and PTSD: Building a common perspective. Taped presentation at the Second National Conference on the Treatment of Post-Traumatic Stress Disorder, Dayton, Ohio: Human Resource Initiatives, 1983.

Ermalinski, R., Hanson, P.G., & O'Connel, W.E.: Toward resolution of a generation-gap conflict on a psychiatric ward. *International Journal of Group Tensions*, 2:77-89, 1972.

Evans, J., Jenkins, E., & Rueth, T.: Developing a comprehensive PTSD treatment program in a community mental health center. Taped presentation at the Second National Conference on the Treatment of Post-Traumatic Stress Disorder, Dayton, Ohio: Human Resource Initiatives, 1983.

Ewalt, J.R.: What about the Vietnam veteran? *Military Medicine*, 146:165-167, March 1981.

Fairbank, J.A., Keane, T.M., & Malloy, P.F.: Some preliminary data on the psychological characteristics of Vietnam veterans with posttraumatic stress disorders. *Journal of Consulting and Clinical Psychology*, 51(6):912-919, 1983.

Fairbank, J.A., Langley, K., Jarve, G.J., & Keane, T.M.: A selected bibliography on posttraumatic stress disorders in Vietnam veterans. *Professional Psychology*, 12(5):578-586, 1981.

Falk, A.: The role of guilt feelings in war neurosis. In C. Spielberger, I Sarason, & N. Milgram (Eds.), *Stress and anxiety*, Vol. 8. Washington, D.C.: Hemisphere, 1982, pp. 163-169.

Faude, K., & Weston-Zarit, J.: Vietnam era veterans and family relationships. Paper presented to the American Psychological Association, Los Angeles, 1981.

Fendrich, J.M.: The returning Black Vietnam era veteran. In V.A., *Viet Vet*, pp. IV-72-82, 1972.

Ferenczi, S., Abraham, K., Simmel, E., & Jones, E.: *Psychoanalysis and the war neurosis.* New York: International Psychoanalytic Press, 1921.

Fiedler, L.: Who really died in Vietnam? *Saturday Review*, Nov. 18, 1972, pp. 44-49.

Figley, C.R.: Contrasts between combat and non-combat Vietnam veterans regarding selected indices of interpersonal adjustment. Paper presented at the annual meeting of the American Sociological Association, San Francisco, August 1975.

Figley, C.R.: The Vietnam veteran in family therapy: Implications from the research. Paper presented at the annual meeting of the American Personnel and Guidance Association, Chicago, March 1976.

Figley, C.R.: Combat experience and veterans' perceived interpersonal adjustment within four life periods. Unpublished material, 1976.

Figley, C.R.: The American legion study of the psychological adjustment among Vietnam veterans. Lafayette, IN: Purdue University, 1977.

Figley, C.R. (Ed.): *Stress disorders among Vietnam veterans: Theory, research, and treatment.* New York: Brunner/Mazel, 1978.

Figley, C.R.: Symptoms of delayed combat stress among a college sample of Vietnam veterans. *Military Medicine*, 143:107-110, February 1978.

Figley, C.R.: The residue of Vietnam. *The American Legion Magazine*, Sept., 1978.

Figley, C.R.: Strangers at home: The war, the nation, and the Vietnam veteran. Paper presented at North Dakota University, Nov. 1978.

Figley, C.R.: The Spartans and the Spartacans: The Vietnam veteran experience in social-historical perspective. Paper presented at Wabash College, Crawfordsville, Iowa, April 1979.

Figley, C.R.: Combat as disaster: Treating combat veterans as survivors. Presentation to annual meeting of the American Psychiatric Association, Chicago, May 14, 1979.

Figley, C.R.: Confusing the Warrior with the War. Editorial in *APA Monitor*, 10(4):2, 1979.

Figley, C.R.: Vietnam veteran mental health treatment: Alternative conceptualizations and new directions. *Evaluation*, Fall, 1979.

Figley, C.R.: Welcoming back the Vietnam veteran survivor: Review and application of post-traumatic stress disorder. Paper presented at 133rd annual meeting of the American Psychiatric Association, San Francisco, May 1980; in V.A., *Resource Manual*, Pt. 1.

Figley, C.R.: Traumatic stress and the role of the family and social support system. Taped presentation at the National Conference on the Treatment of Post-Vietnam Stress Syndrome, Dayton, Ohio: Human Resource Initiatives, 1982.

Figley, C.R.: Toward a generic view of traumatic stress. Taped presentation at the Second National Conference on the Treatment of Post-Traumatic Stress Disorder, Dayton, Ohio: Human Resource Initiatives, 1983.

Figley, C.R. (Ed.): *Trauma and its wake*. New York: Brunner/Mazel, 1985.

Figley, C.R. Burge, S.K., Kishur, R., Segal, S.A., & Gilbert, K.: Catastrophic stress and the family: Implications for the clinician. Taped presentation at the Second National Conference on the Treatment of Post-Traumatic Stress Disorder, Dayton, Ohio: Human Resource Initiatives, 1983.

Figley, C.R., & Leventman, S. (Eds.): *Strangers at home: Vietnam veterans since the war*. New York: Praeger, 1980.

Figley, C.R., & Southerly, W.T.: Residue of war: The Vietnam veteran in mainstream America. Paper presented at the annual meeting of the American Psychological Association, San Francisco, August 1977.

Figley, C.R., & Sprenkle, D.H.: Delayed stress response syndrome: Family therapy indications. *Journal of Marriage and Family Counseling, 4*:53-60, July 1978.

Fiman, B.G., Borus, J.F., & Stanton, M.D.: Black-white and American-Vietnamese relations among soldiers in Vietnam. *Journal of Social Issues, 31*(4):39-48, 1975.

Fisher, C., Kahn, E., Edwards, A., et al.: A psychophysiological study of nightmares and night terrors. *Archives for General Psychiatry, 28*:252-259, 1973.

Fisher, V., Bucuvalas, M. & Schulman, M.A.: *Advance survey of the general public's attitude toward Vietnam veterans: A study of the Veterans Administration* (Study No. 792801). Washington, D.C.: Lou Harris and Associates, 1979.

Fitzgerald, F.: *Fire in the lake: The Vietnamese and the Americans in Vietnam*. New York: Random House, 1973.

Flaherty, J.A., Gaviria, F.M., & Pathak, Dev. S.: The measurement of social support: The social support network inventory. *Comprehensive Psychiatry, 24*(6):521-529, 1983.

Fleet Marine Force, Pacific (Forward), Personal Response Project. *Assessment of attitudes of third marine amphibious force toward the Vietnamese*. June, 1967.

Fleming, R.: An interdisciplinary approach to understanding the Vietnam/Vietnam veteran experience. Taped presentation at the National Conference on the Treatment of Post-Vietnam Stress Syndrome, Dayton, Ohio: Human Resource Initiatives, 1982.

Ford, C.V., & Spaulding, R.C.: The Pueblo incident: A comparison of factors related to coping with extreme stress. *Archives of General Psychiatry, 29*:340-343, September 1973.

Fox, R.P.: Post-combat adaptational problems. *Comprehensive Psychiatry, 13*:435-443, 1972.

Fox, R.P.: Narcissistic rage and the problem of combat aggression. *Archives of General Psychiatry, 31*:807-811, December 1974.

Foy, D.W., Sipprelle, R.C., Rueger, D.B., & Carroll, E.M.: Etiology of posttraumatic stress disorder in Vietnam veterans: Analysis of premilitary, military, and combat exposure influences. *Journal of Consulting and Clinical Psychology, 52*(1):79-87, 1984.

Frank, I.M., & Hoedemaker, F.S.: The civilian psychiatrist and the draft. *American Journal of Psychiatry, 127*(4):497-502, 1970.

Frankl, V.E.: *Man's search for meaning: An introduction to logotherapy*. Boston: Beacon Press, 1963.

Freud, S.: Identification with the aggressor. In *The ego and mechanisms of defense*. New York: International Universities Press, 1946.

Freud, S.: Beyond the pleasure principle. In J. Strachey (Ed.), *Standard edition*, Vol. 18. London: Hogarth Press, 1955 (originally published in 1920).

Freud, S.: Introductory lectures on psychoanalysis. In J. Strachey (Ed.), *Standard edition*, Vol. 16. London: Hogarth Press, 1955 (originally published in 1917).

Freud, S.: Psychoanalysis and the war neurosis. In J. Strachey (Ed.), *Standard edition*, Vol. 17. London: Hogarth Press, 1955 (originally published in 1919).

Freud, S.: Inhibitions, symptoms and anxiety. In J. Strachey (Ed.), *Standard edition*, Vol. 20. London: Hogarth Press, 1955 (originally published in 1926).

Freud, S.: Moses and monotheism. In J. Strachey (Ed.), *Standard edition*, Vol. 23. London: Hogarth Press, 1955 (originally published in 1939).

Freud, S.: Mourning and melancholia. In J. Strachey (Ed.), *Standard edition*, Vol. 14. London: Hogarth Press, 1957 (originally published in 1912), 237-258.
Freud, S.: On the history of the psycho-analytic movement. In J. Strachey (Ed.), *Standard edition*, Vol. 14. London: Hogarth Press, 1957 (originally published in 1913).
Freud, S.: Totem and taboo. *Standard edition*, Vol. 14. London: Hogarth Press, 1957 (originally published in 1913).
Freud, S.: Reflections upon war and death. In P. Reiff (Ed.), *Character and culture*. New York: Macmillan, 1963.
Freudenberg, H.J.: The psychology of the Vietnam veteran and drug addiction. *Psychiatric Opinion, 12*:34-38, 1975.
Friedman, M.J.: Post-Vietnam syndrome: Recognition and management. *Psychosomatics, 22*(11):931-943, 1981.
Friedman, P., & Zinn, Z.: The psychiatry of disaster. *American Journal of Psychiatry, 114*(Supp 5):426, 1957.
Frye, J.S., & Stockton, R.A.: Discriminant analysis of posttraumatic stress disorder among a group of Vietnam veterans. *American Journal of Psychiatry, 139*(1):52-56, 1982.
Fussell, P.: *The great war and modern memory*. New York: Oxford University Press, 1975.
Futterman, S., & Pumpian-Mindlin, E.: Traumatic war neuroses five years later. *American Journal of Psychiatry, 108*:401-408, December 1951.
Gault, W.B.: Some remarks on slaughter. *American Journal of Psychiatry, 128*(4):450-454, 1971.
Geen, R., Stonner, D., & Shope, G.: The facilitation of aggression: A study in response inhibition and disinhibition. *Journal of Personal and Social Psychology, 31*:721-726, 1975.
Geer, J.H., & Silverman, I.: Treatment of a recurrent nightmare by behavior-modification procedures: A case study. *Journal of Abnormal Psychology, 72*(2):188-190, 1967.
Gelb, L.H., & Betts, R.K.: *The irony of Vietnam: The system worked*. Washington, D.C.: Brookings Institution, 1971.
Gelinas, D.J.: The persisting negative effects of incest. *Psychiatry, 46*(4):312-332, 1983.
Gerdeman, E.: A multiple phase and bioenergetic approach to the treatment of posttraumatic stress disorder in Vietnam veterans. Taped presentation at the National Conference on the Treatment of Post-Vietnam Stress Syndrome, Dayton, Ohio: Human Resource Initiatives, 1982.
Getsinger, S.H.: The Vietnam veteran with a psychiatric disability: Vocational assets and liabilities. *Newsletter for Research in Mental Health and Behavioral Sciences, 18*:25-28, 1976.
Giles, S.L.: Post-traumatic stress disorders in rural Vietnam veterans: Crude epidemiologic estimates based on casualty figures. Taped presentation at the National Conference on the Treatment of Post-Vietnam Stress Syndrome, Dayton, Ohio: Human Resource Initiatives, 1982.
Gillispie, R.D.: *Psychological effects of war on citizen and soldier*. New York: W.W. Norton, 1942.
Gillooly, D., & Bond, T.C.: Assaults with explosive devices on superiors: A synopsis of reports from confined offenders at the US disciplinary barracks. *Military Medicine, 141*(10):700-702, 1976.
Glass, A.J.: Psychotherapy in the combat zone. *American Journal of Psychiatry, 110*:725-731, 1954.
Glass, A.J.: Principles of combat psychiatry. *Military Medicine, 117*:27-32, 1955.
Glass, A.J.: Psychological aspects of disaster. *Journal of the American Medical Association, 171*:222-225, 1959.
Glasser, R.J.: *365 days*. New York: Braziller, 1971.
Gleser, G.C.: Quantifying interview data on psychic impairment of disaster survivors. *Journal of Nervous and Mental Disease, 166*:209-216, 1978.
Gleser, G.C., Green, B.L., & Winget, C.: *Prolonged psychological effects of disaster: A study of Buffalo Creek*. New York: Academic Press, 1981.
Glover, H.: Survival guilt and the Vietnam veteran. *Journal of Nervous and Mental Disease, 172*(7):393-397, 1984.

Glover, H.: Themes of mistrust and the posttraumatic stress disorder in Vietnam veterans. *American Journal of Psychotherapy, 37(3):445-452, 1984.*

Goldman, N.L., & Segal, D.R. (Eds.): *The social psychology of military service.* Beverly Hills, CA: Sage, 1976.

Goldman, P., & Fuller, T.: What Vietnam did to us. *Newsweek, 98:*24 (Dec 14, 1981) 46, *passim.*

Goldman, P., et al.: *Charlie company: What Vietnam did to us.* New York: Morrow, 1983.

Goldsmith, W., & Cretekos, C.: Unhappy odysseys: Psychiatric hospitalizations among Vietnam returnees. *Archives of General Psychiatry, 20:*78-83, January 1969.

Goodwin, D.W., Davis, D.H., & Robins, L.N.: Drinking amid abundant illicit drugs, the Vietnam case. *Archives of General Psychiatry, 32:*230-237, February 1975.

Gordon, R.: *Dying and creating: A search for meaning, Vol. 4 of The Library of Analytical Psychology.* London: The Society of Analytical Psychology, 1978, pp. 35-39.

Gottlieb, B.H.: Social support as a focus for integrative research in psychology. *American Psychologist, 38(3):*278-287, 1983.

Grant, Z.: *Survivors.* New York: W.W. Norton, 1975.

Grauer, H.: Psychodynamics of the survivor syndrome. *Canadian Psychiatric Association Journal, 14:*617-622, 1969.

Green, B.L.: Prediction of long-term psychosocial functioning following the Beverly Hills fire (Doctoral Dissertation, University of Cincinnati, 1980). University Microfilms No. 8107489, *Dissertation Abstracts International,* 41, 3919B, 1981.

Green, B.L.: Assessing levels of psychological impairment following disaster: Consideration of actual and methodological dimensions. *Journal of Nervous and Mental Disease, 170:*544-552, 1982.

Green, B.L., & Gleser, G.C.: Stress and long-term psychopathology in survivors of the Buffalo Creek disaster. In D. Ricks & B.S. Dohrenwend (Eds.), *Origins of psychopathology: Problems in research and public policy.* New York and Cambridge: Cambridge University Press, 1983.

Green, B.L., Grace, M., & Lindy, J.: Issues in evaluation: Diagnosis, treatment outcome and research. Taped presentation at the National Conference on the Treatment of Post-Vietnam Stress Syndrome, Dayton, Ohio: Human Resource Initiatives, 1982.

Green, B.L., Grace, M., & Lindy, J.: Mediating variables between stress and outcome in PTSD research. Taped presentation at the Second National Conference on the Treatment of Post-Traumatic Stress Disorder, Dayton, Ohio: Human Resource Initiatives, 1983.

Green, B.L., Grace, M.C., Lindy, J.D., Titchener, J.L., & Lindy, J.: Levels of functional impairment following a civilian disaster: The Beverly Hills supper club fire. *Journal of Consulting and Clinical Psychology, 51(4):*573-580, 1983.

Green, D.B., Jones, R., & Hinton, B.: The non-white Vietnam veteran: Anxieties and frustrations with continuing education. *Journal of Non-White Concerns in Personnel and Guidance, 3:*104-112, 1975.

Greenberg, R., Pearlman, C.A., & Gampel, D.: War neurosis and the adaptive function of REM sleep. *British Journal of Mental Psychology, 45:*27-33, 1972.

Grinker, R.R.: Psychiatric disorders in combat crews overseas and in returnees. *Medical Clinics of North America, 29:*729-739, May 1945.

Grinker, R.R.: *Men under stress.* Philadelphia: Blakiston, 1945.

Grinker, R.R., & Spiegel, J.P.: Brief psychotherapy in war neuroses. *Psychosomatic Medicine, 6:*123, 1944.

Groesbeck, C.J.: The archetypal image of the wounded healer. *The Journal of Analytical Psychology, 20(2):*122-145, 1975.

Groesbeck, C.J.: Dreams of a Vietnam veteran—A Jungian analytic perspective. *Psychiatric Annals, 12(11):*1007-1008, 1010, 1982.

Groom, W.: *Better times than these.* New York: Summit Books, 1978.

Gunderson, E., & Rahe, R.H.: *Life stress and illness*. Springfield, IL: Charles C Thomas, 1974.

Gunther, M.S.: Freud as expert witness: Wagner-Jauregg and the problem of the war neurosis. *Annual of Psychoanalysis, 2*:3-23, 1975.

Haacker, L.P.: Time and its effects on casualties in World War II and Vietnam. *Archives of Surgery, 98*:39-40, 1969.

Halberstam, D.: *One very hot day*. New York: Avon Books, 1973.

Halberstam, D.: *The best and the brightest*. New York: Fawcett, 1973.

Haldeman, J.W.: *War year*. New York: Holt, Rinehart & Winston, 1972.

Haley, S.A.: When the patient reports atrocities: Specific treatment considerations of the Vietnam veteran. *Archives of General Psychiatry, 30*:191-196, 1974.

Hammer, M.: Social supports, social networks, and schizophrenia. *Schizophrenia Bulletin, 7*(1):46-57, 1981.

Hampton, P.T., & Vogel, D.B.: Personality chaacteristics of servicemen returned from Vietnam identified as heroin abusers. *American Journal of Psychiatry, 130*(9):1031-1032, 1973.

Hanson, F.R. (Ed.): Combat psychiatry. *Bulletin of U.S. Army Medical Dept., 9*, Nov., 1949.

Harrington, D., & Jay, J.: Beyond the family: Value issues in the treatment of Vietnam veterans. *Family Therapy Networker, 6*:13-15, 44-45, 1982.

Harrow, M., & Amdur, M.J.: Guilt and depressive disorders. *Archives of General Psychiatry, 25*:240-246, September 1971.

Hartmann, K., & Allison, J.: Expected psychological reactions to disaster in medical rescue teams. *Military Medicine, 146*:323-327, 1981.

Hartzell, I.J., Paige, A.B., & Fitzgibbons, K.: Vietnam combat veterans' attitudes toward the war: A pilot study. *Newsletter for Research in Psychology, 14*:2-4, 1972.

Hasford, G.: *The short timers*. New York: Harper & Row, 1979.

Hayes, F.W.: Military aeromedical evacuation and psychiatric patients during the Vietnam war. *American Journal of Psychiatry, 126*(5):658-666, 1969.

Hayes, F.W.: Psychiatric aeromedical evacuation patients during the Tet and Tet II offensives, 1968. *American Journal of Psychiatry, 127*(4):503-508, 1970.

Haynes, S.N., & Mooney, D.K.: Nightmares: Etiological theoretical, and behavioral treatment considerations. *The Psychological Record, 25*:225-236, 1975.

Heide, F.J.: Relaxation-induced anxiety: Paradoxical anxiety enhancement due to relaxation training. *Journal of Consulting and Clinical Psychology, 51*(2):171-182, 1983.

Heide, F.J., & Borkovec, T.D.: Relaxation-induced anxiety: Mechanisms and theoretical implications. *Behavior Research and Therapy, 22*(1):1-12, 1984.

Helzer, J.E., Robins, L.N., & Davis, D.H.: Antecedents of narcotic use and addiction. A study of 898 Vietnam veterans. *Drug and Alcohol Dependence, 1*:183-190, 1976.

Helzer, J.E., Robins, L.N., & Davis, D.H.: Depressive disorders in Vietnam returnees. *Journal of Nervous and Mental Disease, 163*(3):177-185, 1976.

Helzer, J.E., Robins, L.N., Wish, E., & Hesselbrock, M.: Depression in Vietnam veterans and civilian controls. *American Journal of Psychiatry, 136*(4B):526-529, 1979.

Henderson, S.: A development in social psychiatry: The systematic study of social bonds. *Journal of Nervous and Mental Disease, 168*(2):63-69, 1980.

Henderson, S., Duncan-Jones, P., McAuley, H., & Ritchie, K.: The patient's primary group. *British Journal of Psychiatry, 132*:74-86, 1978.

Hendin, H.: Psychotherapy for Vietnam veterans with posttraumatic stress disorder. *American Journal of Psychotherapy, 37*(1):86-99, 1983.

Hendin, H.: Combat never ends: The paranoid adaptation to posttraumatic stress. *American Journal of Psychotherapy, 38*(1):121-131, 1984.

Hendin, H. & Haas, A.P.: Combat adaptations of Vietnam veterans without posttraumatic stress disorders. *American Journal of Psychiatry, 141*(8):956-960, 1984.

Hendin, H., & Haas, A.P.: *The wounds of war*. New York: Basic Books, 1984.

Hendin, H., Haas, A.P., Singer, P., Gold, F., & Trigos, G.:The influence of precombat personality on posttraumatic stress disorder. *Comprehensive Psychiatry, 24*(6):530-534, 1983.

Hendin, H., Haas, A.P., Singer, P., Houghton, W., Schwartz, M., & Wallen, V.: The reliving experience in Vietnam veterans with posttraumatic stress disorder. *Comprehensive Psychiatry, 25*(2):165-173, 1984.

Hendin, H., Pollinger, H.A., Gold, F., Ulman, R., & Trigos, G.: Evaluation of posttraumatic stress in Vietnam veterans. *Journal of Psychiatric Treatment and Evaluation,* in press.

Hendin, H., Pollinger, A., Singer, P., & Ulman, R.: Meanings of combat and the development of posttraumatic stress disorder. *American Journal of Psychiatry, 138*(11):1490-1493, 1981.

Herbert, W.: Seventeenth-century stress. *Psychology Today,* October 1983, p. 74.

Herr, M.: *Dispatches.* New York: Knopf, 1977.

Herr, M.: Sending the war home. *Esquire,* June, 1983, p. 265.

Hibler, R.J.: Battlefield stress: Management techniques. *Military Medicine, 149*(1):5-8, 1984.

Hirsch, B.J.: Natural support systems and coping with major life changes. *American Journal of Community Psychology, 8*:159-172, 1980.

Hocking, F.: Human reactions to extreme environmental stress. *Medical Journal of Australia,* 2:477-483, 1965.

Hocking, F.: Extreme environmental stress and its significance for psychopathology. *American Journal of Psychotherapy, 24*:4-26, 1970.

Hocking, F.: Psychiatric aspects of extreme environmental stress. *Diseases of the Nervous System, 31*:542-545, 1970.

Hogben, G.L., & Cornfield, R.B.: Treatment of traumatic war neurosis with phenelzine. *Archives of General Psychiatry, 38*:440-445, April 1981.

Holloway, H.C., & Ursano, R.J.: The Vietnam veteran: Memory, social context and metaphor. *Psychiatry, 47*:103-108, May 1984.

Holmes, T.H., & Rahe, R.H.: The Social Readjustment Rating Scale. *Journal of Psychosomatic Research, 11*:213-217, 1967.

Hooper, T., & Spilka, B.: Some meanings and correlates of future time and death among college students. *Omega, 1:49-56, 1970.*

Hoppe, K.: The psychodynamics of concentration camp victims. *Psychoanalytic Forum, 1*:76-80, 1966.

Horne, A.D. (Ed.): *The wounded generation, America after Vietnam.* Englewood Cliffs, NJ: Prentice-Hall, 1981.

Horowitz, M.J.: Psychic trauma: Return of images after a stress film. *Archives of General Psychiatry, 20*:552-559, May 1969.

Horowitz, M.J.: Phase oriented treatment of stress response syndromes. *American Journal of Psychotherapy, 27*:506-515, 1973; in V.A. *Resource Manual,* Pt. 6.

Horowitz, M.J.: *Stress response syndromes.* New York: Aronson, 1976.

Horowitz, M.J.: Psychological response to serious life events. In V. Hamilton & D.M. Warburton (Eds.), *Human stress and cognition.* New York: Wiley & Sons, 1979.

Horowitz, M.J.: Self-righteous rage and the attribution of blame. *Archives of General Psychiatry, 38*:1233-1238, November 1981.

Horowitz, M.J., & Becker, S.S.: The compulsion to repeat trauma, experimental study of intrusive thinking after stress. *The Journal of Nervous and Mental Disease, 153*:32-40, 1971.

Horowitz, M.J., & Becker, S.S.: Cognitive response to stress: Experimental studies of a "compulsion to repeat trauma." *Psychoanalysis and Contemporary Society, 1*:258-305, 1972.

Horowitz, M.J., & French, R.: Interpersonal problems of people who describe themselves as lonely. *Journal of Consulting and Clinical Psychology, 47*:762-764, 1979.

Horowitz, M.J., Krupnick, J., Kaltreider, N., Wilner, N., Leong, A., & Marmar, C.: Initial psychological responses to parental death. *Archives of General Psychiatry, 38*:316-323, March 1981.

Horowitz, M.J., Schaefer, C., Hiroto, D., Wilner, N., & Levin, B.: Life event questionnaires for measuring presumptive stress. *Psychosomatic Medicine, 39*(6):413-431, 1977.

Horowitz, M.J., & Solomon, G.F.: A prediction of delayed stress response syndromes in Vietnam veterans. *Journal of Social Issues, 31*(4):67-80, 1975.

Horowitz, M.J., & Wilner, N.: Stress films, emotions and cognitive response. *Archives of General Psychiatry, 33*(11):1339-1344, 1976.

Horowitz, M.J., Wilner, N., & Alvarez, W.: Impact of event scale, a measure of subjective strength. *Psychosomatic Medicine, 41*:209-218, 1979.

Horowitz, M.J., Wilner, N., Katreider, N., & Alvarez, W.: Signs and symptoms of post-traumatic stress disorders. *Archives of General Psychiatry, 37*:85-92, January 1980.

Horowitz, M.J., Wilner, N., Marmar, C., & Krupnick, J.: Pathological grief and the activation of latent self-images. *American Journal of Psychiatry, 137*(10):1157-1162, 1980.

Howard, S.: The Vietnam warrior: His experience and implications for psychotherapy. *American Journal of Psychotherapy, 30*:121-135, 1976.

Huffman, R.E.: Which soldiers break down: A survey of 610 psychiatric patients in Vietnam. *Bulletin of the Menninger Clinic, 34*:343-350, 1970.

Huggett, W.T.: *Body count.* New York: Dell, 1974.

Huey, L.: Alcoholism and post-Vietnam stress syndrome: Some initial interventions. Taped presentation at the National Conference on the Treatment of Post-Vietnam Stress Syndrome, Dayton, Ohio: Human Resource Initiatives, 1982.

Hughes, L.: *You can see a lot standing under a flare in the republic of Vietnam: My year at war.* New York: Morrow, 1969.

Illman, J.: The hazards of surviving. *World Medicine, 13*:57-61, 1978.

Ingraham, L.H.: "The Nam" and "The World": Heroin use by US Army enlisted men serving in Vietnam. *Psychiatry, 37*(2):114-128, 1972.

Jaffe, R.: Dissociative phenomenon in former concentration camp inmates. *International Journal of Psychoanalysis, 49*:310-312, 1968.

Janis, I.L.: *Psychological stress: Psychoanalytic and behavioral studies of surgical patients.* New York: Wiley, 1958.

Jaremko, M.E., & Brown, R.C.: *The role of the values structure in etiology and treatment of stress-related disorders in Vietnam veterans.* Unpublished manuscript, 1981.

Jenkins, C.D., Hurst, M.W., & Rose, R.M.: Life changes, do people really remember? *Archives of General Psychiatry, 36*(4):379-384, 1979.

Jernigan, A.J., & Kidd, R.: Interview survey of 220 Vietnam era patients. *Newsletter for Research in Psychology, 14*:40-41, 1972.

Joanning, H.: The academic performance of Vietnam veteran college students. *Journal of College Student Personnel, 16*:10-13, 1975.

Johnson, R.: Treatment of post-traumatic stress disorder in Vietnam combat veterans. Taped presentation at the National Conference on the Treatment of Post-Vietnam Stress Syndrome, Dayton, Ohio: Human Resource Initiatives, 1982.

Jones, D.R.: What the repatriated prisoners of war wrote about themselves. *Aviation, Space, and Environmental Medicine, 52*:615-617, 1980.

Jones, F.D.: Experiences of a division psychiatrist in Vietnam. *Military Medicine, 132*:1003-1008, December 1967.

Jones, F.D., & Johnson, A.W., Jr.: Medical and psychiatric treatment policy and practice in Vietnam. *Journal of Social Issues, 31*(4):49-65, 1975.

Kales, A., Soldatos, C.R., Caldwell, A.B., Charney, D.E., Kales, J.D., Markel, D., & Cadieux, R.: Nightmares: Clinical characteristics and personality patterns. *American Journal of Psychiatry, 137*(10):1197-1201, 1980.

Kaminski, R.C.: Saying good-bye, an example of using a "good-bye technique" and concomitant psychodrama in resolving a family grief. *Journal of Group Psychodrama and*

Sociometry, 34:100-111, 1981.

Kaplan, B.H., Cassell, J.C., & Gore, S.: Social support and health. *Medical Care, 15*:47-58, 1977.

Kardiner, A.: *The traumatic neurosis of war.* New York: Paul B. Heober & Sons, 1941.

Kardiner, A.: Traumatic neuroses in war. In S. Arieti (Ed.), *American handbook of psychiatry.* New York: Basic Books, 1959.

Kardiner, A., & Spiegel, H.: *War stress and neurotic illness.* New York: Hoeber, 1947.

Karnow, S.: *Vietnam: A history.* New York: Viking Press, 1983.

Karotkin, K.M.: A comparison of Vietnam veterans, Vietnam-era veterans, and non-veterans in terms of political alienation, purpose in life and life stress (Doctoral Dissertation, Texas A&M University, 1976). *Dissertation Abstracts International, 36*:7952-7953, 1976.

Keane, T.M., & Fairbank, J.A.: Survey analysis of combat-related stress disorders in Vietnam veterans. *American Journal of Psychiatry, 140*(3):348-350, 1983.

Keane, T.M., Fairbank, J.A., Caddell, J.M., Zimmering, R.T., & Bender, M.E.: A behavioral approach to assessing and treating posttraumatic stress disorders in Vietnam veterans. In C.R. Figley (Ed.), *Trauma and its wake.* New York: Brunner/Mazel, 1985.

Keane, T., Fairbank, J., Caddell, J., Zimmering, R., & Russell, S.: Progress in the behavioral assessment and treatment of PTSD in Vietnam veterans. Taped presentation at the Second National Conference on the Treatment of Post-Traumatic Stress Disorder, Dayton, Ohio: Human Resource Initiatives, 1983.

Keane, T.M., & Kaloupek, D.G.: Imaginal flooding in the treatment of post-traumatic stress disorder. *Journal of Consulting and Clinical Psychology, 50*(1):138-140, 1982.

Keane, T.M., Malloy, P.F., & Fairbank, J.A.: Empirical development of an MMPI subscale for the assessment of combat-related posttraumatic stress disorder. *Journal of Consulting and Clinical Psychology, 52*(5):888-891, 1984.

Keane, T.M., Scott, W.O., Chavoya, G.A., Lamparski, D.M., & Fairbank, J.A.: Social support in Vietnam veterans with posttraumatic stress disorder: A comparative analysis. *Journal of Consulting and Clinical Psychology,* in press.

Keehn, R.J., Goldberg, I.D., & Beebe, G.W.: Twenty-four year mortality follow-up of army veterans with disability separations for psychoneurosis in 1949. *Psychosomatic Medicine, 36*:27-46, 1974.

Keerdoja, E.: Some of the wounds have healed. *Newsweek,* May 9, 1983, p. 13.

Keerdoja, E.: A Vietnam vet's toughest battle. *Newsweek,* July 18, 1983, p. 9.

Kelman, H.C.: Violence without moral restraint: Reflections on the dehumanization of victims and victimizers. *Journal of Social Issues, 29*(4):25-61, 1973.

Kentsmith, D.K.: Minimizing the psychological effects of a wartime disaster on an individual. *Aviation, Space and Environmental Medicine, 51*:409-413, 1980.

Keown, M.: PTSD as a legal defense: Credo, caveat and case management. Taped presentation at the Second National Conference on the Treatment of Post-Traumatic Stress Disorder, Dayton, Ohio: Human Resource Initiatives, 1983.

Kestenberg, J.: Psychoanalysis of children of survivors from the Holocaust: Case presentation and assessment. *Journal of American Psychoanalytic Association, 28*:775-804, 1980.

Kidder, T.: Soldiers of misfortune. *Atlantic, 241*:41-52, 87-90, 1978.

Kinney, L., Kramer, M., & Schoen, L.S.: Sleep in delayed stress victims. *Sleep Research,* in press.

Kinston, W., & Rosser, R.: Disaster: Effects on mental and physical state. *Journal of Psychosomatic Research, 18*:437-456, 1974.

Kinzie, J.D., Fredrickson, R.H., Ben, R., Fleck, J., & Karls, W.: Posttraumatic stress disorder among survivors of Cambodian concentration camps. *American Journal of Psychiatry, 141*(5):645-650, 1984.

Kipper, D.A.: Behavior therapy for fears brought on by war experiences. *Journal of Consulting and Clinical Psychology, 45*(2):216-221, 1977.

Klama, E.: Identification and treatment of post-traumatic stress disorder in a hospital setting. Taped presentation at the National Conference on the Treatment of Post-Vietnam Stress Syndrome, Dayton, Ohio: Human Resource Initiatives, 1982.

Kleiger, J.H.: Chronic PTSD among active-duty Vietnam veterans. Taped presentation at the Second National Conference on the Treatment of Post-Traumatic Stress Disorder, Dayton, Ohio: Human Resource Initiatives, 1983.

Kleiger, J.: Chronic post-traumatic stress disorders among active duty Vietnam veterans: Case reports. *Military Medicine*, 149(3):159-161, 1984.

Klein, R.: *Wounded men, broken promises*. New York: Macmillan, 1981.

Klonoff, H., McDougall, G., Clark, C., Kramer, P., & Horgan, J.: The neuropsychological psychiatric, and physical effects of prolonged and severe stress: 30 years later. *Journal of Nervous and Mental Disease*, 163(4):246-252, 1976.

Kohn-Dor-Shav, N.: On the long range effects of concentration camp internment on Nazi victims: 25 years later. *Journal of Consulting and Clinical Psychology*, 46(1):1-11, 1978.

Kolb, L.C.: Healing the wounds of Vietnam. *Hospital and Community Psychiatry*, 33(11):877, 1982.

Kolb, L.C.: Return of the repressed: Delayed stress reaction to war. *Journal of American Academy of Psychoanalysis*, 11:531-545, 1983.

Kolb, L.C.: The post-traumatic stress disorders of combat: A subgroup with a conditioned emotional response. *Military Medicine*, 149(3):237-243, 1984.

Kolb, L.C., & Mutalipassi, L.R.: The conditioned emotional response: A sub-class of the chronic and delayed post-traumatic stress disorder. *Psychiatric Annals*, 12(11):984-987, 1982.

Koppel, T.: Nightline, ABC News. Show #552, June 21, 1983, Post-traumatic stress disorder.

Koranyi, E.: Psychobiological correlates of battlefield psychiatry. *Psychiatric Journal of Ottawa*, 2(3), 1977.

Kovic, R.: *Born on the fourth of July*. New York: McGraw Hill, 1976.

Kral, V.A.: Long-term effects of a prolonged stress experience. *Canadian Psychiatric Association Journal*, 12:175-181, April 1968.

Kramer, M.: Dream disturbances. *Psychiatric Annals*, 9:750-768, 1979.

Kramer, M., Schoen, L.S., & Kinney, L.: The dream experience in posttraumatic stress. In B.A. Van der Kolk (Ed.), *Adult psychic trauma—Psychological and physiological sequelae*. Washington, D.C.: American Psychiatric Press, in press.

Kramer, R.: Achieving intimacy and resolving grief: The Vietnam veteran's newest battle. Taped presentation at the National Conference on the Treatment of Post-Vietnam Stress Syndrome, Dayton, Ohio: Human Resource Initiatives, 1982.

Kroll, J.: Racial patterns of military crimes in Vietnam. *Psychiatry*, 39(1):51-64, 1976.

Krupnick, J.L., & Horowitz, M.J.: Stress response syndromes: Recurrent themes. *Archives of General Psychiatry*, 38:428-435, April 1981.

Krystal, H.: *Massive psychic trauma*. New York: International Universities Press, 1968.

Krystal, H.: Trauma and affects. *Psychoanalytic Study of the Child*, 33:81-116, 1978.

Kubie, L.S.: The retreat from patients. *Archives of General Psychiatry*, 24:98-106, 1971.

Lacoursiere, R.B., Godfrey, K.E., & Ruby, L.M.: Traumatic neurosis in the etiology of alcoholism: Vietnam combat and other trauma. *American Journal of Psychiatry*, 137(8):966-968, 1980.

LaGuardia, R.L., Smith, G., Francois, R., & Bachman, L.: Incidence of delayed stress disorder among Vietnam era veterans: The effect of priming on response set. *American Journal of Orthopsychiatry*, 53(1):18-26, 1983.

Langer, H.P.: The making of a murderer. *American Journal of Psychiatry*, 127(7):950-953, 1971.

Langley, M.K.: Post-traumatic stress disorders among Vietnam combat veterans. *Social Casework*, 63:593-598, 1982.

Lavie, P., Hefez, A., Halperin, G., & Enoch, D.: Long-term effects of traumatic war-related events on sleep. *American Journal of Psychiatry, 136*(2):175-178, 1979.

Leahy, M.R., & Martin, I.C.: Successful hypnotic abreaction after twenty years. *British Journal of Psychiatry, 113*:383-385, 1967.

Leiken, S.: Traumatic war neuroses revisited. *Military Medicine, 131*(9):789-795, September 1966.

Leopold, R.L., & Willon, H.: Psychoanatomy of a disaster: A long term study of post-traumatic neuroses in survivors of a marine explosion. *American Journal of Psychiatry, 119*:913-921, 1963.

Lerner, D.: PTSD in heart attack victims. Taped presentation at the Second National Conference on the Treatment of Post-Traumatic Stress Disorder, Dayton, Ohio: Human Resource Initiatives, 1983.

Levav, I., Greenfeld, H., & Baruch, E.: Psychiatric combat reactions during the Yom Kippur war. *American Journal of Psychiatry, 136*(5):637-641, 1979.

Levenson, H.: Brief psychotherapy of post-Vietnam stress syndrome with and without the use of medication. Taped presentation at the National Conference on the Treatment of Post-Vietnam Stress Syndrome, Dayton, Ohio: Human Resource Initiatives, 1982.

Leventman, S.: Official neglect of Vietnam veterans. *Journal of Social Issues, 31*(4):171-179, 1975.

Leventman, S., & Camacho, P.: The "gook" syndrome, the Vietnam war as a racial encounter. In C.R. Figley & S. Leventman (Eds.), *Strangers at home: Vietnam veterans since the war.* New York: Praeger Publications, 1980.

Lewis, C.N.: Memories and alienation in the Vietnam combat veteran. *Bulletin of the Menninger Clinic, 39*:363-369, 1975.

Lewis, C.N.: Memory adaptation to psychological trauma. *American Journal of Psychoanalysis, 40*(4):319-323, 1980.

Lewis, N.D.C., & Engel, B. (Eds.): *Wartime psychiatry: A compendium of the international literature.* New York: Oxford University Press, 1954.

Lieberman, E.J.: War in the family: The psychology of antigrief. *Modern Medicine,* 179-183, 191, 1971.

Lifton, R.J.: *Death in life: Survivors of Hiroshima.* New York: Simon & Schuster, 1967.

Lifton, R.J.: Psychological effects of the atomic bomb in Hiroshima—the theme of death. *Daedalus, 92*(3):172-197, 1967.

Lifton, R.J.: Vietnam: Betrayal and self-betrayal. *Transaction, 6*(11):6-7, 1969.

Lifton, R.J.: Why civilians are war victims. *U.S. News and World Report,* Dec. 15, 1969, p. 25.

Lifton, R.J.: Guilt of the survivor, A profile of the Vietnam veteran. Testimony before the Subcommittee on Veterans Affairs of the Committee on Labor and Public Welfare, United States Senate, Vol. 6, Jan. 27, 1970.

Lifton, R.J.: The scars of Vietnam. *Commonwealth, 91*:554-556, 1970.

Lifton, R.J.: Statement. In V.A., *Viet Vet,* pp. IV-29-43, 1972.

Lifton, R.J.: Home from the war: The psychology of survival. *Atlantic Monthly, 230*:56-72, 1972.

Lifton, R.J.: The consequence of war: The gook syndrome and numbered warfare. *Saturday Review,* November 18, 1972, pp. 66-72.

Lifton, R.J.: *Home from the war.* New York: Simon & Schuster, 1973.

Lifton, R.J.: The sense of immortality: On death and the continuity of life. *American Journal of Psychoanalysis, 33*:3-15, 1973.

Lifton, R.J.: "Death Imprints" on youth in Vietnam. *Journal of Clinical Child Psychology, 3*:47-49, 1974.

Lifton, R.J.: The postwar war. *Journal of Social Issues, 31*(4):181-195, 1975.

Lifton, R.J.: On death and the continuity of life. *Omega, 6*(2):143, 1975.

Lifton, R.J.: *The life of the self.* New York: Simon & Schuster, 1976.

Lifton, R.J.: From analysis to formation towards a shift in psychological paradigm. *Journal* of the American Academy of Psychoanalysis, 4(1):63, 1976.

Lifton, R.J.: *The broken connection.* New York: Simon & Schuster, 1979.

Lifton, R.J.: The psychology of the survivor and the death imprint. *Psychiatric Annals,* 12(11):1011-1012, 1014-1017, & 1020, 1982. (Reprinted from *The Broken Connection,* New York: Simon & Schuster, 1979).

Lifton, R.J., & Olson, E.: The human meaning of total disaster: The Buffalo Creek experience. *Psychiatry, 39:*1-18, 1976.

Lin, H., Dean, A., & Ensel, W.M.: Social support scales: A methodological note. *Schizophrenia Bulletin, 7*(1):73-89, 1981.

Lindemann, E.: Symptomatology and management of acute grief. *American Journal of Psychiatry, 101:*141-148, 1944.

Linden, E.: The demoralization of an army: Fragging and other withdrawal symptoms. *Saturday Review,* Jan. 8, 1972, pp. 12-17.

Lindley, F., Jr.: The history of Vietnam veterans. *The Stars and Stripes,* November 11, 1982.

Lindy, J.D.: Treatment of survivors of man-made disasters: The Vietnam war and civilian catastrophes. Taped presentation at the National Conference on the Treatment of Post-Vietnam Stress Syndrome, Dayton, Ohio: Human Resource Initiatives, 1982.

Lindy, J.D.: PTSD and the working alliance. Taped presentation at the Second National Conference on the Treatment of Post-Traumatic Stress Disorder, Dayton, Ohio: Human Resource Initiatives, 1983.

Lindy, J.D., Grace, M.C., & Green, B.L.: Survivors: Outreach to a reluctant population. *American Journal of Orthopsychiatry, 51:*468-478, 1981.

Lindy, J.D., Green, B.L., Grace, M.C., & Titchener, J.L.: Psychotherapy with survivors of the Beverly Hills supper club fire. *American Journal of Psychotherapy, 37,* 1983.

Lindy, J.D., & Titchener, J.: Acts of God and man: Long-term character change in survivors of disasters and the law. In *Behavioral Sciences and the Law.* New York: Van Nostrand Reinhold, 1983.

Lindy, J.D., Wilson, J.P., Green, B.L., & Grace, M.C.: Post-traumatic stress disorder following civilian disaster and combat in Vietnam. *Frontiers in Psychiatry,* Oct. 1981.

Lineman, M.M., Goodstein, J.L., Nielsen, S.L., & Chiles, J.A.: Reasons for staying alive when you are thinking of killing yourself: The reasons for living inventory. *Journal of Consulting and Clinical Psychology, 51*(2):276-286, 1983.

Linn, D. & Linn, M.: *Healing of memories.* New York: Paulist Press, 1974.

Lipkin, J.O., Blank, A.S., Parson, E.R., & Smith, J.: Vietnam veterans and posttraumatic stress disorder. *Hospital and Community Psychiatry, 33*(11):908-912, 1982.

Lorenzer, A.: Some observations on the latency of symptoms in patients suffering from persecution sequelae. *International Journal of Psychoanalysis, 49:*316-318, 1968.

Lorr, M., Peck, C.P., & Stenger, C.A.: Interpersonal styles of Vietnam era veterans. *Journal of Personality Assessment, 39*(5):507-510, 1974.

Ludwig, A.O.: Neuroses occurring in soldiers after prolonged exposure. *Bulletin of the Menninger Clinic, 11:*15-23, January 1947.

Lumry, G.K., Cedarleaf, C.B., Wright, M.S., & Braatz, G.A.: Psychiatric disabilities of the Vietnam veteran. *Minnesota Medicine, 55*(11), 1972.

Lumry, G.K., & Braatz, G.A.: The Vietnam era veteran and psychiatric implications. In V.A., *Viet Vet,* pp. IV-97-106, 1972.

Lynn, E., & Belza, M.: Factitious posttraumatic stress disorder: The veteran who never got to Vietnam. *Hospital and Community Psychiatry, 35*(7):697-701, 1984.

MacHovec, F.J.: Use of hypnosis in the treatment of post-traumatic stress disorder. Taped presentation at the National Conference on the Treatment of Post-Vietnam Stress Syndrome, Dayton, Ohio: Human Resource Initiatives, 1982.

Mackey, D.: Establishing a therapeutic alliance with Vietnam combat veterans: An exploration of the special challenges faced by non-veteran therapists. Taped presentation at the Second National Conference on the Treatment of Post-Traumatic Stress Disorder, Dayton, Ohio: Human Resource Initiatives, 1983.

MacLean, G.: Psychic trauma and traumatic neurosis. *Canadian Psychiatric Association Journal*, 22(2):71, 1977.

MacPherson, M.: *Long time passing, Vietnam and the haunted generation.* Garden City, N.Y.: Doubleday, 1984.

Mahedy, W.: We've got to get out of this place. *Christian Century*, Sept. 26, 1979, p. 922.

Maillet, E.L.: The severely damaged veteran of the Vietnam war: Some problems in social role. In V.A., *Viet Vet*, pp. IV-149-159, 1972.

Malloy, P.F., Fairbank, J.A., & Keane, T.M.: Validation of a multimethod assessment of posttraumatic stress disorders in Vietnam veterans. *Journal of Consulting and Clinical Psychology*, 51(4):488-494, 1983.

Mantell, D.M.: Soldiers in and after Vietnam: Introduction. *Journal of Social Issues, 31*(4):1-2, 1975.

Marin, P.: Coming to terms with Vietnam. *Harpers*, December, 1980, pp. 41-56.

Marin, P.: Living in moral pain. *Psychology Today*, November 1981, pp. 68-80.

Marin, P.: What the Vietnam vets can teach us. *The Nation*, November 17, 1982, p. 545.

Marlowe, C., & Crowne, D.P.: Social desirability and response to perceived situational demands. *Journal of Consulting Psychology*, 25:109-115, 1961.

Martin, L., & Kramer, R.: Psychological adjustment counseling: A multiple treatment plan for combat veterans experiencing post-Vietnam stress syndrome. Taped presentation at the National Conference on the Treatment of Post-Vietnam Stress Syndrome, Dayton, Ohio: Human Resource Initiatives, 1982.

Maughon, J.S.: An inquiry into the nature of wounds resulting in killed in action in Vietnam. *Military Medicine, 135*(1):8-13, 1970.

Mayfield, D.G., & Fowler, D.R.: Combat experience plus twenty years: The effect of previous combat experience on psychiatric patients. *Military Medicine, 134*(11):1348-1354, 1969.

McCarty, M.: *The seventeenth degree.* New York: Harcourt Brace Jovanovich, 1974.

McCormick, W., & Ritter, R.: Bringing war home—Vets who have battered. Taped presentation at the National Conference on the Treatment of Post-Vietnam Stress Syndrome, Dayton, Ohio: Human Resource Initiatives, 1982.

McCormick, W., & Ritter, R.: Masculinity as a treatment model for Vietnam veterans. Taped presentation at the National Conference on the Treatment of Post-Vietnam Stress Syndrome, Dayton, Ohio: Human Resource Initiatives, 1982.

McCubbin, H.I., Dahl, B.B., & Lester, G.R.: Coping repertoires of families adapting to prolonged war-induced separations. *Journal of Marriage and the Family, 38*:461-471, 1976.

McCubbin, H.I., Dahl, B.B., Lester, G.R., & Ross, B.: The returned prisoner of war: Factors in family reintegration. *Journal of Marriage and the Family*, 471-478, August 1975.

McCubbin, H.I., Hunter, E.J., & Dahl, B.B.: Residuals of war: Families of prisoners of war and servicemen missing in action. *Journal of Social Issues, 31*(4):95-109, 1975.

McGee, R.: Flashbacks and memory phenomena, a comment on "flashback phenomena—Clinical and diagnostic dilemmas." *Journal of Nervous and Mental Disease,* 172(5):273-278, 1984.

McLeod, B.: In the wake of disaster. *Psychology Today, 18*(10):54-57, 1984.

Meerloo, J.A.M.: Persecution trauma and the reconditioning of emotional life: A brief survey. *American Journal of Psychiatry*, 125(9):1187-1191, 1969.

Meguro, K.: War neurosis: A 20-year follow-up study. *Foreign Psychiatry*, 1:165-203, 1972.

Mellet, T.P.: Attitudes and personal values of Vietnam veterans. *Newsletter for Research in Mental Health and Behavioral Sciences*, 15(2):4-9, 1973.

Mennell, J.M., & Smith, D.: The work values of veterans and some implications for educational therapy. *Newsletter for Research in Mental Health and Behavioral Sciences,* 15:4-9, 1973.

Merbaum, M.: Some personality characteristics of soldiers exposed to extreme war stress: A follow-up study of post-hospital adjustment. *Journal of Clinical Psychology, 33*:558-562, 1977.

Merbaum, M., & Hefez, A.: Some personality characteristics of soldiers exposed to extreme war stress. *Journal of Consulting and Clinical Psychology, 44*(1):1-6, 1976.

Metres, P.J.: Reverse culture shock in returning Vietnam veterans. Unpublished Master's thesis, United States International University, 1971.

Middleton, D.: Vietnam and the American military. *New York Times Magazine,* Jan. 10, 1982, p. 37.

Milgram, N.A.: Psychological stress and adjustment in time of war and peace: The Israeli experience as presented in two conferences. *Israel Annals of Psychiatry and Related Disciplines, 16:*327-338, 1978.

Milgram, S.: Behavioral study of obedience. *Journal of Abnormal and Social Psychology, 67*(4):371-378, 1963.

Milgram, S.: *Obedience to authority.* New York: Harper & Row, 1974.

Miller, W.R., & DiPilato, M.: Treatment of nightmares via relaxation and desensitization: A controlled evaluation. *Journal of Consulting and Clinical Psychology, 51*(6):870-877, 1983.

Mineka, S., & Kihlstrom, E.: Unpredictable and uncontrollable events: A new perspective on experimental neurosis. *Journal of Abnormal Psychology, 87:*256-271, 1978.

Minton, B., & Spilka, B.: Perspectives on death in relation to powerlessness and form of personal religion. *Omega, 7:*261-267, 1976.

Mintz, J.: The impact of Vietnam service on heroin-addicted veterans. *American Journal of Drug and Alcohol Abuse, 6:*39-52, 1979.

Mitchell, J.: Conducting critical stress debriefings for emergency personnel. Taped presentation at the Second National Conference on the Treatment of Post-Traumatic Stress Disorder, Dayton, Ohio: Human Resource Initiatives, 1983.

Modlin, H.C.: Traumatic neurosis and other injuries. *The Psychiatric Annals of North America, 6*(4):661-682, 1983.

Monroe, S.M.: Life events and disorder: Event-symptom associations and the course of disorder. *Journal of Abnormal Psychology, 91*(1):14-24, 1982.

Morgenthau, T.: The troubled Vietnam vet. *Newsweek,* March 30, 1981, p. 24.

Morrell, D.: *First blood.* New York: M. Evans & Co., 1972.

Morris, H.: Guilt and punishment. *Personalist, 52:*305-321, 1971.

Morris, H.: Guilt and suffering. *Philosophy East and West, 21:*419-434, 1971.

Morris, L.E.: "Over the Hump" in Vietnam: Adjustment patterns in a time-limited stress situation. *Bulletin of the Menninger Clinic, 34:*352-362, 1970.

Morrow, L.: The forgotten warriors. *Time,* July 13, 1981, pp. 18-25.

Moses, R., Bargal, D., Calev, J., et al.: A rear unit for the treatment of combat reactions in the wake of the Yom Kippur war. *Psychiatry, 39:*153-162, 1976.

Moskos, C.C., Jr.: The American combat soldier in Vietnam. *Journal of Social Issues, 31*(4):25-37, 1975.

Moskos, C.C., Jr.: Why men fight, American combat soldiers in Vietnam. *Trans-Action,* 13-23, 1969; in V.A., *Viet Vet,* pp. III-8-17, 1972.

Mott, F.: *War neuroses and shell shock.* London: Oxford University Press, 1944.

Mucha, T.F., & Reinhardt, R.F.: Conversion reactions in student aviators. *American Journal of Psychiatry, 127*(4):493-497, 1970.

Muller, R.: Wounds that will not heal. *Time,* July 13, 1981, p. 22.

Mullis, M.R.: Vietnam, the human fallout. *Journal of Psychosocial Nursing, 22*(2):27-31, 1984.

Musser, M.J., & Stenger, C.A.: A medical and social perception of the Vietnam veteran. *Bulletin of the New York Academy of Medicine, 48*(6):859-869, 1972.

Myers, E.R.: Counseling today's veterans: A program and its implications. *Personnel and Guidance Journal, 52*(4):233-238, 1973.

Nace, E.P., & Meyers, A.L.: The prognosis for addicted Vietnam returnees: A comparison with civilian addicts. *Comprehensive Psychiatry, 15*(1):49-56, 1974.

Nace, E.P., Meyers, A.L., O'Brien, C.P., Ream, N., & Mintz, J.: Depression in veterans two years after Vietnam. *American Journal of Psychiatry, 134*(2):167-170, 1977.

Nace, E.P., Meyers, A.L., & Rothberg, J.M.: Addicted Vietnam veterans: A comparison of self-referred and system-referred samples. *American Journal of Psychiatry*, 130(11):1242-1245, 1973.

Nash, J.L., & Walker, J.I.: Stress disorders in Vietnam returnees: The problem continues. Case Report. *Military Medicine*, 146:582-583, August 1981.

Newman, C.J.: Children of disaster: Clinical observations at Buffalo Creek. *American Journal of Psychiatry*, 133(3):306-312, 1976.

Niederland, W.G.: Psychiatric disorders among persecution victims. *Journal of Nervous and Mental Disease*, 139:458-474, 1964.

Niederland, W.G.: Clinical observations on the "survivor syndrome." *International Journal of Psychoanalysis*, 49:313-315, 1968.

Nordheimer, J.: From Dak To to Detroit: Death of a troubled hero. *New York Times*, May 26, 1971, p. 1.

Nordheimer, J.: Post-Vietnam war syndrome (series of three articles). *New York Times*, August 1972.

Norman, M.: A wound that will not heal. *New York Times Magazine*, November 11, 1979, pp. 134-141.

Noyes, R.: The experience of dying. *Psychiatry*, 35:174-184, 1972.

Noyes, R., & Kletti, R.: Depersonalization in response to life-threatening danger. *Comprehensive Psychiatry*, 18(4):375-384, 1977.

O'Brien, T.: *If I die in the combat zone, box me up and send me home*. New York: Delacorte Press, 1973.

O'Brien, T.: *Going after Cacciato*. New York: Dell, 1979.

O'Brien, T.: The violent vet. *Esquire*, December, 1979, pp. 96-97.

Ochberg, F.: Post-traumatic therapy: Clinical paradigms. Taped presentation at the Second National Conference on the Treatment of Post-Traumatic Stress Disorder, Dayton, Ohio: Human Resource Initiatives, 1983.

O'Neill, D.J., & Fontaine, G.D.: Counseling for the Vietnam veteran. *Journal of College Student Personnel*, 14:153-155, 1973.

Oppenheim, H.: *Die Traumatischen Neurosen*. Berlin, 1889, pp. 86-122.

Oswald, P., & Bittner, E.: Life adjustment after severe persecution. *American Journal of Psychiatry*, 124:1393-1400, 1968.

Palmieri, R.G., & Suarez, Y.: The future outlook of Puerto Rican Vietnam-era hospitalized psychiatric patients. *Journal of Clinical Psychology*, 28:394-399, 1972.

Panzarella, R.F., et al.: Psychiatric syndromes, self-concepts, and Vietnam veterans. In C.R. Figley (Ed.), *Stress Disorders*, pp. 148-172.

Parson, E.R., & Harris, H.: The "gook" identification: Its role in stress pathology in minority Vietnam veterans. Taped presentation at the National Conference on the Treatment of Post-Vietnam Stress Syndrome, Dayton, Ohio: Human Resource Initiatives, 1982.

Paykel, E.S., Prusoff, B.A., & Uhlenhuth, E.H.: Scaling of life events. *Archives of General Psychiatry*, 25:340-347, October 1971.

Peck, C.P.: The Vietnam veteran. In V.A., *Viet Vet*, pp. IV-1-4, 1972.

Peck, C.P., & Stenger, C.A.: Interpersonal styles of Vietnam era veterans. *Journal of Personality Assessment*, 39(5):507-510, 1975.

Pelfrey, W.G.: No laurels for legionnaires. *The New Republic* (1970); in V.A., *Viet Vet*, pp. IV-52-55, 1972.

Penk, W.E., et al.: Adjustment differences among male substance abusers varying in degree of combat experience in Vietnam. *Journal of Consulting and Clinical Psychology*, 49:426-437, 1981.

Perlman, M.S.: Basic problems of military psychiatry: Delayed reaction in Vietnam veterans. *International Journal of Offender Therapy and Comparative Criminology*, 19:129-138, 1975.

Peter, H.M.: Effects of open admission on the academic adjustment of Vietnam veterans. *Journal of College Student Personnel*, 16:14-16, 1975.

Peterson, C., & Seligman, M.E.P.: Learned helplessness and victimization. *Journal of Social Issues,* 39(2):103-116, 1983.

Pettera, R.L., Johnson, B.M., & Zimmer, R.: Psychiatric management of combat reactions with emphasis on a reaction unique to Vietnam. *Military Medicine,* 134:673-678, November 1969.

Phillips, R.E.: Impact of Nazi holocaust on children of survivors. *American Journal of Psychotherapy,* 32(3):370-377, 1978.

Pilisuk, M.: The legacy of the Vietnam veteran. *Journal of Social Issues,* 31(4):3-12, 1975.

Pink, W.T., Freund, E.H., & Stormo, E.G.: A resocialization strategy for Black Vietnam veterans. *Journal of Negro Education,* 48:500-512, 1979.

Polner, M.: Vietnam war stories. *Trans-Action,* November 1968, pp. 8-20; in V.A., *Viet Vet,* pp. IV-43-51, 1972.

Polner, M.: *No victory parades: The return of the Vietnam veteran.* New York: Holt, Rinehart & Winston, Inc., 1971.

Powell, S.: 5 years later—Have the scars healed? *U.S. News and World Report,* April 28, 1980, pp. 30-33.

President's Commission on Mental Health. *Report of the special working group: Mental health problems of Vietnam era veterans.* Washington, Feb. 15, 1978.

Prosen, M., Clark, D.C., Harrow, M., & Fawcett, J.: Guilt and conscience in major depressive disorders. *American Journal of Psychiatry,* 140(7):839-844, 1983.

Pucclik, F., & Germano, D.: Within every poison lies the cure (innovation treatment, prevention language therapy, meta therapy), Part I & II. Taped presentation at the National Conference on the Treatment of Post-Vietnam Stress Syndrome, Dayton, Ohio: Human Resource Initiatives, 1982.

Rado, S.: Pathodynamics and treatment of traumatic war neurosis (traumatophobia). *Psychosomatic Medicine,* 42:362-368, 1942.

Rahe, R.H., & Arthur, R.J.: Life-change patterns surrounding illness experience. *Journal of Psychosomatic Research,* 11:341-345, 1968.

Rahe, R.H., & Genender, E.: Adaptation to and recovery from captivity stress. *Military Medicine,* 148(7):577-585, 1983.

Rahe, R.H., McKean, J.D., Jr., & Arthur, R.J.: A longitudinal study of life-change and illness patterns. *Journal of Psychosomatic Research,* 10:355-366, 1967.

Rangell, L.: Discussion of the Buffalo Creek disaster: The course of psychic trauma. *American Journal of Psychiatry,* 133(3):313-316, 1976.

Rapoport, D.: *Emotions and memory.* New York: International Universities Press, 1971.

Reich, D.: One year in Vietnam: A young soldier remembers. The state Historical Society of Wisconsin, *Wisconsin Magazine of History,* 64(3):163-180, 1981.

Renner, J.A.: The changing pattern of psychiatric problems in Vietnam. *Comprehensive Psychiatry,* 14(2):169-181, 1973.

Rich, R.: Providing services to victims: An empirical investigation. Taped presentation at the Second National Conference on the Treatment of Post-Traumatic Stress Disorder, Dayton, Ohio: Human Resource Initiatives, 1983.

Richards, P. (Ed.): *Made in America sold in the 'Nam.* Fort Wayne, IN: DMZ Publishing, 1984.

Roberts, W.R., Penk, W.E., Gearing, M.L., Robinowitz, R., Dolan, M.P., & Patterson, E.T.: Interpersonal problems of Vietnam combat veterans with symptoms of post-traumatic stress disorder. *Journal of Abnormal Psychology,* 91(6):444-450, 1982.

Robins, L.N.: A follow-up study of Vietnam veterans' drug use. *Journal of Drug Issues,* 4:61-63, 1974.

Robins, L.N., Davis, D.H., & Nurco, D.N.: How permanent was Vietnam drug addiction? *AJPH Supplement,* 64:38-43, 1974.

Robins, L.N., Helzer, J.E., & Davis, D.H.: Narcotic use in Southeast Asia and afterward: An interview study of 898 Vietnam returnees. *Archives of General Psychiatry,* 32:955-961, August 1975.

Rosenheim, E., & Elizer, A.: Group therapy for traumatic neuroses. *Current Psychiatric Therapies*, 17:143-148, 1977.

Rosenman, S.: The paradox of guilt in disaster victim populations. *Psychiatric Quarterly*, 30 (Suppl.): 181-220, 1956.

Rosenthal, I.: Vietnam war soldiers and the experience of normlessness. *Journal of Social Psychology*, 96:85-90, 1975.

Roth, R.: *Sand in the wind*. Boston: Little, Brown, 1973.

Rottman, L. (Ed.): *Winning hearts and minds: War poems by Vietnam veterans*. Montclair, NJ: East River Anthology, 1972.

Sajer, G.: *The forgotten soldier*. (Trans. Lily Emmet) New York: Harper & Row, 1971.

Salasin, S.: Treating Vietnam veterans as survivors: An interview with Charles Figley. *Evaluation and Change* (Special Issue: *Services for Survivors*) 135-141, 1980; in V.A., *Resource Manual*, Pt. 6.

Salasin, S., & Rich, R.: Serving the victims of disaster: Treatment and policy concerns. Taped presentation at the Second National Conference on the Treatment of Post-Traumatic Stress Disorder, Dayton, Ohio: Human Resource Initiatives, 1983.

Santoli, A.: *Everything we had: An oral history of the Vietnam war by thirty-three American soldiers who fought it*. New York: Random House, 1981.

Sarason, I.G., Levine, H., Bashaw, R., & Sarason, B.: Assessing social support: The social support questionnaire. *Journal of Personality and Social Psychology*, 44:127-139, 1983.

Savage, P.L., & Gabriel, R.A.: Cohesion and disintegration in the American army: An alternative perspective. *Armed Forces and Society*, 2:340-376, 1976.

Scarano, T.P.: Family therapy: A viable approach for treating troubled Vietnam veterans. *Therapist*, 3(3):9-15, 1982.

Schindler, F.E.: Treatment by systematic desensitization of a recurring nightmare of a real life trauma. *Journal of Behavior Therapy and Experimental Psychiatry*, 11:53-54, 1980.

Schlosberg, A., & Benjamin, M.: Sleep patterns in three acute combat fatigue cases. *The Journal of Clinical Psychiatry*, 39:546-549, June 1978.

Schnaier, J.: Female Vietnam veterans and post-traumatic stress disorders : Assessment and implications. Paper presented at National Conference on the Treatment of Post-Vietnam Stress Syndrome, Dayton, Ohio: Human Resource Initiatives, 1982.

Schneider, R.J., & Luscomb, R.L.: Battle stress reaction and the United States Army. *Military Medicine*, 149(2):66-69, 1984.

Scruggs, J.C., Berman, A.L., & Hoage, C.: The Vietnam veteran: A preliminary analysis of psychosocial status. *Military Medicine*, 145:267-269, April 1980.

Scurfield, R.: Post-traumatic stress: Comprehensive overview of issues, etiology, assessment and treatment implications. Taped presentation at the National Conference on the Treatment of Post-Vietnam Stress Syndrome, Dayton, Ohio: Human Resource Initiatives, 1982.

Segal, D.R.: Illicit drug use in the U.S. Army. *Sociological Symposium*, 18:66-83, 1977.

Segal, J., Hunter, E.J., & Segal, Z.: Universal consequences of captivity: Stress reactions among divergent populations of prisoners of war and their families. *International Social Science Journal*, 28:594-609, 1976.

Seligman, M.E., & Garber, J.: *Human helplessness*. New York: Academic Press, 1980.

Seligman, M.E., & Maier, S.F.: Failure to escape traumatic shock. *Journal of Experimental Psychology*, 74:1-9, 1967.

Selye, H.: Confusion and controversy in the stress field. *Journal of Human Stress*, 1(2), 1975.

Shabecoff, P.: Prisoner killing divides soldiers. *New York Times*, April 5, 1970.

Shatan, C.F.: How do we turn off the guilt? *Human Behavior*, 56-61, February 1973.

Shatan, C.F.: The grief of soldiers: Vietnam combat veterans' self-help movement. *American Journal of Orthopsychiatry*, 43(4):640-653, 1973.

Shatan, C.F.: Inside the Vietnam veteran: A psychological time bomb. *Human Behavior*, 56-61, 1973.

Shatan, C.F.: Through the membrane of reality: "Impacted grief" and perceptual dissonance in Vietnam combat veterans. *Psychiatric Opinion*, 11:5-14, 1974.

Shatan, C.F.: Bogus manhood, bogus honor: Surrender and transfiguration in the United States Marine Corps. *Psychoanalytic Review*, 64:585-610, 1977.

Shatan, C.F.: Veterans problems. Letter to the Editor. *Psychiatric News*, April 17, 1981.

Shatan, C.F.: The tattered ego of survivors. *Psychiatric Annals*, 12(11):1031-1038, 1982.

Shen, W.W., & Park, S.: The use of monoamine oxidase inhibitors in the treatment of traumatic war neurosis: Case report. *Military Medicine*, 148(5):430-431, 1983.

Sherman, C.J., & Caffey, E.M., Jr. (Eds.): *The Vietnam veteran in contemporary society.* Washington, D.C.: U.S. Government Printing Office, 1972.

Sierles, F.S., Chen, J., McFarland, R.E., & Taylor, M.A.: Posttraumatic stress disorder and concurrent psychiatric illness: A preliminary report. *American Journal of Psychiatry*, 140(9):1177-1179, 1983.

Sigal, J.J., Silver, D., Rakoff, V., & Ellin, B.: Some second-generation effects of survival of the Nazi persecution. *Journal of Orthopsychiatry*, 43:320-327, April 1973.

Silver, S.M.: Post-traumatic stress reaction and family of creation variables among Vietnam veterans (Doctoral Dissertation, Temple University, 1981), *Dissertation Abstracts International*.

Silver, S.M.: Posttraumatic stress disorders in Vietnam veterans: An addendum to Fairbank et al. *Professional Psychology*, 13(4):522-525, 1982.

Silver, S.M.: Factor-analytic support for DSM-III's post-traumatic stress disorder for Vietnam veterans. *Journal of Clinical Psychology*, 40(1):5-14, 1984.

Silverman, I., & Geer, J.H.: The elimination of a recurrent nightmare by desensitization of a related phobia. *Behavior Research and Therapy*, 6:109-111, 1968.

Sims, T.C.: Gulag and Kyrie. *Lutheran Church in America: Partners*, 5(3):8-12, 22, 1983.

Singer, M.T.: Vietnam prisoners of war, stress, and personality resiliency. *American Journal of Psychiatry*, 138(3):345-346, 1981.

Slattery, J., Doyle, D., & Cohen, G.: Vietnam veterans in Virginia state prisons: Research and treatment issues. Taped presentation at the Second National Conference on the Treatment of Post-Traumatic Stress Disorder, Dayton, Ohio: Human Resource Initiatives, 1983.

Sledge, W.H., Boydston, J.A., & Rabe, A.J.: Self-concept changes related to war captivity. *Archives of General Psychiatry*, 37(4):430-443, 1980.

Sloan, J.P.: *War games.* New York: Avon Books, 1973.

Smith, J.R.: The roles, stages and structure of rap groups in the treatment of post-traumatic stress reactions. Paper, Dartmouth Symposium on Post Vietnam Syndrome, Hanover, NH, Nov 21, 1980.

Smith, J.R.: A review of 120 years of the psychological literature on reactions to combat from the civil war through the Vietnam war: 1860-1980. Unpublished manuscript, Duke University, 1981.

Smith, J.R.: Personal responsibility in traumatic stress reactions. *Psychiatric Annals*, 12(11):1021-1025, 1029-1030, 1982.

Smith, J.R.: Diagnostic issues in the treatment of post-Vietnam stress syndrome. Taped presentation at the National Conference on the Treatment of Post-Vietnam Stress Syndrome, Dayton, Ohio: Human Resource Initiatives, 1982.

Smith, J.R.: From nostalgia to stress disorders: Reactions to war and catastrophe in the twentieth century. Taped presentation at the National Conference on the Treatment of Post-Vietnam Stress Syndrome, Dayton, Ohio: Human Resource Initiatives, 1982.

Smith, J.R., Parson, E.R., & Haley, S.H.: On health and disorder in Vietnam veterans: An initial commentary. *American Journal of Orthopsychiatry*, 53(1):27-33, 1983.

Smith, R.W., & Young, K.H.: Symptom patterns of psychiatrically diagnosed veterans who request treatment and those who do not. *Psychological Reports*, 22:1001-1005, 1968; in V.A., *Viet Vet*, pp. IV-122-126, 1972.

Sohlberg, S.C.: Stress experiences and combat fatigue during the Yom Kippur war (1973). *Psychological Reports*, 38:523-529, 1976.

Solomon, J.C.: *Soldiers and psychiatry in war.* Washington, D.C.: U.S. Government Publications, 1918.

Solomon, G.F.: Psychiatric casualties of the Vietnam conflict with particular reference to the problem of heroin addiction. *Modern Medicine, 38*:199-201, 211, 215, 1971.
Solomon, G.F., Zarcone, V.P., Yoerg, R., Scott, N.R., & Maurer, R.G.: Three psychiatric casualties from Vietnam. *Archives of General Psychiatry, 25*:522-524, 1971.
Spero, M.H.: Psychophysiological sequelae of holocaust trauma in a Jewish child. *American Journal of Psychoanalysis, 40*(1): 53-66, 1980.
Stanton, M.D.: Understanding the Vietnam veteran: Some social-psychological considerations. In V.A., *Viet Vet*, pp. III-17-21, 1972.
Stanton, M.D.: Drugs, Vietnam, and the Vietnam veteran: An overview. *Journal of Drug and Alcohol Abuse, 3*:557-570, 1976.
Stanton, M.D., & Bardoni, A.: Drug flashbacks: Reported frequency in a military population. *American Journal of Psychiatry, 129*:751-755, 1972.
Stanton, M.D., et al.: Heroin addiction as a family phenomenon: A new conceptual model. *American Journal of Drug and Alcohol Abuse, 5*:125-150, 1978.
Starr, P.: *The discarded army: Veterans after Vietnam.* New York: Charterhouse, 1973.
Stein, J.: The forgotten vets. *The Progressive,* June, 1980, pp. 14-15.
Steinberg, H.R., & Durell, J.: A stressful social situation as a precipitant of schizophrenic symptoms: An epidemiological study. *British Journal of Psychiatry, 114*(514):1097-1105, 1968.
Steiner, M.D., & Neuman, M.: Traumatic neurosis and social support in the Yom Kippur war returnees. *Military Medicine, 143*:866-868, 1978.
Stenger, C.: The Vietnam era veteran. *The Counseling Psychologist, 2*:77-82, 1971.
Stenger, C.: Life style shock: The psychological experience of being an American prisoner of war in the Vietnam conflict. *Newsletter for Research in Psychology, 15*:1-4, 1973.
Stenger, C.: The Vietnam veteran. *Psychiatric Opinion, 11*(6):33-37, 1974.
Stenger, C.: *American prisoners of war.* Washington, D.C.: U.S. Veterans Administration, 1977.
Sterba, J.P.: The hours of boredom, the seconds of terror. *New York Times Magazine,* Feb. 8, 1970.
Stern, G.M.: From chaos to responsibility. *American Journal of Psychiatry, 133*(3):300-301, 1976.
Stierlin, E.: *Uber der medizinischen Folgezustande der Katastrophes von Courrieres.* Berlin, 1901.
Stone, R.: *Dog soldiers.* Boston: Houghton Mifflin, 1974.
Straker, M.: The Vietnam veteran: The task is re-integration. *Diseases of the Nervous System, 37*:75-79, February 1976.
Strange, R.E.: Combat fatigue versus pseudo-combat fatigue in Vietnam. *Military Medicine, 133*:823-826, 1968.
Strange, R.E.: Psychiatric perspectives of the Vietnam veteran. *Military Medicine, 139*(2):96-98, 1974.
Strange, R.E., & Arthur, R.J.: Hospital ship psychiatry in a war zone. *American Journal of Psychiatry, 124*(3):281-286, 1967.
Strange, R.E., & Brown, D.E., Jr.: Home from the war: A study of psychiatric problems in Vietnam returnees. *American Journal of Psychiatry, 127*(4):488-492, 1970.
Strauss, H.: Das Zusammenschruecken. *Journal of Psychological Neurology, 39*: 111-231, 1929.
Strayer, R., & Ellenhorn, L.: Vietnam veterans: A study exploring adjustment patterns and attitudes. *Journal of Social Issues, 31*(4):81-93, 1975.
Strom, A. et al.: Examination of Norwegian ex-concentration camp prisoners. *Journal of Neuropsychiatry, 4*:43-62, 1962.
Strümpfer, D.J.W.: Fear and affliction during a disaster. *Journal of Social Psychology, 82*:263-268, 1970.
Stuen, M.R., & Solberg, K.B.: The Vietnam veteran: Characteristics and needs. In V.A., *Viet Vet*, pp. IV-115-122, 1972.
Swank, R.L.: Combat exhaustion: A descriptive and statistical analysis of causes, symptoms and signs. *Journal of Nervous and Mental Disease, 109*:475-508, 1949.

Symonds, M.: Victims of violence: Psychiatric effects and after-effects. *American Journal of Psychoanalysis*, 35:19-26, 1975.

Talbott, J.A.: Vietnam as metaphor. *Hospital and Community Psychiatry*, 35(7):655, 1984.

Tanay, E.: The Dear John syndrome during the Vietnam war. *Diseases of the Nervous System*, 37:165-167, March 1976.

Taylor, G.O.: American personal narrative of the war in Vietnam. *American Literature*, 52:294-308, 1980.

Teggin, A.F., & Van Niekerk, J.P.: Manifestations and management of stress. *South African Medical Journal*, 59:751-752, 1981.

Templer, D.I.: The construction and validation of a death anxiety scale. *Journal of General Psychology*, 82:165-177, 1970.

Terr, L.C.: Psychic trauma in children: Observations following the Chowchilla school bus kidnapping. *American Journal of Psychiatry*, 138:14-19, 1981.

Terr, L.C.: The Chowchilla school bus kidnapping: Three-Year follow-up. Presentation at the Neuropsychiatric Institute, University of California, Los Angeles, June, 1982.

Terry, W.: Bringing the war home. *The Black Scholar*, November 1970; in V.A., *Viet Vet*, pp. IV-63-72, 1972.

Terry, W.: *Bloods: An oral history of the Vietnam war by black veterans*. New York: Random House, 1984.

Thienes-Hontos, P.: Stress-disorder symptoms in Vietnam and Korean war veterans: Still no difference. *Journal of Consulting and Clinical Psychology*, 51(4):619-620, 1983.

Thienes-Hontos, P., Watson, C.G., & Kucala, T.: Stress-disorder symptoms in Vietnam and Korean war veterans. *Journal of Consulting and Clinical Psychology*, 50(4):558-561, 1982.

Thoits, P.A.: Conceptual, methodological, and theoretical problems in studying social support as a buffer against life stress. *Journal of Health and Social Behavior*, 23(2):145-159, 1982.

Tiffany, W.J., Jr · Mental health of army troops in Vietnam. *American Journal of Psychiatry*, 123(12):1585-1586, 1967.

Tiffany, W.J., & Allerton, W.S.: Army psychiatry in the mid-60s. *American Journal of Psychiatry*, 123:810-821, 1967.

Titchener, J.L., & Kapp, F.T.: Family and character change at Buffalo Creek. *American Journal of Psychiatry*, 133(3):295-299, 1976.

Tobin, J., & Friedman, J.: Spirits, shamans, and nightmare death: Survivor stress in a Hmong refugee. *American Journal of Orthopsychiatry*, 53:439-448, 1983.

Trautman, E.: Violence and victims in Nazi concentration camps and the psychotherapy of the survivors. In H. Krystal & W. Niederland (Eds.), *Psychic traumatization*. Boston: Little, Brown & Co., 1971, pp. 115-133.

Trimble, M.R.: *Post-traumatic neurosis: From railway spine to the whiplash*. New York: John Wiley & Sons, 1981.

Turner, R.J.: Social support as a contingency in psychological well-being. *Journal of Health and Social Behavior*, 22:357-367, December 1981.

Tyhurst, J.S.: Individual reactions to community disaster: The natural history of psychiatric phenomena. *American Journal of Psychiatry*, 107:764-769, 1951.

Tyhurst, J.S.: The role of transition states—including disasters—in mental illness. In *Symposium on preventive and social psychiatry, Walter Reed Army Institute of Research*, U.S. Government Printing Office, 1957, pp. 149-169.

Ursano, R.J.: The Vietnam era prisoner of war: Precaptivity personality and the development of psychiatric illness. *American Journal of Psychiatry*, 138(3):315-318, 1981.

Ursano, R.J., Boydstun, J.A., & Wheatley, R.D.: Psychiatric illness in U.S. Air Force Vietnam prisoners of war: A five-year follow-up. *American Journal of Psychiatry*, 138(3):310-314, 1981.

Van Der Kock, B.A.: Intrusion and numbness: Clinical implications of the Rorschach in posttraumatic stress disorder. In B.A. Van Der Kock (Ed.), *Adult psychic trauma—psychological and physiological sequelae.* Washington, D.C.: American Psychiatric Press, in press.

Van Der Kock, B.A., Blitz, R., Burr, W., Sherry, S., & Hartmann, E.: Nightmares and trauma: A comparison of nightmares after combat with lifelong nightmares in veterans. *American Journal of Psychiatry*, 141(2):187-190, 1984.

Van Der Kock, B.A., Burr, W., Blitz, R., et al.: Characteristics of nightmares among veterans with and without combat experience (abstract). *Sleep Research*, 10:179, 1981.

Van Devanter, L.: Women: The forgotten veterans. *The New American*, January 26, 1982.

Van Devanter, L.: *Home before morning.* New York: Beaufort Books, 1983.

Van Putten, T., & Emory, W.H.: Traumatic neuroses in Vietnam returnees: A forgotten diagnosis? *Archives of General Psychiatry*, 29(11):695-698, 1973.

Veterans Administration, Dept. of Medicine and Surgery. *The Vietnam veteran in contemporary society, Collected materials pertaining to the young veteran.* IB 11-22, May, 1972.

Veterans Administration, Board of Veterans Appeals. Memorandum No. 01-78-12, 18 Aug. 1978. *Posttraumatic disorder.* In V.A., *Resource Manual,* Pt. 2.

Veterans Administration, Dept. of Medicine and Surgery, Readjustment Counseling Service. *Operation Outreach, Program Guide.* G-13, M-1, Part 1, June 16, 1982.

Volkan, V.D.: Symptom formation and character changes due to upheavals of war: Examples from Cyprus. *American Journal of Psychotherapy*, 33:239-262, 1979.

Von Franz, M.-L.: *Puer aeternus, a psychological study of the adult struggle with the paradise of childhood,* 2d ed. Santa Monica, CA: SIGO Press, 1981.

Walker, J.I.: Case report. *Postgraduate Medicine*, 69(2):82-84, 1981.

Walker, J.I.: The psychological problems of Vietnam veterans. *Journal of the American Medical Association*, 246(7):781-782, 1981.

Walker, J.I.: Vietnam combat veterans with legal difficulties: A psychiatric problem? *American Journal of Psychiatry*, 138(10):1384-1385, 1981.

Walker, J.I.: Post-traumatic stress disorder after a car accident. *Postgraduate Medicine*, 69:82, 84, 86, 1981.

Walker, J.I.: Chemotherapy of traumatic war stress. *Military Medicine*, 147:1029-1033, December 1982.

Walker, J.I.: Techniques in group therapy for post-Vietnam stress syndrome. Taped presentation at the National Conference on the Treatment of Post-Vietnam Stress Syndrome, Dayton, Ohio: Human Resource Initiatives, 1982.

Walker, J.I., & Cavenar, J.O.: Vietnam veterans: Their problems continue. *Journal of Nervous and Mental Disease*, 170:174-180, 1982.

Walker, J.I., & Nash, J.L.: Group therapy in the treatment of Vietnam combat veterans. *International Journal of Group Psychotherapy*, 31(3):379-389, 1981.

Warnes, H.: The traumatic syndrome. *Canadian Psychiatric Association Journal*, 17:391-396, 1972.

Watkins, J.G.: *Hypnotherapy of war neuroses.* New York: Ronald Press, 1947.

Webb, J.: *Fields of fire.* Englewood Cliffs, NJ: Prentice-Hall, 1978.

Weber, D.S.: Some characteristics of Vietnam era patient. *Newsletter for Research in Psychology*, 13(1), 1971.

Weinstein, E.: The function of interpersonal relations in the neurosis of combat. *Psychiatry*, 10:307-314, 1947.

Weisbrod, J.: Stress management and movement therapy: Treatment techniques with post-traumatic stress disorder (PTSD) clients. Taped presentation at the National Conference on the Treatment of Post-Vietnam Stress Syndrome, Dayton, Ohio: Human Resource Initiatives, 1982.

Weissman, M.M., & Klerman, G.L.: Sex differences and the epidemiology of depression. *Archives of General Psychiatry*, 34:98-111, 1977.

Weppner, R.S.: Drug abuse patterns of Vietnamese war veterans hospitalized as narcotic addicts. *Drug Forum*, 2:43-54, 1972.

White, N.: PTSD: Psychic scarring. Taped presentation at the Second National Conference on the Treatment of Post-Traumatic Stress Disorder, Dayton, Ohio: Human Resource Initiatives, 1983.

Wilkinson, C.B.: Aftermath of a disaster: The collapse of the Hyatt Regency Hotel skywalks. *American Journal of Psychiatry*, 140(9):1134-1139, 1983.

Williams, C.: Group treatment with women partners of Vietnam veterans. Taped presentation at the National Conference on the Treatment of Post-Vietnam Stress Syndrome, Dayton, Ohio: Human Resource Initiatives, 1982.

Williams, C.: The Vietnam vet family system: Assessment and intervention. Taped presentation at the National Conference on the Treatment of Post-Vietnam Stress Syndrome, Dayton, Ohio: Human Resource Initiatives, 1982.

Williams, C.: The mental foxhole: The Vietnam veteran's search for meaning. *American Journal of Orthopsychiatry*, 53(1).4-17, 1983.

Williams, M., & Jackson, R.C.: A small-group living program for Vietnam-era veterans. *Hospital and Community Psychiatry*, 23:141-144, May 1972.

Williams, T. (Ed.): *Post-traumatic stress disorders of the Vietnam veteran*. Cincinnati, OH: Disabled American Veterans, 1980.

Williams, T.: The clinical decision: What modality of treatment to use. Taped presentation at the National Conference on the Treatment of Post-Vietnam Stress Syndrome, Dayton, Ohio: Human Resource Initiatives, 1982.

Williams, T.: Group therapy with Vietnam veterans (Processes in getting started). Taped presentation at the National Conference on the Treatment of Post-Vietnam Stress Syndrome, Dayton, Ohio: Human Resource Initiatives, 1982.

Williams, T.: Treating post-Vietnam stress syndrome: An overview. Taped presentation at the National Conference on the Treatment of Post-Vietnam Stress Syndrome, Dayton, Ohio: Human Resource Initiatives, 1982.

Wilmer, H.A.: Origins of a Jungian-oriented therapeutic community for schizophrenic patients. *Hospital and Community Psychiatry*, 27(5):338-342, 1976.

Wilmer, H.A.: Post-traumatic stress disorder. *Psychiatric Annals*, 2(11):995-1003, 1982.

Wilmer, H.A.: What do you say when a patient tells you a dream? *Texas Medicine*, 78:46-48, 1982.

Wilmer, H.A.: Vietnam and madness: Dreams of schizophrenic veterans. *Journal of the American Academy of Psychoanalysis*, 10(1):47-65, 1982.

Wilmer, H.A.: Dream seminar for chronic schizophrenic patients. *Psychiatry*, 45(4):351-360, 1982.

Wilmer, H.A.: The healing nightmare: An unconscious history of the Vietnam war. Taped lecture presentation, San Francisco, CA: C.G. Jung Institute, 1984.

Wilson, D.P., & Horack, J.: Military experience as a determinant of veterans' attitudes. In V.A., *Viet Vet*, pp. IV-15-17, 1972.

Wilson, J.P.: Identity, ideology and crisis: The Vietnam veteran in transition. Testimony given before the United States Senate Subcommittee on Veteran Affairs, June 22, 1977, Washington, D.C.

Wilson, J.P.: *Identity, ideology, and crisis: The Vietnam veteran in transition. Part I, Identity, ideology and crisis: The Vietnam veteran in transition. Part II: Psychosocial attributes of the veteran beyond identity: Patterns of adjustment and future implications. Forgotten Warrior Project.* Cleveland State University, 1978. (Reprinted by the Disabled American Veterans, Cincinnati, Ohio, 1979).

Wilson, J.P.: Towards an understanding of post-traumatic stress disorders among Vietnam veterans. Testimony before U.S. Senate Subcommittee on Veterans Affairs, May 21, 1980, Washington, D.C.

Wilson, J.P.: Stress response syndrome among Vietnam veterans: The need for continued outreach programs. Testimony before U.S. Senate Sub-Committee on Oversight in Government Spending, October 19, 1981, Washington, D.C.

Wilson, J.P.: The dimensions of post-traumatic stress disorders among Vietnam veterans: Implication for psychotherapy. Taped presentation at the National Conference on the Treatment of Post-Vietnam Stress Syndrome, Dayton, Ohio: Human Resource Initiatives, 1982.

Wilson, J.P.: *Post-traumatic stress disorders (PTSD): Collected papers.* Cleveland OH: Cleveland State University, 1983.

Wilson, J.P.: Post-traumatic stress syndromes among Vietnam veterans: The implications for future research. Testimony before U.S. House Veterans Affairs Sub-Committee on Hospital and Health Care, March 24, 1983.

Wilson, J.P.: New theoretical dimensions on PTSD. Taped presentation at the Second National Conference on the Treatment of Post-Traumatic Stress Disorder, Dayton, Ohio: Human Resource Initiatives, 1983.

Wilson, J.P., & Krauss, G.E.: *The Vietnam era stress inventory.* Cleveland, OH: Cleveland State University, 1981.

Wilson, J.P., & Prabucki, K.: The relationship of post-traumatic stress disorder to drug and alcohol use among Vietnam combat veterans. Submitted to *Journal of Consulting and Clinical Psychology.*

Wilson, J.P., & Zigelbaum, S.D.: The Vietnam veteran on trial: The relation of post-traumatic stress disorder to criminal behavior. *Behavioral Sciences and the Law, 4,* August 1983.

Winnick, H.Z.: Psychiatric disturbances of holocaust ("shoa") survivors. *Israel Annuals of Psychiatry and Related Disciplines, 5:*91-100, 1967.

Winnicott, D.: The use of an object. *International Journal of Psychoanalysis, 50:*711-716, 1969.

Worthington, E.R.: The Vietnam era veteran, anomie and adjustment. *Military Medicine,* 141:169-170, March 1976.

Worthington, E.R.: Post-service adjustment and Vietnam era veterans. *Military Medicine,* 142:865-866, November 1977.

Wyant, W.K., Jr.: Coming home with a habit. *The Nation,* July 5, 1971, pp. 7-10; in V.A., *Viet Vet,* pp. IV-187-190, 1972.

Yager, J.: Personal violence in infantry combat. *Archives of General Psychiatry,* 32:257-261, February, 1975.

Yager, J.: Postcombat violent behavior in psychiatrically maladjusting soldiers. *Archives of General Psychiatry,* 33(11):1332-1335, 1976.

Yager, J., Laufer, R., & Gallops, M.: Some problems associated with war experience in men of the Vietnam generation. *Archives of General Psychiatry,* 41(4):327-333, 1984.

Yalom, I.D.: *Existential psychotherapy.* New York: Basic Books, 1980.

Young, W.M.: When the negroes in Vietnam come home. *Harpers Magazine,* June, 1967; in V.A., *Viet Vet,* pp. IV-56-63, 1972.

Zarcone, V.P., Jr., Scott, N.R., & Kauver, K.B.: Psychiatric problems of Vietnam veterans: Clinical study of hospitalized patients. *Comprehensive Psychiatry, 18*(1):41-53, 1977.

Zeeman, E.C.: Catastrophe theory. *Scientific American,* 234(4):65-83, 1976.

Zilberg, N.J., Weiss, D.S., & Horowitz, M.J.: Impact of event scale: A cross-validation study and some empirical evidence supporting a conceptual model of stress response. *Journal of Consulting and Clinical Psychology,* 50:407-414, 1982.

Zilboorg, G.: Psychiatric problems in the wake of war. *Rhode Island Medical Journal,* 27:385-386, 413, 417, 945, 1944.

Zlotogorski, Z.: Offspring of concentration camp survivors: The relationship of perceptions of family cohesion and adaptability to levels of ego functioning. *Comprehensive Psychiatry,* 24(4):345-354, 1983.

APPENDIX B

A Guide to Self-History-Taking with Particular Reference to Post-Traumatic Stress Disorder (PTSD)

W. PETER SAX, M.D.

Help us put the picture together clearly and in the veteran's own words. Include the following:

The Trouble Now: Presenting problems, complaints, when symptoms began, together with the time, duration, and recurrence. When and for what reason was it essential to "get help."

Past History: This is to include pre-military: family, school, jobs, behavior, outlook, reputation, community attitudes, and general health prior to the onset of the present difficulties. The same area post-discharge should be covered.

Work History: This should describe the veteran's adjustment to his or her employment, both before and after service. This needs to be in detail and describe the experience of working, reasons for change of jobs, educational and vocational background and training, whether the veteran has entered, since service, any training or institutional type education. Is the veteran currently employed? How is he or she getting along on the job? Has he/she been promoted; if not promoted or if passed over, why? Include social adaptability or lack of it and how it affects his/her work capacity. How does veteran get along with his or her supervisors and fellow workers on the job?

Military History: Branch of service, units, and locations to which person was ordered. Training in service, military occupational specialty, significant facts, and circumstances surrounding the occurrence of any disability during service. Were the present symptoms first experienced during military service or after discharge? A description of the subjective (personal experience of it) and objective symptoms (observable by others, describable results and findings) upon which the picture of PTSD is based. Is there any evidence of a traumatic or life-threatening episodé (stressor)? (PTSD may occur under combat or other circumstances such as natural disasters, serious vehicular and airplane crashes with severe injuries and loss of life.) Give date, time, and place stressor occurred and unit to which assigned when it took place. Describe episode(s) in detail: (a) What was the personal experience of the event and your reactions to it, behavior, feelings, and thoughts? (b) As an imaginary historian might describe it (the proverbial fly on the wall), what happened: natural disaster, ambush, crashes, fire fight, type of weapons and explosives used? Describe the terrain and casualties, the number killed or injured and the severity of it, close friends or buddies. Was veteran wounded, where, how extensive, subsequent treatment?

History Afterwards: Include any reexperiencing of the events in the form of recollection, dreams, or actions, together with the frequency and circumstances under which these may occur and ways in which they can be lessened. Any numbing of feelings, sense of detachment, changes of ways of looking at life and people, loss of interests, or difficulty with attention, follow-through, concentration, or memory. Report any unusual startle reactions, guilt about surviving, shame about war, problems with sleep, and ways of trying not to remember. Describe any episodes of seeing or hearing people or events which in fact are not present to other observers. Describe circumstances in which the experience of being monitored or controlled or directed by outside forces occurs. Describe depression with thoughts or attempts at suicide or self-injury. Describe concern with personal health, including worries about transmission of bad effects, bad vibes, or disease to or from other people. Other unusual events or changes in ways of feeling or functioning? Does any known event cause these things to happen? Are they related to circumstances within one's self, or actions such as drinking or using drugs? Is there impairment in the learning capacity and to what extent are social and industrial adaptability impaired?

An accurate setting forth of these questions and recollections can be of great help in letting the staff know what is happening and in letting the veteran review and survey what has happened and where he or she is.

APPENDIX C

A Suggested Overview Reading List of Material on Vietnam Veterans and PTSD

STEVEN M. SILVER, Ph.D.

This bibliography is not comprehensive; there are now literally hundreds of articles on Vietnam War veterans and post-traumatic stress disorder (PTSD) and its antecedents. However, many articles available in the professional literature were flawed in their methodology or have since been incorporated in later work. A code follows each listing:

E—Describes the Vietnam War experience;
D—Provides data or descriptions of Vietnam War veterans;
T—Addresses treatment approaches to PTSD;
H—Relates to the history of the development of the concept of PTSD;
*—An exceptionally excellent source of information.

Obviously, the judgments expressed here are subjective. They are based on the experiences of being a Vietnam War veteran (Marines, RVN 1969–1970) and being a mental health professional who has conducted research and treatment of PTSD, and continues to do so.

Archibald, H.C., Long, D.M., Miller, C., & Tuddenham, R.D. Gross stress reaction in combat: A 15-year follow-up. *American Journal of Psychiatry*, 1962, *119*, 317-322. (T,H)
Archibald, H.C., & Tuddenham, R.D. Persistent stress reaction after combat: A 20-year follow-up. *Archives of General Psychiatry*, 1965, *12*, 475-481. (T,H)

Borus, J.F. Incidence of maladjustment in Vietnam returnees. *Archives of General Psychiatry*, 1974, *30*, 554-557. (D,H)

Brende, J.O. Combined individual and group therapy for Vietnam veterans. *International Journal of Group Psychotherapy*, 1981, *31*, 367-378. (T)

Brende, J.O., & Benedict, B.D. The Vietnam combat delayed stress syndrome: Hypnotherapy of "dissociative symptoms." *American Journal of Clinical Hypnosis*, 1980, *23*, 34-40. (T)

Caputo, P. *A rumor of war.* New York: Holt, Rinehart & Winston, 1977. (E*)

Card, J.J. *Lives after Vietnam.* Lexington, MA: Lexington Books, 1983. (D*)

Cavenar, J.O., Jr., & Nash, J.L. The effects of combat on the normal personality: War neurosis in Vietnam returnees. *Comprehensive Psychiatry*, 1976, *17*, 647-653.

Chamberlain, B.C. The psychological aftermath of disaster. *Journal of Clinical Psychiatry*, 1980, *41*, 238-244. (T)

DeFazio, V.J. The Vietnam era veteran: Psychological problems. *Journal of Contemporary Psychotherapy*, 1975, *7*, 9-15. (D)

Egendorf, A. Vietnam veteran rap groups and themes of post-war life. *Journal of Social Issues*, 1975, *31*, 111-124. (D,T)

Figley, C.R. (Ed.). *Stress disorders among Vietnam veterans: Theory, research and treatment.* New York: Brunner/Mazel, 1978. (E,D,T,H*)

Figley, C.R., & Leventman, S. (Eds.). *Strangers at home: Vietnam veterans since the war.* New York: Praeger, 1980. (D,T)

Haley, S.A. When the patient reports atrocities: Specific treatment considerations of the Vietnam veteran. *Archives of General Psychiatry*, 1974, *30*, 191-196.

Horowitz, M.J. *Stress response syndromes.* New York: Aronson, 1976. (T,H*)

Horowitz, M.J., Wilner, N., Kaltreider, N., & Alvarez, W. Signs and symptoms of post-traumatic stress disorders. *Archives of General Psychiatry*, 1980, *37*, 85-92. (H)

Keane, T.M., & Kaloupek, D.G. Imaginal flooding in the treatment of post-traumatic stress disorder. *Journal of Consulting and Clinical Psychology*, 50(1):138-140, 1982. (T)

Kovic, R. *Born on the fourth of July.* New York: McGraw-Hill, 1976. (E)

Lacoursiere, R.B., Godfrey, K.E., & Ruby, L.M. Traumatic neurosis in the etiology of alcoholism: Vietnam combat and other trauma. *American Journal of Psychiatry*, 1980, *137*, 966-968. (T,D)

Lifton, R.J. "Death imprints" on youth in Vietnam. *Journal of Cinical Child Psychology*, 1974, *3*, 47-49. (D)

Marin, P. Living in moral pain. *Psychology Today*, 1981, *15* (Nov.), 68-80. (D)

Santoli, A. *Everything we had.* New York: Random House, 1981. (E*)

Shatan, C.F. Through the membrane of reality: "Impacted grief" and perceptual dissonance in Vietnam combat veterans. *Psychiatric Opinion*, 1974, *11*, 5-14. (D,T)

Spiegel, D. Vietnam grief work using hypnosis. *American Journal of Clinical Hypnosis*, 1981, *24*, 33-40. (T)

Stanton, M.D. Drugs, Vietnam, and the Vietnam veteran: An overview. *Journal of Drug and Alcohol Abuse*, 1976, *3*, 557-570. (D)

Walker, J.I., & Nash, J.L. Group therapy in the treatment of Vietnam combat veterans. *International Journal of Group Psychotherapy*, 1981, *31*, 379-389. (T)

Webb, J. *Fields of fire.* Englewood Cliffs, NJ: Prentice-Hall, 1978. (E*)

Williams, T. (Ed.). *Post-traumatic stress disorders of the Vietnam veteran.* Cincinnati: Disabled American Veterans, 1980. (E,D,T,H*)

Wilson, J.P. *Identity, ideology, and crisis: The Vietnam veteran in transition, Parts I & II.* Cleveland: Cleveland State University, 1978. (D)

Name Index

Acosta, F.X., 185, 188
Adams, M.F., 250, 252, 261
Amery, J., 13-14, 27
Archibald, H.E., 19, 21
Argeropoulos, J., 85, 88

Balsley, S., 158
Balson, P.M., 202
Barnes, F., 72
Beck, S., 81
Behrends, R., 174
Benedict, B.D., 201-207, 216
Bergman, A., 176
Berman, E., 72
Bersoff, D., 81
Blanck, G., 174
Blanck, R., 174
Blank, A.S., 153, 269
Blos, P., 56-57, 68-69
Boscarino, J., 92
Boulanger, G., 170, 182
Bourne, P.G., 45, 149
Bowlby, J., 59-60
Brende, J.O., 172, 200-208, 216
Breuer, J., 194, 196
Brewin, R., 48
Burnstein, A., 72

Campbell, J., 46
Caputo, P., 44, 52, 63, 92, 140, 247
Carrington, P., 204
Cavenar, J.O., 200
Clark, K., 178
Constantinople, A., 138
Coppola, F., 18
Crawford, D., 259

Delvecchio, J., 140
Dempster, C.R., 202

Egendorf, A., 72, 149, 151, 252
Eisenhart, R.W., 201

Eitinger, L.S., 21
Ellenberger, H.E., 194, 196
Emerson, G., 140
Ephron, H.S., 204
Epstein, A.W., 183
Erickson, M.H., 195
Erikson, E., 51, 137, 141, 145
Evans, L., 188
Ewalt, J.R., 259

Fairbank, J.A., 203
Fenichel, O., 194, 197
Figley, C.R., 149, 155-156, 171, 200, 251-252
Fine, B., 173, 175
Fisher, C., 72
Forman, B.D., 171
Fox, R., 59
Fraiberg, S., 174
Freud, A., 176, 197
Freud, S., 31-32, 56, 58, 104, 172, 194, 196-197, 228-230
Fromm, E., 200
Furey, J.A., 250, 252
Furst, S.S., 36
Futterman, S., 72

Geller, J., 174
Gill, M.M., 195
Gitlow, S.E., 246
Glass, A.U., 55
Glasser, R., 154
Gleser, G.C., 103-104
Glueck, V.C., 204
Godfrey, K., 205
Goldstein, A., 184
Goodwin, J., 250-254, 268
Gosliner, B., 176
Grant, J.C.B., 16
Green, B., 103, 105, 108
Greenacre, P., 177
Grinker, R.R., 55, 198-199

329

Haley, S.A., 22, 60-61, 66, 149, 161, 171, 212-213, 252, 257, 260-261, 265, 271
Harbert, K., 167-168
Hare, R.D., 145
Harrison, I., 185
Hartley, D., 174
Hellmuth, J., 181
Helzer, J.E., 144
Hendin, H., 73
Herr, M., 44
Hesselbrock, M., 144
Holiday, B., 27
Hollingshead, A., 184
Horowitz, M.J., 55, 57-58, 104-105, 107, 142, 149, 193-194
Horsley, J.S., 220
Houston, S., 181
Howard, K., 185
Howard, S., 73
Hunt, J., 181
Huppenbauer, S.L., 250, 252

Jackson, H.C., 250
Jacobs, D., 199-200
Jacobson, E., 173-174, 176
Jaffe, R., 72
Janet, P., 194
Jaynes, J., 17
Jensen, A., 181
Joel, B., 168
Jung, C., 194-195

Kadushin, C., 170, 182
Kapp, F.T., 104
Kardiner, A., 15, 81, 113-114, 180
Kavlor, W., 237
Kernberg, O., 55
Klein, E., 199
Klein, G.S., 173, 175
Kohut, H., 55, 69
Krauss, G.E., 116, 118, 153
Kreigh, H.L., 260, 262
Krystal, H., 171
Kubie, L.S., 195
Kucala, T., 230
Kuhn, T.S., 45

Lachman, F., 72
Leahy, M.R., 213
Leventman, S., 155-156, 251
Lewis, O., 181
Lidz, T., 72
Lifton, R.J., 45, 60, 86, 90, 102-104, 114-115, 141, 149, 183, 194, 196

Lindy, J.D., 13, 105, 108
Lipin, T., 172
Lipkin, J.O., 254
Lorion, R.P., 184
Luparello, T., 72

Mahler, M., 31, 55, 176-177
Maoz, B., 200
Marron, J., 150, 155-156, 160, 163, 166
Martin, I.C., 213
Martin, J., 170, 182
Martinez, G., 156, 166
Masterson, J.F., 145
McCann, I.L., 200-201, 203-204, 206, 208
McGinley-Schneider, C., 158
Merluzzi, T., 186
Modell, A., 58
Moore, B., 173, 175
Morrier, E., 61
Moses, R., 205-206
Moynihan, D.P., 181
Myrdal, G., 38

Nash, J.L., 200
Nefzger, M.D., 21
Nemiah, J., 72
Niederland, W.C., 21, 72, 103-104, 114

Orlinsky, D., 185
Ott, J., 167
Ovesey, L., 180

Parloff, W., 185
Parson, E.R., 69, 171-173, 180, 182-183, 185, 187, 203-204
Perko, J.E., 260, 262
Perry, J.C., 199-200
Pincus, C., 200
Pinderhughes, E., 179
Pine, F., 176
Pollinger, A., 73
Polner, M., 86, 88, 90
Prabucki, K., 138
Pumpian-Midlin, E., 72

Rado, S., 72
Redlich, F.C., 184
Reiff, R., 193
Reiser, M., 215
Resing, M., 251-252
Rinsley, D., 204
Robbins, L., 144
Rorschach, H., 81
Rosenblatt, B., 175

Rosenman, S., 171
Russell, B., 38
Rustin, S., 20

Salmon, T.W., 55
Sandecki, R., 167
Sandler, J., 175
Saul, L., 228
Scheerer, M., 193
Schmidt, L., 186
Schnaier, J., 150-152, 157-158, 166
Schofield, W., 185
Schwartz, H.J., 234
Sedler, M.J., 194, 197
Shapiro, D., 194
Shatan, C., 15, 18-22, 26, 50, 60, 86, 90,
    92, 95, 141, 171, 206, 251-253
Shellabarger, C., 157
Shorr, J.B., 85
Sillen, S., 181
Silver, S.M., 245
Simenon, G., 26
Smith, J., 22, 55, 92, 96-97, 189
Smith, R., 92, 96-97
Sonnenberg, S., 72
Spiegel, D., 198-199, 202
Spiegel, J., 55
Spiegel, S., 186
Staples, R., 177
Stolorow, R., 72
Stroebel, C.F., 204
Strong, S., 186
Stroud, J., 167

Suhl, Y., 26
Sundberg, N.D., 185

Tanay, E., 19, 36
Thienes-Hontos, P., 230
Thomas, A., 181
Titchener, J., 104
Triana, R., 174
Trimble, M.R., 235
Tuddenham, R.D., 19, 21

Vail, A., 185
Van der Kolk, B., 81
Veith, I., 194

Watkins, J.G., 199, 204-205
Watson, C.G., 230
Waugh, E., 14
Webb, J., 140
Weitzenhoffer, A.M., 195
Wexler, H., 56-57
Williams, T., 250, 252-254, 261
Wilson, J.P., 51, 103, 105, 109, 116, 118,
    137-138, 141-143, 145, 149, 153, 253
Winget, C.N., 103
Winnicott, D.W., 176-177, 184
Wish, F., 144
Wolberg, L.R., 220

Yamamoto, J., 188

Zea, P.H., 21
Zetzel, E.R., 55

Subject Index

Abreaction, 194-196, 204-208, 223-224, 226-227, 263, *see also* Hypnosis/hypnotherapy
  drug-induced, 199-200, 220
  non-chemical techniques for, 200-202
Acting-out behavior, 229, 269
Adaptability, impaired, 15
Adolescence, 55, 57-58, 85, 250
Adrenal depletion syndrome, 55
Advocacy, 262
Affect disorders, 245
Affect-bridge, 205
Afro-Americans, 170-190
Agency for International Development, 150
Aggression, 31, 33, 57, 60, 68, 114-115
  inpatient setting and, 268-270
Aggressor, identification with the, 58, 60, 63, 68, 206
Alcoholism, 18, 39-41, 87, 91-92, 288-289, *see also* Drug abuse
  high rate of in Vietnam veterans, 98
  inpatient PTSD program and, 266
  reliving experiences and, 74, 79, 81, 82
  used to block intrusive images, 95, 255-256
  women veterans and, 160
Alienation, 85-86, 92, 99, 119-120, 122
  women veterans and, 151
Altered consciousness, 72
Ambivalence, 182
Amnesia, 72, 77, 159, 165, 207, 232, *see also* Dissociative states; Memory
  recurrent episodes of, 217-229
Amphetamines, 18
Amytal interviews, 55, 199-200, 213, 220, 222
Anger, 86, 237, *see also* Rage
  acting out, 78
  number of weeks in combat and, 143
Annihilation anxiety, 55, 59, 64, 68
Anniversary dates, 94

Antidepressants, 247, 265
Antisocial behavior, 115-116, 136-138, 145, 208
Anxiety, 119, 141
  annihilation, 55, 59, 64, 68
  biofeedback and, 283
  hypnosis and, 203, 216
  inpatient setting and, 271
  orgasmic dysfunction and, 161
  reactive numbing and, 173
  separation and, 64, 68
Arrests, 119
Atrocities, 33, 37-38, 48, 54, 63, 66
Atypical post-traumatic seizure disorder, 218
Authority conflict, 119-120, 123, 263
Automatic incursive phenomena, 171-172
Autonomic nervous system arousal, 104
Autonomic physiological reactions, 172, *see also* Startle reactions

Behavioral contract, 271
Benzodiazepines, 265
Bi-cultural psychic orientation, 178-179, 183
Biofeedback, 283, 288
Blacks, 170-190
Borderline traits, 208, 279

Catastrophic stress, 55-59, 67-68, 102-103, *see also* Stress
Catharsis, 47, 166, 212
Center for Policy Research, 4, 9
Chaplain, 282
Character disorders, 108, 279
Child abuse, 86
Child development, 176-178
Childhood trauma, 228
Cleland, Max, 8
Cognitive functioning, 105
Combat fatigue, 235-236
Combat grief, 60

Combat neurosis, 218, 227
Combat roles, 109-111, 116, 118, 120, 124-126, 129-132
  as best predictor of PTSD, 146
  severity of PTSD and, 140, 143-144
Combat-related stress disorder, 15
Communality, 21-23, 25-26, 141
Communication problems, 92-94, 288
Concentration camp survivors, 17-27, 29-30, 32, 37, 114
  dissociative states and, 72
  intergenerational transmission of survivor images, 183
  post-concentration camp syndrome, 171
Conflicts
  between repression and confession, 82
  Oedipal, 226
Congress, 3-11
Consciousness, altered, 72
Control, 212, 214, 237
  loss of, 242, 269
Coping mechanisms, 107, 109, 277-278, 290
Counseling, vocational, 285-286, 289, *see also* Treatment
Countertransference, 54, 57, 60, 67, 187, 189, 260 261, *see also* Transference
  black veterans and, 187, 189
Culture shock, 159-160

Dalmane, 265
Death
  from non-hostile causes, 153
  of a soldier's buddy, 55, 59-60, 221
  stress of exposure to, 111-112, 118-119, 127-132, 144
  unending threat of, 14
Death experience, 102-103, 116
Death imprint, 46, 183
Death instinct, 56
Defense mechanisms, 107, 109, 142, 227, 229
  adolescence and, 57
  dissociative states and, 72
  reactive numbing and, 173
Dehumanization, 32, 36-37
Delayed stress, 4, 18, 230, *see also* Stress
Delayed stress response, 217-229
Denial, 32, 57, 104, 107-108, 142
  hypnosis and, 213
  of psychic trauma, 38-42
  versus intrusive traumatic memories, 194
  of war atrocities, 37-38

women veterans and, 159
Department of the Army Civilians, 150
Depersonalization, 282
Depression, 34, 40-41, 87, 104, 246-247
  end of therapy and, 285
  endogenous, 279
  loss and, 141
  management in an inpatient setting, 270-271
  number of weeks in combat and, 143
  predictors of PTSD and, 119-121, 126, 132
  reactive numbing and, 173
  since leaving Vietnam, 254
  suicide potential and, 61-62
  unemployment and, 22
  women veterans and, 151, 159
Desensitization, 198, 227, 232, 243
Despair, 59-60
Detachment, 59-60
Differentiation phase, 177
Disabled American Veterans, 25
Discharge, less-than-honorable, 18
Dissociative states, 72-83, 104, 220
Dreams, *see* Nightmares
Drug abuse, 48, 92, 98, 119, 122, 154, 244, *see also* Alcoholism
  correlated with post-traumatic stress disorder, 135-136
  inpatient PTSD program and, 266
  low resistance to orders and, 18
  reliving experiences and, 77, 82
  women veterans and, 160
Drug-induced abreactions, 199-200, 220
Drugs (medication), 246-247, 265-266, 280
DSM-III, 17, 19, 71, 80, 104, 118, 136, 171, 230, 238, 276-279

Edgar, Bob, 6
Education
  for nurses treating PTSD, 251-252, 272
  patient, 243
Ego, 12, 14-15, 17, 33, 55, 61, 174, *see also* Superego
  adolescent, 57-58
  constriction, 246
  contraction of the, 114
  defenses, 103, 107, 142, 197, 229
  development, 103, 145-146
  hypnotic suggestions to enhance the, 215
  identity, 109
  identity and skin color, 178
  regression in service of the, 203

strength, 107, 114-115, 179, 186
Egosyntonic/egodystonic, 33, 36-37
Environment
    for recovery, 108, 113
    as stressor in Vietnam, 112
Euphoria, 19
Existential crisis, 34, 183

Family, 88-89, 93-94, 96-97, *see also* Wives
    involvement in therapy, 283-285
Family therapy, 288
Fatigue, 73, 81-82
Fear, 159
Flashbacks, 17, 19-24, 72, 157, 214, *see also*
    Reliving experience
    management in an inpatient setting,
    266-268
Free association, 196, 200

Gender identity, 163-164
Gestalt therapy, 246
"Gook" identification, 182, 188
Grief, 12, 19, 26, 87, 237-238
    hypnosis and, 207, 216
    loss of buddies and, 259
Gross stress reaction, *see* Post-traumatic
    stress disorder
Group therapy, 231, 238, 240-241, 243-245,
    see also Treatment
    to deal with isolation, 50
    hypnosis and, 200-201
    women and, 167-168
Guilt, 24, 32-33, 47, 66, 87
    awareness of, 75, 82
    hypnosis and, 204, 207-208, 215, 221-
    222, 224-225
    reactive numbing and, 173
    religion and, 282
    survivor's, 26, 56, 104, 189, 258, 282
        concentration camp survivors and, 32
        the triage process and, 154

Hallucinations, 16, 72, 80
Heroin, 18
History-taking format, 258-259
Holocaust survivors, *see* Concentration
    camp survivors
Homecoming experience, 5, 34-35, 113,
    116-120, 134-136, 140-141, 144, 253
    for women veterans, 155-158
Homicidal impulses, 61-62
Homosexual, 163
Hyperalertness, 19, 104, 157, 172, 268, 289
Hypervigilance, 23

Hypnoid states, 194, 196
Hypnosis/hypnotherapy, 24, 51, 55, 202-
    208, 211-232, 246
    as a diagnostic tool, 216-217
    hazards of, 228-229
    psychoanalysis and, 196-198
Hysteria, 194, 196, 226
Hysterical-conversion symptoms, 104

Ibuprofen, 247
Identification with the aggressor, 58, 60,
    63, 68, 206
Identity confusion, 120-121, 145
Identity formation, 137-138
Imipramine, 266
Impacted stress, 182
Impotence, 161
Imprinting, 16-17
Infertility, 24
Inhibition, against killing, 34-35
Inpatient program, 234-247
Insomnia, 76-77, 104, 173, 244
    management in an inpatient setting,
    266-268
    women veterans and, 159
Intimacy, 12, 19-20, 104, 119-120, 124, 126,
    133-134
    fear of loss and, 143
    female therapists and, 253
    predicting PTSD and, 119-120, 124, 126,
    133-134
    women veterans and, 161
Intrusive imagery, 119-120, 123, 126, 133,
    136, 138-139, 183, 194
    alcohol used to block out, 256
    black veterans and, 183
    denial and, 194
    phenelzine and, 247
    World War II veterans and, 56
Isolation, 56-57, 119, 134, 136, 146
    as the best predictor of post-traumatic
        stress disorder, 141-142
    defense mechanisms and, 108
    rap groups and, 50
    reactive numbing and, 173
    severe symptoms of post-traumatic
        stress disorder and, 144
    women veterans and, 159

Korean war veterans, 59, 230, *see also*
    Vietnam veterans

Legal problesm, 119, 244
Libido, 114

Lithium, 247
Loss, 141
  of communality, 21-22
  denied, 19
  of interest in work and relationships,
    104
  of memory, 194, 217, *see also* Amnesia
  of a soldier's buddy, 55, 59-60
  traumatic, 72

Magical thinking, 58-59
Manic depressive disorder, 280
Medevac system, 154
Medical personnel, 153-155
Medication, 246-247, 265-266, 280
Meditation, 203-204
Memory, 105, 172, *see also* Amnesia:
    Dissociative states
  impairment of, 104, 119-120, 122
  loss of, 194, 217
  suppressed, 214
Military life, 31-32
Minnesota Multiphasic Inventory, 218,
    245
Mythos, warrior, 44-48

Narcissism, 55, 64, 115-116, 136-139, 145,
    208, 245
Narcosynthesis, 199, 220, 231-232
Negroes, 170-190
Neurosis, 108
Nightmares, 25, 39-41, 63, 66, 103-104,
    244, 255, 259
  family understanding of, 93
  hypnosis and, 213-214, 216
  management in an inpatient setting,
    266-268
  phenelzine and, 247
  reliving experiences and, 76, 80-81
  triggered by the environment, 20
  women veterans and, 159-160
Nurses and nursing, 249-274, *see also*
    Women
  interventions, 264-272
  nurse-patient relationship, 251-160
  treatment team and, 260-262
  veteran's attitude toward women and,
    261

Object relations, 55, 173
Object-representations, 175-178, 180, 188
Obsessions, 103
Occupational therapy, 282-283, 288
Oedipal conflict, 57, 226

Outlaw mythos, 48-49
Outreach clinics, 276

Paranoia, 14, 19, 30, 116, 136-138, 145
Paresthesia, 104, 119
Passivity, 61
Patient education, 243
Peer group, 36, 58, *see also* Group therapy
Pentothal, 200
Perceptual dissonance, 15-17, 19, 21
Personality changes, 14
Personality disorders, 118, 136-139
Personality traits, 103, 109
Phenelzine, 247
Phenothiazines, 265
Physical exercise, 283, 288
Post-traumatic stress disorder
  applicability to women veterans, 151
  characteristics of veterans with, 277
  Congressional legislation and, 3-11
  defined as service-connected disability,
    9
  diagnosis of, 71, 252, 276-279
  financial aspects of, 290
  four types of, 254
  homecoming experience and, *see*
    Homecoming experience
  hypnosis and, 202-208, 211-217
  inpatient program for, 234-247
  interactional theory of, 115
  latent period and, 21-22
  misdiagnosis of, 164-165
  model for the development of, 105-109
  nursing care for, 249-274
  patient assessment and, 273
  percentage of black veterans with, 170
  prediction of, 102-146
  preexisting intrapsychic conflict and,
    228
  premorbid character flaws and, 113-116
  premorbid personality disorder and,
    136-139
  psychological isolation as the best
    predictor of, 141
  severity correlated with combat stress,
    140
  severity correlated with isolation, 144
  symptoms of, 19-21, 96-97, 104, 171-173
  treatment of, 187-190, 276-291
  World War II veterans and, 217-232
Power, 103, 212
Premorbid personality characteristics, 109,
    113-117, 145
Premorbid personality disorder, 136-139

Pro-social humanitarian behavior, 103
Projection, 32
Propranolol, 247
Psychic integration, 16
Psychic numbing, 56, 60, 103, 143, 157,
   161
  hypnoid states as a form of, 194
Psychic overload, 107-108
Psychic reality, 14-17
Psychic representations, 173-178
Psychic trauma, 12, 36-37
  denial of, 38-42
Psychoanalysis, 94, 174
Psychoanalytic theory, 114-115, 197
Psychoformative processes, 103
Psychological parallels, 85
Psychopathology, post-war, 145
Psychosis, 108, 243, 279
Psychotherapy, see also Treatment
  black veterans and, 186-190
  with minority patients, 184-186
  survivor strength and, 51-52
Psychotic distortion, 39

Racism, 33-34, 179, 182-183, 187-188
Rage, 12, 14, 87, 119-120, 123, 126, 133,
      see also Anger
  at those back home, 34
  helplessness and, 206
  hypnosis and, 221-222
  inpatient setting and, 268-270
  loss of love object and, 59-60
  political nature of the war and, 259
  primitive, 55
  veteran's fear of uncontrolled, 26
  violence and, 37
  women veterans and, 159, 165
Rap group therapy, 50, 201, 231
Rape trauma syndrome, 171
Rapprochement, 177-178
Reactive numbing, 172-173
Readjustment Counseling Program, 4-5, 8-
   10
Readjustment problems, 4, 9, 12
Reality, psychic, 14-17
Red Cross, 150
Regression, 16, 55-56, 58-59, 68, 173
  in the service of the ego, 203
  integrative, 200, 204
Rehearsing the past, 193-194
Relaxation techniques, 203, 268, 283
Religion, 282
Reliving experience, 71-83, 229, see also
   Flashbacks

Repetition compulsion, 142
Representational world, 173-178, 183, 186-
   190
Repression, 47, 114, 197
  conflicted with confession, 82
  delayed stress and, 230
  hypnosis and, 213
Resistance, 200, 208
  group, 245
  hypnosis and, 213
  passive, 242
Revivification, 195, 200-201, 207-208, 220
Rorschach response, 81

Sadism, 55-56, 58
Sadomasochism, 31, 66
Scapegoat, 19, 48, 86, 254
Schizophrenia, 80, 164, 174
Self-actualization, 103
Self-esteem, 137, 145, 183, 258
Self-representations, 175-178, 180, 188
Self-repudiation, 88
Senate Veterans Affairs Committee, 3-4
Sensation seeking, 119-120, 123, 126, 142,
   145
Separation anxiety, 64, 68
Separation-individuation phase, 31, 55,
   57-58, 72, 177
Sex
  adolescence and, 57
  deprivation and military life, 31-32
  problems and the Vietnam experience,
     160-163
  release of repressed urges, 114
  reliving experiences and, 74, 76, 80
Sexual harassment, 163
Shell shock, 55, 235
Short-timer syndrome, 112, 119, 128, 132-
   133
Sibling rivalry, 224-225
Sleep disturbances, see Insomnia;
   Nightmares
Sociopathy, 279
Sodium amytal, see Amytal interviews
Somatic problems, 119, 122, 142, 145, 172
  in an inpatient population, 243-244
Somnambulistic state, 81
Splitting, 194, 196, 207
Startle reactions, 19, 25, 63, 104, 172
  compared to reliving experiences, 72
  hypnosis and, 203
Stress, see also Post-traumatic stress
   disorder
  catastrophic, 55-59, 67-68, 102-103

combat role and, 126, 132-134, 140
delayed, 4, 18, 230
exposure to injury and death, 111-112,
  116, 118-119, 127-132, 144
impacted, 182
physical exercise and, 283
return of maladaptive behavior and, 278
traumatic loss and, 72
unpredictable Vietnam environment
  and, 112
unresolved problems and, 91
Stress Assessment Questionnaire, 144
Stress Assessment Scale, 138-139
Stress response syndromes, 55
Substance abuse, *see* Alcoholism; Drug
  abuse
Suicide, 14, 41, 57, 61-62, 67, 87, 91
  concentration camp survivors and, 22
  factors which contribute to, 88-89
  high rate among Vietnam veterans, 27
  inpatient care and, 254
  management in an inpatient setting, 270
  women veterans and, 151, 166
Superego, 55-56, 60-61, *see also* Ego
  guilt and, 33, 36
  identification with the aggressor and, 68
  sadomasochism and, 31
Survivor guilt, 26, 32, 56, 104, 189, 258,
  282
Survivor mode, 180
Survivor strength, 51-52
Survivor's syndrome, 171
Symbiosis, 176

Tension reduction, 216
Therapeutic alliance, 60, 237, 251, 253, 271
  family involvement in therapy and, 284
Therapeutic milieu, 259-264, 273
Therapist
  difficulties in working with PTSD
    patients and, 63, 260-261
  minority patients and, 185-186
  non-intrusive posture of the, 189
  previous combat experience and, 281
  risk in treating combat veteran and, 69
Thought disorders, 245
Transference, 57, 60, 66, 260, *see also*
  Countertransference
  hypnosis and, 197-200, 226, 232
  inability to form a, 174
Transient situational disturbances, *see*
  Post-traumatic stress disorder
Transient stress reaction, 113
Transitional object, 55, 58-60

Trauma, *see also* Post-traumatic stress
  disorder
  adaptation outcomes to, 108
  childhood, 228
  integration and assimilation of, 105-108,
    140-141
  memory function and, 172
  nature of the, 107-108
  reexperiencing of, 103
Traumatic neurosis, 114, 139, 235-236
Traumatic psychosis, 80
Traumatic stress syndrome, 142
Traumatic triggering factors, 18
Traumatic war neurosis, 55-56
Treatment, 276-291, *see also* Group
  therapy; Psychotherapy; Vocational
  counseling
  of black Vietnam veterans, 187-190
  difficulty in engaging in, 254
  environmental considerations for, 262-
    264
  plan for, 259
  rejection of, 281
  success in, 280
  team, 260-262
  women veterans and, 164-168
Triage process, 154, 212
Tricyclic antidepressants, 247, 265
Trust, 21, 27, 160
  hypnosis and, 203-204
  nurse-patient relationship and, 251

Values, 34, 98, 109, 157
Veterans Administration, 4-10, 34, 156,
  239, 253
Veterans organizations, 6-8, 157, 285-286
Victim identification, 205-208
Victim system, 179-180
Vietnam Era Stress Inventory (VESI), 116-
  120, 132, 141, 143-144, 146
Vietnam veterans, *see also* Korean war
  veterans; Post-traumatic stress
  disorder; World War II veterans
  abandonment by society, 47
  age of, 151
  bitterness of, 98
  blacks, 170-190
  characteristics of those with PTSD, 277
  characterization of, 140
  compared to concentration camp
    survivors, 17-27, 29-30, 32, 37
  compared to World War II veterans, 5,
    230-232

critical of U.S. involvement in the war,
    35
educational level of, 151
experience of military service in
    Vietnam and, 33-34
family and, 88-89, 93-94, 96-97, 283-285
family background and maladjustment,
    85-86
high suicide rate and, 27
homecoming experience, *see*
    Homecoming experience
most likely to benefit from an inpatient
    program, 244-245
mythos of, 44-52
number of women veterans, 150
overt violence of, 37
readjustment problems of, 4, 9, 12
reasons for seeking inpatient care, 253-
    254
self-repudiation and, 88
society's attitude toward, 86, 88, 97-99,
    141-142, 156, 212, 231, 290-191
wives of, *see* Wives

women, 148-168
Vietnam Veterans Against the War, 6, 25
Vietnam Veterans of America Women
    Veterans Project, 159
Violence, 37
    inpatient setting and, 268-270
Vocational counseling, 285-286, 289

War atrocities, 33, 37-38, 48, 54, 63, 66
War Participation Syndrome, 34
Warrior mythos, 44-48
Withdrawal, *see* Isolation
Wives, 88, 99-100, 256-257, 284, 288, *see
    also* Family
    description of veterans' problems, 96-97
    problems of, 97
Women, 148-168, 252-253, 261, *see also*
    Nurses and nursing
World War II veterans, 5, 56, 59, 217-226,
    230-232, 236, 250, *see also* Vietnam
    veterans

Zombie reaction, 235